TO LIVE'S TO FLY

ALSO BY JOHN KRUTH

Bright Moments:
The Life and Legacy of Rahsaan Roland Kirk

TO LIVE'S TO FLY

THE BALLAD OF THE LATE, GREAT
TOWNES VAN ZANDT

JOHN KRUTH

DA CAPO PRESS
A Member of the Perseus Books Group
New York

The publisher would like to thank the Van Zandt family for their generous contribution of
the use of Townes's lyrics.
Jeanene Van Zandt—Silver Dollar Music, Columbine Music, Townes Van Zandt Songs
John Townes Van Zandt II—JTVZ Music
William Vincent Van Zandt—Will Van Zandt Publishing
Katie Belle Van Zandt—Katie Belle Music

And to Butch Hancock for the right to quote the lyrics of his song, "Toast of the Townes,"
published by Two Roads Music (ASCAP) administered by BUG Music.

Cataloging-in-Publication data for this book is available from the Library of Congress.
ISBN-10: 0-306-81553-2
ISBN-13: 978-0-306-81553-9

First Da Capo Press edition 2007

Design by Jane Raese
Text set in 11.5-point Granjon

Published by Da Capo Press
A Member of the Perseus Books Group
http://www.dacapopress.com

Da Capo Press books are available at special discounts for bulk purchases in the U.S. by
corporations, institutions, and other organizations. For more information, please contact
the Special Markets Department at the Perseus Books Group, 11 Cambridge Center,
Cambridge, MA 02142, or call (800) 255-1514 or (617) 252-5298, or e-mail
special.markets@perseusbooks.com.

1 2 3 4 5 6 7 8 9—11 10 09 08 07

CONTENTS

Days up and down they come
Like rain on a conga drum
Forget most remember some
But don't turn none away
Everything is not enough
Nothing is too much to bear
Where you been is good and gone
All you keep is the getting there
TVZ, "To Live's to Fly"

STILL LOOKIN' FOR YOU

AN INTRODUCTION

I picked up the phone and took my best shot. Hell, Townes was a gambler who continually took all kinds of foolish risks with his psyche, body, and wallet. So I called Jeanene Van Zandt cold from New York City and told her what I had in mind. I asked for her blessing. I wanted her to know I was a "right guy," even if I happened to be a Yankee. I gave her my guarantee that I wasn't out to lionize her husband for all the wrong reasons—his drinking, drugging, and depression. I learned to stop glorifying tragedy years ago when I was a student at the University of Minnesota and my old English professor, the Pulitzer Prize–winning poet John Berryman, threw himself off the Washington Avenue Bridge one frozen January day. And I'm hardly any kind of moralist, Old Testament, Christian Right, or otherwise, looking for some sinful singer-songwriter to condemn. If anything (like journalist Jerry Leichtling, who actually once called Townes a saint in the *Village Voice,* albeit "a slightly berserk, chronically dissipated, drunk, self-destructive hobo saint"), I've tended to err on the side of hagiography, as in the case of my first book, a tome to the blind multi-instrumentalist Rahsaan Roland Kirk.

I guess my career as a hagiographer unwittingly began as a kid, growing up idolizing ballplayers like Mickey Mantle and Willie Mays and then those wacky mop tops from Liverpool, the Beatles. Then came the self-destructive—tortured-artist types like Vincent Van Gogh. My mom, a frustrated painter turned interior decorator, loved art. On our living room wall hung a self-portrait by Russian-born Ashcan-school painter Raphael Soyer in wire-rimmed glasses, overcoat, and hat, looking like he could use some lunch. His dark eyes followed me everywhere, watching every move I made from the time I could crawl until I left home. Thank God he couldn't talk! So from a young age I was indoctrinated not just by the power of paintings but by the dramatic life stories of these artists who dredged such precious expressions from the depths of their souls, often at terrible cost to themselves.

Then came my sister's high school boyfriend, a guy named Steve Brick who recited the poems of Dylan Thomas, William Blake, and Allen Ginsberg off the top of his head. One Sunday afternoon he offered to take my sister to the Village to see the Reverend Gary Davis, but she was more interested in buying shoes at Altman's. So she went shopping, and Steve took me to MacDougal Street, where I would discover gyros, cappuccino, and the music of Dave Van Ronk, Richie Havens, and the Blues Project. I soon ordered a subscription to *Sing Out!* magazine that I religiously took to bed each night along with guitar catalogs and copies of *Playboy*. While my friends were still flipping baseball cards, I memorized the names of a new generation of folk heroes. Beyond Bob Dylan and Joan Baez—whom *everybody* knew—was Leonard Cohen, Buffy Sainte-Marie, Fred Neil, Phil Ochs, and Eric Andersen, names that with a bit of clever advertising and neat graphics became like those of saints to me. Their songs, although recently written, seemed like the Holy Grail when published in the pages of *Broadside* or *Sing Out!* They were songs that I believed could stop wars, world hunger, and poverty and make young women pledge their undying love to me.

Eventually, I caught wind of an outsider, a dark horse who occasionally rode into town from Texas to sing at Gerdes' Folk City. His reputation preceded him and had already begun to mushroom into legend—which, in my book, was equally important to his poetry and pickin'. Although some thought him to be a space cowboy, Townes Van Zandt was more like a fearless pioneer of the last frontier—the damp, dark alleys of the human psyche where no one but Cohen and Dylan had dared tread.

Speaking of treading, I arrived in Smyrna, Tennessee (twenty-two miles outside of Nashville), the morning after a multiple murder at a fish restaurant at the local strip mall. Three people were shot dead. One body was found in a cooler, another in a parked car. They never found out exactly what happened to the third person.

I was driving slowly, searching for the Van Zandt estate while being followed by a young redneck in a white '67 GTO. The guy tailgated me while repeatedly gunning his engine. Every so often he'd pop the clutch and lay some rubber with a screech, then stop short, just before ramming my rear end. Lost and looking for the house, I pulled a U-turn on a dead end. He just sat there in the middle of the road, staring me down. All of a sudden he stomped on the accelerator while pointing his car directly at me. At the last second, just before crashing into me headfirst, he swerved, ran the car into a ditch, smashed into a mailbox, and then rolled his car. I didn't stop and stick around to see if he was okay.

This was only the beginning. It wasn't long before I found myself wading through a pool of sharks. The situation was volatile, to say the least. In the wake of Townes's death, a hail of derogatory names, bitter curses, and heinous accusations started to fly from all directions at once—among friends, businessmen, and family members alike. A good part of the animosity, but not the entire feud, revolved around the issue of finances, of course. All involved parties claimed their fair share of rights and credits to Townes's publishing and recorded legacy. Everyone involved had a story to tell, whether they were willing to talk or not.

Townes was apparently *everybody's* best friend, and many a deal had been agreed upon by word of mouth, with a handshake, or over a drink, or four or five. The principal players in this drama (which still rages on to this day) are the Eggers brothers—Kevin, Townes's producer and owner of Poppy (and later Tomato) Records, along with his younger brother Harold, Townes's road manager and handler for more than fifteen years. (Unfortunately, Harold declined to be interviewed, as he plans to write his own book someday.) Then there is Jeanene, Townes's third wife, a feisty spitfire from Texas, whom many resent for barging in and trying to straighten out the shambles of Van Zandt's career. Her main concern, since Townes's death, has been to make sure that Townes's children Will and Katie Belle are provided for, as well as furthering her husband's musical legacy (although many claim she is in it only for her personal advantage).

No matter which side of the fence you're on, when it comes to Jeanene, I can personally vouch that the woman is *thoroughly* devoted to her dead husband, to the point of obsession. It's almost spooky. When I stayed at the "Ponderosa" (the house that Jeanene and Townes shared in the last years of their marriage) for a couple of nights while interviewing her, I felt like I had entered "the house where time stood still." The only records she played were by Townes, except an occasional track by somebody else covering a Van Zandt song. Posters and photographs of

Townes were everywhere. On the living room wall hung a ghostly portrait of Townes by Jett Whitt, titled *Snake Eyes,* that appeared on the cover of *No Deeper Blue.* Van Zandt's favorite old books of poetry, western novels, and Indian lore that date back to his school days still sit on the shelves, waiting patiently for his daughter, Katie Belle (who at age thirteen has already written a handful of poems and plays), to open them to discover and share her father's love of literature. An antique credenza sits beside a tank inhabited by three bearded dragons from Australia that live above a pair of ball pythons. Made of mahogany, it is a treasure chest filled with old notebooks full of Van Zandt's lyrics, unfinished poem fragments, press clippings, miscellaneous files, hoodoo trinkets, and various Indian relics all meticulously archived. In no time the theme song from *The Addams Family* began echoing in my head—"Their house is a museum when people come to see 'em."

Then there's J. T., a fly fisherman, boat builder, singer-songwriter, and guitarist in his own right, living in Austin, who, although soft-spoken, has some pretty stringent opinions of his own, not only about how the pie should be cut but also about who Townes's friends *really* were and who has attached themselves to his dead father for their own personal gain.

Last but not least are the Clarks, Susanna and Guy. (Unfortunately, Susanna declined to be interviewed. For whatever reason, she took the Fifth.) If we were making a buddy film here, Guy would clearly have been cast in the role of the Sundance Kid to Van Zandt's Butch Cassidy. This is by no means a slight on Clark's finely crafted songwriting, but more like the natural order of the universe. As Old Chief Rolling Papers put it: "The guy was a giant among his peers. The way I look at it, Townes Van Zandt was a Texas legend. Everybody else is just a Texas songwriter." Or as Townes's old friend and "guru" Darryl Harris said, "While most of us consider ourselves the main character in our own lives, with Townes, he had such a powerful effect on people that you were, at best, a supporting player in *The Townes Van Zandt Story.*"

PROLOGUE

THE SUN IS BURNING OUT

It all started innocently enough one day back in 1952 when Townes Van Zandt's third-grade teacher presented a routine lesson on the solar system. The teacher began by introducing all nine planets to the children, describing their sizes, colors, and unique characteristics. Then came trickier concepts like gravity. She explained how the planets revolve around the sun, the enormous distances from earth to other planets, and the weather unique to each sphere. A couple of kids began wriggling nervously in their seats, while others slouched, lost in daydreams. Oddly enough, the biggest daydreamer of them all, Townes Van Zandt, was surprisingly attentive. His large ears perked up, and his dark, sparkling eyes dilated in amazement.

"Now, the sun is a star, and all stars eventually burn out. Just like people, stars die too," the teacher gently explained to the class. A moment later, Townes's arm shot into the air. The teacher ignored him. She never could quite figure this kid out. He was usually off on cloud nine, and then suddenly, for no apparent reason, he was bursting with questions and clever comments. She continued with the lesson, while Townes stretched his lanky limb as far as he could, all the while huffing and groaning and waving his hand in desperation. Finally, the teacher gave in and called on him, assuming the boy needed to rush down the hall to use the toilet.

"Excuse me, ma'am, but did you just say the sun is a star and that *all stars* eventually burn out?" Townes asked incredulously.

"Yes, that's right, Mr. Van Zandt," the teacher snapped. "We've already discussed that."

"Now, hold it a minute," Townes demanded. "If the sun's burning out, then what are we doing *here*? I mean, why do we have to go to school and be here on time and get good grades and not cuss and comb our hair and eat vegetables and everything, if the sun is burning out? It just doesn't make any sense."

It goes without saying that Townes's teacher was totally unprepared for this sort of question. No matter how cleverly she tried to debate this precocious eight year old, her answers simply weren't good enough. From that day forth, Townes Van Zandt would never be the same. He had just discovered the sun was burning out.

CHAPTER 1

WHERE I LEAD ME

There ain't much I ain't tried,
Fast livin', slow suicide.
— TVZ, "Still Lookin' for You"

Wherever the road led him on his brief fifty-two-year tour of this sad and beautiful planet, Townes Van Zandt's reputation had a way of preceding him. Word of him traveled down the pike long before he blew into town, with his dusty, scuffed-up cowboy boots, old guitar, and aw-shucks, gold-tooth grin. He was a living legend, albeit more often than not an unknown one. Van Zandt was a notorious rambler, gambler, hell-bent drunk of the first order, and arguably the greatest American songwriter of his day. The first time Emmylou Harris laid eyes on him at Gerdes' Folk City in Greenwich Village in the midsixties, she swore he was the reincarnation of Hank Williams, "but with a twist." That "twist" to which Emmylou referred was Townes's incandescent lyrics, expressed with pristine imagery, well-crafted wordplay, and stark honesty.

Yet no matter how his friends and the press raved about him, Townes simply wanted no part of it. When his old pal Texas songwriter Guy Clark dubbed him "the Van Gogh of country music," Van Zandt quipped, "Actually, Guy said that because I have no ear."

Perhaps the grandest (and most preposterous) acclaim for Townes's lyrics came from his friend singer-songwriter Steve Earle, who as a kid was in such awe of Van Zandt that he used to carry Townes's guitar case around just to be in the man's presence. "Townes Van Zandt's the best songwriter in the world, and I'll stand on Bob Dylan's coffee table in my cowboy boots and say that," Earle once declared. Although Townes appreciated the sentiment, after taking one look at Dylan's bodyguards, he assured Steve he didn't think it would be such a good idea. "It makes me nervous," Van Zandt joked in his typically self-deprecating fashion. "I've met Bob Dylan's bodyguards, and if Steve Earle thinks he can stand on Bob Dylan's coffee table, he's sadly mistaken."

Whenever anyone would try to tag him with that "world's greatest songwriter" handle, Van Zandt would shrug his bony shoulders and reply, "What about Mozart? What about Paul Simon? What about Bob Dylan?" and then quote the comedian and free-speech activist Lenny Bruce, who once said, "Flattery isn't bad, if you can hold your breath long enough."

Accolades aside, Van Zandt knew very well where he stood in the larger scheme of things, citing competition with "Beethoven, Lightnin' Hopkins, the Rolling Stones, and the Lord." If by chance the word *legend* happened to be mentioned in the same breath as his name, Townes would clarify that only people of such caliber as Albert Schweitzer, Vincent Van Gogh, Chuck Yeager, Elvis Presley, and Bob Dylan deserved a reserved seat in such rarefied atmosphere.

In addition to the overly enthusiastic Earle, Norah Jones, Lyle Lovett, the Cowboy Junkies, Hoyt Axton, and Doc Watson have all recorded fine renditions of Townes's songs. Van Zandt's verses have also inspired a couple of chart-topping duets over the years. Emmylou Harris and Don Williams's cover of Townes's lilting love song "If I Needed You" went to number three on the country music charts in 1981, while "Pancho and Lefty," Van Zandt's classic outlaw ballad, first covered by Emmylou in 1977 on her *Luxury Liner* LP, was recorded by Willie Nelson and Merle Haggard and topped the country charts at number one in 1983. More Van Zandt–inspired duets followed: Nanci Griffith and Arlo Guthrie cut a stirring rendition of "Tecumseh Valley," Townes's tragic ballad of Caroline, the miner's daughter. And Jimmie Dale Gilmore kicked out the jams on "White Freight Liner Blues," backed by the Seattle grunge rockers Mudhoney.

John Townes Van Zandt came kicking and screaming into this world on March 7, 1944, in Fort Worth, Texas. The son of a fourth-generation oil family, Townes wasn't born to money as much as he'd been born to history. In 1848, Van Zandt County (named in honor of Townes's great-great-grandfather Isaac Van Zandt) was created on 850 square miles of land, 50 miles east of Dallas. From 1822 to 1839 it was owned and colonized by the Cherokees, but during the Civil War the county became known as "the Free State of Van Zandt."

Jacob Van Zandt Sr., born around 1750, emigrated from Holland to Pennsylvania with the Moravian Colony shortly before the American Revolution. He then moved to Winston-Salem, North Carolina, where he married a Virginian named Catherine Moon, who gave birth to a son, Jacob Van Zandt Jr. Shortly before 1800, the peripatetic Jacob Sr. packed up his family once more and moved to Tennessee, near Winchester, in Franklin County.

In Franklin, Jacob Jr. married Mary Isaacs, who gave birth to a son, Isaac, on July 10, 1812. Isaac first became a merchant, studied law, and soon after passing his bar moved to East Texas. Isaac Van Zandt was soon elected to congress, where he figured prominently in the diplomatic affairs of what became the Lone Star State. In 1842, Sam Houston, the president of the Republic of Texas, appointed Isaac to the position of chargé d'affaires to the United States. As a member of the congress of the Republic of Texas, Isaac represented his country in the annexation negotiations with the Union. The United States had rejected the notion twice before a deal was finally cut. Frustrated with the long-drawn-out proceedings, Van Zandt sent a dispatch to the Honorable Anson Jones, secretary of state, dated October 16, 1843, inquiring, "Are we ready to negotiate a treaty of annexation or not?" A savvy yet compassionate man, Isaac was concerned with the treatment of "wild Indians" in Texas and complained of the "illicit trade" practices and poor treatment of native peoples in a dispatch in September 1843. Not only did Isaac represent the Republic of Texas as its first ambassador to the United States under Sam Houston, but he also served as its ambassador to France from 1835 to 1845. Five years later, at age thirty-eight, he would die of yellow fever while running for governor.

Isaac's first son, Khleber Miller Van Zandt, born November 7, 1836, was variously a general, legislator, merchant, banker, and community leader and had a reputation as a quiet and genteel man. An old photograph portrays a dignified southern gentleman in a three-piece suit with tie and watch chain. His pomade hair, graying at the temples, is neatly parted on the left side. What is instantly striking about him, beyond his meticulously groomed white goatee, is a pair of dark eyes that reflect the pain of witnessing the horror of war and the destruction of his beloved Confederacy.

There is little known about Khleber's younger brother, Isaac Lycurgus Van Zandt, Townes's great-grandfather, who was born in 1840. The black sheep of the family, Isaac Lycurgus was rumored to have wasted the family fortune and run off with the Indians (hence the speculation that Native American blood ran through Townes's veins).

Traditionally, a first son is named for the father, but as Khleber was named after a favorite clerk who worked in his father's mercantile shop (Khleber Miller), the honor was bestowed upon Isaac Lycurgus. While Townes gained a deep appreciation for his great-great-granddad, the rest of the family rarely, if ever, spoke his name.

At ninety-three, Khleber finished his autobiography, *Force without Fanfare,* within a few months of his death in 1930. The book recalled how the Van Zandts left Washington, D.C., in 1856 and joined the first migration west, leaving behind "the debt ridden and stifling society of the antebellum South. Seeking a newer, freer society," the family settled "on the edge of the prairies" of what would soon become the city of Fort Worth, whose population at the time barely reached 250.

Khleber Van Zandt paints the dreary scene:

Forth Worth as I first saw it late on an August afternoon in 1865 presented a sad and gloomy picture. The town had lost much of its former population due to the war. The young men had nearly all gone into the Confederate army. Many of them had fallen on the field of battle and those who had returned home had fallen prey to the apathy of the old men who remained at home and became weary with four long years of watching and waiting. It is apparent that if Fort Worth was to become a city something had to be done very soon.

Taking the bull by the horns, he founded the town's first newspaper, the *Fort Worth Democrat,* with fellow Confederate officer B. B. Paddock by trading a wagonload of wheat for an old printing press from the *Quitman Herald.* Khleber then became founder and president of the Fort Worth National Bank and was also instrumental in bringing the railroad to Fort Worth.

"Business was prospering and I had the opportunity of becoming a wealthy man," he wrote. "But I was interested in other values before money." The general believed that "men gained by giving." Putting his money where his mouth was, Van Zandt, upon his death, donated his farm to the growing city. Today, the cultural hub of Fort Worth thrives where his old homestead once stood.

On the other side of the family was Townes's great-grandfather, judge and law professor John Charles Townes, to whom the main building of the University of Texas at Austin School of Law, Townes Hall, is dedicated. Born in Tuscumbia, Alabama, on January 30, 1852, John Charles was four years old when his parents, Eggleston Dick Townes and Martha Cousins (Betts), moved to Travis County, Texas, where he grew up, attended Baylor University, and received an honorary LL.D. degree.

On December 28, 1871, John Charles married Kate Rector Wildbahn, who bore him four children, including John Charles Jr. Three years later Townes was admitted to the bar and practiced law in Austin until 1877. The family moved once again, this time to San Saba County, where John Charles was elected judge of the Thirty-third Judicial District.

As a professor of law at the University of Texas, John Charles Townes became its first dean in 1902, but a year later he resigned and returned to teaching. In 1907 he was appointed dean once more and held that position until resigning in August 1923. Later that year he died in Austin. During his lifetime John Charles Townes published five books on the study of law. After his death his former students donated a portrait and bust of him to the University of Texas law school, while the University Baptist Church named its Bible chair in his honor.

John Charles Townes Jr., Townes's grandfather, was born in Georgetown, Texas, on July 4, 1886. Originally a liberal arts student at the University of Texas, he ultimately followed in his father's footsteps, switching his major to law in 1906, and received a LL.B. degree in 1909. A year later, John Jr. married Helen Markle of Palestine, Texas. They had three daughters.

From 1909 to 1917 John Jr. practiced law privately in Houston until joining the army at the outbreak of World War I. After the war he became the general attorney for Humble Oil and Refining Company until resigning in January 1929. Following the death of his first wife, he married Mozelle Barnhart on June 9, 1944, and practiced law privately until his death on February 22, 1948.

A photograph of John Charles Townes Jr. depicts him standing in a grove of enormous ponderosa pines, wearing a straw hat, holding a leashed pair of harlequin Great Danes with their long tongues dangling from their mouths. With a cigar stub planted firmly in the corner of his mouth, he bore a striking resemblance to Sydney Greenstreet in *Casablanca*.

With a family filled with distinguished congressmen, high-ranking soldiers, and high-powered lawyers on both sides, Townes soon discovered he had a lot to live up to. But beyond the remarkable and intimidating history of his forefathers was a more subtle, soulful influence that came from an unexpected source.

As an infant, Townes's parents employed a black nanny named Frances Edwards, who had an enormous influence on the child's development. While the Van Zandts regularly attended the local white Baptist church every Sunday, Frances spirited her son, Jimmy, and young Townes across town to the black Pentecostal church, where he was thrilled by the driving rhythm of gospel music.

One year for Christmas, Frances presented the Van Zandt family with a small handwritten book titled *My White Family*. Filled with precious memories and anecdotes of her years with the Van Zandts, Ms. Edwards composed a handful of short vignettes recalling each child's personality and adventures. The chapter on Townes began: "Townes was a pistol. He was so lively and always busy."

On the occasion of Townes's first birthday, Frances recalled that "Mrs. Van" was out of town for the baby's party. Inviting Mr. Van's mother and sister over for dinner, Frances "baked a white cake and fixed the table real pretty," with "real silver glasses for drinking water." She dressed the child in a little white gown and set him in his high chair. "After dinner the cake was served. Townes had fun with his cake. He was one year old."

"Mr. and Mrs. H. W. Van Zandt were a really nice couple," Frances wrote. "They were known to their friends as Van and Dotsy. Mrs. Van needed a maid. That was the beginning of many years of service. She was expecting a baby. When the baby came, he was Mr. Townes Van Zandt. I really did not want to be a babysitter," Frances confessed. "One night the white lady couldn't come. I told them I would sit that night. That was the beginning of many nights of sitting. I did general housework, but cooking was my hobby, collecting and saving recipes."

Frances recalled how Townes at two years old "could run so fast. He would go down the driveway and down the walk, past four or five houses. He knew I could not catch him. He would laugh, and I would want to sit down and cry. He played with a pretty little dog named Sandy. I did not like Sandy. He would play so rough, but Townes loved him. I would worry about him. He would climb the cyclone fence, and his foot would get [caught] in one of those little holes."

One morning on Washington Terrace, Frances was working in the kitchen while young Townes played outside. "He came in and asked me for a nickel. He came back several times for a nickel. I asked Townes what was he doing with so many nickels? Nickels was getting low! He said there was a little boy down the street selling Kool-Aid for five cents a glass. I said, 'Townes, it would be cheaper for me to make you a pitcher of Kool-Aid for five cents a package.'"

Gauging by Frances's memoir, it seems that Townes's bad habits began at a very early age: "During the war, we could not get much laundry soap," Frances recalled. In lieu of store-bought detergent, she whipped up some homemade soap with bacon grease that she stirred with a wooden spoon. "Townes climbed up in a chair and licked the spoon. His little mouth was blistered. I was sorry. We found him one day sitting on the bathroom floor with a can of Sani-Flush. Thank the Lord, he hadn't eaten any.

"He began to grow up," Frances continued. "I read so many cowboy books. He loved stories. He liked pancakes and cherry pie. The children liked to take the bedspreads and blankets and make tents over the card table and take the big pretty cushions from the divan and place them in a long row and play train. Sometimes it seemed as if a cyclone came through."

In return for her many years of loyal service, the Van Zandts helped Frances's sister pay for her college tuition. In her careful handwriting, she quoted from Psalm 41, verses 1, 2, and 3: "Blessed is he that considereth the poor. The Lord will do wonderful things for him."

"I can never thank them enough," she added. Townes's well-known generosity and compassion for the poor undoubtedly were inspired by his parents' example. "The Van Zandt home was a haven to Jimmy [Frances's son]. They would give him Townes's cowboy shirts he had outgrown. He loved those shirts better than new ones."

Family snapshots of Townes as a Cub Scout reveal a gangly boy with a mischievous grin and shining dark eyes. "I think his childhood was pretty ordinary, with a family that loved him. He was a happy-go-lucky, funny kid," Townes's older sister, Donna Spence, recalled.

According to Jeanene Munsell Van Zandt, Townes's third wife, Townes spoke of his father as "a great, compassionate man who he really respected." Harris Van Zandt had been the company lawyer for Pure Oil until he was promoted to the position of vice president. One day, a young Townes came home to discover his father in tears. He had never seen Van so emotionally distraught before. Clearing his throat, his father explained, "Son, today I had to lay off three hundred men." Torn apart over the matter, Harris soon resigned from the job.

Townes's first eight years, the most stable in his life, were spent in Fort

Worth, until a series of moves made every few years permanently up-rooted him. First the family moved to Midland, Texas. Then a year later, the Van Zandts packed their bags again and headed north to Billings, Montana. At that point, Frances sadly chose to stay behind. Four years later the family would relocate once again, this time to Barrington, an affluent Chicago suburb, for a three-year stretch.

"We would move a lot," Donna reminisced. "Mom used to laugh and say that before the truck was empty and the furniture was put in the house Townes would've rounded up a friend for him and a friend for me and a friend for our younger brother Bill in the new neighborhood. He was an easy person to like, friendly, outgoing and caring, a nice, silly little brother, but his life took a different turn later on."

"I had a nice childhood and all that," Van Zandt once joked. "I don't remember it, but that's what I've been told." Townes's remark isn't nearly as flippant as it seems. His memory had been permanently fogged by a series of electric- and insulin-shock treatments he received after being diagnosed as a manic depressive with schizophrenic tendencies in the wake of a nervous breakdown suffered during his sophomore year of college.

Counter to what Van Zandt claimed, his youth in Texas was not a complete blank. Bits and pieces of memories came drifting back years later when columnist and author Cynthia Heimel pressed him for some substantial answers. "I remember smells," he said hesitantly, "hot sun after a rain mixed with cow manure and grass." Townes also recalled the first song his father sang to him and began to hum a few bars of "By the Beautiful Sea." There was an uncle who liked to sing "Ragtime Cowboy Joe." And at his first roundup at the age of four, Townes got an eyeful of the first naked girl he ever saw, bathing in a water trough. Her name was Bonnie, the daughter of the foreman on his uncle Brownie's ranch.

"What was it like in the mental institution?" Heimel probed. As if out of a hazy dream, Van Zandt began describing a scene sounding like something from an Ingmar Bergman film: images came rushing back of long corridors filled with strange, silent people in white gowns, standing around in the soft light of dawn. Van Zandt recalled his parents coming to visit him and the doctor having to reintroduce his mother to him as "the one with the long hair."

CHAPTER 2

STRUCK BY LIGHTNIN', TOUCHED BY FROST

I asked Lightnin' one time what the blues were.
And he said, "Well, son, I think they're a cross
between the greens and the yellows."
—TVZ

On the evening of September 9, 1956, a twelve-year-old Townes Van Zandt sat glued before the family TV set, one of the few on the block at the time, breathlessly awaiting the arrival of "the King" on *The Ed Sullivan Show*. Townes, like the rest of his generation, was about to be all shook up by the sound and sight of Elvis Presley in a plaid jacket and slick pompadour, hiccuping his new hit song, "Don't Be Cruel."

For Townes, the phenomenon of Elvis didn't come out of nowhere. He'd already heard plenty of country music on the radio growing up in Texas, driving from oil field to oil field with his father. Although fond of country stars like Hank Snow, Hank Williams, Lefty Frizzell, and Roy Acuff, whose high-lonesome sound came reverberating through the little dashboard speaker of his daddy's car, they were simply no match for a supernova like Presley.

"It definitely started with Elvis," Townes later explained, citing his original inspiration. "That just flipped me out. He didn't quite seem real, you know?" It wasn't only Elvis's music that moved Van Zandt that night. Watching his sister Donna and her two screaming girlfriends' reactions to the King, Townes had a sudden revelation: "I realized that guy's doin' nothin' but playin' guitar and he's got every Cadillac in the world. He's obviously got the heart of every girl in the world, judgin' by my sister and her buddies. And he wears clothes like that, so he must have all the money he wants. I gotta get me a guitar."

"We were in Billings at the time," Donna recalled with a laugh. "We were just being like everybody else our own age, going crazy about Elvis Presley."

In the wake of Presley's television debut, an incurable case of rockin' pneumonia spread among America's youth in pandemic proportions. Overnight, Van Zandt became completely obsessed with rock and roll. Ricky Nelson, Jerry Lee Lewis, and the Everly Brothers were among his favorites, as well as the hard-knocks country crooner Johnny Cash. That Christmas, Townes wrote Santa a letter, promising to learn his father's favorite song, Bobby Helm's "Fraulein," if old Saint Nick would just bring him a guitar. On the morning of December 25, Van Zandt awoke to discover a brand-new Harmony six-string lying under the family's shimmering tree. True to his word, Townes would eventually record the sweet but corny ballad of "the old German's daughter" on his sixth album, *The Late, Great Townes Van Zandt,* years later, in tribute to his late father.

Soon after moving to the Chicago suburbs, Townes, the new kid on the block, played his first gig at a weekend sock hop in response to a friendly dare. After dropping her son off at the junior high school, Townes's mom, Dorothy (whom everyone called Dotsy), turned the corner, parked the car out of sight, and then sneaked back to peer through the cafeteria window to watch her son perform three songs by each of his heroes, Elvis, Ricky Nelson, and Hank Williams. As he began to sing, the girls in the crowd, as he'd secretly hoped, started to scream. By the end of his short set, Townes had become an instant celebrity.

"[As] I went through the crowd, everybody patted me on the back. I fell in with all the best guys and girls immediately," Van Zandt later recalled. In the meantime, Townes continued teaching himself the rudiments of guitar. "By the time he was in junior high the guitar had become more and more important to him and he got better all the time," Donna Spence recalled.

"I learned my first chord at fifteen and my second when I was twenty," Townes once joked.

Grabbing him by the arm one afternoon, Townes dragged his dad into his bedroom to listen to his rendition of "Blowin' in the Wind." Mildly impressed with his son's earnest singing and strumming skills, Van made a suggestion that would forever change the boy's life. He told Townes he thought he should write his own songs.

At times, the stories of Van Zandt's early life seem to draw a parallel to those of Holden Caulfield, the irreverent protagonist of J. D. Salinger's classic novel of adolescence, *The Catcher in the Rye*. Holden, much like Van Zandt, was extremely bright but applied himself only when absolutely necessary. Both kids came from good families but constantly wound up in trouble and either dropped out or were kicked out of a series of schools until they were finally institutionalized after nervous breakdowns.

Both boys, fictitious and real, were deeply troubled by their rootless upbringings. As the Van Zandt family moved regularly, from Texas to Montana to Illinois, during his formative years, Townes was able to build few, if any, lasting relationships. It's not hard to imagine Van Zandt harboring the same regrets as Holden Caulfield while he stood on a chilly winter hillside, watching the football game below after getting the boot from some snooty private school, trying to reach some kind of resolution or closure.

The job of the catcher in the rye, as Salinger explained, is to prevent children at play from running off the edge of a cliff. For Van Zandt, his songs would eventually fulfill the same function. Over the years, Townes regularly received fan letters from people thanking him for pulling them out of the black hole of addiction, insanity, and suicide.

But unlike Caulfield, who felt that everyone he met was a phony, Townes Van Zandt wasn't completely jaded by cynicism. He believed his purpose on earth was to "write songs that really do make a difference" and would fervently devote himself to the idealistic mission of saving the world with a song.

"I'd like to alter the course of the universe, make it a happier place," Townes once said. "No death. No disease. No depression. Nobody getting older. All the babies would get older, but once they start getting too much older they die. I'm not sure how exactly to do this. I haven't made my move yet."

In 1960, at age sixteen, Townes was shipped off to Shattuck Academy in Faribault, Minnesota, about fifty miles south of Minneapolis, where he received what he later described as a "real serious private prep school ivy-covered education."

"He didn't talk about his past much. He had alluded to having gotten into some mischief with a girl back at Barrington High," Van Zandt's old classmate and friend Marshall "Marsh" Froker said. "I don't think he was too happy about where he was. But then again not many of us were.

"Shattuck was a military academy with an ROTC program. We had to wear uniforms, gray pants with a black stripe down the side and gray shirts with black ties and cadet-rank insignias on our arms or collars," Froker recalled. "The academic program was modeled after English public schools. The teachers were called 'Masters.' Architecturally, the place looked like an English school in the countryside, with tan limestone buildings and a clock tower as Anglican as can be."

Townes and Marsh lived in the same dormitory but on different floors. One night Froker heard music coming from Van Zandt's room and knocked on his door. "Townes was listening to some comedian from the South that I'd never heard of. We got acquainted, and he found out that I played the bongos recreationally," Marsh recalled.

Townes wanted some rhythm to go with his guitar, so we ended up hanging out together. On free nights we'd go off someplace where we could make a racket. We actually played a couple of gigs together. Our big number was [Ray Charles's] "I Got a Woman." We also did a rendition of [Elvis Presley's] "Mystery Train." It was probably the most ridiculous thing those people ever heard in their lives. At the first gigs he played he was kind of shy and didn't say much. Later on, it struck me how talky he was in between songs. He'd rattle on, telling jokes, or he'd come back after a break and start to sing "Amazing Grace," and by the second verse he'd smile and say, "Just kidding. I won't subject you to that."

While many of the boys at Shattuck Academy would continue on to military colleges, become officers in the army, and end up in Vietnam, Townes didn't fit in too well with the gung-ho crowd. Although he was something of a misfit, Van Zandt was never outwardly disrespectful. His proper southern upbringing had taught him to politely (and wisely) keep his stronger opinions to himself. It was his appearance that clearly projected an air of rebellion.

"Townes was kinda cool and wore his hat at a rakish angle," Froker recalled. "You were supposed to have a glass shine on your shoes, but he wasn't into that. I was an officer, and he was in my platoon. Eventually I got tired of reminding him that he needed to improve, so I made him the platoon sergeant," Marsh chuckled. "That way he'd have to be in front of the platoon whenever we drilled or marched. I would give the command,

and he'd have to execute it. So he had to pay attention or he'd make an ass out of himself. We were friends, so it was hard to be a hard-ass with him."

For his duration at Shattuck, until graduating in 1962, Townes seemed content to remain at the lowest rank of sergeant. He showed absolutely no ambition or hopes of earning more stripes, nor was he the type that enjoyed bossing others around.

"As a senior everyone was supposed to call you 'Sir,' but Townes didn't want any part of that. He'd say, 'No, don't do that. I thought we were buddies.' The freshmen would just about fall over," Marsh chuckled.

"We were assigned as roommates for our junior year at Shattuck," classmate Luke Sharpe recalled. "Townes was a smart guy, not an avid student but a pretty good athlete. He weighed between one forty and one fifty, pitched baseball, played football and wrestled, which I happened to do too. Townes had good reflexes. He was tall, had pretty good leverage and was pretty strong in a wiry sort of way."

"He was in good shape although he smoked," Marsh Froker added.

Back then *everybody* at boarding school used to smoke as an act of rebellion. He was a smoker, but he'd knock it off during the football season. Where Townes really excelled was on the wrestling team. He had these ropy forearms and was really strong and well coordinated. He was in the same weight class as the captain of the team. They didn't get along very well. Townes thought he was an arrogant, gung-ho military type. Each week they'd have a match to see who was going to wrestle the opposing team member in their class, and Townes would always beat him. So the captain of the wrestling team wound up warming the bench while Townes wrestled. I think he was kind of proud of that.

The guys really looked up to Townes. He had a lot of natural charisma. There was a story that went around the school. I never heard it from him directly, but people said that during a tournament in Minneapolis, Townes managed to do the deed with some girl from St. Mary's in a janitor's closet. I knew this girl. She'd gone out with me once just because I knew Townes. She was hot for him, and I guess it was her way of getting next to him.

Whatever it was, charisma, mojo, or what the TV commercials back in the sixties referred to as "sex appeal," Townes had it in spades. Van Zandt's effect on women was nothing short of intoxicating. And tales of his "scoring" with the hottest babes only added to his already considerable reputation at Shattuck.

With his sharp wit and gregarious personality, Van Zandt became the ringleader of a band of obnoxious prep-school hell-raisers whose pranks included tossing cherry bombs down dormitory toilets, causing the pipes to burst and freeze over in the dead of winter.

"Most of the trouble he got into was during his senior year when he hung out with a different crowd who were up to no good," Marsh recalled. "There was one kid who could actually put explosives together. Nothing big, but occasionally he'd manage to rock the campus."

"Oh, it was pretty good entertainment," Luke Sharpe chortled. "They made homemade bombs from potassium permanganate which they stole from the chemistry lab. It's a great oxidizer, but it always left behind a big purple stain."

During his senior year Townes roomed with John Roehl, who along with Tom Barrow formed what they conceived of as "a kind of counter-culture group" called the Syndicate. "They amused themselves by not going along with school policies and drinking everything they could get their hands on," Luke Sharpe laughed. "I was a lot straighter than Townes, which is a pretty low bar. But bein' his old roommate and a southern boy, he felt kindly towards me and let me tag along sometimes."

Cadets disciplined for bad behavior were usually put on "walk squad," which meant they were forced to march back and forth in front of the armory for hours at a time while toting their rifle. Although Van Zandt was frequently found trudging that well-worn path, he frequently had plenty of company.

"After our senior year at Shattuck, Townes came down to stay with me in Checotah, [Oklahoma]," Luke Sharpe reminisced.

He was kind of drifting around at the time, and his dad was trying to hammer him in line. He tried to put him on a seismograph cruise, goin' around the country, setting off charges for oil exploration and reading the results.

Townes could probably get into trouble faster than anyone I've ever seen. He had a gift for it. One summer I picked him up at the airport and said, "Hey, Van Zandt, I'll take you to this dance and show you how the locals have fun here in Oklahoma." He walked in and eyeballed a couple of girls when one of their dates walked over and said, "Hey, I saw you lookin' at my girlfriend." Townes said, "Which one is she?" He pointed out the girl, and Townes said, "That dog. Are you kiddin' me?" And the fight was on. I said, "Oh, c'mon, Townes, I gotta live in this town."

"You'd never know which Townes was going to show up on any given day," Marsh Froker explained.

He could be very social and outgoing and telling jokes. Then at other times he was pretty withdrawn, but there was nothing even close to psychotic behavior. He loved to gamble, even back then. Townes played a lot of poker, but he wasn't like other kids his age who'd bet a couple chips here and there. When you played with him, he wasn't afraid to push the whole pile in. Townes would put everything on the draw of a card or the flip of a coin. Eventually I lost enough money that I stopped playing with him.

Marsh appreciated his friend's carefree sense of daring and was often surprised by his impulsive generosity and lack of attachment to material things: "Townes liked to give stuff away. He'd suddenly get this urge and just give you something that he had like a valise or an attaché case. No matter what it was he'd never regret it. I would ask him what [his sudden burst of generosity] was all about, and he'd say, 'It just seemed like a good idea at the time.'"

"Townes was a rich kid who didn't care much about material things," Luke Sharpe surmised. "His dad could've given him the inside track to a big executive job, but he was more concerned about how he would be thought of musically. He told me he thought he would be the second-most-famous alumnus at Shattuck. He said he didn't think he could beat out Marlon Brando. I don't think anyone at Shattuck was surprised about what Townes did and how well he did it, or how he ended up."

"Townes was *very* dedicated and serious about music," Marsh Froker said. "He was influenced by Elvis, but mostly he played records by Josh White and Johnny Cash. He paid a lot of attention to the guitar playin' on Johnny Cash's records. His taste could be very eclectic. He also liked Dave Brubeck's album *Time Out* a lot."

"He loved music and had an amazing knowledge of it," Luke Sharpe marveled. "He introduced me to Leadbelly, and of course he was a big Elvis fan and a good Elvis mimic too. He let his sideburns grow *way* too long. Townes played guitar and wrote songs continually. He had a note-book of 'em. I think the music was something that he just had naturally, and it wasn't ever gonna go away. It was *all* he cared about."

Of all the music that Townes listened to, it was the blues of Mance Lipscomb and Lightnin' Hopkins that resonated with him on the most profound level. Although both men hailed from the Lone Star State, their music was as different as night and day. Lipscomb's laconic picking supported a rustic, earthy vocal delivery, whereas Lightnin's fiery style was inspired from some place hotter and more supernatural than the Piney Woods.

"Townes *loved* Mance Lipscomb," Guy Clark recalled. "Mance was a really nice seventy-year-old gentleman sharecropper who fell into the folk scene and wound up playin' for college kids and drunks. I'm sure he was wonderin' what the white man was gonna fool him with next. But Lightnin' was a drinkin', gamblin', guitar-playin' crazy guy all his life. That's *all* he ever did. And I think, in many ways, Townes felt a little closer to him."

While on break from school, Townes would hunt down Hopkins's obscure albums in record shops in Chicago and Minneapolis and then soon wear out the grooves of the treasured vinyl, attempting to learn Lightnin's slippery licks. But it wasn't just Hopkins's guitar style and weary voice that captivated Townes; the raw poetry of the blues man's hard life as a sharecropper and ne'er-do-well gambler spoke to his soul like mystical scripture from a forgotten religion.

Despite his small-town Centerville origins, Sam "Lightnin'" Hopkins was rather urbane. He wore his hair conked, drove a pink-and-black Dodge, and carried a pint of gin in his hip pocket. Lightnin' dressed slick, "on the pimpy side," as the Bentonia blues man Skip James once described him. With a tilted porkpie, a pair of Ray-bans and a cigarette perpetually dangling from his lips, Hopkins had plenty of style to spare. His never-play-it-the-same-way-twice approach set him apart from all other blues men of his day with the exception of John Lee Hooker of Clarksdale, Mississippi. Both men were famous for changing chords on their guitars whenever they "felt like it." Their bold approach to improvisation always kept their blues fresh and adventurous. Even though he idolized Hopkins, very little of Van Zandt's music was ever improvised. Chance became a factor in Townes's music only as his sobriety diminished.

"When he was coherent he was a great guitar player. Townes always said Lightnin' influenced him, but I never heard that. I heard Bob Dylan," musician and journalist Paul Kopasz (a.k.a. Paul K.) pointed out. "There were times when Townes would apologize to his crowd for having to sit down at a gig. But then he'd recall one of Lightnin' Hopkins' old adages: 'If you're gonna play the blues, you shouldn't even be *able* to stand up.' Lightnin' taught Townes to become a blues sponge, but blues and booze weren't all that Townes regularly soaked up," Paul said, referring to Van Zandt's unquenchable thirst for drama and misery. "His sad songs had that wonderful capacity to make a depressed person actually feel better."

Although Townes worshiped Lightnin' and considered him a major influence, his fingerpicking style was firmly rooted in the blues of the Mississippi Delta. Van Zandt's "Colorado Girl" and "Rex's Blues" reveal the influence of Mississippi John Hurt's gentle, spinning melodies like "My Creole Belle" more than the loose, boozy groove of a Lightnin' Hopkins tune. Echoes of Skip James's classic "Cypress Grove" can be heard in Van Zandt's slinky guitar picking on "Brand New Companion," whereas numbers like "Where I Lead Me" and "I Ain't Leavin' Your Love" both evoke the low-down, funky rumble of Bo Diddley, whose "Who Do You Love?" Townes often relied on to kick his shows into overdrive.

"Townes's guitar playing was pristine. He wasn't flashy, but boy, was he accurate in his fingerpicking and his slapping flat-pick style," old friend Rex "Wrecks" Bell said. "I have his fingerpicks and use them all the time."

At the Eighth Annual Townes Van Zandt Wake, held on January 1, 2005, at Bell's club, the Old Quarter, in Galveston, Wrecks ceremoniously placed a fifth of cheap vodka beside a bottle of Orange Crush on the stage so that performers wanting to commune with Townes could take a swig of booze and then chase it with his favorite mixer. If they really wanted to do a ghost dance with Van Zandt's spirit, they could also wear his old fingerpicks while performing one of his songs.

"I appreciated his guitar picking when I was young," Townes's oldest son, John "J. T." enthused.

He was an incredible guitar picker back then. He wore metal picks on all four of his fingers and a thumb pick, and he could just play [like a] piano on the strings down there. It would sound like a couple of guitars. On his early albums, they're kind of overproduced, but you can hear that his playing was phenomenal. As he got older, he still could do it, but I think it was somewhat diminished just from the drinking and traveling and all the tough years. But at the beginning he was an outstanding fingerpicker.

"Townes had two different styles of playing guitar," Guy Clark explained. "He used either a thumb pick with metal fingerpicks or a flat pick. His flat-pick style was one of the coolest things I'd ever heard. He'd take a flat pick and drive it into the next string so that it would pop off the string. It's called a support stretch, and I never heard anybody do it like him. It was deceptively simple and made this beautiful roll. Some of his songs are really hard to play. When he was on—he was on *fire*," Clark enthused. "But most of the time he didn't play very good because he was drunk. His style was sparse, but his timing was dead on. At least he didn't try to play more than he knew. Townes, more than anybody, understood the economy of movement. He was like, I'll move over there just as soon as I finish this watermelon."

"The way Townes played is to let the pick travel through one string and then hit the string behind it," Steve Earle said. "Combined with a hammer on, it gives a distinct percussive effect."

Van Zandt claimed that "Dollar Bill Blues" from his album *Flyin' Shoes* was originally inspired by Doc Watson's banjo picking on his recording of "The Coo-Coo Bird."

"Townes adored Doc Watson," Earle added. Chip Phillips, an old high school buddy and one-time musical collaborator of Steve's back in Houston, recalled hanging out backstage at Nashville's Exit Inn one night with Doc Watson when Van Zandt appeared:

> Doc was talking about listenin' to the same whippoorwills and trains that Hank Williams once listened to, when all of a sudden Townes came walkin' through the door. We were at the back of a cluttered shotgun room, and Doc raised his head with those glazed-over eyes of his—he's blind, y'know—and says, "Well, Townes Van Zandt, you old son of a gun, I haven't seen you . . . ever." We all laughed, and Townes said, "How'd you know it was me, Doc?" Doc said, "The mixture of vodka and cheap cologne [Old Spice] was unmistakable."

Watson often worried over Townes's hell-raising ways much in the same way that Van Zandt was concerned about Steve, whom he called "the Kid." Earle, barely seventeen when they first met in 1972, had already developed an unhealthy appetite for self-destruction. Townes soon found it quite a challenge trying to protect Steve from himself as well as all the pitfalls of the troubadour's life.

In many respects Townes Van Zandt embodied the "everyman" of his generation. As a teenager he strongly related to the antihero, the young, bold individualist as personified by 1950s movie stars James Dean and Marlon Brando. Rebellion at the time wasn't merely a fad but the yardstick by which many of the "war babies" measured their personal worth.

Millions of well-meaning parents soon discovered their kids were not about to quietly accept the mundane blueprint of American life laid out before them by the church, the public school system, or Hollywood. The sound advice of pipe-smoking, sweater-clad TV dads portrayed by Ozzie Nelson and Robert Young soon gave way to the mad, rambling, amphetamine-fueled visions of a new America described by Beat writers Jack Kerouac, Allen Ginsberg, and William Burroughs.

Rock and roll was one of the few detours from the well-trodden path jammed with pin-stripe-suited, briefcase-toting commuters, who worked nine to five, five days a week, to provide for the wife and two-point-five children.

In 1995, Townes told Irish journalist Patrick Brennan how he came to be "another guy on the Lost Highway." "Actually I was all set up by my folks to go into real estate but then I saw Elvis Presley on television. That Christmas I asked and got an electric guitar and that was that, really.

"My people, along with some others, were the founders of Fort Worth. They had pretty big ideas for me too but as soon as I got that guitar in my hand I knew I wasn't gonna ever do anything else. I think I was a big disappointment to them."

But by the end of the 1950s, rock and roll had taken a left hook square on the jaw and was down for the count. Elvis was never the same once the army and Colonel Tom Parker had their way with him. Buddy Holly and the Big Bopper had tragically died in a plane crash. Denouncing rock and roll as well as his flaming homosexuality, Little Richard proclaimed, "God didn't make no Adam and Steve" and repented for his evil ways, while Jerry Lee Lewis was nearly crucified after marrying his thirteen-year-old cousin.

Meanwhile, squeaky-clean heartthrobs like Pat Boone sapped the soul from black music, pasteurized it, and made it as safe (and white) as milk for suburban teenagers, whose fearful parents didn't allow none of that rock and roll music 'round their happy homes.

By the early sixties, college campuses across the United States began to smolder with the first sparks of student rebellion. The battle for civil rights came to a head as churches burned in Alabama. Blacks attempting to vote in Mississippi were lynched, while Kennedy and Khrushchev brought the world to the brink of nuclear annihilation.

In the midst of this constant turmoil came a new folk craze spear-headed by a raspy-throated, surrealist hobo poet from Minnesota named Bob Dylan along with the barefooted, raven-haired Madonna of Harvard Square, Joan Baez. Their striking images and booming record sales immediately eclipsed that of old-school troubadours like Woody Guthrie and Pete Seeger.

Although Van Zandt adored Woody's dust-bowl ballads and his uplifting socialist anthems, it was Dylan's "The Times They Are a-Changin'" that hit him like a bucket of ice water in the face. Bob's prophetic poetry drew bold lines between old and young, apathy and activism, and pointed its nicotine-stained finger in a new direction, not just for Townes but for an entire generation of songwriters to follow.

At the same time Townes was enthralled by blues and folk music, he also became obsessed with twentieth-century American poetry. Mr. Below, "a serious, serious old English teacher," as he later described him, first introduced Townes to the ephemeral verse of Emily Dickinson and Robert Frost. Discovering Frost's "My November Guest" was one of the most significant experiences Van Zandt gleaned during his time at Shattuck Academy. Years later, Frost's influence would reveal itself in Van Zandt's "She Came and She Touched Me," a gentle, spinning waltz, brimming with shimmering imagery and alliteration. Looking back at the lyric years later, Townes remarked, "Robert Frost once said, 'Worry about the phonetics, and the meaning will take care of itself.' I hope he was right."

Under Mr. Below's tutelage, Van Zandt wrote his first play and experimented with odd-metered sonnets. This love of literature was nothing new for Townes, who had grown up on a steady diet of Shakespeare and cowboy stories lovingly read to him at night by his aunt Sudie (Mildred Cantral Perryman).

"The professors, or 'Masters' as we called them at Shattuck, were old guys who had been around forever and were somewhat distinguished in their fields," Marsh Froker recalled. "Mr. Below, whose first name was Frank, but everyone called him Buzzy—but not to his face—was a white-haired Shakespearean scholar who had us read the classics and memorize soliloquies. We spent a lot of time studying Samuel Taylor Coleridge's 'Rime of the Ancient Mariner' and 'Kubla Khan.' Later on when I first heard Townes's 'Silver Ships of Andilar' it reminded me of old Buzzy. It sounded like our senior-year English class, but on acid," Marsh laughed.

"At the time I never thought of Townes as this very creative guy," Froker reminisced. "I don't think he was writing much of his own music yet. Outside of class he didn't talk about Shakespeare or literature or anything. But in his senior year he wrote a spoof of a Tennessee Williams play. I picked it up and looked at it and said, 'Townes, this is seriously good.' But he just blew it off. This was a real eye-opener because academically he wasn't that motivated; he just did enough to stay out of trouble most of the time."

"Poetry ran in his family," Van Zandt's first wife, Fran (Peterson Van Zandt) Lohr, explained. "Ida Van Zandt Jarvis had published a book of Texas poetry around the end of the nineteenth century. And Townes grew up on the classics. He read incessantly. He would laugh at Shakespeare while most everybody else struggled through it because it had been assigned."

Van Zandt also loved Canadian bard Robert Service's rhyming ballads like "The Shooting of Dan McGrew" and "The Spell of the Yukon," which plumbed the dark hearts of the desperate men who battled one another, as well as the harsh elements of North America's wild frontier.

Influenced by old English folk ballads, many of Van Zandt's first lyrics possessed an underlying formality that few of his peers could match. Townes would often employ double prepositions like "for to go," which gave his verses a distinct Elizabethan flavor.

"We were both big fans of Dylan Thomas. Thomas used language to its absolute fullest. He always brought you up to another level. I always aspired to write with the same economy and abandon," Guy Clark explained. "Anytime we started feelin' cocky about ourselves, like when it got to the point where Townes would ask me, 'Guy, who do you think is the best songwriter? You or me?' we'd listen to an old Dylan Thomas record, and it would give us some immediate perspective." Besides the brilliance of his mad, rambling poetry, there is little doubt that tales of Mr. Thomas's infamous binges and outrageous behavior spurred the pair of young aspiring songwriters on to new levels of craziness and debauch ery as well.

In 1962, Townes enrolled at the University of Colorado at Boulder, intending to major in economics, a peculiar choice considering his lifelong disdain of money. Van and Dotsy just hoped their son would one day lead a "normal" life and harbored dreams of him becoming a lawyer or perhaps a politician and settling down to raise a family in Texas.

Back in his college days at the University of Colorado, Harris Van Zandt had joined a fraternity known as Sigma Nu. In turn this made Townes, a legacy, an automatic pledge. "He hated fraternities and never, *ever* would have joined if it had not been for his parents," Van Zandt's college roommate, Bob Myrick, recalled. "He didn't want to have a thing to do with it. He just wanted to go home, listen to Jimmy Reed records, and play his guitar."

Myrick recounted the misadventure that led to Van Zandt writing his brilliant satire "Talking Fraternity Blues," which later appeared on his classic album *Live at the Old Quarter, Houston, Texas:*

> We had been drinkin' all afternoon and were drunker than skunks until we finally we ran out of booze. They were having a formal dance next door at the Sigma Nu house. They always gave Townes shit for being their worst pledge. They didn't hate him, but they didn't think he was a very good pledge. And he wasn't. Townes *never* wore his pledge pin. So we strolled over to the Sigma Nu house to say hi to everybody and hit the punch bowl. Townes didn't even have his shirt on. No shoes, no socks, just a pair of jeans. They started givin' him plenty of shit right away. So he pulled his pledge pin out of his pocket and damn if he didn't pin it right through his skin. There was this little dribble of blood runnin' down his chest. He said, "Okay, look you guys, I'm wearin' it." Then he walked over to the punch bowl and start drinkin'. Those goddamn actives were *horrified.*

Bob laughed: "He totally blew them away. A month later he was no longer a pledge."

"When Townes first played 'Fraternity Blues' everybody thought it was the funniest goddamn thing they'd ever heard," Myrick recalled. Delivered over a fingerpicked, old-timey medicine-show chord progression, Van Zandt recounted how he tried to impress his frat brothers by mastering "the entire Greek alphabet" by whipping "through that son of a Beta backward in five seconds." Townes didn't fit in with the perky preppy set any more than he did with the gung-ho crowd at Shattuck Academy. He was immediately pegged as "a trouble causer" for his cheap wine, slouching posture, and grouchy attitude. Ultimately, he was shunned for failing to properly "bubble with enthusiasm."

Back in Houston, visiting the folks while on break from college, Townes went down to the Bird Lounge to witness his hero, Lightnin' Hopkins, live, in the flesh. Van Zandt sat mesmerized as he watched Hopkins's long, black, snakelike fingers chase each other up and down the neck of his old Gibson guitar while he sang about the real people and events that directly shaped his life. There were plenty of cruel boss men, corrupt cops, and no-good lyin' women, always giving "Po' Lightnin'" more than his fair share of trouble. But in the retelling of the daily injustices he witnessed and experienced as a black man in his hometown of Houston, Hopkins would unintentionally become something of a spokesman for the civil rights movement.

Little did he know, but just a few short years later Townes would appear as Hopkins's opening act at the Jester Lounge, Houston's "Folk Mecca." Eventually, they got to know each other pretty well over the years. Townes always got a kick out of how the old blues man mangled his name. But it was no big deal. Wrecks Bell played bass with Hopkins for nearly ten years, and no matter how many times he corrected him, Lightnin' still managed to call him "Rick." "They both make the same mistakes at the same time," Townes once remarked, mystified by Bell's ability to follow the totally unpredictable Hopkins.

"I played with him. Visited his house a couple times," Townes later told Patrick Brennan. "I knew [Lightnin'] when he was a sixty-year-old black blues player who came through hard times from wandering around the country and from white people who were ripping him off steadily. So he didn't have much trust in white people. He liked me because I wasn't there to rip him off."

"He was so influenced by Lightnin' Hopkins who was a poor black man with incredible courage and spite for the white man," J. T. explained. "Townes looked at where he came from: privileged background, private school, and wealthy parents, and he walked away from all that and hit the road without any second thoughts."

Worried about his credibility as a white, college-educated, blues-singing troubadour, Townes eventually blew off all the comforts and opportunities of his upper-middle-class background, believing that real-life experience was infinitely more valuable than a paycheck or emotional stability. He was simply not the kind of writer to observe human nature safely through a keyhole. Life, in all its messy drama, fueled his songs, and he threw himself into the thick of it every chance he got.

Townes always claimed he scored his first matchbox full of marijuana from Lightnin' Hopkins back in Houston. Years later, roaring drunk, Van Zandt and Clark headed down to the Ash Grove in Los Angeles to catch up with their pal Po' Lightnin'.

"Here were these two white boys from Houston raisin' hell," Guy reminisced. "We stormed into his dressing room, and his family was there. He could hardly even remember our names. Then Townes proceeded to tell everybody in the room about how Lightnin' sold him a joint. Lightnin' said, 'Excuse me, but this here is my *aunt.*' They didn't exactly throw us out bodily, but they sure made it seem like we had somewhere else to go in a hurry," Clark said with a husky laugh.

"Lightnin's persona was totally different on stage than it was at home or in a car," Townes's guitarist Mickey White explained. "He was a real southern gentleman, a *completely* different guy when he wasn't dealing with all the competition. All the old black bluesmen were *very* competitive. Mance Lipscomb used to say, 'Lightnin' is good. . . . He can play in E and A. But I can play in all five keys—E, A, D, G, and C.'"

Back at the University of Colorado, things were far from normal for Townes. Without a word to anyone he had taken to locking himself up in his room for a week at a time. Leaving the phone off the hook, he'd down a bottle of Bali Hai wine and play guitar for hours on end. Repeatedly spinning his favorite records by Lightnin', Hank Williams, and Bob Dylan, Townes would study their every nuance.

After a week of self-imposed isolation, Townes was ready to party. One night he sat teetering on the edge of a fourth-floor balcony, leaning over backward, "just to see what it felt like all the way up to when you lost control," he'd later recall. Townes realized that if he was going to fully experience the sensation, he'd have to actually let himself fall. Then, like some half-crazed scientist from an old horror movie, he proceeded with his grim experiment and let himself tumble backward, nearly forty feet down to the ground below.

I started leaning back really slow, and really paying attention. I fell over backwards and landed four stories down flat on my back. I remember the impact and exactly what it felt like and all the people screaming. I had a bottle of wine, and I stood up. Hadn't spilled any wine. Felt no ill effects whatsoever. Meanwhile all the people jammed onto the elevator, and when the doors opened, they knocked me over coming out. And it hurt more being knocked over than falling four stories.

Knowing his old friend's propensity to exaggerate, Darryl Harris voiced his doubts concerning this oft-repeated tale: "When you think about it, you couldn't be sittin' on a rail and fall off four stories and then land on your back. Most likely you'd land on your head. Maybe it was more like two stories or a first-floor balcony. What's that old saying?" Darryl said with a grin. 'Leaks get worse and stories get better.'"

"It was the *third floor* of Varsity Manor. *And he didn't fall—he jumped,*" Bob Myrick emphasized. "I was standing right next to him when he did it. He was hanging his legs over the edge of the balcony and said, 'I wonder what would happen if I jumped? Do you think I'd get hurt?' He was being kind of a pain in the ass at the time, so we said, 'There's only one way to find out.' We didn't think he'd do it, but he did."

Soon after surviving this maniacal stunt Van Zandt moved in with Myrick, who gave him a job checking IDs at Tulagi's, one of Boulder's oldest and most beloved watering holes where students downed 3.2 beer by the pitcher-full.

Fran Lohr recalled first meeting Townes during their sophomore year at Boulder in 1963: "He was nineteen and I was eighteen, working as a maid to the president of the university. At the time I lived in a garage apartment right behind the president's house. We met when a girlfriend and I were going to happy hour at Tulagi's. Townes was the bouncer," she laughed.

> He told me I couldn't get in unless I gave him a kiss as a cover charge. He called me later to apologize for being so forward and fresh. Then he asked me out.
>
> We started dating and fell in love right off the bat. Townes got drunk one night and sent me flowers the next day, a beautiful Mexican heather plant, to apologize and promised he would be better from then on. Of course, he broke that promise many times over.
>
> He had a guitar and played it occasionally, but we listened to music all the time, mostly to blues, a lot of Lightnin' Hopkins and Muddy Waters and of course plenty of Hank Williams. Townes wasn't much into the Beach Boys. I don't remember him playing guitar at parties in college. Mostly he played just when we were by ourselves.

Van Zandt soon began performing regularly at a little folk club called Barefoot Charlie's, which happened to be managed by his pal Bob

Myrick. "I would always request the 'Ballad of Ira Hayes,' which was a very dramatic tune that he did really well," Bob said. "He did some Dylan songs as well as delta blues and folk music. He hadn't really started writing his own songs yet."

"We were just regular old college students for the most part," Fran continued. "We liked to go into the mountains on picnics with friends. Although Townes liked hiking, he was very amateurish and would always end up hurting himself somehow. Once he nearly froze on top of a mountain and got real embarrassed with himself, so he threw away all his hiking equipment after that."

"Townes was *so* smart. You'd hang on every word he said," Fran continued.

He was so funny and so far out that it was hard keeping up with him. He *was* truly the pied piper, and everybody followed him. Once we were riding in his blue Chevy 409 and he was waving at everybody when he accidentally ran into the back of a policeman. The cop got out of his car to give Townes a ticket and told him he thought he probably wouldn't live long enough to pay it, so he let him off. Townes was certainly living a charmed life back then. But I was quite different. I grew up real strict and straight-laced, a Southern Baptist, just like his mom and sister. I didn't even *know* about marijuana. He didn't want me in the drug scene. Townes hated it if I got drunk. All I needed was two beers, and it was over. So our relationship was different than he had later on with other women. He was very protective. There were some wild things going on that I didn't see. He would throw some wild parties, but at the same time Townes would make everybody behave and treat me with respect.

He'd already fallen off the balcony before we met, and he laughed about that. Back in high school Townes had a hankering to hop railcars to go find out how poor people lived. He'd gone on a pretty serious drinking binge and was about to do it again during the second semester of our sophomore year. His parents worried a lot about his drinking and wanting to take off again. So they came and got him and brought him down to Galveston, to the hospital, and gave him insulin- and electric-shock therapy. The thinking back then was that if you had a bad experience they would burn out that part of your brain. They managed to destroy most of his childhood memories. But it wasn't obvious to me at the time that he had real problems.

"Poor Harris was nearly driven to distraction by Townes. His dad played college football and was a straight-line operator, a real pillar-of-the-community-type guy," Luke Sharpe said.

Townes was a lot more like his mom who was a free-spirit type, the antithesis of a Houston socialite. His dad took me aside a couple of times and said, "You lived with him, Luke. What can I do to straighten him out?" I said, "Mr. Van Zandt, I'm sorry, he is what he *is,* and there's just nothin' anyone can do to change it." Townes was always pushing the limit. He was always up for any sort of adventure and any sort of stimulant, from codeine to sniffing glue. In the Shattuck school yearbook there was a picture of him with a pair of socks hanging out of his mouth.

(Van Zandt's favorite technique for sniffing glue was to wrap a tube of the toxic cement up in a ball of socks and either hold it under his nose or pop it in his mouth to get the most out of the mind-bending fumes.)

But it wasn't their concern over Townes's excessive drinking that finally triggered his doting parents to come to Boulder and retrieve their wild child. Van Zandt and his buddy from Billings, Montana, Tom Barrow, who graduated valedictorian at Shattuck and would also later enroll at the University of Colorado, had concocted a crazy scheme to finally free Townes from the drudgery of his academic obligations.

"Townes refused to study. He just wanted to drink and learn the guitar and cruise along," Bob Myrick explained. "Tom was an absolute genius who was incredibly talented. He graduated from CU in architectural engineering, built homes in Santa Fe, and later became known as one of the world's best-known balloonists. We used to call him 'the Godfather.'"

Back in the days of "the Syndicate," one of the many talents Tom Barrow so keenly honed was the ability to fabricate driver's licenses for his fellow students at Shattuck Academy. At Townes's request Tom would forge both Van Zandt's parents' signatures to a letter stating they had granted their son permission to drop out of school. Barrow then slipped the envelope into the dean's mailbox, complete with an expertly rendered out-of-state postmark.

"I remember looking at the letter and Townes asking me if I thought they'd buy it. I said, '*Sure,*'" Myrick laughed.

They thought they'd never hear another word about it. *Wrong*. The dean did *not* buy it and went ahead and took it upon himself to call his parents. He called Mr. Van Zandt and asked him if he wrote the letter. When his folks found out, they came to get him in a heartbeat and pitched him into the hospital in Galveston where they diagnosed him as manic depressive. They wouldn't let me communicate with him, but somehow Townes got Little John, a dealer on the University of Houston campus, to smuggle him in bottles of Bali Hai and Thunderbird wine.

Clever and charming as it all sounds, Van Zandt soon wound up with a serious case of what he, years later, described as "The Sanitarium Blues." Haunted by the memory for the rest of his life, Townes recalled the grueling experience in his last song, released on the 1999 posthumous album *A Far Cry from Dead*.

The folks, they just can't take no more
Throw you in the back seat, slam the door
No stopping as down the road you go
Got no time to lose

Gigantic one-way gate ahead
You're thinkin' man I'd as soon be dead
They decided to give you life instead
The sanitarium blues

Big ole nurse all dressed in white
Slaps you on the table in the middle of the night
Then he straps you down real tight
You're wonderin', what'd I do?

They hose you down, make sure you're clean
Wrap you up in hospital green
Shoot you full of Thorazine
The sanitarium blues

Committed to the University of Texas Medical Branch Hospital in Galveston, Townes went through a three-month program of electric- and insulin-shock therapy. Fran considered his treatment "an extreme measure" for what she believed was just the wild escapades of "a normal college student."

"Back then people did what doctors told them to," Jeanene Van Zandt said with a shrug. "A lot of people gave his parents a bad rap for putting Townes in a mental institution. But those were the same folks that let him fall off a four-story balcony, for God's sake."

"Townes had a reputation for being wild. And he *was*. But I always had the impression he knew exactly what he was doing and just how far it was goin', even when he was drunk. It was just his sense of humor, which was a real Texas sense of humor," Guy Clark explained.

Throughout his life Van Zandt suffered from frequent debilitating bouts of depression. Although it eventually became clear to friends, family, and doctors that his condition was unstable, Townes later made the entire incident sound like a clever ploy to intentionally evade the draft board when he confided to music journalist and author Robert Greenfield that he'd staged "a student breakdown" in Boulder in order to avoid being sent to Vietnam.

Yet Van Zandt's description of his desperate battle for sanity sounds more like a terrifying passage from Edgar Allen Poe, another of his favorite authors. "Boy, there's been a lotta times when depression with me just became physical, it hurt so bad," he told journalist Lola Scobey. "It was wrenching me apart, wrenching me apart, wrenching my brain apart, my whole body, to the point where I was holding my head and screaming. There's been times when my hands, I look at them, and I have the feeling, a very strange feeling, that if I had a machine and could chop my hands off, then everything would be fine."

"Now that's heavy," exclaimed Chris Robinson, lead singer of the Black Crowes, in response to Van Zandt's nightmarish vision. "Townes actually wished a metallic box would float down outta nowhere and chop his hands off so he wouldn't have to play guitar and write songs anymore. The only thing that could stop him from dealing with such intense human feelings wasn't even human—it was a floating metallic box with knives. That story has been permanently tattooed on my brain," he said.

"Townes carries the terror and the sorrow of a sensitive man who has looked into the abyss and seen. . . the abyss," Scobey observed. Yet for all of the darkness that enveloped Townes, Scobey felt Van Zandt was "consistently friendly" and spoke with a "dignified reserve and little placid silences that suggest an underlying well of gentleness."

"Both Dostoyevsky and Kerouac delved into the idea of salvation through suffering," multi-instrumentalist and composer David Amram pointed out. "Jack, who had a Catholic background, spoke of the *pentitentes* in Mexico, where people whipped themselves, not because they were masochists but perhaps in that moment of pain they might reach a higher level of spirituality. Townes did not drink to punish himself. He didn't want to be in pain; it was to anesthetize himself, to end the pain. When Townes wrote tragic songs it wasn't to glorify suffering. He wasn't a postmodern tourist in Gloomsville."

"It was amazing how many people Townes helped through his tragedy. I can't tell you how many I've met," Fran said, recalling one troubled stranger in particular and the effect her ex-husband's music had on his life.

> In September 2004, my niece and I were at a hotel, sitting in the bar, having lunch, when a guy in his sixties came in and sat next to us and struck up a conversation. He told us that his son was bipolar and had recently committed suicide. He said most people don't understand that disease. I said, "I have a feeling about it because my first husband was bipolar." We talked for half an hour. It turned out that music helped him understand his son better. They loved the same music. It kept them really close. I told him that my husband was a musician, and he asked me his name. I said, "Townes Van Zandt," and he burst into tears, sobbing uncontrollably for ten minutes. I finally said, "I'm sorry if I brought back somethin' bad." He said, "No, no, that was the music we used to listen to."

Upon his release from the mental institution, Van Zandt was so thoroughly disoriented that the doctor had to reintroduce him to his family, explaining that the young woman was his fiancée and the lady was his mother. Before the whole terrible ordeal, Townes and Fran had been engaged to be married.

During the spring semester of her junior year Fran left Boulder to be with Townes in Galveston. That summer she spent the weekends with the Van Zandt family at their beach house, still clinging to her dream of a "normal life" with her soon-to-be husband—a law student, who she hoped would one day pass the bar and become a lawyer.

Years later Fran joked with Jeanene, "At least you knew what you were getting," she said. "I thought I was marrying a lawyer."

"My progress towards being a lawyer was a little shaky anyway. It wasn't like I threw away a glittering law career," Townes confessed in a 1992 interview on Dutch television.

It would take a while for Townes to return to his "normal" self again. "When he came back to Boulder he knew my name, but there were a lot of people he worked with at Tulagi's who he couldn't recall," Bob Myrick explained. "And Townes never forgot anything. But he eventually got his memory back, and he started to write and play again, and that's *all* he wanted to do."

In January 1964 Townes and Fran enrolled together at the University of Texas in Houston. Townes once again switched majors, hopping from economics to law to liberal arts and philosophy over the course of his college career. But it was in English literature that he truly excelled. "He blew the professors away," Lohr said. "They couldn't keep up with him. They'd save his papers."

In a heroic attempt at normalcy, Townes married Fran Peterson on August 24, 1965. "The wedding was a trip," Luke Sharpe recalled with a laugh. "I don't remember it all that well as I served the punch. Tom Barrow was there with his wife. The four of us stayed in Townes's apartment while everyone was getting ready for the wedding. But Townes was less than avid about the whole deal."

"We had a big wedding and stayed at a beautiful suite at the Warwick Hotel that his parents had gotten for us," Fran reminisced. "The next night we drove back to Colorado with our friends Tom and Joyce and stopped in Dallas and stayed at some hovel right out of *Psycho*. We woke up in the middle of the night, and the place was infested with roaches. So we went screaming out of there at one in the morning, only to find another motel that looked like *Psycho II*," Fran laughed. "Townes woke up a couple hours later, running into the next room frantically screaming at Joyce and Tom that I was gone. He thought I had been abducted. But I decided to go out and sleep in the backseat of the car because the place was so seedy.

"You'd be surprised, but Townes was quite a domestic guy," Lohr continued. "The summer before we got married he worked, doing hard labor at a cement plant, and made a lot of money for us so we'd have the cash for a down payment on our apartment. He had a real eye for decoration and would refinish furniture for our place. Townes liked to bake bread on Sunday mornings, and we would take it over to my parents' house with pats of butter and have hot bread with the family. He loved my mom and called her 'Granny Good Witch.' She would cook him fried eggs. He ate so many you would get sick just watchin' him."

CHAPTER 3

THE GLINT OF THE RANDALL KNIFE

When the legend becomes fact—
Print the legend.
> —Maxwell Scott, editor of the *Shinbone Star:*
> *The Man Who Shot Liberty Valance*

It was eleven in the morning, a bit on the early side to be drinking, when Guy Clark answered his front door with a bottle in his hand. "I'm gettin' drunk just so I can do this interview for you," he grumbled and took a long pull off a fifth of tequila. "I would *love* to have people know what Townes was all about. But I suggest you go talk to Susanna first, as she probably knew him better than anybody," Clark said and pointed me in the direction of the bedroom. I found her sitting up in bed, watching TV in a bathrobe with her hair piled up on top of her head, cigarette in one hand and what looked like a glass of brandy in the other. "Not today," Susanna said, with a wave of her hand. "I'm just not feelin' up to it."

I had been told by producer, author, and musician Jim Rooney that Susanna and Townes had a special relationship, tighter both spiritually and intellectually than either one shared with their spouses. No matter where he was, or what his condition, Townes religiously called Susanna every morning to check in. A lovely and talented woman in her own right, Susanna contributed lyrics to Van Zandt's "Heavenly Houseboat Blues" and has written songs with her husband and Carlene Carter, as well as painted album covers for Willie Nelson, Nanci Griffith, and Guy over the years.

I had just driven fifteen hours to Nashville from New York and was blown off in a matter of moments. So much for the inside story from "the one who knew Townes best."

A minute later Guy waved me through the living room and downstairs to the basement. Clark sighed heavily as he sat down. He squinted at me for a minute, sizing me up. "If you burn me on this, I'll slit your throat and drink your blood like wine," he snarled. It seemed like a fair-enough deal, so I thanked him for the extra-added incentive I might need to finish the book.

Over the door to his workshop, where he handcrafts fine nylon-string classical guitars that resonate with a deep, rich tone, hung a black-and-yellow sign that pegged him perfectly: "Hard Head Area." Susanna gave it to him for a Christmas present.

Clark was a complex guy—friendly one minute but antagonistic the next. He clearly had mixed feelings about rehashing the old days with his runnin' buddy Townes. Sitting at a knee-high coffee table, he determinedly worked his way through a pack of Merits, stubbing them out, one after the next, in a skull ashtray. I found myself throwing every pitch I had, hoping he'd eventually take a swing at something . . . anything. Clark would only occasionally brake his stony silence with a chuckle and a brief "Ahh, yeah," the kind of response that doesn't help much when gathering information for a book.

I suppose Guy had every right to be guarded. It would take nearly an hour and half a bottle of tequila before he unshackled his armor and spoke directly from his sore heart. Apparently, there was still plenty of pain, unfinished business, and old ghosts lurking down at the dark end of Memory Lane.

Although he made fun of my plaid shorts and Doc Marten boots, we talked for several hours. All the while he begrudged me as "a little Yankee journalist."

In his unflinching memoir, *The Gulf Coast Boys,* the New Mexican–born singer-songwriter Richard "Ricardo" Dobson described Guy as "never one to suffer fools, gladly or otherwise." Although Clark was ornery, I tried not to take his remarks personally.

At some point I recalled an old article written about Townes for *Melody Maker* back in 1987. "You're a Yankee, you're probably Jewish and you're all mixed up but I like you," Van Zandt told a bewildered journalist who had just flown down to Music City, USA, to be "verbally abused by an American cult legend." The piece described Townes as "unspeakably brilliant" but "an infuriating self-destructive alcoholic." No matter how great the author felt Van Zandt was, he confessed that "he'd rather smash in his teeth than kiss his behind."

"He was my best friend—*ever*," Clark growled, sounding more like a warning than some sort of warm, fuzzy sentiment. "And the best man at our wedding thirty-five years ago. . . . Let's see if we can get a Townes vibe goin' in the room," Guy said, taking another pull off the bottle. He grabbed an old cassette tape recorded at his house on Christmas Eve 1976 and popped it into the machine: "It was me, Susanna, Townes, [Van Zandt's second wife] Cindy, and Steve Young." Mayhem ensued as a swirling unidentified bluegrass number burst loose from the speakers like a merry-go-round, spinning out of control. Steve picked a dizzying riff with mad abandon, while Cindy's laughter bubbled like cheap champagne. A minute later Clark yanked the tape out of the deck. So much for the party atmosphere. . . "Well, it seemed important at the time," Guy said, furrowing his bushy silver eyebrows. "The next day I woke up with a hangover."

"Do you know what Townes would say if he saw you comin'?" Clark goaded. "Watch me skin this Yankee." A moment later Guy reached into his pocket and pulled out a quarter. "Twenty bucks," he said. "C'mon, call it—heads or tails." I'd grown up around gamblers and learned from a young age that the best way to stay ahead of the game was to keep your money in your pocket. Besides, we were in Tennessee, so what kind of odds did a Yankee have laying a bet on a portrait of Old Hickory? Clark even once lived on Old Hickory Lane in Nashville, for God's sake.

"Uh, those stakes are a bit high for me," I stammered. "How about a Lincoln?" The coin landed in his hand. I lost, rolled my eyes, and peeled off a five spot. All the while, a stark black-and-white portrait of Van Zandt taken by Nashville photographer Jim McGuire peered down at us from the wall. Every pore on his leathery face was magnified. Puffy and hungover, with a small scar beneath his eye, Townes looked as cold and lonely as the man in the moon.

"Townes wrote the kind of songs that everybody was scared to write and you'll never hear again." Clark said, hunting for an example to illustrate his point. Guy Clark reached for a copy of Van Zandt's obscure 1993 release *The Nashville Sessions* and spun "The Spider Song," a ballad in E minor plainly picked on acoustic guitar, complete with a humming Greek chorus drenched in reverb.

There is a spider in my dreams
Long and silent is his name
Cold as lightning is his smile
Final is his sting

"Nobody cuts it that close to the bone. I s'pose everybody cuts it as close as they can. It's not a competitive sport," Clark imparted. "It's more like how close can you cut it to your own bone? Did you break your own heart? Did you scare the shit out of yourself? That's what matters. Townes went for the passion, not a bunch of clever bullshit. He sounded like himself. I learned that from Townes, or maybe I knew it before, I don't know. . . . What we had in common was to truck no bullshit and applaud craziness."

Reaching for a copy of *Live at the Old Quarter, Houston, Texas,* the Holy Grail of Van Zandt's oeuvre, Guy cued up Townes's surrealistic ballad "Two Girls," reciting the song's opening lines before it began to play: "The clouds didn't look like cotton / They didn't even look like clouds." "Now this song is a yardstick," Clark proclaimed. "That's how good it's gotta be. The only other guy whose songs affected me like that is Ramblin' Jack Elliott. Have you ever heard his '912 Greens'?"

"Sure," I replied. "I know Ramblin' Jack."

"Oh you do, do ya?" Guy goaded. "Well, let's just see about that." With that Guy reached over, grabbed the phone, and punched Jack Elliott's number with the intent of putting me on the spot. "Jack," he barked, "I got this little Yankee journalist here who says he knows you." Then he handed me the phone with a steely glare.

I had crossed paths with Ramblin' Jack a number of times over the years, but like the old blues singer that can't recall your name that Guy immortalized in his tune "That Old Time Feelin'," I wasn't sure if Jack would remember me. Clark watched impatiently as I fumbled with the receiver. It was one of those moments when time stood still long enough for me to wonder what I had gotten myself into and to contemplate finding another line of work.

"Hey, Jack," I began hesitantly, telling him my name, although I was certain he wouldn't recall me. Then I recounted how I'd seen him play a couple times at Passim, up in Cambridge and at Folk City, back in the day. "And then a few years ago in Floyd, Virginia, my pal Old Chief Rolling Papers brought you to town," I said, suddenly jarring his memory.

"Oh, yeah," Jack said cheerfully. "How's the Old Chief doin'?" His innocent inquiry led me to recall the tragic saga of how Old Chief Rolling Papers had recently died in jail. Arrested for drunk driving, his plumber rolled over on him and told the cops how the Old Chief had a couple of trailers filled with marijuana plants hanging up to dry back in the woods. A couple days later, after the kids left for school, a SWAT team surrounded his house and dragged Old Chief Rolling Papers off in chains. To make a long story short, some birds don't live very long locked up in a cage.

"Oh, man, I'm sorry to hear it," Jack whispered.

Elliott then began to reminisce about a string of gigs he and Townes played together back in 1996, driving around California in Van Zandt's old pickup truck he called "the Colonel." Jack recalled how Townes holed up in his motel room one afternoon, scratchin' on his fiddle for hours while a gaggle of gorgeous ladies lounged around the swimming pool. Finally persuading Van Zandt to put down "the damn violin" and go for a dip, Elliott loaned Townes some swimming trunks and coaxed him into the daylight.

"Come on, it's a beautiful day out there," Jack said.

"Yeah, if you like days," Townes groaned.

"Townes was shy about his skinny legs, so he put on some sunglasses, closed his eyes, and pretended to be Ray Charles while I led him over to the pool. He kept askin' me, 'How much further?' 'Just one more step,' I told him. 'About another six inches, . . .'" Jack said, as they neared the edge. "That was all Townes needed to know, and then he shoved me right into the water," Elliott said with a raspy laugh.

A moment later, Guy grabbed the phone from my hand. "Hey," he growled, "I'll talk to you later." Clark hung up the receiver, hoisted himself off the stool, and went off in search of another pack of cigarettes. He offered me a drink, but when I declined, he just rolled his eyes and let out a groan of disgust. A couple minutes later, Guy returned to find me picking a blues riff on one of his homemade guitars.

"Oh, I thought you were just a little Yankee journalist. I didn't know you were a *musician too,*" he sneered.

Although it was clear that Clark couldn't give a damn what I had to say, I told him I'd cut a half-dozen albums and been playing gigs for the past twenty-five years.

"Yeah, yeah," he said, dismissing me with a wave of his hand. "Well, then, why don't we step outside, and you can play me a song, Mr. Little

Yankee Journalist." We repaired outdoors on his back porch and pulled up a couple of chairs. It was July in Nashville, hellishly hot and humid. As soon as we sat down, he leaned over and got right in my face and growled, "Okay now, Mr. Little Yankee Journalist, play me the best fuckin' song you ever learned." With that I closed my eyes, took a deep breath, swallowed hard, and started to sing Leonard Cohen's "Sisters of Mercy."

"Goddamn! Leonard Cohen!" he hooted before I'd finished the first verse. "Shit. He wrote all those great songs to my favorite movie—*McCabe and Mrs. Miller.*" I had to agree with him. Not only was Cohen's soundtrack a classic, but Robert Altman's existential western starring Warren Beatty as the gambler John "Pudgy" McCabe and Julie Christie as Mrs. Miller, the beautiful, opium-addicted madam with sky-blue eyes and corkscrew hair, was an all-time favorite of mine as well. But somehow, at the moment, I felt more like Jimmy Stewart in John Ford's *The Man Who Shot Liberty Valance,* when Lee Marvin (with bullwhip in hand) barks at him, "You got a choice, dishwasher—either you get out of town, or tonight you be on that street alone." It seemed that a showdown was imminent, and I had no shotgun-toting John Wayne standing in the shadows, ready to back me up.

"Alright now, Mr. Little Yankee Journalist Songwriter," Guy sneered, surlier than ever. "Play me the best goddamn song you ever wrote in your *life.*" With that I played him a ballad of sorrow and regret about an old Indian chief who lived with the tragic memory of his murdered tribe. It wasn't necessarily the best song I'd ever written but one I thought he might appreciate. And surprisingly enough, he did, except for a couple lines here and there, which he pointed out that I might improve upon. (And, of course, he was right.)

For the moment I tried to relax in the sweltering heat, thinking perhaps he'd get off my back now that I'd proved myself to be something more than a "little Yankee journalist." That's when Guy pulled out his knife. "You ever heard my song 'The Randall Knife'?" he growled. I had to admit that although I was familiar with his famous tunes "L.A. Freeway" and "Desperados Waiting for a Train," I hadn't heard the song in question. I tried to tell him that in recent years I had gotten into jazz and was in a different world.

"I don't care what world you've been in," he snapped. With that he pointed his knife in the general vicinity of my nose. Clark was pretty drunk. I wasn't sure if the close proximity of the blade to my face signified a real threat or if it was just his way of offering me the opportunity to observe its fabled tip a bit closer.

"Alright, Guy," I said, raising my hands in the air, "you've got my undivided attention. Let's hear the song." He slipped the blade back into its sheath and proceeded to sing one helluva tune about a knife that was "made for darker things" with a blade that was "probably forged in hell."

As I listened, I pictured Clark as a sweating, burly Buddha, begrudgingly passing down a double shot of crazy wisdom from his pal Townes, the disembodied troubadour, directly on to me. At the same time he resembled an old-time preacher (like the guy on the Quaker Oats box but hardly as benevolent), trying to put the fear of Townes in me. Either way, he made his point.

CHAPTER 4

HOUSTON TOWNES

**If you say Buddy Holly is the father of Texas rock,
then you have to say that Townes is the father of Texas folk.**
—Michael Murphey

"This whole folk movement was really a North-eastern thing. Down in Texas it was a different world, and there was this group of songwriters who got started in a little coffeehouse and club in Houston that Townes Van Zandt used to frequent," Nanci Griffith explained. "Lightnin' Hopkins was their guru, the guy from the older generation they latched onto. Townes also had a great feel for the old English ballads. He was extraordinarily talented as a writer," said Griffith, who along with Lyle Lovett and Robert Earl Keen constituted the next generation of Lone Star songwriters to carry on the tradition.

Nanci's father, "Griff," first introduced her to Van Zandt's music when he took his teenage daughter to a small club in Austin and told her to pay close attention, as Townes was "the greatest folksinger Texas ever gave birth to and that's only because Woody Guthrie was born in Oklahoma." Nanci sat transfixed, "nailed to her seat," as Townes sang "Tecumseh Valley."

"Townes sacrificed everything for his art," Griffith said. "The beauty of Townes and the hallmark of his work is that he had the courage as a writer to go places, physically . . . to physically be there and feel it, so the rest of us wouldn't have to. But then Townes couldn't do it any other way."

Through an outstanding command of language and an uncanny ability to process his life into impeccably crafted verse, Townes both inspired and dared dozens of other Houston singer-songwriters to look within and find their own voice.

"I hung around in Houston with a bunch of really talented guys—Townes Van Zandt, Mickey Newbury, Jerry Jeff Walker. And there was a camaraderie about it, a feeling we had for one another," Guy Clark told *Country Style* magazine.

"Townes was the biggest single influence on my writing," Guy confessed. "Working around a poet like him you learn not to throw away a phrase or a rhyme, or a word for a pattern. You learn to keep your work clean, or at least that's what you're aiming for."

While hitching around Texas sometime in early 1965, a rounder by the name of Ron Crosby from Oneonta, New York, would transform himself into Jerry Jeff Walker. At the Rubaiyat Club in Dallas, Walker met Allen Damron, a fixture on the Lone Star folk scene at the time, known for his storytelling and banjo and guitar picking. Allen also had a knack for getting audiences to join him on Pete Seeger–type sing-alongs. Damron asked Walker if he'd been to Austin yet, and when the young drifter shook his head, they piled into Allen's old car and headed south down Route 35.

Austin, the state capital and home of the University of Texas, has long been an oasis of liberalism in a land of fire-spitting oil rigs and redneck cow wranglers. In the midsixties the city had yet to earn its reputation as the "Live Music Capital of the World." These days you can find cowboy singers, blues wailers, folk strummers, slick-haired rockabilly cats, nouveau bluegrassers, Mexican mariachis, grungy punks, jazz jammers, and psychedelic renegades all rocking the populace every night of the week at any one of the dozens of local watering holes.

From Austin, the pair lit out for Houston, where Jerry Jeff soon crossed paths with Townes Van Zandt at the Jester Lounge. Singer-songwriter Don Sanders recalled the burgeoning scene:

> The Jester was your basic beer and wine lounge. In those days you couldn't buy liquor by the drink down here, so you'd bring in a bottle of whiskey and pay for what they called "a set-up," which was basically a glass of Coca-Cola with some ice in it. It was a huge scene. Mac Webster, who owned the Jester, was a real character. He'd stand at the door and take money and would sing a little bit himself. He was a pretty good entertainer. There was no other place like it in town to hang out, so Mac had a great business. He would fill the room a couple times a night with young men and women who thought they were part of the *Playboy* set.

By 1964 the folk boom had reached its peak, and the stage at the Jester became something of a conveyor belt, ushering a procession of five to six singers across its weathered planks each night. Before a perpetually packed house, performers of widely varying degrees of skill rushed through short sets of three or four songs each. The club even released a compilation album called *Look It's Us* on its own label, Jester Records, featuring tracks by Oil City's finest—Lightnin' Hopkins, Guy Clark, and K. T. Oslin.

"Sometimes big-name acts would come by after they played one of the larger venues in town and would play the last set. You'd never know who you'd see. But you always had Townes and Jerry Jeff Walker and Guy Clark and his first wife, Susan, and Don Sanders. They made all of ten dollars a night," Fran chuckled. "To earn some extra money, Mac Webster asked if I wanted to work as a waitress. Townes's mom and dad were appalled. They said, 'Call us and let us know when you're working, and we'll come another night," Fran laughed again. "I worked one night and then quit, but Mac needed me that Friday and Saturday night. I wound up dumpin' a pitcher of beer in Townes's lap. He said, 'You gotta stop because it's gonna cost us more money than you can make.' It made Townes a nervous wreck for me to be workin' there. He said, 'I'm gonna have to hit somebody for pinchin' you.'"

"I first met Townes and his wife Frannie on the steps of the University of Houston Library. He'd already written some songs but was still taking a couple of courses at the time," Don Sanders recollected. "I had played a few gigs, mostly doing social commentary songs like Pete Seeger's 'Waist Deep in the Big Muddy,' Tom Paxton's 'What Did You Learn in School Today?' and of course some Dylan tunes. Or maybe I'd sing a Clancy Brothers song like 'Whiskey in the Jar.' I had written just one song at that point."

Townes and Jerry Jeff soon discovered how tiny the Texas folk scene was, as they compared notes on clubs and opening shows for established performers like Doc Watson, Lightnin' Hopkins, and Allen Damron. Not only was Van Zandt impressed by Damron's stage presence and his professionalism, but he also confessed to being "awestruck" by Allen changing into a fresh shirt between sets. Impressive as Damron's costume changes might have been, Jerry Jeff Walker was the first of Townes's peers he'd met to actually write and sing his own songs, which included "Little Bird" and "Ramblin' Gamblin.'"

"At the time Townes was goin' to school and was married to his first wife, Frannie," Jerry Jeff recalled.

Guy Clark was playing and touring a bit but hadn't really written anything. None of us were doing full sets of original material yet. We were still gaining confidence in our own songs. Townes had written a couple things, but he still had one foot in the academic world. He said to me, "Man, you're travelin' on the road, livin' the songs, and then playing them." We both agreed that's what you *had* to do. You had to make a total commitment. And suddenly it seemed that we both made that transition from sittin' on the outside, lookin' at it from a distance, to travelin' and livin' the music every day.

Townes and Jerry Jeff would play their first concert together on February 24, 1966, at the Houston Jewish Community Center (JCC). Wanting to have a new song for the occasion, Walker penned a long protest number called "The Ballad of the Hulk," while Van Zandt composed the gentle, reassuring "Close Your Eyes, I'll Be Here in the Morning."

In the past the JCC had sponsored blues concerts with Lightnin' Hopkins and Leadbelly and was taking a risk by presenting a new breed of folk singer. An article in a newsletter dated February 18, 1966, announced the Folksong Series that featured the upcoming show with "two newcomers to the Houston scene. Both Townes Van Zandt and Jerry Jeff Walker write the great majority of songs they sing," it went on to explain.

They are well in the tradition of the folksong process, for they sing about the lives they lead, the places they go, and the things they see. Their style is similar, but the range of topics is very broad. They pull no punches, preferring instead to sing as they feel and leave judgment to the audience. Folk music today is expanding and a whole new era of song-making is upon us. Townes Van Zandt and Jerry Jeff Walker are part of this unending process. They are developing the folksongs of tomorrow upon the realities of today.

Finishing with a somewhat desperate-sounding plea, the author, as if hoping not to lose any stature within the community by presenting a pair of radical underground folksingers, added, in italics: *The Center urges all persons interested in folk music, all interested in social comment, all interested in an entertaining evening of new talent, to attend this concert."* The admission for the show was $1.00 for members and $1.50 for guests.

Soon after the big concert Jerry Jeff hit the road again, returning to New York City, where he cut a pair of albums for Vanguard Records as a member of an electric rock band called Circus Maximus.

While the scene at the Jester thrived, a nonalcoholic venue called the Sand Mountain Café opened, in hopes of drawing high school–aged kids into folk music.

"In 1966 I had been opening shows for people like Jerry Jeff Walker, Don Sanders, and Townes Van Zandt at the Sand Mountain Café," Wrecks Bell recalled. "It was *the* place to play at the time, but there was no alcohol allowed. In the back room Mrs. Carrick introduced me to Townes. As soon as she left Townes asked me, 'Do you drink?' I said, 'Sure.' And he opened up the window, and there was a gallon of wine hangin' on a rope. We took a couple of shots, and we were friends ever since,'" Wrecks grinned.

"The first place I played was a club on Westheimer called the Jester Lounge," Van Zandt later recalled in an interview in *Omaha Rainbow*.

That was the first place I ever got paid real money for singing. This guy who turned out to be Don Sanders, came up to me in there and said I also oughta try this place called Sand Mountain. I went over there with him and we did a little short set. Mrs. Carrick was at her desk keeping an eye on the proceedings and the place was almost empty at the time. There was this song I used to do at the time called "The KKK Blues" and I sang it that night. It was a talking blues about dropping out of the second grade to join the Ku Klux Klan and the guy [in the song] said, "You got too much education." Then I did another one called "The Vietnamese Blues" which had a chorus line about leaving Vietnam to the Vietnamese. Anyway, I got through singing and Mrs. Carrick said, 'Well, that was real good, but we just don't do things like that around here." I said, "Well, this is a fine place but I just can't stay here then." Next day she sent Don as an envoy again and she said she wanted us to come back.

"John Carrick started the club with the help of his mother, who everybody called 'Ma.' Then he joined the Marine Corps, leaving his mom in charge of the place," Don Sanders recounted. "Ma Carrick was a fierce, powerful personality who was always gossiping, always had an opinion, and always knew what was best."

"Mrs. Carrick was a real character," Fran Lohr concurred. "She ran a straight coffeehouse—no drinkin' and no dope, but she was a lot of fun. She was so helpful to all the singers and songwriters."

"They presented a lot of 'entertainers,' mostly girls with pretty voices and guys with deep voices, who did a 'show' with patter. At the time Guy was married to Susan Spaw, a smart, cute girl who did a beautiful version of 'The Handsome Cabin Boy.' I couldn't stand her because she had such a gorgeous voice," Sanders said with a laugh.

"Of course the pay was pitiful," Don groaned.

Mickey Newbury would come through every once in a while, and even though he'd had a couple hits he was still sleepin' in his car. Jimmy Post was around back then before he and his wife [a duo known as Friend and Lover] had that big hit in the summer of 1968 ["Reach Out in the Darkness"]. At the same time John A. Lomax was promoting concerts with Mance Lipscomb who'd come down from Navasota. The Hill brothers, Rocky and Dusty, had a band called American Blues. Then Dusty went on to play bass with ZZ Top. The Winter boys, Edgar and Johnny, used to play a joint down on South Main Street. Johnny would come in and play acoustic at the Sand Mountain every now and then. Janis Joplin also performed there a number of times. She was really wild. Nobody knew *what* to make of her, although John Carrick liked her a whole lot. And there was K. T. Oslin [who, before turning folksinger, had acted and toured as Carol Channing's understudy in *Hello Dolly*]. Kay had a duo with a brilliant guy called Frank Davis, a great entertainer, just weird as hell. They sounded great together. Frank's voice was just as rough as Kay's was smooth and polished.

"Kay Toinette Oslin and I went through junior high, high school, a year of junior college, and the Jester Lounge together," Darryl Harris recollected fondly. "Frank Davis was a regular at the Jester. He mounted a Fender Stratocaster neck onto a snare drum head, called the instrument 'Daddy Banjo,' and played Leadbelly songs. I met Townes at the Jester, which was the first and for a while the only folk joint in Houston. Mac Webster, who owned several bars around town, took this little cinder-block building, way out on West Pine, and started having music there."

Harris worked for Mac in the dual capacity of dishwasher and flamenco guitarist, although the hot water was hell on his calluses. "It was a very happening place. Everybody who was playing folk music at the time played there," Darryl said, recalling the club's early days. "Judy Collins came out and played one night. John Denver played there. In 1963, when the New Christie Minstrels were in town to do a hootenanny at the high school football stadium they all came over to the Jester. Sometimes a dozen people would play over the course of a night. Eventually Mac went to a more sane format with just one person playing at a time."

"Townes actually played there after the club's heyday," Harris pointed out.

> He was doin' knock-offs of Lightnin' Hopkins tunes like "Mustang Blues" and "Candy Man." I was recently divorced and in school and would run into him on campus at the University of Houston. Townes was pre-law at the time, and we'd talk each other into cutting class. We were pretty much hangin' out from that point on, drinkin' and takin' drugs. When we first hung out together we'd smoke pot or split a jug of wine, and Townes would just fall asleep. He wasn't a big drinker then. He was married to Fran Peterson, who I knew in high school. They were livin' upstairs above the Sand Mountain at the time.

"Townes was a scoundrel and had some girlfriends on the side, and that didn't mix too well with bein' married," Darryl said with a wink.

A bootleg tape that has been in circulation for years until finally being released in 2004 titled *Live at the Jester, 1966* offers a glimpse of Townes's live set at the time. Van Zandt performs a handful of his earliest songs, including "Black Crow Blues" and "Colorado Bound," which later appeared on the 2003 release of Townes's first demo sessions called *In the Beginning*. His heroes were also well represented, with "Hello Central" by Lightnin' Hopkins, Jimmie Rodgers's "T for Texas," and "I'm So Lonesome (I Could Cry)" by Hank Williams. Townes also treated the small crowd to a couple of talking blues numbers that covered everything from birth control to karate. "Talking Thunderbird Blues" was a rambling stream-of-consciousness narrative chronicling Van Zandt's life as a floundering college student and an aspiring derelict. His driving, flat-picking guitar rhythm and tongue-in-cheek delivery were clearly inspired by Ramblin' Jack Elliott and early Bob Dylan records. Townes also told a couple of his trademark deadpan jokes about catching gorillas and a nun who knowingly orders a "martin-eye" with her lunch.

"The music Townes used to play at the Jester was a lot of fun," Fran reminisced. But as his songwriting developed, Van Zandt began to use

his poetry to different effect. Writing witty and whimsical topical numbers soon gave way to dark, disturbing portraits of bewitching women
and desperate, down-and-out drifters.

"I started writing funny songs, not dirty songs, but funny bar room
type just to get the audience," Van Zandt recalled in a 1977 interview. "I
was playing these beer joints and used to play folk songs and it got a bit
rowdy. They wanted some funny songs and I hadn't got any, so I wrote
some. Then I wrote serious songs. It used to be a problem that they were
too serious."

"Townes told me he thought that the first serious tune he ever wrote
was '(Quicksilver Daydreams of) Maria,'" Darryl Harris said. Van Zandt
soon found writing and performing "serious" songs was a whole different ball game.

Shunning the finger-pointing politics of Phil Ochs's and Bob Dylan's
early protest songs, Townes became the quiet champion of the dispossessed. His stunning "Waitin' 'round to Die" was inspired after drinking
beer with an old man he'd met one afternoon at the Jester, who, as
Townes later recalled, "kinda put out these vibrations."

Driven by a droning A-minor chord reminiscent of Appalachian coal
mining ballads, Van Zandt delivered the lyric with an eerie sense of ac-
ceptance and detachment:

Sometimes I don't know where
This dirty road is taking me
Sometimes I can't see even the reason why
But I guess I'll keep a ramblin'
Lots of booze and lots of gambling
It's easier than just waitin' 'round to die

"We'd been married just a few months when Townes first started
writing," Fran recalled. "I remember when he walked out of that little
closet he used go in to be alone and play guitar, and he said, 'Hey, babe,
listen to this,' and then played me 'Waitin' 'round to Die.' I wanted to say
it was really great, but I was *appalled*. It wasn't exactly the love song I was
hoping for. He looked at me and said, 'It's kinda macabre, huh?' I asked
him, 'What's *that* about?' And he laughed and said, 'I don't know. . . It
just came out.' A month later he wrote 'Close Your Eyes, I'll Be Here in
the Morning,' which was beautiful."

"When he was younger, I think [his songs] just blitzed him out of nowhere, and he just did what he could to write down all those thoughts," J. T. said, shedding some light on the nature and workings of his father's Muse.

He and my mom had this small apartment, and there was this room in it that was as small as the smallest closet, and most of the songs that he wrote that were on his early albums were written in that closet. His songs just started surfacing. No one witnessed any of that. They were just all under Townes's hat. His interpretation of how he wrote them was that he was just sort of a medium for all those songs—like the songs were around before he was, and he was just there when they popped out. That was just the explanation everyone was given. He never gave a straight answer on where they came from.

While his contemporaries sang glorified visions of the driftin' way of life, Townes thrived, living on the edge, and somehow miraculously survived to write and sing about it. Frank Beard, drummer for ZZ Top, recalled flopping by a hippie crash pad one night in Houston back in the early seventies and discovering Townes "lying face down on a mattress with no sheets on it." Van Zandt had recently downed a pint of Southern Comfort and was out cold just hours before a gig. Although Beard prodded him a couple times with the pointed toe of his boot, he still couldn't rouse more than a groan out of Townes. "Right then I knew I had to go see him that night 'cause I knew he was gonna be good," Frank said.

Although still married to Fran, Townes was hardly the ideal husband. He was frequently found crashed out on friend's couches and floors and was even said to eat dog food when things got rough, although Jeanene would later refute the story as blatant sensationalism perpetuated by a journalist after Townes supposedly shared a Gaines burger with his beloved half-husky/half-wolf Geraldine during a particularly exasperating interview.

"The Great Dog Food Controversy," fueled by *Time* magazine's obituary of Townes, stated: "Born to wealth, Van Zandt spent part of his teens institutionalized for manic depression. At one point he became so poor he subsisted on dog food." This callous bit of reportage was swiftly rebutted by Townes's friends and family in lieu of a round of well-deserved buckshot in the nameless editor's backside.

"Townes never ate dog food," guitarist Mickey White claimed. "Townes never ate dog food," echoed Darryl Harris. "The only way Townes *might* eat dog food would be on a bet, during an incoherent period," painter Jet Whitt said. "Why would Townes eat dog food?" Jan Holle mused. "I know a lot of women that would have gladly fed him, not to mention his friends and family." "I fed him for sixteen years, and I never served up dog food," Jeanene exclaimed. "Of all the things *Time* could write about Townes, wasting space with a ridiculous lie that he ate dog food is an insult to the memory of a genius songwriter and friend," Wrecks Bell groused.

"I used to wonder if Townes didn't have defective taste buds," Wrecks laughed. "I've heard a million stories about people who got drunk with Townes, but I never heard about anybody *ever* having dinner with him. When we were on the road Mickey and I would always be lookin' for food, but Townes didn't care. A peanut butter or bologna sandwich was fine with him. He'd go into the grocery store with five thousand dollars in his pocket and come out with a package of bologna and some white bread. He never cared about food—*ever.*"

Townes had a typical alcoholic's view toward food. Whether breakfast, lunch, or dinner, in a greasy diner or a fancy mansion, it was all "slop" to him. "He always used to say to me, 'What kind of slop are you servin' tonight?'" Jeanene said, shaking her head.

In January 1966 Townes's father, Harris, suddenly died of a heart attack at age fifty-two, leaving him with a slew of unanswered questions and unresolved emotions to sort out.

"His dad was in the hospital with an ulcerated esophagus," Fran recalled. "He was a dynamic, fabulous man, but when we went in to see him the last time he was frail and pale gray. Townes hugged him and kissed him, and then he had a heart attack. Townes's father had been a big supporter of his music, and his death was very hard on him."

"Our father's death hit him very hard," Donna Spence concurred. "They were relating better then they had for a while, and it was hard for Townes to lose him at that point. Their relationship had gotten better, not that it was bad, but they were seein' each other more clearly at that point. I've had a lot of people ask me if my dad tried to pressure him to be something else, but I think Townes put just as much pressure on himself as anybody else did."

Van Zandt had hoped his father would live long enough to see him become a successful folksinger, but, sadly, it was never to be. For years he tried to please Van, making many of his most important decisions based on an overwhelming sense of obligation toward his family. "I think Townes always needed someone to be proud of him," Jeanene sighed. "I'm sure Van's death was very difficult for him."

For years Townes wrestled with the lofty dream of becoming a traveling troubadour and the nagging obligation to finish college, settle down, and lead a "normal" life with Fran. In a desperate attempt to solve his daunting dilemma in one fell swoop, Townes tried to enlist for a stint in the Air Force but was rejected after the doctor diagnosed him as "an acute manic-depressive who has made minimal adjustments to life." Fran believed her troubled husband not only hungered for the kind of adventure he'd find in the wild blue yonder but also yearned for the sense of camaraderie and discipline he once knew as a cadet at Shattuck Academy and was hoping to find in the armed forces.

"Townes had only been out of the hospital for a year when he dropped out of college and tried to join the service," Lohr recalled. "The letter said he had acute schizophrenia. I was furious. I later ran into an intern [who worked under the doctor who diagnosed Townes] that had quit because he felt the doctor had doomed him. Basically they told him he was 'legally crazy.' At first it shocked him, but then, unfortunately, he kind of believed it and began to act it out."

"From the time he first started playing at the Jester up until when his dad died was a magic time that lasted about a year and a half," Fran reminisced.

Townes wasn't drinkin' that much. He'd get drunk here and there, at parties, but most of the time he was just a lot of fun. We had good times in Galveston with his family. His whole family was really super. Everyone was extremely intelligent. Townes and his brother Bill were very close when we were dating and would play a lot of chess together. We would go to the beach house on Friday nights, which was "game night." His mother always wanted to play mah-jongg, which we hated. His dad liked to play hearts or spades, and Bill would choose spoons. It was a hoot. It was an innocent, fun time. We were college students, just married at that time. He seemed almost . . . content then. He'd found his groove and was startin' to write and was very excited about it. But after that letter was written . . . Boy, I'd love to dig up that psychiatrist and beat the shit out of him.

I think after his dad died he felt like he should've been the man of the family, but he just wasn't ready for that. Pressure always took Townes to extremes. He already had a lot of guilt over not living up to his mom's expectations. She knew he'd never lead a "normal" life in the suburbs. She said he'd either be very poor or rich and probably wouldn't become famous until after death. They never believed he'd become the governor of Texas, like some people say. He was a pre-law student when I met him, and I can tell you it was a pretty big leap to becoming a singer-songwriter.

Shortly after his father's funeral, Townes dropped out of college and took that leap once and for all. He was also determined to get out of Houston as well, fearing he'd become trapped there and considered nothing more than a "local" artist. Van Zandt's description of the petrochemical capital of Texas reflected his own grim state of mind at the time, portraying a murky vision of "Oil City" to something akin to Hieronymus Bosch's demonic world. "If you can't catch the blues in Houston, man, you can't catch them anywhere," he joked. "I figure there's heaven, hell, purgatory and the blues. I've always been in the blues, just reaching up for hell."

Meanwhile, two floors down from hell, Townes experienced a mad flood of inspiration, knocking out one great song after another. By a flickering candlelight in the room above the Sand Mountain Café where Mrs. Carrick allowed performing musicians to crash for five dollars a week, Townes composed the elegant "For the Sake of the Song."

That August Fran took a job working for Shell Oil but would quit eight months later to join Townes on the road for the next six months. "At that time we either lived in the RV or at 'Ma' Carrick's above the Sand Mountain," Lohr recalled. "Then when Townes went back on the road again I went back to work at Shell."

"Townes never felt comfortable with just being part of the Texas scene," singer-songwriter Eric Andersen explained. "He was always willing to pack up his guitar and head off to Boston or Europe and venture out as a solo artist. He had a very devoted following all over the world. Those songs meant a lot to people. Townes was arguably the most important southern song-poet since Hank Williams. He had a lot of sympathy for the human condition. He wasn't interested in tryin' to get rich or make money. He just wanted to play."

And have a damn good time as well. Eric recounted one of Van Zandt's most hilarious antics at a gig that took place years later at Rockefeller's in Houston, when he split the bill with banjo ace, fiddler, and songwriter John Hartford. Townes showed up early looking for his old friend but found nobody around, so he left his guitar in the dressing room and took off in search of a drink. He returned again, but Eric had yet to arrive. The club had recently laid a new rug down on the stage floor and rolled the old one up and leaned it against the back wall. Feeling kind of "gray and hazy" after a couple vodkas, Townes rolled himself up in the old rug and took a little nap. By the time the audience arrived and took their seats, he was out cold and didn't come to until suddenly hearing the emcee call his name.

"We know he's here, ladies and gentlemen. His guitar's in the dressing room. Townes, you must be around here somewhere." Van Zandt just laid there for a moment, pondering his next move: "Do I crawl outta this thing now or wait till the show's over and everybody leaves? Well, I don't want to lay here all night," he reckoned. A moment later Townes began to squirm around, shrugging his shoulders, from side to side until he built up enough momentum to heave himself out of the rug and make a grand entrance. The audience nearly laughed their heads off as he took a bow. They just couldn't believe it. Then somebody handed him his guitar, and he opened the show, lookin' a little bleary eyed.

"There was a real bohemian edge to Houston that spilled out of St. Thomas University, the Sand Mountain, and Club La Maison. Mayo Thompson's free-form freak-out band, Red Krayola, started in Houston back in sixty-six," said Bill Bentley, publicist at Warner Bros. Records.

There was a psychiatrist at St. Thomas University, whose name I won't mention, that gave out LSD to famous people who flew into Houston to be part of a Ken Kesey–style acid test. Sand Mountain was a beatniky folk hangout on Richmond Avenue. I was young and didn't like the music as much as rock and roll because it was too quiet. But Townes had the heaviness, the songs, and the personality. It was not just entertainment with him. He was *possessed* by it. It was almost like a burden that he had to share these incredibly emotional songs. It wasn't like Townes sat down to write those songs. *They wrote him.* He didn't just live those songs. They *were* him. When he played live it wasn't like he was singing, it was like he was telling you about his inner soul. That was just his way to communicate. It was almost eerie the way he could pull you in. You got the feeling like you were inside him when you listened to him sing. Even with the funny songs, he took you right inside himself. Townes had that way to make you feel exactly what he was singing about. Not many people could do that. There weren't that many musicians that were out on the edge like that. Maybe Billie Holiday or Roky Erickson from the 13th Floor Elevators.

If you've ever doubted that truth is stranger than fiction, consider that Roky Erickson, the notoriously wild front man of the 13th Floor Elevators, was once Townes Van Zandt's roommate. The lead singer for America's weirdest psychedelic band slept on the living-room floor on a makeshift bed made from stacks of albums from Townes's prized record collection. Desperate for a bassist, Roky once begged Townes to join his band of Lone Star lunatics even though Van Zandt had never picked the instrument up before. "That don't make any difference," Erickson rationalized. "[If] you can play guitar like that, then you can play bass in a second," he said.

A couple of weeks went by, and Townes somehow managed to scrounge together the bread to buy a Gibson electric bass. But while auditioning for the Elevators, their amplified-jug player, Tommy Hall, was so unimpressed with Van Zandt's playing that he was instantly canned.

"He's a fine young man from a fine family," Townes once said about Roky. "I never met a more straighter, more moral human being than him. He'd never stab you in the back. We're blood brothers," Townes joked, claiming he even had the scars to prove it. "I became blood brothers with Roky and caught hepatitis and the clap at the same time."

Erickson and Van Zandt were indeed brothers of sorts. Both had been in and out of schools, jails, and mental hospitals so often it was as if the buildings had been fitted with revolving doors. (After his second conviction for pot, Roky was dealt an unusually harsh hand, sentenced to the Rusk State Mental Hospital for the Criminally Insane in 1969 for possessing six joints.)

"Once we went to a wild party with the 13th Floor Elevators," Fran recalled. "I was sitting in a corner by the pool with Townes, who was just playing his guitar. Everybody thought I was stoned, but I hadn't even had water. They played *Sergeant Pepper's Lonely Hearts Club Band* over and over again, trying to decode it. They were convinced that there was some secret message in there about going to an island where the Beatles were." (A rumor circulated that the flowers on the album cover spelled out BE AT LESO when the large period was perceived as the letter *O*. Leso is an island off the coast of Greece, where the Beatles considered buying property to escape the very madness that created these type of rumors.)

"I would come home from work and that whole crew would be in our apartment," Lohr continued. "Townes would bring 'em all over to jam, and all of a sudden there would be an impromptu party taking place. It was a real surreal scene. I love music, but I never heard *that* as music."

Townes's and the Elevators' convoluted jams would often last up to half an hour at a time, transforming old rock and roll tunes like "Who Do You Love?" or "Mystery Train" into a barrage of incomprehensible psychedelic gobbledygook.

While Townes articulated his depression with razor-sharp precision, Roky expressed his madness in an explosion of abstract noise and fragmented poetry that bordered on incoherence. Rock journalist Richie Unterberger once described Erickson's unbridled vocal style as "pure dementia that veered off into hair-raising yelps and fire engine screams."

"I loved it when Townes and his friends just sat around and played, but it was hard to keep your lease whenever the 13th Floor Elevators came over. The place would be semidestroyed. There was always a lot of cleanup involved. I was unfortunately the grown-up of the group and would have to get up and go to work the next day," Fran said. "He was still a struggling singer-songwriter, which was fine as long as I was working. But after J. T. was born I became known as 'the Grinch,'" Lohr sighed.

"At that time if you worked for Shell Oil you couldn't be pregnant. As long as there was money coming in, the pressure was off him. We were living in a little old cottage house on Duke and University at the time. I had just been to the doctor the night before J. T. was born. He didn't think I was due for another five or six weeks. So that night we went to a party for Townes's brother Bill who was getting married, and I splurged and had iced tea and strawberry pie for dessert," Fran said, chuckling at the memory.

About two or three o'clock that morning my water broke. I didn't know what was goin' on. I thought it was a false alarm. By five A.M. I woke Townes up and said, "You've gotta take me to the hospital." He was berserk. Here we were, five minutes from the hospital, and he couldn't figure out which way to go. But he was there with his mask and gown on. It was a special time for both of us, but there were a lot of challenges to our relationship after the baby was born. I couldn't support him in the same way I had been. And I didn't want drugs in the house. About three or four months later I became a schoolteacher, we separated, and Townes really went downhill after that. I think he felt a lot of guilt for not doing what he felt was "the right thing" as a southern gentleman. The person I knew for most of the time we were married was funny, sweet, and thoughtful. I still saw that in him over the years.

CHAPTER 5

MUDD, GOLD, AND SONGS FROM THE SKY

Bukka White said he reached up
and grabbed 'em out of the sky.
He called 'em "Sky Songs."
But, man, it seems to me
that they reach down
and grab me off the Earth.
  —TVZ

"The Houston scene originally revolved around the Jester and the Sand Mountain Café. But then the Old Quarter came along," Don Sanders said in reverie. "The crowd was an interesting mix. It not only attracted young people, but you had winos coming in off the streets that lived in the run-down resident hotels in the neighborhood. Instead of being a privileged middle-class suburban kid, you suddenly felt like you were *living the life*."

"Sometimes an old crazy guy would come in and start makin' noise, but by and large the Old Quarter had listening crowds that would be quiet and very attentive," Darryl Harris recalled.

Owned and operated by Wrecks Bell and his partner, Dale Soffar, the Old Quarter was located on the corner of Austin and Congress, across the street from the city jail in a seedy section of downtown Houston. Funky as it was, the OQ was a dream come true for Wrecks: "I had gotten out of the service in '65, and my goal was to start a folk club of my own. Shortly after that I opened up the Old Quarter, and Townes started playing there," Bell recalled.

"The first thing that attracted me to Townes was hearing his songs the way that Wrecks played them. Wrecks and I became instant friends. Our personalities just meshed," Mickey White said, recalling meeting his old friend and bandmate.

Wrecks noticed that I was an up-and-coming fingerpicker and said, "Man, if you like fingerpickin' you gotta hear Townes." Then he pulled out a guitar and played me "Columbine." My jaw just dropped. Then he played that lick from "Lungs," the way that Townes did it. It was great stuff.

I was livin' in Austin at the time, crashing in empty dorm beds at a co-op. I went down to the record store, and *Our Mother the Mountain* had just come out [in autumn of 1969]. The guy behind the counter pulled the record out and played me "Second Lover's Song," and that was the first time I ever heard Townes play. It just blew my mind.

The following Wednesday night White found Townes on the Old Quarter stage, sitting on a stool, playing to a small crowd with his eyes shut, lost in deep concentration.

"That first night I saw Townes play is indelibly etched in my memory. It was a real life-changing moment for me," Mickey recalled.

His physical presence was unreal. He was a stunningly good-looking guy, so stoic. Townes never translated that well to TV or huge venues, but put him in a club with a hundred people and boy . . . He sure put a crimp in my aspiration to become a songwriter.

I'd dropped out of UT, where I'd gone for a semester or two. I'd been in the music school, but they couldn't teach me how to fingerpick so I quit and enrolled at the University of the Old Quarter. I had my preppy clothes on and was singin' "Everybody's Talkin' at Me" [Fred Neil's anthem of alienation from *Midnight Cowboy,* made famous by Harry Nilsson]. Fortunately, Dale Soffar liked what he heard, and he gave me two or three dates.

Townes was only playing to about fifteen people. The Old Quarter sat about sixty people, including the bar stools, but you could stuff nearly a hundred in there, shoulder to shoulder, wall to wall. He was playing

"You Are Not Needed Now," and it didn't take long to gain an appreciation for his poetry and guitar picking.

"Townes had a special way of writing, which almost bordered on the formal," Eric Andersen explained. "He wasn't a vernacular songwriter or conversational in the sense of Joni Mitchell. He had a great ability to employ poetical devices and was more stylistically akin to writers like Charles Dickens and Delmore Schwartz than most contemporary songwriters."

Van Zandt's commitment toward his art was so intense that it often frightened people. Anyone harboring illusions of grandeur was immediately set straight by Townes with the grim prospects of the songwriter's life. "[First] you have to get yourself a guitar or a piano; guitars are easier to carry," Townes would point out. "And then you have to blow off everything else. You have to blow off your family. You have to blow off comfort. You have to blow off money. You have to blow off security. You have to blow off your ego. You have to blow off everything except your guitar. You have to sleep with it. Learn how to tune it. And no matter how hungry you get, stick with it. You'll be amazed at how many people turn away."

For Guy Clark, Van Zandt's dedication and discipline were a shove in the right direction. Guy's set until then mostly consisted of interpretations of old traditional English ballads like "Handsome Molly" and the occasional Bob Dylan tune. Townes's first songs not only changed Clark's life but also inspired many of the local folkies to drop their well-worn repertoire of sea chanties and Kingston Trio tunes and start expressing their feelings and personal experiences with their own words and chords. Without realizing it, Van Zandt blew open the door of new possibility for everyone around him.

"They were great songs, and he was on fire with it," Guy said. "He got a publishing deal soon after that. Mickey Newbury became his champion for all the right reasons. I figured, Jesus Christ, if he can do it, then so can I. So I started writing. I knew Jerry Jeff and he was a good writer, but he wasn't writin' *those* kinds of songs," Guy exclaimed. "I suddenly got it— like it was *okay* to do this. It wasn't that I needed anybody's permission. I liked Townes's approach. It was mostly askew, but that's the way he saw it."

Eventually, the pair tried writing together, but like their earlier attempt at forming a blues band, nothing much came of it. A little ditty about a hippie MD called "Dr. Rippy" remained unfinished. Clark admitted they never got past the first verse, figuring his contribution was pointless, as Van Zandt didn't need anyone's help when it came to songwriting.

"I've never really written with anybody because I just can't," Van Zandt said in a 1977 interview. "My songs come out at times, like, when I'm in upstate New York in a motel room and it's freezing out and I don't know anybody and the gig's not been going very good and I haven't seen anybody I even know for weeks. . . . To sit down and write with somebody, I've never even considered . . . I just never have tried to write anything real serious with anybody."

But Townes actually wrote a couple songs with Mickey Newbury called "The Queen" and "Mister Can't You See," which was covered by Buffy Sainte-Marie and provided him with his first real paycheck as a songwriter.

Considering Van Zandt perpetually wandered through most of his life in a fog of vodka (or whatever mind-altering substance was readily within reach), his keen sense of observation and razor-sharp wit were downright startling. He seemed to live in a continuous state of receptivity, grabbing melodies out of thin air and improvising lyrics off the top of his head.

"His songs zapped him into a place that he didn't necessarily want to be in," J. T. explained. Although it was difficult for his friends and particularly his family to understand Townes's creative process, J. T. claimed he "started getting into the lyrics when I was about sixteen. It was then that I started understanding how wise he was. By twenty, I knew that he was hot shit with a pen."

"Some take craftsmanship; others just hit you on top of the head," Townes once said, attempting to explain the workings of his Muse.

Some take a year; some take thirty minutes. They can come straight through you, and you don't know what they're about or where they're coming from. You just write 'em down and play 'em. Most everybody could write songs. I've heard kids dancing around a maypole, making up as pretty a song as I could ever do. Because I've been doing this for twenty-five years, I'm aware of when a song comes along. I'm aware of the little clues that come together to make a song.

Some of them, I work on for days, weeks. And then some, like "Mr. Mudd & Mr. Gold," it was like my hand was cramped. I was tryin' to get what was comin' down. It was hitting me so fast, it was like my hand couldn't keep up with the flashes [of inspiration]. I didn't sit down with that one and say "er . . . wicked King of Clubs, uh. . . ." It took me a week just to read the damn thing.

"Townes had this tremendous output even when he was completely dead drunk around the clock. I don't know how he did it," Texas troubadour Jimmie Dale Gilmore exclaimed. "It was a mystery how he could write all those songs when he was so drunk all the time. To me 'Mr. Mudd and Mr. Gold' is impossible. I think the DNA code is in that song," Jimmie Dale joked.

"I wanted to *be* Townes," Steve Earle confessed. "The way I play guitar came from Townes more than probably anybody else. The way I wrote came from Guy more than anybody else, 'cause story songs are Guy's strong suit."

In 1972 Steve Earle hitchhiked from San Antonio up to Austin to crash Jerry Jeff Walker's thirty-third birthday party in hopes of getting a firsthand glimpse at his hero. Just seventeen at the time, Earle, the self-conscious stranger, immediately found a corner, pulled his hat down over his eyes, and tried to act inconspicuous. Sometime around three in the morning, "Townes blew in like a tornado through a trailer park looking positively *mythic*," Steve would recall at Van Zandt's funeral on January 3, 1997. "Suddenly there was no one else in the room."

Arriving with dice in hand, Townes immediately stirred up some action. Earle watched in awe as Townes soon lost all of his money along with a beautiful beaded buckskin jacket that Jerry Jeff had given to him for his birthday just a few weeks earlier.

Two weeks later, while on stage at the Old Quarter, Earle came face-to-face with Townes. The small audience was composed of a handful of rowdy drunks. Leading the pack was Van Zandt, who sat in the front row, relentlessly heckling the poor kid over and over again to play "The Wabash Cannonball." After each of Steve's songs Townes would shout, "Play 'The Wabash Cannonball,'" until Earle finally admitted he didn't know the famous A. P. Carter tune. "You call yourself a folk singer, and you don't know 'The Wabash Cannonball'?" Van Zandt asked incredulously. In order to shut him up, Steve broke into a torrid rendition of Townes's own "Mr. Mudd and Mr. Gold."

According to Van Zandt, the surrealist ballad of a poker game between Mr. Mudd and Mr. Gold suddenly came to him after a long night of drinking and partying. Everyone had gone to bed, while Van Zandt sat with his guitar, plunking out a simple repetitive chord-pattern rhythm that inspired a mad rush of lyrics.

"It felt like my right arm was going to drop off," Townes later explained. By six in the morning the flood of visions had ended, the first draft of the song was complete, and the floor was covered with wadded-up balls of yellow legal paper. Townes dragged himself off to bed, exhausted. Later that afternoon he awoke, groggily grabbed his guitar, reread the lyrics, and worked his way through the song. After tinkering with a couple of verses, he got the phrasing right, and the tune was finished.

The tale of "a game of stud" "'tween a man named Gold and a man named Mudd" goes far beyond the typical cowboy ballad of such legendary poker games as Kenny Rogers's "The Gambler." Van Zandt's use of meter and imagery is astounding. Townes not only tells a story but also paints a surrealistic portrait of men consumed by "greedy vapors." Mudd and Gold ultimately become warped by their passion, while their "eyes like bullets burned."

According to Bob Myrick, Van Zandt's "Mr. Mudd and Mr. Gold" was such a milestone among the small clique of Houston musicians that "Guy totally stopped writing and could hardly play."

"It was a weird song, but it showed me just how far you could take a recitation piece," said David Olney, the Rhode Island–born singer-songwriter who migrated to Nashville in the early seventies. "I never would have written 'Jerusalem Tomorrow' without hearing 'Mr. Mudd and Mr. Gold.'"

J. T. Van Zandt sat at the busy lunch counter of a Mexican café on Congress Street in Austin. His eyes, dark, intense pools, gleamed just like his father's. Over the years he's heard more than his fair share of apocryphal stories about his old man's drinkin' and druggin' and was looking to clear the air a bit: "All those stories mean nothing when he was in that other zone where he was writing," he said.

"The annoying assumption is that somehow there's a correlation between his substance abuse and his writing, but those two things were totally removed from each other," John once told journalist Richard Skanse. "His ability to write was there long before he was a substance abuser. Alcoholism didn't take effect until the last ten years of his life and then maybe only at his live shows."

Whether or not he was inspired by stimulants, Townes was always modest and quick to credit "a greater power" as the source of his songwriting abilities. He believed he was merely "a secretary to the spirits," as

Ishmael Reed described the poet's job, writing down his luminous verse as it was dictated by the Muse.

"Townes didn't like to talk about what his lyrics meant," Bob Myrick said. "He always spoke as if there was something or somebody else writing them for him. But I think that was just his way of getting out of discussing it."

Townes, describing the workings of his relentless Muse, often felt "slammed upon, hit between the eyeballs, out of the blue." He claimed to have actually written his hit song "If I Needed You" while sound asleep. Dreams have always been a great source for writers, musicians, and painters. But upon awakening, we are often left with fragmented, meaningless images that, although glowing with inspiration from another dimension, are useless on the earth plane.

One time after everyone had come down with the flu at Guy and Susanna Clark's East Nashville house, Townes was elected, after drawing the short straw, to stroll down to the corner drugstore and retrieve a pint of codeine cough syrup. The trio soon polished off the sticky narcotic cocktail and then bid one another goodnight.

Townes stretched his long legs out on a mattress in Susanna's closet-sized art studio and immediately conked out. Stumbling down the sidewalk of his subconscious, Van Zandt had a remarkable dream that night, "in blazing Technicolor," as he later recalled it. He dreamed he was a folksinger on stage, singing a beautiful new song. As the dream faded he woke up barely long enough to scribble down the lyrics just as they had come to him only moments before. The melody was so clear he knew he'd have no trouble remembering it, so he pulled the blanket over his head and fell back to sleep.

The next morning Susanna and Guy sat hovering around the kitchen table in a fog, sipping mugs of steaming black coffee, when Townes sauntered in with his guitar. "Hey, y'all, listen to this," he said as the new song rolled off his tongue and fingertips as if he'd been playing it for years. Of course, they loved it. "When did you write that?" they asked. "Last night," Townes replied. The bemused couple told him it wasn't possible, as he'd gone off to bed before them, and in their tiny house they would've undoubtedly heard him through the walls, working in the middle of the night.

Born from a high temperature and narcotic slumber, Townes's lilting portrait of undying love "If I Needed You" was first covered by Doc Watson on his 1973 Grammy-winning album *Then and Now*. The song would eventually climb to number three on the country charts thanks to Emmylou Harris and Don Williams. One of Townes's most popular and enduring tunes, "If I Needed You" is routinely played at weddings around the South and West (including Mr. and Mrs. Ricky Skaggs's nuptial ceremony).

If I needed you
Would you come to me,
Would you come to me,
And ease my pain?

If you needed me
I would come to you
I'd swim the seas
For to ease your pain

In the night forlorn
The morning's born
And the morning shines
With the lights of love

You will miss sunrise
If you close your eyes
And that would break my heart in two

Lady's with me now
Since I showed her how
To lay her lily hand in mine

Loop and Lil agree
She's a sight to see
And a treasure for the poor to find

Loop and Lil were a pair of parakeets that Townes took with him wherever he went. Loop (depending on whom you ask) was either named after the North Loop pharmacy in Austin where Townes regularly bought codeine cough syrup or the Chicago train system. Lil was christened in honor of a lady friend. Townes couldn't bear caging the birds, so he carried them with him, even while on the road. They fluttered freely about his car, in motel rooms, and around friends' houses. Townes supposedly sneaked Loop and Lil with him onto airplanes, snapping shut the pearl buttons to the breast pocket of his cowboy shirts to keep them from flying off. But one cold winter day Loop escaped from an open window at (producer and owner of Poppy, and later Tomato, Records) Kevin Eggers's brownstone apartment. Distraught, Van Zandt spent hours combing the Brooklyn Heights neighborhood searching for his lost feathered friend. Lil, after pining for her mate, died of a broken heart a week later.

Guy Clark believed his friend's lyrics transcended the function of songwriting and achieved the stature of literature. "Some of his songs are easier to understand on paper than they are listening to them. But they work both ways. Nothing was thrown away in his writing just to get a rhyme. It was all pretty much stream-of-consciousness.

"Townes was a brave soul," Clark sighed heavily. "Very few people are willing to go that deep and take a hard look at the darkness. One time he was playin' a set of the saddest stuff, and some woman in the audience said, 'Townes, could you play a happy song?' And he said, 'Man, *these are* the happy songs. You don't want to hear the sad ones.'"

"I have a few [songs] that aren't sad—they're hopeless. They're not sad. That's just the way it goes. . . . You don't think life's sad?" Van Zandt goaded an interviewer on Dutch television in 1992. Time stood perfectly still as his dark eyes waited for an answer from the bewildered journalist. Townes then grinned knowingly and picked up the conversation once more: "But from recognizing the sadness you can put it aside and be happy and enjoy the happy side of life. Blues is happy music.

"I'm pretty happy. I'm subject occasionally to what they call . . . violent mood swings," Van Zandt continued, playing with the poor fellow. "I'm pretty happy. Just kinda sittin' around waitin' for the axe to fall."

"There's a lot of sadness in people's lives that needs to be addressed," Jerry Jeff Walker reckoned. "I've always worked towards an optimistic conclusion myself. I always try and lift people up. It just makes the goin' a lot easier. Like Anthony Quinn shows you in *Zorba the Greek,* in tragedy you have to learn to dance. If you're full of sadness you've got to spin that dark mood out of yourself. But Townes had a way of dwelling down there and mining those areas. For some people that serves a purpose, but I can't stay there for a long time. Maybe that's why Townes always used to tell those corny jokes—to relieve some of the tension that would build up in the room after eight or nine of those songs."

Paul K. sees Van Zandt as an alchemist, believing the magic of his songwriting came from the way Townes transmuted his pain into beauty: "Van Zandt's most beautiful songs were often the most painful. Everybody says how depressing his music is, but if they felt that kind of pain and dealt with it the way he did, then we wouldn't need someone like him. Townes went through it all so we wouldn't have to be depressed. Most people can't take their pain and turn it into a song like Townes," he said.

"Townes's music reaches out to troubled people. He lets them know they aren't alone, that somebody cares and has been through it as well. He never wallowed in self-pity," David Amram pointed out.

He was an incredible poet, like a modern-day Texas version of Fyodor Dostoyevsky. Dostoyevsky's books documented the soulful qualities of nineteenth-century Russian people who were neglected or on the outside of society but had beautiful qualities that made them very precious. Dostoyevsky himself had such struggle in his own life but managed to create something beautiful from it that was uplifting. Whenever I think about Townes, I feel inspired. He was a true musician-poet-troubadour who found the most spiritual qualities in everyday life, in people that society dismissed as total misfits and losers. His songs never dwelled on the negative or worshiped sleaze. I think Townes saw the world a lot like Dostoyevsky. Once I mentioned this to a young songwriter sitting around the campfire at the Kerrville Folk Festival, and the guy said [Amram affects a Texas twang], "Dusty who?" I told him, "I don't mean Dusty Springfield, buddy," and said, "You better go get a copy of *The Brothers Karamazov* and *The Gambler*." The following year I ran into Townes again at Kerrville and told him this story, and he just roared with laughter.

"I saw him in Houston and in Austin in the 1960s, and my impression right from the first was that he had a unique aura which I came to believe was rooted in his poetic soul," Dan Rather surmised. "He had the ability to mesmerize a live audience, even in the cheapest honky-tonk or dingiest dive. What became clear as the years went by was that he had a companion ability to mesmerize on his recordings. In the pantheon of Texas songwriters I can say of him what Bum Phillips once said about Earl Campbell, which was 'I don't know how long the list is but however long it is, he's on it.' With the possible exception of Willie Nelson, no songwriter in his generation conveys the Texas id better than Townes Van Zandt."

Norah Jones, who recorded Townes's "Be Here to Love Me" for her second album, *Feels Like Home* (2004), concurs, praising Van Zandt as "one of the most poetic songwriters I can think of. His songs just sing themselves," she said.

Van Zandt's poetry has always had the power to carry the listener to some metaphysical place beyond the earth plane where it's just the two of them, the listener and Townes, the storyteller. A few years back, I was at a party with a bunch of young rappers in Brooklyn when one guy said, "Hey, you look like you'd know something about folk music. You ever heard of some guy named Tom Van Somethin' from Austin, Texas?" "You mean Townes Van Zandt? Sure, what about him?" "You ever heard that song 'bout a poker game?" "You mean 'Mr. Mudd and Mr. Gold'?" "The dude's phat, man. I never heard no shit like that before." I suggested that he cover the song, do a rap version of it. He fell out laughing. "Yeah," he agreed, "that would be the bomb." There I was in my old blue jeans, boots, and flannel shirt. He had on his uniform too—big shiny bling-bling hanging around his neck, football jersey, and his pants hangin' low. I was amazed how Townes managed to get his lyrics heard in the 'hood without the bludgeoning beat of drum machines.

Mickey Newbury maintained that Townes Van Zandt's songs will be remembered a hundred years from now: "Anybody who can't recognize the genius of Townes Van Zandt, I don't want to spend more than five minutes talking to them about music," Newbury once proclaimed. "How can it get much better than 'No Place to Fall' or 'Our Mother the Mountain' or '(Quicksilver Daydreams of) Maria'?" Newbury claimed he beat his brains out trying to get Johnny Cash to cut Townes's "St. John the Gambler." "It would have been a smash by him," he lamented.

Mickey thought Townes "looked a little like Hank Williams and even wrote like Hank probably would have written. But I think Townes is better. I consider him in the same category as Dylan and McCartney. Townes's songs contained some of the most beautiful imagery I've ever heard in my life. You've got to wonder why he wasn't successful. But he just didn't get the break. He didn't have the right people working his deal. There's no doubt that *he* worked. The man was a road warrior. He was the Real Deal."

Just four years Townes's senior, Mickey Newbury, born in 1940, began traveling around the country in an old Pontiac, as soon as he came of age, sleeping in all-night laundries, reading poetry, and playing guitar in beatnik coffeehouses. Newbury's smash hit, "I Just Dropped in to See What

Condition My Condition Was In," reached number five on the pop charts in 1968 for Kenny Rogers. Inducted into the Nashville Song-writer's Hall of Fame in 1980, Mickey's tunes have been covered by three generations of singers, including Elvis Presley, Willie Nelson, Waylon Jennings, Ray Charles, Joan Baez, Jerry Lee Lewis, B. B. King, Roy Or-bison, John Denver, and the Everly Brothers. The list gets more diverse as it goes on, including everyone from the Grateful Dead to Gene Vin-cent and Andy Williams. His song "An American Trilogy" was the final encore that Elvis Presley performed at his last concert, in Indianapolis in 1977. He is the only American singer-songwriter to have four number-one hit songs on four different charts in the same year.

For Mickey, as for Townes, music was a necessary escape from a life-long battle with depression. "How many people have listened to my songs and thought, 'He must have a bottle of whiskey in one hand and a pistol in the other.' Well, I don't. I write my sadness," Newbury confessed.

Journalist William Hedgepath first learned about Townes Van Zandt from Mickey Newbury in 1971. "The person who's influenced me more'n just about anybody else is somebody I'm sure you've never heard of, a guy by the name of Townes Van Zandt. An incredible poet," Mickey told him.

Newbury, who had signed a publishing deal with the prestigious Acuff/Rose Agency based in Nashville, had been playing the same circuit of small Texas clubs as Townes, including the Sand Mountain Café and the Jester as well as the Id and the 11th Door in Austin. Mickey and his uncle Jay Boyette would introduce Townes to Doyle Jones who owned a recording studio in Houston, where, in early 1966, Van Zandt cut a demo of the stark and stunning "Tecumseh Valley" along with an introspective meditation on vanishing youth titled "Sixteen Summers and Fifteen Falls."

Newbury recalled that when he first met Van Zandt, he seemed torn between two worlds. The previous autumn, at age twenty-two, Townes had just bought a motor home and was on the verge of quitting college after experiencing an intense creative streak that produced a pair of his best songs, the poetically lush "(Quicksilver Daydreams of) Maria" and the harrowing "Our Mother the Mountain."

"That was the best writing he ever did," Mickey exclaimed. "He wanted to be a songwriter, but he was studying law, wearing starched dress shirts with cufflinks and a corduroy jacket with blue jeans."

Mickey convinced Townes that if he wanted a record deal he'd have to go to Nashville to get it. "Sure, Mick, I'll go anywhere," Van Zandt replied enthusiastically and soon found himself in "Music City," where Newbury introduced him to the legendary producer Cowboy Jack Clement. But Cowboy Jack and his partner, Jim Malloy (head engineer at RCA Records who recorded Elvis Presley), recalled the story a bit differently: "We made a little pilgrimage to Houston and got with my old buddy Doyle [Jones]. He started telling us about this guy Townes Van Zandt and how great he was. He played some tapes he'd cut, just voice and guitar," Cowboy Jack told John Lomax III. "That piqued our interest so we got Townes in and listened to him and decided we'd work with him. I thought Townes had a sort of specialized kind of thing. It wasn't something for everybody, but I thought it was really good. So did Malloy."

"Jack and I got half loaded and went out to Texas to see Townes playing at a club somewhere in Houston," Jim recollected. "I was used to traditional country music. When I first heard those songs, I said to Jack, 'I don't know *what* this is.' Townes wasn't really country. We didn't have a clue what those songs were about," Malloy confessed. "It was really wild to us. Jack said, 'Hell, let's sign him to a publishing contract, and we'll get a record cut on him. So we signed Townes to a publishing deal and made some tapes right there in Doyle's studio."

"People have tried to put a tag on my music but it hasn't stuck. It's not really country and it's not really anything. It's not top 40, for sure. I always call it folk music because live I play alone, but on records it's different," Van Zandt said in 1977.

The demo session, as John Lomax III later described, was the "opening act" for Townes's 1968 debut album, *For the Sake of the Song*. But the tapes went missing for thirty-six years until they were recently discovered in the files of Jack Clements's Silver Dollar Music. They were then remixed and released in 2003 as *In the Beginning*. The album comprises ten Van Zandt originals: a handful of ballads played solo, along with a couple of funky electric blues numbers that featured a bunch of unidentified jammers (which included Charlie McCoy wailing on harmonica). Although Van Zandt's songwriting had yet to reach the caliber of his first release, there is something compelling about the honest, no-frills production of *In the Beginning*. All the images and themes heard throughout Townes's career were clearly there. "Black Widow Blues" is reminiscent of the boastful lyrics sung by bluesmen like Muddy Waters and Bo Diddley, who claimed to possess supernatural powers with magical talismans like black cat bones, John the Conqueror root, and cobra snake neckties.

In contrast, the lovely "Maryetta's Song" is a delicately fingerpicked ballad filled with sexual innuendo and metaphors in which Van Zandt paints a portrait of "a virgin mistress" who "stands all alone with her sorrow like a bird that's afraid to sing." Townes reveals Maryetta's dark moods, singing of "the winds that howl behind her face," while lusting for her "scarlet jasmine" that's "tucked away 'neath her vest of purest gold."

"Big Country Blues" is the diary of a rambler whose hard traveling has taken him from "Mississippi to Manitoba." Following in the tradition of Woody Guthrie and Bob Dylan, Townes recounts his experiences among the poor and dispossessed. The song ultimately sounds like it was written by someone well beyond Van Zandt's age and experience.

With "Black Crow Blues" Townes goes from being old before his time to singing from the grave. He seems to take pleasure in morbid sentimentality, as his disembodied spirit calls to his grieving lover:

Find a big man to stand beside you
Take him down to the river and show him my bones
Tell him there lies a friend I once knew

Oddly enough, this demo session compiled and released as *In the Beginning* was one of the most successful experiences Townes would ever have in a recording studio. Thrilled and optimistic about his future, Van Zandt told a journalist, "The next thing I know, I'm in a studio surrounded by some of the coolest cats and best players in the world making a record. I didn't have to go through back doors. I just came straight down the freeway. And it was because of Mickey."

But to this day, Mickey regrets having brought Townes to Nashville, as it led Van Zandt to what Newbury and others have described as a long and complex relationship with Kevin Eggers.

CHAPTER 6

WELCOME TO GNASHVILLE

That's Nashville with a *G,* son.

—Mickey Newbury

"There's an old saying in Texas: 'You can climb a tree for a dishonest nickel to leave an honest dollar on the ground,'" John Lomax III grumbled. "Kevin Eggers is a good promoter of himself. He makes you *want* to believe him. Years later *I still want to believe him*. Kevin's been spectacularly unsuccessful. He had great ears, but he never had the big score that good karma brings you."

Just a month or so before he passed away of cancer, I interviewed Mickey Newbury by phone at his home in Springfield, Oregon. Although he was seriously ill, he still had enough fire left in him to want to punch Kevin Eggers in the nose one time before he got his hat. "Promise me one thing," Newbury said in earnest. "If you ever get within six feet of Kevin, land one on his face for me." Although I haven't been in a fight since junior high school, I heard myself promising Mickey Newbury that he could rest easy. Though it's tough denying a dying man's request, when the opportunity arose, I must confess I chickened out.

I arrived at Eggers's apartment at New York's infamous Chelsea Hotel (home to a slew of the world's most famous rockers, poets, and artists over the years) just as the sun was beginning to set. A big rust-orange cat, a bunny in a cage, and a crazy skinny puppy named Basil were his roommates. Kevin sat on a brocade sofa with his back to the window as the sunlight poured through. Patterns were everywhere, from Kevin's flowery Hawaiian shirt to red velvet wallpaper, faux leopard-skin and zebra pillows, and a swirling carpet on the floor. I wasn't sure if it was by design or by chance, but the moment I sat down, I realized I couldn't see his face. It was just a silhouette framed by the fading light of the New York afternoon. As he spoke in a fast, breathy Brooklyn staccato, I soon discovered that Eggers was a master of spin.

Before launching Poppy Records in 1968, Kevin had worked as an assistant to promoter Sid Bernstein, who brought the Beatles to Carnegie Hall. Eggers also claims to have booked the first Rolling Stones U.S. tour and worked with every British Invasion band, including the Who, the Kinks, and Donovan.

In creating Poppy, Kevin "looked for people who had their own point of view and could produce a major body of work." Yet no matter which musician's name came up during the course of our conversation, the story soon revolved around him and the invaluable part he played in the creation in each of these artists' careers and works.

Kevin Eggers first heard Townes Van Zandt one afternoon when Lamar Fike spirited him over to Cowboy Jack Clement's bungalow to listen to a new Charlie Pride record he'd just cut. "Lamar was a close friend who I met playing touch football with Ricky Nelson and Elvis Presley in Bel Air," Kevin recalled. "He was a member of the Memphis Mafia and handled Elvis's publishing company. He was a real powerhouse. He just about walked on water. Jack was a big-time Charlie in Nashville, a crazy man but very intelligent and very creative. I respect Jack enormously. He was always bigger than life. Most people aren't aware of the fact that he was once a Marine Honor Guard at the White House," Eggers said.

By the mid- to late sixties there was plenty of music being cut in Nashville aside from commercial country hit records. Rock musicians began to flock to Tennessee hot on the heels of Bob Dylan, who recorded a string of his finest albums there, including *Blonde on Blonde, John Wesley Harding,* and *Nashville Skyline*. Although it bears little trace of Music City's distinctive stamp, Simon and Garfunkel's masterpiece *Bookends* was also cut in Nashville, as was the Gram Parsons–led incarnation of the Byrds, who migrated from L.A. to Tennessee to make their dubious debut on the Grand Ol' Opry and cut their country-rock opus *Sweetheart of the Rodeo* in 1968.

In 1954 Cowboy Jack was hired by legendary producer Sam Phillips (who first recorded Elvis Presley, Johnny Cash, Roy Orbison, and Jerry

Lee Lewis) to engineer and eventually produce sessions at his Sun Studios in Memphis. Jack would write "Ballad of a Teenage Queen" for Johnny Cash and produce Jerry Lee Lewis's smash hit "Whole Lotta Shakin'." Clement was also credited with discovering Don Williams and Charlie Pride.

Despite the sudden influx of liberal longhairs, Nashville remained a very conservative place, still wrestling with issues of racism. Nobody knew it better than Charlie Pride, who shocked the country music world when his fans learned of his African heritage.

Kevin recalled going to Cowboy Jack's studio for a preview of Charlie Pride's "Snakes Crawl at Night": "Jack said, 'It's gonna be a number-one record. I just made a deal with ["Mr. Guitar," head of RCA Records] Chet Atkins. They want a picture of the artist, but they don't know he's a nigger.' True story," Eggers said with a chuckle. "Nashville in those days was a very racist, very white town. At that time a black country artist was not only unheard of—it was completely off the charts. Well, the record was a complete success, and they would cut many platinum albums together."

It was Cowboy Jack who'd play Eggers the audition tape of "Tecumseh Valley" that Van Zandt recorded at Doyle Jones's Houston studio in 1966. Instantly impressed by Townes's well-crafted lyrics and penny-plain delivery, the wheels in Kevin's head began to spin. Before the tragic ballad ended Eggers was ready to cut a deal. "I thought it was an absolutely classic song. When I heard it I said, 'This is a brilliant songwriter.' I told Jack right then and there that I would sign Townes and make a record with him. Townes was brilliant from day one. He was always a great songwriter and well respected among artists, but his sales were dismal—that's the irony," Kevin confessed.

Suddenly, contracts were flying everywhere. Mickey and his uncle Jay (who also managed Newbury) had already inked a deal with Townes to manage him. Meanwhile, Cowboy Jack and Jim Malloy had formed a production company together called 7 Come 11 and signed a contract with Townes to publish his songs. And although he had no official record company to speak of, Kevin offered a naive and hungry Townes Van Zandt his first record deal.

"We started plannin' an album with Townes when along comes this guy Kevin Eggers. I don't have much good to say about him," Cowboy Jack groused. "I think he was bad news for Townes . . . worst thing that ever happened to him. Townes needed a really good manager. I can't blame it *all* on Kevin. But a lot of it.

"So we went over to the Quonset Hut and cut *For the Sake of the Song*," Clement continued. "It was his first album, and I thought it was pretty good. But Kevin just jumped right in and started tellin' us what to do. And after a while he homed in on the publishing. He had good instincts, but he had some bad instincts too. Kevin was mostly good with concepts and graphics."

"Around that time he was offered a pretty big contract," Fran Lohr recalled. "Townes came back from Nashville and said, 'Babe, I've signed a record deal. Things are gonna be great. We can do all the things we dreamed of.' Then I'm not really sure what happened, but that check for eighty thousand dollars got torn up or disappeared. We could barely pay the hospital bill when J. T. was born."

Everyone interviewed regarding Van Zandt's initial record deal quoted different figures, ranging anywhere from ten to eighty thousand dollars. One thing was certain, whether Townes drank, gambled, or gave away his big advance, as some claimed, or was taken advantage of, as others said, he returned to Texas empty-handed.

"I grew up on the streets and could see that deal comin' from day one," Mickey Newbury said.

I would've liked to have gotten Townes a record contract with somebody outside of Nashville, but unfortunately he got tied up with Kevin Eggers before I had a chance to make a move. In the end Townes went ahead and signed with Kevin who was slick enough to snooker him. It was the worst move he ever made in his life.

Everything happened real fast. Jack went ahead and worked out a deal with Kevin. I thought they'd understand what to do with him. I didn't want to step in and be a hard-ass, but I wasn't getting any support from Jack or Jim Malloy or anyone else. *I* did *not* ask Jack to be his producer. I stayed a silent partner in that deal and probably should've stepped out front and put my foot down. I knew Townes was makin' big a mistake.

Although they remained good friends over the years, Mickey would never do business with Van Zandt again after he signed with Eggers. "If Clive Davis had gotten hold of him, his career would've gone to a whole 'nother place. He woulda been dead rich and mighta still been here, to-day. I'm sure there's a plan somewhere for everything, but I sure hated to see him suffer over it. Every time he did, I bled with him. Townes was frustrated, and he had every right to be. He had lousy record deals and lousy contracts," Mickey lamented.

But not everyone involved sees eye-to-eye with Newbury: "This idea that Kevin got rich off of Townes and ripped him off is just stupid," Mickey White exclaimed. "Maybe Townes sold twenty thousand copies of an album at best during his heyday. There wasn't any profit made. Townes never accused Kevin of ripping him off, but then again, he never stepped up to his defense either. He could have put a nix on that. There was money in gigs and publishing. Townes was doin' okay, certainly better than the rest of us."

"Mickey Newbury was an up-and-coming songwriter at the time, very flashy. There's bad blood between us because I wouldn't sign him to my label," Kevin Eggers countered. "He was in awe of Townes yet never recorded any of his songs. 'Our Mother the Mountain' was one of his favorites. He said after he heard it he couldn't write for five months. But I think there was a lot of jealousy there in a funny way."

Released shortly before Christmas 1968, Townes's first album, *For the Sake of the Song,* was the flagship release of Eggers's new Poppy Records. With record jackets drawn and designed by sixties graphics guru Milton Glaser and a roster of blues and folk musicians that included Lightnin' Hopkins, the Dillards, Chris Smither, and Eric von Schmidt, the label was clearly successful on an artistic level, but commercially it was a failure.

Over the years Kevin Eggers has been criticized for taking liberties with Townes by using his albums as a venue for his own concepts and aesthetic choices. On the inside flap of the *Late, Great Townes Van Zandt* album sleeve, above producer Jack Clement's name, reads the credit "A Kevin Eggers Record." And it is Eggers's sophomoric poetry, not Townes's finely crafted lyrics, that appear on the original inside sleeve of *Our Mother the Mountain*. But Kevin was hardly the only one guilty of overstepping his boundaries when it came to Townes's records.

"The first album I released was by Townes, produced by Jack Clement and Jim Malloy. I love Jack. He is an amazingly talented songwriter and producer. Jack had turned me on to Townes, but then we had an artistic disagreement when he took 'Tecumseh Valley,' one of Townes Van Zandt's masterpieces, and cut the ending off it because he thought the lyric was too much for the fans and disc jockeys to handle. That was the end of that creative relationship for the time being," Kevin said.

The verse in question went:

She turned to whoring out on the streets
With all the lust inside her
It was many a man
Returned again
To lay himself beside her

Townes described Nashville as a "pretty straight" place, and his "lewd and offensive" lyric describing young Caroline's whoring "just horrified everybody," he explained. As no one felt it could possibly be said on a record at the time, the line "whoring out on the streets" was changed to the vague and innocuous "walking in the streets." "In terms of a song I thought 'whoring in the street' was a little too strong," Clement said, defending his decision.

To remedy this debacle Townes would recut the song in its original form the following year on his second album, *Our Mother the Mountain*. But the dispute over "Tecumseh Valley" was just the tip of the iceberg that all but sank Van Zandt's maiden voyage.

Listening to the record now, it seems apparent that Clement and Malloy were at a serious loss as to how to produce Townes's music. "Townes was so different. He didn't fit the country profile. He was a unique songwriter, very poetical. 'The Silver Ships of Andilar' was more like a movie than a song," Cowboy Jack said. "I'm not all that analytical as a producer. I hear somethin' and just do what comes natural. That first album was experimental. It's just how it fell into place at the time. I wasn't tryin' to do anything different from what I usually did. Townes wasn't too flappable. We just made everything work around him. I dunno . . . Maybe I overproduced it a little bit. But that wouldn't be the first time I've done that," Clement chuckled.

In lieu of twangy Telecasters, fiddles, and pedal steel guitars, which actually might've suited him better, the pair of perplexed producers concocted a southern Gothic sound employing ethereal organs, gossamer harpsichord fills, and medieval recorders. In the hands of the brilliant multi-instrumentalist Brian Jones these instruments worked wonders for the Rolling Stones on their midsixties hits "Lady Jane" and "Ruby Tuesday." But in Van Zandt's case, it was nothing short of disastrous.

Clement and Malloy took the brooding odes of a blue-jeaned cowboy poet and gussied them up beyond recognition. The studio musicians that

Van Zandt claimed to have been awestruck by sound like they had little or no clue whatsoever what he was singing about. The campy, way-out-West vamp employed on "Tecumseh Valley" sounds more like the soundtrack to *Seven Brides for Seven Brothers* than an attempt to evoke the dire straits faced by a destitute young girl. A *Star Trek*–style Greek choir of backup vocals meant to evoke a haunted mood just sounds silly and out of place. A high-lonesome harmonica whines, reminiscent of a spaghetti western soundtrack or a dog food commercial. But perhaps the producers' greatest sin comes in the handling of Townes's voice, which on the title song is so saturated in reverb it seems to be burbling up from the bottom of some deep, dark well. Sadly, the effect nearly obscures the artful complexity of the lyric.

The overproduction of Van Zandt's music ultimately had a boomerang effect, alienating Townes's small but devoted following of folk "purists" who attended his live shows at coffeehouses and bars. His albums were a far cry from the fingerpicked guitar and stark poetry that originally hypnotized Townes's fans, who believed he was the genuine article, "the Real Deal," the last link in a long line of troubadours that stretched back to Woody Guthrie and Jimmie Rodgers.

"I was literally brought here [Nashville], sat on a stool and told to play the song," Van Zandt told *Goldmine.* Instead of being the focal point of the album, Townes and his songs were lost in a Phil Spector–like "Wall of Sound." Once the party was over, Van Zandt claimed he could barely listen to the album, not only because of the schmaltzy production but because his guitar was so out of tune. "I was a kid, a stone freak from Texas. I wasn't too happy with what they did with the album," he later complained.

Thirty-four years after the fact, I arrived at Cowboy Jack's studio looking for some answers. Suddenly, it was apparent how Townes, the "stone freak," was swept up in Clement's charisma and watched silently as his songs were given the full Nashville treatment. Record producers can be an intimidating bunch, especially when you're new to the game. And Jack Clement can get you jumping through hoops without lifting a finger. Cowboy looks something like Santa Claus's southern brother, with a big ol' grin that could charm a throng of gullible townsfolk into buying snake oil by the gallon. It's not Jack's appearance that strikes fear into your heart. It's the man's résumé. Not only did he write hits for the Man in Black, but Clement also engineered the first song I remember hearing, Jerry Lee Lewis's "Great Balls of Fire."

I was no more than four years old at the time, playing down in the rec room, when my sister tossed a 45 on the old RCA. Suddenly, a volcanic blast of wild rhythm came blaring through the speaker. "The Killer's" maniacal howl, "Oooh, feels good," scared the hell out of me. It was the first clue I had that the devil existed. And *I liked it.* A moment later I ran upstairs as fast as I could, frantically searching for my mother.

And now the man behind the bogeyman who first introduced me to the power and passion of rock and roll was wondering if I'd had lunch yet. He was cooking up a big pot of his famous soup, which was enjoyed around a big kitchen table by the entire crew of his infamous Cowboy Arms Hotel and Recording Spa.

After a tasty meal we repaired to Jack's office for a couple questions, but I soon found myself distracted by the most beautiful Gibson J-200 I'd ever seen, hanging on the wall behind him.

The J-200 is an entity unto itself—the Cadillac of six-string guitars. And like every Caddy that's ever chauffeured nobility—from presidents, kings, sheiks, and despots to movie stars and rock and rollers, in black, gold flake, scarlet, or pink—the Gibson J-200 is its equal as a status symbol in every way. Its va-va-va-voom Playmate-of-the-Month curves gently surrender in Bob Dylan's hands on the cover of his country opus *Nashville Skyline.* The Reverend Gary Davis named his beloved J-200 "Miss Gibson" and relied on her sweet, resonant maple voice to drive home his hallelujah ragtime blues. Both Townes and Gram Parsons, like Elvis before them, had a blonde model, although Van Zandt claimed to own the worst one Gibson ever made.

Suddenly, the tough questions I had planned to confront Jack with (like what was he was thinking when he drowned Van Zandt's first album in a wash of sonic gravy?) slipped away, and I found myself downright charmed by the scoundrel. Besides, I wanted to play that guitar in the worst way. Of course, it felt and sounded like a dream. It also turned out to be the very same ax strummed by Johnny Cash on his classic hit "Ring of Fire." I nearly fell out of my chair when Jack said so.

As a recording artist Van Zandt had a chip on his shoulder that ultimately damaged his career. He simply had no or very little interest in the record-making process at all. Perhaps this self-destructive attitude was something he picked up from his hero Lightnin' Hopkins, whose philosophy was "Just give me the money, and I'll play the damn songs."

Yet for all of its flaws, his first album, *For the Sake of the Song,* is rather impressive when you consider how it was recorded. "We cut it all live over at Bradley's Barn. Back in those days you couldn't overdub. We only had a three-track recorder," Jim Malloy explained.

Whether you like them, hate them, or ignore them (as in the case of Wrecks Bell, who claimed, "I don't even hear all that stuff. All I hear is Townes"), those over-the-top Nashville baroque arrangements were played live and, surprisingly, were not the end result of obsessive over-dubbing. But the controversy over how Van Zandt's career and albums were handled still rages on today.

"I still don't get it," Guy Clark sighed.

It breaks my heart to hear the way they overproduced some of his stuff. He was not unaware of it. Townes is really the one who's responsible. It's nobody's fault but his. You can't let him off the hook. He didn't have time to mix the fuckin' records 'cause he was too busy drinkin' and shootin' dice. The way Townes looked at it, his job was writin' songs and playin' 'em for people, not puttin' 'em on tape and makin' records out of 'em. Unfortunately, he wound up workin' with people that didn't know shit about that. It was a travesty. His attitude was 'I wrote these songs; you *can't* fuck 'em up.' There were times that I wanted to produce his records the way I heard 'em.

"Townes's first album was pretty well done," Jerry Jeff Walker countered. "It mighta bothered him when they overdid it. Sometimes they'll make tracks that you can't hardly sing to if you've never led a group before in the studio. I used to let somebody else play my guitar parts 'cause I was ashamed of my guitar playing," Jerry Jeff confessed. "But later on I realized my style actually helped the other guys in the band get a lick off of it."

"A lot of his recordings were not really great," Texas singer-songwriter Joe Ely admitted.

You could tell he just barely made it through some of 'em and that clearly hurt him career-wise. Townes wasn't much into the recording process. I always listened to his records and thought, goddamn, he probably hated makin' this record. He'd much rather be out in some club drinkin' and playin' songs. Some of his live albums caught him in that special light. I don't think he really liked the recording studio. The only time I was in the studio with him was when we cut "Where I Lead Me" [for the posthumously released collection *Texas Rain*]. I could tell he didn't really like bein' there. It was like goin' to the dentist office.

"I will not vilify Kevin Eggers," Mickey White exclaimed.

Townes and Kevin were creative partners, collaborators. Kevin was as big a believer in Townes Van Zandt's music as anyone on the face of this earth, and Townes exercised a lot more creative control than people thought. People thought he wasn't professional, that he didn't care about the business, that he didn't have a game plan or want success, and that's just bullshit. Townes wanted to be successful but on his own terms. But he was never able to accomplish that. I just think that style of production was the trend. They wanted to make a product that was gonna sell and make him a star.

Producer and engineer Eric Paul, who worked on three of Van Zandt's best posthumous records, explained the dynamic between Kevin and Townes as he saw it: "Townes approved of everything Kevin was do-ing. There was trust there. An artist decides who they're going to work with. Who are we to judge or decipher who an artist trusts? And Townes trusted Kevin. They were very friendly," Eric claimed.

"You generally think of accompaniment as adding to the music, but in Townes's case it obliterated the clarity of his songs," said Nina Leto, for-mer press secretary at Eggers's second record company, Tomato. "I think Kevin was trying his damnedest to get Townes accepted by the Nashville crowd by producing those albums that way."

Once you cut through the excessive production you'll find Townes's poetry at the heart of the music. His "Sad Cinderella" recalls the swirling mercurial imagery of Bob Dylan's "Like a Rolling Stone," though it lacks Dylan's venomous spite. Van Zandt gently warns a socialite whose world is on the edge of crumbling to beware of lurking opportunists who can be likened to Dylan's sleazy diplomat, who "carries on his shoulder a Siamese cat," although she is slow to discover that he has already taken everything he can steal. Van Zandt sings:

When the bandits have stolen your jewelry and gone
And your crippled young gypsy, he's grown tall and strong
And your dead misconceptions have proven you wrong
Well then, princess, where you plannin' to turn to?

When your magazine memory has spun you around
And you realize your lovers were just painted clowns
And outside your window you start hearing sounds
Where they're building a cross for to burn you

Bill Bentley once gave Elvis Costello a cassette of Townes's songs to check out while the angry young man of punk was learning to drive in Los Angeles. Elvis was so moved by "Sad Cinderella" that he was said to have curbed the car and could only listen in awe.

Built on a loping, syncopated guitar vamp, "For the Sake of the Song" reveals the complexity of an unrequited relationship burdened by self-doubt and the pitfall of desire. The lyric contains a sophisticated internal rhyme scheme that sings like a country song while reading like poetry on the page. Townes tries to steer his way clear, navigating through a web of guilt and illusion woven by an alluring but troublesome woman.

Does she actually think I'm to blame
Does she really believe that some word of mine
Could relieve all her pain
Can't she see that she grieves
Just because she's been blindly deceived by her shame

While serving as the title to Van Zandt's first album, the phrase "for the sake of the song" (which described a woman's pent-up emotional state and inability to express herself) seemed to neatly sum up Townes's life. Van Zandt often confessed he had little choice but to follow his Muse, no matter where it led him or what the personal cost. "Maybe she just has to sing for the sake of the song / Who do I think that I am to decide that she's wrong?"

The next verse draws parallels to the Rolling Stones' "Ruby Tuesday," in which Mick Jagger bemoans the loss of a fly-by-night girl who can't understand the merit of "a life where nothing's gained and nothing's lost."

Nothing's what it seems
Maybe she'll start someday to realize
If she abandons her dreams
Then all the words she can say are only lies
When will she see that to gain is only to lose
All that she offers me are her chains and I got to refuse

The song's protagonist sits by, unable to get a word in edgewise, assuring himself, "If she could see how I feel then I know that she'd understand." We are given a front-row seat to the internal workings of Townes's thought process while this self-centered woman babbles on, full of self-doubt, uncertain what she's looking for, whether it is "soft sympathy," as Van Zandt suggests, or perhaps something more. Ultimately, the singer must choose self-respect rather than take advantage of a lady in distress. Better to go home alone than to be "nothing more than a tool."

Although both the Stones and Townes played plenty of funky honky-tonk, they also, oddly enough, shared a similar baroque aesthetic, a classical formality that peaked in the midsixties with the Beatles' forays into what Beach Boy Brian Wilson once dubbed "pocket symphonies." Arrangements that paired Paul McCartney's introspective crooning against pristine string sections on "Yesterday" and "Eleanor Rigby" would soon morph into psychedelic sonic collages. Suddenly, cellos, harpsichords, recorders, and Bach piccolo trumpets on "Penny Lane" and "Strawberry Fields Forever" were given the same kind of prominence once reserved exclusively for electric guitars, keyboards, bass, and drums.

Attempting to get to the heart of his music, Townes explained his "closer-to-home country approach." Van Zandt often relied on simple song forms based on two- and three-chord progressions with no diminished or augmented voicings. "It's much closer to the music you'd play on your front porch," he said. Or the music you'd hear your "grandmother play or stepfather play and his buddies than it is to sittin' in a studio with a clarinet player from Julliard or a bass player from the Lower East Side. There's no electronics involved—no echo and wah wah. You can tell the difference between me sittin there singin' a song and a Beatles record. It's closer to a front porch."

CHAPTER 7

FROM GOAT HILL TO CARNEGIE HALL

**I bought *Our Mother the Mountain* in 1969. That look in his eye
told me it was gonna be somethin' special.**
   —Danny "Ruester" Rowland

"Townes didn't seem to do anything for any reason except for the purpose of writing another song. He came on this earth to play music. It didn't matter what shape he was in, he always damn well fulfilled his goal. And he affected a lot of people by doing it," Joe Ely exclaimed.

Ely, who has been dubbed "the heir to Buddy Holly's mantle," first crossed paths with Townes Van Zandt in 1971 when he saw him wandering alone down a hot, dusty road outside of Lubbock with his guitar in tow. Van Zandt was on the last leg of a long journey back to Houston from San Francisco, standing in a no-man's-land out on the Clovis Highway, desperate for a lift, when Ely spied him.

Joe knew the dude had no chance of getting a ride where he was. He'd been out hitchhiking around California recently himself and sympathized with the poor devil. "So I gave him a ride to the other end of town," he said. "As I was letting him off, he opened up his backpack, but there weren't any clothes in there, not a stitch. Instead there were about twenty-five albums, neatly stacked." Townes reached in and grabbed a brand-new copy of *Our Mother the Mountain* and handed it to Ely in return for his kindness. A moment later they decided to stop by the nearest liquor store to pick up a six-pack, drink a couple of beers, and shoot the shit in Joe's Volkswagen Beetle before saying farewell.

Joe Ely and Jimmie Dale Gilmore had been only casual acquaintances until the following afternoon, when Joe phoned to tell him about the strange hitchhiker he had picked up carrying a backpack full of his own records. "Joe called me up and said, 'You gotta hear this guy.' And, of course, it was Townes Van Zandt's *Our Mother the Mountain*," Jimmie Dale recalled. "I guess you could say Townes's music was the catalyst for our lifelong friendship."

"We just fell in love with that record and played it over and over all night," Ely remembered. "I think what affected us most was his intelligence. We went over and found Butch Hancock. Now that I think about it, Townes was probably the catalyst for the Flatlanders gettin' together and writin' songs. Me and Butch and Jimmie had a strange bond with Townes from listenin' to that record so intensely. We figured we knew him inside and out. The three of us stayed real close to him up until he died," Joe added.

"Well, Joe remembers it a little differently," Jimmie Dale said with a laugh. "That was back in the sixties, a long time before we got together with Butch. Joe and I were mutual fans of each other's, but we came from very different worlds. He called me up and told me about Townes's record; then we got together and played it and were both so blown away. Townes was like a combination of Hank Williams and Bob Dylan. Here was this guy with a country pine doin' this folk stuff. That was the two worlds I was in at the time."

"When they played me that record it just paralyzed me," Butch Hancock recalled.

It was like he was speaking from inside my head. It instantly put the stamp of approval on what we were doin', but at the same time he gave us a high-end benchmark to hold things up against.

A few years later when I finally moved down to Austin, Townes came to my debut gig at the Split Rail. The next week I found out about it in the paper. I didn't even know it at the time. It was a noisy room, and somebody said he was listenin', payin' attention to the words. I was deeply honored he'd been at my first gig.

By the winter of 1971, the Flatlanders had finished recording their debut album and headed to Austin to begin building their legend, slugging it out on the strip of clubs on Sixth Street. "Townes didn't know us, but he'd already heard my song 'Dallas' in some joint in Dallas and enjoyed it. He just kept pumpin' quarters into the jukebox until the people at the bar got furious at him for playin' the song over and over again. That was the Flatlanders' recording of it," Jimmie Dale said proudly.

"Townes had a *huge* effect on me," Gilmore confessed. "There was such a high level of quality in his lyrics. He affected us all—Guy Clark and Rodney Crowell. He set the standards. He was relentlessly great. I cannot understand why people don't appreciate him. I don't think he's better than Bob Dylan, but I think the two stand out above everybody else . . . and Leonard Cohen too, of course. It's funny how people overlook him," Jimmie Dale mused.

"Townes was a naturally soulful, humanistic person who sang with complete sincerity and always put himself into the song, whether it was his own or someone else's," David Amram imparted. "There was power, poetry, and beauty to his lyrics. Townes appreciated the poetry of everyday Texas speech, places with poetic names like Dripping Springs and Cut and Shoot."

David admired Townes's love of people and the down-home Texas way of life, a way of life that Van Zandt saw vanishing into a sprawl of shopping malls, motels, and fast-food restaurants. "Jack Kerouac felt the same way," Amram explained. "He was so hurt when those beautiful, simple things were ignored, or when they were eventually acknowledged, they were co-opted and destroyed by so-called progress."

A recent victim of somebody's idea of progress is the small, out-of-the-way neighborhood of Austin called Clarksville, originally a ten-acre parcel of land bought by a co-op of emancipated slaves who built their homes and raised their families there following the Civil War.

"I lived in Clarksville from the time I first moved to Austin in 1972. It was the greatest little neighborhood, a little world unto itself. It was so *unsupervised,*" Darryl Harris said with an impish grin. Townes used to live there, in a trailer on a little lot on the corner of Charlotte and Eleventh Street. We built a tree house in a live oak where we'd sit and drink and smoke joints all day. It was great. He had some goats, so we called his place 'Goat Hill.'"

Around the corner lived the neighborhood guru, Uncle Seymour Washington, an old blacksmith known for his wisdom and his tasty barbecue. Seymour lived in Clarksville for more than forty years, and his old porch, home to Pepe and Jim, a Chihuahua and hound dog, respectively, was the neighborhood's focal point, where people would stop by for a few minutes or a whole afternoon.

"It was an interesting mix of hippies and old black people who'd been there all their lives. Everybody got along pretty well. There was no conflict or friction. It's been so gentrified since then," Harris groaned.

Driving around the neighborhood in the winter of 2005, I circled back and forth, zigzagging through the tiny streets, when I stopped to talk with an old-timer in a baseball hat. I asked him if he recalled where Seymour Washington once lived. "Sure," he said, with a blinding-white dentured grin. "'Round the corner there on Twelfth Street, but the place burned down. The neighborhood has changed quite a bit since those days."

The building of Route 1 and Mo-Pac (named for the Missouri-Pacific Railway) took out half of Clarksville. With new condominiums squeezed between the old houses wherever possible, it rapidly became what real estate agents enthusiastically refer to as "a desirable neighborhood."

"By the time I moved there the houses were already cleared out," Darryl recollected. "Mo-Pac just sat there, nothing but a big pile of dirt for many years."

Only patches of head-high weeds, giant live oaks, and blackbirds and grackles perched on bare branches, silhouetted against the gray winter sky, have remained the same since Uncle Seymour once held court. And thankfully so has Nau's Soda Fountain. With its old-fashioned green Formica lunch counter and salmon-red swivel chairs, wooden booths, and fans lazily spinning overhead, Nau's, famous for cheeseburgers, BLTs, and malts, is a vision of America's past. Like something out of a Norman Rockwell painting, the quaint old corner drugstore with its wooden magazine racks and shelves filled with model airplane kits remains a precious oasis in a land now sprawled with strip malls.

Townes lived in Clarksville in 1974 when filmmaker Jim Szalapski came to town to shoot his underground classic, *Heartworn Highways*. The movie featured performances by Townes, Guy Clark, David Allan Coe, Rodney Crowell, Gamble Rogers, Steve Young, the Charlie Daniels Band, as well as Richard Dobson and a teenage Steve Earle. Szalapski's footage of Townes is clearly the film's centerpiece. In one scene Van Zandt, full of booze and mischief, proudly gives the camera a tour of his hillbilly ranch. Accompanied by his dog Geraldine, whom he introduces before his girlfriend (and future second wife) Cindy, a giggling, frecklefaced, redheaded teenager, Townes pointed out an enormous hole in the ground, claiming his property was infested with giant rabbits ("The bigger, the bunnier," he puns with a gold-tooth grin). A moment later he is in the clutches of said mythical beast, being dragged down the dusty, dark hole, where he will either be gruesomely gnawed to death by a pack of rabid bunnies or have a spot of tea and swap stories and stimulants with Alice.

The next time Townes appears he is in the company of Uncle Seymour, who earnestly offers advice on whiskey consumption while Van Zandt slaps his thighs, doubled up with laughter. A moment later Townes pulls out his guitar, hammers an A-minor chord, and falls into a solemn rendition of "Waitin' 'round to Die," as the old man begins to weep.

"They just came and filmed us for a couple of days and it all happened at the same time as I started a big gig in Austin where we lived for a time," Townes told a reporter from *Omaha Rainbow*. "It was winter and they wanted to have a Seymour-style barbecue where we lived, Seymour's house being famous for barbecues. He's this old black man. He was eighty-two at the time and a real ham. A couple of friends and I tried to get a fire going. There were people driving past looking at us like we were nuts."

"Townes stayed in Clarksville while they shot *Heartworn Highways*. He and Cindy lived in a little trailer, down the block from Uncle Seymour's house. It wasn't a very productive time for him. He didn't do too many gigs. He mostly sat around drunk all the time. He and Cindy were constantly at each other's throats," Mickey White recalled.

"I remember the day the film crew showed up," Darryl Harris said. "We were all just sittin' around when Townes came out of the back bedroom in this long blond wig and lipstick. I don't know if they even saw it. Cindy hit him like a Doberman pinscher, got him back in that bedroom, and took that shit off him as quick as she could."

The next time Joe Ely ran into Townes was nearly as mythical as their original meeting. A big fire was blazing in Seymour's front yard when he arrived. Van Zandt apparently (hadn't heeded a single word of Uncle Seymour's advice and) had been drinking whiskey all day and was fit to be tied. He'd gotten into an argument and was about to take a slug at his pal Chico when he tripped over a log and fell backward into the blazing barbecue pit. "Everybody ran over to pull him out," Joe recalled with a laugh. "When we picked him up, I noticed he hadn't spilled a drop from that pint of whiskey he had in his hand. Townes would drink and fight and write songs. He followed his emotions, which I don't think was always the best thing to do. He was mischievous and ornery. He'd tell a story, and then he'd go out and live it, or sometimes he'd live it and then tell it afterwards. You'd never know which came first. Sometimes I think songwriting might have been his worst enemy," Ely said, chuckling at the thought.

"Joe and Jimmy and I had gone over to Uncle Seymour's house where they were roasting a goat for Chico's birthday when Townes and Chico got into a fight. Both of 'em were fallin' over into the fire from different directions. Uncle Seymour, who was a warm soul and somethin' of a front porch philosopher, said, 'Oh, it's alright, let 'em fight—It's Chico's birthday.' Well, they finally got themselves dusted off when Townes took that bottle, took a big swig off it, and tossed it over to Chico and said, 'Happy birthday, man,'" Butch Hancock recalled with a laugh.

The album-cover head shot for *Our Mother the Mountain* by Allen Vogel is a revealing portrait of Van Zandt's dual nature. Townes's chin rests on his hand, rolled into a fist, more dangerous to himself than anyone else. His young face is expressionless except for one eye that stares at you, dark and unfathomable, through the lens of his wire-rimmed glasses. The other eye, along with the entire left side of his face, is enveloped in darkness. The honey glow of the setting sun, or perhaps the flickering light of a campfire, brushes his sullen right cheek.

His hat rises out of the shadows like a distant mountain atop his head. There is no trace of "the gentle person named Townes" whom Kevin Eggers described in his liner notes. You are face-to-face with the dark stranger, the unpredictable drifter, the moon-faced poet who remains unknowable.

There are few artists whose records have entered the marketplace without their names emblazed across the cover. They are usually of the stature of Frank Sinatra, Bob Dylan, and John Lennon. And although Van Zandt was a legend in the making, he was still far from that point in his career. If he was "unknowable" from the cover photo, the man's identity remained in question until you flipped the record jacket over and saw his name in yellow block letters across the top. Whether this was a deliberate ploy by Kevin Eggers to create an aura of mystery around Townes or an aesthetic choice by Milton Glaser, it didn't help him get one inch ahead of where he was already in the public eye.

"The idea was always provocation," Glaser explained.

Our motto at Poppy was "There's something unusual going on here." We wanted to be, for better or worse, out of the mainstream. We tried to establish a position that was abstract, more ambiguous, more obscure, because we knew that our audience would respond to those kinds of things. So we did a lot of oblique communication. The album cover for *Our Mother the Mountain* was about provoking people's interest. To get them to ask, "What the hell is that?" Either they got it or they didn't. If they didn't know who Townes was, his name wouldn't mean anything if they were compelled to buy it. These were basically cult records bought by a small group of passionate people.

Inside the original LP was a black-and-white Vogel photo of Van Zandt that portrayed a different side of Townes altogether: the English-lit major in sports jacket and dress collar. This time, Van Zandt's obsidian eyes squint at some distant specter, perhaps William Blake's Avalon.

Following in the footsteps of fellow seekers Woody Guthrie and Jack Kerouac, Townes, along with his pal Bob "Mav" Myrick and Kevin Eggers, would hit the road in late 1968, "to look for America," as Simon and Garfunkel sang.

"Kevin was tired of New York and wanted Townes to make another album," Myrick said, recounting their odyssey. "He had a chauffeur named Billy. So he and Townes and I drove across the country, through the heartland of the United States in a Cadillac limousine, to San Francisco for a couple days and then down along the coast on Route 101 to Malibu. Townes stayed in Malibu for four months while making the album. We were stoned all the way and had long hair, which was not acceptable back then. The Nebraska farmers didn't think much of us when we stopped to get gas and came piling out of the limo in a big cloud of smoke.

"Kevin was a pretty bizarre character, but I liked him a lot," Myrick said. "When we got to Malibu, Tuesday Weld picked him up in a Mercedes, and we didn't see him for a day or two. He knew everybody in Hollywood. *Everybody.*

"As far as we knew Kevin was makin' big money. I don't know, maybe it was all a front. Townes didn't like to talk about money. He didn't even *like* money. He said Kevin had screwed him a couple of times. But Eggers, in fact, *loved* Townes's music. There was no doubt about it."

The basic tracks for *Our Mother the Mountain* were cut in Los Angeles and later "sweetened" in Nashville. With Cowboy Jack and Jim Malloy back in the producer chairs along with Kevin Eggers, there was a somewhat simpler, lighter-handed approach production-wise than with the flawed first album. On board were James Burton (famed guitar picker for Ricky Nelson and Elvis Presley), on lead and Dobro, while Charlie McCoy played everything from harmonica, guitar, bass, and organ to recorder.

"I went to all the sessions at Sunset Studios," Myrick recounted. "They brought in a piano player named Don Randi who called the shots. The original album, the way they cut it, was absolutely dynamite. Randi and the studio musicians were jammin' and had a really good time. They did it so fast it was unbelievable." Randi, a jazz pianist who continues to lead his own group, has recorded with everyone in Los Angeles over the years, from Frank Sinatra to Frank Zappa.

But Myrick was in for a real shock when he laid that new slab of shiny vinyl on his turntable and cranked up the volume: "When the record came out, as a finished product with all those strings and orchestral arrangements on there, I couldn't believe it. I was livid and let Kevin, Jack, and Malloy know it was totally fucked up. Frannie didn't like it much either. But Townes didn't give a shit," Bob said. "He wrote purely for the sake of the song. He didn't care if it made a dime. Hell, he didn't care if he even *had* a dime."

Side two of the album featured the much needed remake of "Tecumseh Valley." Originally written on a five-string banjo, the ballad of Caroline is a heartbreaking portrait of a young immigrant woman whose dream has withered and died. Like "Hollis Brown," Bob Dylan's starving farmer, driven to madness and suicide, and Robbie Robertson's brokenhearted rebel Virgil Kane from "The Night They Drove Old Dixie Down," Caroline will forever stand among the timeless figures of American song.

"Townes just takes you so far into this woman that it hurts deeply," Nanci Griffith explained. Griffith (whose middle name also happens to be Caroline) identifies strongly with the song, calling it "a source of strength and identity. I feel as if I could have been Caroline. That song kept me from being her," she confessed. "Thinking about her downfall and sorrow often saved me from making wrong turns when I felt I had no choice but do so," Nanci said. The song would bring Arlo Guthrie and Griffith to tears when they recorded it for her 1993 album *Other Voices/Other Rooms*.

"Just listen to 'Our Mother the Mountain,'" coproducer Jim Malloy exclaimed. "That right there tells you the whole story." Simply put, the song is otherworldly. Like the best of Van Zandt's dark sagas, this tale of a bewitched lover is a minor-key waltz that limps along like foreboding footsteps approaching in the hall, coming closer, closer, as the song slowly envelops you. It feels as if the walls of your room are closing in as you writhe within the claustrophobic grip of this gruesome story.

Purple moonlight shines through his false lover's black hair, as the singer, transfixed by her beauty, is hypnotized by a medallion that she slowly twirls. Filled with desire he dares to touch her. And that's when sparks start to fly.

> So I reach for her hand
> And her eyes turns to poison
> And her hair turns to splinters
> And her flesh turns to brine
>
> She leaps 'cross the room
> She stands in the window
> And screams that my first-born
> Will surely be blind
>
> She throws herself out
> To the black of the nightfall
> She's parted her lips
> But she makes not a sound
>
> I fly down the stairway
> And I run to the garden
> No trace of my true love
> Is there to be found

If there is any moral to this mysterious parable, it comes when Townes sings, "So walk these hills lightly and watch who you're lovin'." In the end Van Zandt warns, "Love not a woman with hair black as midnight." But this bit of advice is ultimately worthless, as betrayal in Townes's world comes from all directions and in all shapes and colors. By the album's end he bitterly bids farewell to the "yellow-headed misery" he's known in "Snake Mountain Blues."

In "Kathleen" the protagonist finds himself fearfully fleeing across a haunted landscape. What he's running from is not clear. It's his destination that matters most and if he will reach it in time. Townes is alone, vulnerable. He flees in fear but soon finds relief, if not redemption, in the arms of a "sweet" woman, whose name could easily be a metaphor for heroin.

Yet Van Zandt's eerie lyrics and brooding moods, black as they might be, never got in the way of the fun they had cutting the record. "He wasn't somber *all* the time," Jack Clement explained. "Townes was morose in his lyrics, but he was not a morose person. He had a great sense of humor. He was always callin' me up with some joke. One time he went to Europe and brought me back a CD with twenty-six versions of 'La Paloma.'"

Veteran New York disc jockey Vin Scelsa first met Townes early in the winter of 1969. Kevin Eggers, a listener and supporter of WFMU, the fountainhead of New York free-form radio, had called the station in East Orange, New Jersey, to promote Van Zandt's new album, *Our Mother the Mountain*.

"Kevin was like Townes's cheerleader. He was like a speed freak whenever he talked about him," Scelsa recalled. "We were vaguely aware of his first album, but soon everyone at the station was charmed by Van Zandt, his songs and his corny jokes."

Townes and I just clicked, and he spent a couple nights sleeping on my couch. We got high together, and talked, and he played the guitar. He was just another guy at the time that was very talented, but there was something special about him. There were secrets that Townes would allude to, mysteries about him being the black sheep of a prominent Texas family and being institutionalized and having shock therapy.

In September 1969, we shut down WFMU after the college tried to implement some restrictions on us. It was the sixties. We didn't bother to strike; we just shut the station down. And it was months before it was up and running and back on the air again. Around that time, Kevin offered me a job at Poppy Records. The office was at Sixth Avenue between Forty-third and Forty-fourth Street, in the same building as RCA Records, who distributed Poppy. There were a couple people in the office working for Kevin, mostly women and a guy named Sugar Bear, a jolly, happy freak who was always high. I was hired to be the radio promotion guy, which I had neither experience nor any desire to do. I was from a free-form, freaky radio station and didn't know the first thing about commercial radio.

With Nixon in the White House, the war in Vietnam raged on as the hippies' utopian dream culminated in the summer of August 1969. Half a million stoned pilgrims seeking "Three Days of Love, Peace, and Music" swarmed to the Woodstock Music and Art Fair, to dance in the mud and get high on pot and acid, at Max Yasgur's farm in the bucolic Catskill Mountains.

"It was a great time musically. There was a communal sense at Poppy. All the artists knew each other," Kevin Eggers reminisced fondly. "In 1969 we put on a show with Dick Gregory, Mandrake Memorial, and Townes at Carnegie Hall."

The night before Thanksgiving, on Wednesday, November 26, Poppy Records presented a showcase that featured three of their most diverse acts: comedian and activist Dick Gregory, the psychedelic ensemble Mandrake Memorial, and Townes at the most prestigious concert hall on earth.

A Gentle Evening with Townes Van Zandt, finally released by Dualtone Records in 2002, reveals a set of nine songs that Van Zandt performed that evening. Photos of Townes taken during his set that night portray him wearing a flower-embroidered shirt with his long hair parted down the middle, hanging over his shoulders, his face, wooden as a tobacco-store Indian, his eyes, as always, shut tight, in deep concentration while he sang.

After a warm round of applause, Townes nervously mumbled that he planned to start the evening off with "Talking Thunderbird Blues," but as he figured there were "more bigots than winos" in the crowd, he would play (Ma Carrick's favorite) "KKK Talking Blues" instead. The politically correct crowd was taken aback for a moment, as Van Zandt proceeded with his story of how he earned the dubious honor of "bigot of the year."

Reminiscent of Randy Newman's twisted brand of social satire, the song was perhaps the closest Townes had ever come to making an overtly political statement. It never appeared on any of his future albums, studio or live, and seems to have been permanently dropped from his repertoire immediately after he finished singing it. A strange choice to break the ice with, the tune was met with a polite response at best. From there, Van Zandt headed straight for the *Twilight Zone,* debuting a spellbinding new minor-keyed waltz he'd recently written called "Rake." Teeming with supernatural imagery, Townes sings from the viewpoint of a damned soul crying out, though it's unclear whether from behind a row of bars at a carnival freak show, an insane asylum window, or the fiery depths of hell itself.

> You look at me now, don't think I don't know
> What all your eyes are a-sayin'
> Does he want us to believe these ravings and lies
> They're just tricks that his brain's been a-playin'
>
> A lover of women he can't hardly stand
> He trembles, he's bent and he's broken
> I've fallen it's true but I say unto you
> Hold your tongues until after I've spoken

The crowd's judgment comes swiftly in a flood of warm applause as the last chord rings from his guitar. "Nice to be here, y'know?" Townes replies softly to their enthusiastic response. It didn't take long for Van Zandt to charm the crowd after an awkward start.

Van Zandt's nine-song set that night was particularly morose, if not downright funereal, except for a few bits of quirky humor thrown in for momentary relief. A series of three cleanly picked, heartfelt, introspective ballads followed. In "Like a Summer Thursday," Townes knowingly accepts the cycle of life and death, gain and loss, and that finding true love (if it exists) is mostly a waiting game.

> If only she could feel my pain
> But feelin' is a burden
> She can't sustain
> So like a summer Thursday
> I cry for rain
> To come and turn
> The ground to green again

Like a Polaroid snapshot of a fleeting moment, "Second Lover's Song," from Townes's recently released second album, captured the complex emotions running just below the surface of a pair of star-crossed young lovers. Van Zandt refuses to allow his girlfriend's past to destroy the joy they currently share. Ever the southern gentleman courting his fair lady, Townes sings:

Would your eyes more brightly shine?
Would your laughter be so tender
If you'd been only mine
For as long as you remember

I don't want tears from you
Don't build your love on shame
All what we've done is through
And all we can do remains

My lady can't you see
I love not jealously
But for all you are to me
And all you'll be tomorrow

An Olympian feat of surrealist lyricism in which images don't flow but gush from Van Zandt's stream of consciousness, "She Came and She Touched Me" tells a tale of desire and betrayal while "peons pick partners and waltz across ceilings."

Once again Dylan's influence (circa *Highway 61 Revisited/Blonde on Blonde*) is clearly evident. But whereas Dylan relied on a highly personalized vocal style to accentuate the meaning of his fragmented poetry and tales of deceit, Van Zandt's lyrics shined, whether on the written page or sung plainly with a simple guitar accompaniment.

Singing of a mad careening wind that blows through the paneless windows of his soul, Townes evokes the sort of imagery found in the works of such poets as Dylan Thomas and Arthur Rimbaud. The third verse seems set against the backdrop of a hallucinatory ball where the sangria is spiked with psilocybin.

Drunkards drink deeply from cups full of nothing
Ghost lovers laugh at the games that they play
While the moments do somersaults into eternity
Cling to their coattails and beg them to stay,

Saying I got nothin' to hide
Illusions projected on walls made of tiffany
Mad minuets to a sad satin song
Harlequin mandolins harmonize helplessly

Hoping that endlessly won't last for long,
Praying that their Gods ain't died

Then I turn and I see her in a dress made of moonlight
Teardrops like diamonds run slow down her face
Her arms, they surround me like chains made of velvet
The demons fall faithfully into their place,
The rivers run with jewels

As in Dylan's "Desolation Row," where Albert Einstein saws an electric violin and is seen sniffing drainpipes while reciting the alphabet, the topsy-turvy absurdity of Townes's worldview is laid bare for all to see.

Now the morning lies open, the night went quite quickly
Memory harmlessly fractures and fades
All the poets do push-ups on carpets of rubber foam
Loudly they laugh at some joke that's been made,
And the wise men speak like fools

Served up back-to-back, the dark drone of "Lungs" and "Tecumseh Valley" is a particularly frightful duo. They are two of Van Zandt's most intense portraits of alienation and death, in which he portrays America as a land of crushed dreams.

After a particularly gripping rendition of "Tecumseh Valley," Townes offers a much needed moment of comic relief, telling his old joke about the nun who feigns ignorance while ordering a delicious "martin-eye." He then continues on a lighter note with "Talking Thunderbird Blues." Van Zandt closes out the show with Peter LaFarge's "Ballad of Ira Hayes" (popularized by Johnny Cash in 1964), taking no prisoners with his spare delivery of a devastating tale of the drunk and homeless Pima Indian who once helped raise the flag at Iwo Jima and then died in the gutter.

Van Zandt's set walloped the crowd more than wowed it that night at Carnegie Hall. Whether meant as a double dose of existential angst or as a sly bit of gallows humor, Townes hardly created the festive mood Eggers and company had hoped for. Dick Gregory soon hit the stage with his politically charged stand-up shtick, putting the audience in stitches, while a few in the crowd wondered about that odd fellow and his strange, sad songs about vampires, Indians, and the KKK.

For all of his wild antics and spontaneous generosity, Townes was a poor excuse for a hippie. Although fond of a strong toke of Mother Nature and an occasional front-seat ride on Dr. Hoffman's psychedelic express, Van Zandt generally preferred the twilight world of narcotics and depressants. Although Townes scribed such lighthearted ditties as "Brother Flower" and "Columbine," which reflect the musings of a lonely bard contemplating love and life in a pastoral paradise, he was certainly no jasmine-perfumed, velvet-draped Donovan, offering his cosmic verse as a gentle gift "from a flower to a garden." You would never find Townes among the throng of antiwar demonstrators delicately placing daisies into the rifle barrels of National Guardsmen at the Pentagon or Kent State.

"Townes didn't strike me as much of a hippie at all. What makes a hippie? Being a free spirit?" mused Wisconsin folksinger Bill Camplin. "Townes was only interested in heaven once he was down in hell and looking up at it."

Just a few weeks after Poppy's shindig at Carnegie Hall, the Rolling Stones, looking to ride the wave of euphoria still lingering from the previous summer's Woodstock festival, organized a party of their own on December 6, featuring Santana; Crosby, Stills, Nash, and Young; Jefferson Airplane; and the Flying Burrito Brothers at the Altamont Speedway in northern California. In lieu of security guards, Hell's Angels were hired to ward off any glassy-eyed stoner who got too close to the stage.

While Mick Jagger pranced around like Mephistopheles in his jammies howling "Sympathy for the Devil," an eighteen-year-old black man became the feast's sacrificial lamb. Meredith Hunter was stabbed to death while others were beaten back by a pack of leather-clad Angels wielding pool cues, hammered on beer and bad acid.

A week later, the media had a field day with Charlie Manson's twisted family values, as his ghoulish crew was hauled into the light of day for the heinous murder of a pregnant Sharon Tate and six others back in August. As Creedence Clearwater Revival's John Fogerty had predicted, a bad moon was surely on the rise, casting a strange and eerie glow over the Age of Aquarius.

In January 1970, Townes hit the road for eight weeks, playing the college-campus coffeehouse circuit run by the Bitter End, a popular folk club in Greenwich Village. Most troubadours making those rounds traveled solo, driving their own cars, spending a week at a time, performing two sets a night in the big university towns of the Midwest and South.

Townes, according to Vin Scelsa, had been getting over some sort of illness that he believed was hepatitis. Not yet twenty-six, Van Zandt was already faced with the choice to dry up or die. Doctors had repeatedly warned Townes that one more drink could set him off on another binge, which could prove fatal, considering the sorry condition of his liver.

"Kevin, realizing that I was useless around the office, started to wonder what he was paying me for," Scelsa chuckled. "So he sent me out on the road with Townes to babysit him and make sure he didn't drink."

Vin chauffeured Townes from gig to gig while he lounged in the backseat strumming his guitar, picking old blues numbers or ironing out chord changes to new tunes. "Though I can't remember any of the songs specifically, I know he wrote several by the end of that trip, and I was lucky enough to have witnessed their development," Scelsa said.

One morning they woke up early in order to get to the next town where Kevin had wired some money ahead. Bleary-eyed, Vin glanced over at Townes, who sat on the edge of his bed transfixed by the TV set, watching a new show that neither of them had seen before, called *Sesame Street*. Townes began to sing along with a little ditty, designed to teach children how to count. Suddenly, he stopped to mull the situation over for a moment. "Vinny," he said slowly, deliberately, as if on the verge of making an earth-shattering revelation, "this is a *weird* fuckin' country."

"Townes's natural inclination was to go out partying and drinking every night, so I had to find some way to keep him busy. We spent a lot of time going to all the Dairy Queens of the Midwest. We both probably gained ten pounds on that trip," Vin recalled with a laugh. "For Townes to gain any weight at all was extraordinary, as he was pencil thin.

"At that point he was a beautiful young man," Scelsa admitted. "The girl who I was goin' with at the time, who I later married that year, she was in love with him. *Everyone* was in love with him. Every town we went to, he got a girl and sometimes more than one. There was always one who'd hang out with us for the whole week. He had remarkable charisma. I gotta admit I was a little jealous as I wasn't gettin' *any*."

One night in Milwaukee Vin was sure he would score. Scelsa recalled the object of his desire: "She was about ten years older than me and wasn't all that attractive," he chuckled. "I thought I was finally gonna get laid. We sat around late at night, passing the pipe, but nothing was happening between us. The next thing I know I'm sitting there all alone, listening to Townes and her going at it in the next room. The funny thing was, she wasn't his type at all."

Townes later told Robert Greenfield that while on tour he planned on making a detour to his old hometown of Barrington, Illinois, to hunt down some high school girls he used to know. "I'm gonna go get a telephone book and look up names," he said. "It's ten years since I graduated from high school. Whew, ten years. People probably got homes and kids, and I'm goin' out with high school girls all the time. High school girls are outta sight."

But the promise of a little tour nookie was not the only thrill the Land of Lincoln had to offer. One night, after the gig, wide awake and wired on all the free coffee and donuts they'd downed at the college coffeehouse, Vin and Van Zandt packed up the Plymouth and hit the road to get a head start on the next day's journey. It was late and freezing cold as they tooled along an empty two-lane highway, past the ice-glazed barns and desolate cornfields of central Illinois. With mounds of glistening snow piled high around them, it seemed like they were driving through an endless ice tunnel. Suddenly, the glint of a pair of distant headlights ignited their rearview mirror. The piercing high beams illuminated the long, lonely road ahead, a straight black ribbon with not a curve in sight. With nowhere to hide, paranoia soon had them in its ugly stranglehold. The strange car began to gain on them. In the middle of nowhere, the stoned duo somehow convinced each other that a crazed killer was on their trail, stalking them. Having just seen the low-budget hippie road odyssey *Easy Rider,* fear wreaked havoc on their dope-baked brains. They didn't want to die like Dennis Hopper, whose character in the film (a perfect imitation of the Byrds' David Crosby, complete with Yosemite Sam mustache and buckskin jacket) was blown off his customized chopper for popping some trigger-happy redneck the finger.

Suddenly, scarlet spears of light exploded all around them, splashing off the bright-white walls of snow. Townes pulled the Plymouth over. It wasn't a crew of psycho rednecks after all. It was only the law. For a moment he felt oddly relieved. Of course, they were holding. Townes, in those days, always scored some dope along the way to keep the journey interesting.

As the cop approached their car, Van Zandt slipped his buddy the stash. "Here, Vinny," he whispered. "Get rid of this. Quick!" A moment later the cop leaned in the window, waving his flashlight around, when Scelsa spied a couple of gnarly roaches reeking in the ashtray. Luckily, "the man," a little slow on the uptake, didn't.

"Howdy, officer," Townes said a bit too cheerfully. "Is there somethin' wrong?"

"You boys haven't been smokin' pot, have you?" the cop asked, sniffing around.

"No, sir," Townes replied, a goofy grin plastered across his face.

"Where you boys from?" the cop prodded.

"New York," the pair answered in tandem, forgetting their car was registered in the Lone Star State.

"Well, then, what are you doing in a vehicle with Texas plates?" the officer snapped. With that he took Townes's license and registration and returned to the patrol car, where he sat with the lights flashing while Scelsa began to have a meltdown. "Oh, fuck, Townes, WE'RE GOIN' TO JAIL!" he cried. "We'll never get out of Illinois."

"Just be cool, Vinny," Van Zandt, a veteran of a thousand near busts, said.

Meanwhile, Scelsa carefully cracked the passenger-side window open, and a moment later the contraband was gone with the winter wind.

The cop finally returned and handed Townes back his paperwork. "Now, where'd you boys say you're headed?" he asked.

Vin cleared his throat and took his best shot, explaining in his best DJ–road manager voice: "Officer, this is Townes Van Zandt, the legendary singer-songwriter from Austin, Texas. We started out on this tour a couple weeks ago back in New York City," he said, handing him a copy of Townes's latest album. "And that's why we said we're from New York. We just played a show earlier this evening, and we're awfully tired, sir, and then we got lost looking for the motel. Isn't the Interstate up ahead somewhere?"

"Okay, you boys just follow me," the cop said, hypnotized by Townes's black eyes, glaring at him through the cellophane-wrapped cover of *Our Mother the Mountain.*

With the law leading the way, they drove another five miles until the cop signaled them to turn onto the exit ramp.

"I just about wet my pants," Vin said with a nervous laugh.

"See, I told ya not to worry, Vinny, didn't I?" Townes replied as he pulled another dime bag out of his boot. And soon the sweet, sticky smoke permeated the Plymouth once again.

"Oh, that was just business as usual for Townes Van Zandt," Old Chief Rolling Papers said. "After all, the man was a gambler, skilled in the way of the bluff. Townes never made his move too soon."

"He had an incredible face," Scelsa concurred. "As he got older, it developed that Indian-chief kind of look to it. Townes's skin was like the color of beautiful suede, but at a certain point that suede began to crack like old leather, and he looked like an image carved into a mountain."

"He was the only person I knew who could sit completely still," Robert Earl Keen said. "It was almost kind of eerie. He never moved. Didn't fidget or blink or fumble for his cigarettes. It was like sittin' next to an old Indian. One time we were drivin' a rent-a-car through Massachusetts, and he said, 'Let's pull over for a burger,' and I swear his lips never moved."

CHAPTER 8

WEIRD SCENES INSIDE A DOLL'S HOUSE

When things get me so low
I duck when caterpillars pass overhead,
there's always another Van Zandt gem
to ease the pain.
—John Lomax III

With the release of the Beatles' *Sergeant Pepper's Lonely Hearts Club Band* in June 1967, the record album suddenly became an "objet d'art." The album's cover was of utmost importance. It set the tone for the listening experience. First impressions came not from the music itself but from the art or graphic chosen to represent it. One look at Townes's spoon-bending stare on the jacket of *Our Mother the Mountain,* and you knew you weren't going to spend the afternoon "Feelin' Groovy" with the likes of Simon and Garfunkel.

And after breaking the sealed cellophane, if the gatefold opened and contained photos and lyrics or liner notes like some urgent telegram, giving you the latest on your favorite group or singer, all the better. Even the feel of the cardboard would eventually reach a fetishistic level. The rich, pebbled texture of Crosby, Stills, Nash, and Young's album *Déjà Vu* made one feel as if they were holding a prized family heirloom or a modern-day version of the Holy Grail.

"Some of the photography we used at Poppy was very amateurish," Milton Glaser explained. "That shot of Townes in the East Village [by

Ken Beckles, which graced the cover of *Delta Momma Blues*] perfectly captured the mood of the moment. We didn't want it to look too slick. That wonderful picture of Townes with his eyes shut at the table that we used for his third album [the self-titled *Townes Van Zandt*] was shot in my kitchen in Woodstock by Sol Mednick," Milton recollected. "Sol told Townes to sit down and just close his eyes for a while."

Mednick's portrait of Van Zandt took the complete opposite approach of Allen Vogel's snap on Townes's previous album. Where his black eyes once glared so hard you might've wondered if he shattered the photographer's lens, Van Zandt now appears withdrawn. He is there in form, but not in spirit, waiting to be filled with divine inspiration, fragments of poetry, and melodies floating in the ether or through the open blue door to his left. Townes found meaning in life by fashioning elegantly crafted songs from the landslide of emotions and images that came rushing, at times, uninvited into his head. Here he sits resigned, head in hand, in a perfectly painted kitchen where everything is neatly arranged, as in a doll's house.

In Milton Glaser's kitchen Van Zandt momentarily found respite from a world in which he constantly felt at odds. Time appears to stand still, except for his cigarette, burning in the ashtray, as his fingers tap absentmindedly on the tabletop.

Like Robert Johnson before him, Van Zandt also had to keep moving, driven by the "blues falling down like hail." But the "hellhounds" on Townes's trail, more often than not, were of his own making.

Townes Van Zandt, or "*The Kitchen Album*," as it's sometimes been called, begins with a much needed remake of "For the Sake of the Song." On the first verse he is alone with just his guitar and poetry. Townes's picking and singing are pristine. With the second verse, a percussionist falls in playing hand drums that oddly resemble the sound of gulping bullfrogs (echoes of Townes's old pal Marsh Froker banging on bongos back at Shattuck Academy?). To build the dynamic on the third verse, a harpsichord is once more employed (it seems that Mr. Eggers and Mr. Malloy couldn't help themselves).

On the gentle folk hoedown "Columbine" the harpsichord returns, framing the lyric like auditory lace, as a bluesy harmonica chugs along. But the interpretive drum fills just sound silly. "Cut yourself a columbine," Van Zandt sings while the drummer answers him, chopping down the flower with a *thwack, thwack, thwack*.

The third song is another desperately needed remake from the first album. Here Townes's "Waitin' 'round to Die" is dealt a much lighter hand production-wise. The existential adventures of a high-plains lowlife are recounted over Townes's trademark fingerpicking. A wailing blues harp enhances the track that is once again marred by a clueless drummer who sounds as if he drank the bottle of codeine that Van Zandt praises in the lyrics.

"Don't You Take It Bad" could have been a hit on the soul charts if Ray Charles had gotten hold of it. A gentle waltz to failed love, sung directly from the heart, the song has all the key elements of Brother Ray's classic rendition of Don Gibson's "I Can't Stop Lovin' You." In Townes's version a twangy Dobro tastefully echoes the wistful lyrics describing a brokenhearted loneliness and the inevitable new beginning that follows with "the sweetness of springtime and the sound of the rain."

With "Colorado Girl" Townes sings and fingerpicks a classic folk blues number that sounds as if it was written by Mississippi John Hurt himself. But the love Townes sings of in "Colorado Girl" is not yet a reality. She is an ideal he seeks, the very reason he's "going out to Denver" in the first place.

The shockingly stark "Lungs" immediately shatters this plaintive yet optimistic mood with a lyric as haunted as the dark hollows of Appalachia, where the skies are filled "with screams and cries." Townes reveals a chilling self-portrait over a riff that sounds like an old fiddle tune.

> Won't you lend your lungs to me?
> Mine are collapsing
> Plant my feet and bitterly
> Breathe up the time that's passing
> Breath I'll take and breath I'll give
> And pray the day's not poison
> Stand among the ones that live
> In lonely indecision

In a limited-edition songbook titled *For the Sake of the Song* published in 1977, Townes claimed the song was inspired by "the darkness of disease and the fire of frustration."

"I'll Be Here in the Morning" was originally written for Fran back in their early days in Houston. "I could never hit the open road and leave you lyin' there," Townes sings, filled with conflict, wanting to stay with the woman he loves, while knowing all along, no matter how he tries to convince her (and himself) that his poetic promise is ultimately hollow, it's only a matter of time before he'll take to the highway once again.

"Fare Thee Well, Miss Carousel" relates a tale of bitter disappointment in intricate wordplay and metaphor, with a twist of spite that sounds inspired by Dylan. In a mosaic of images and seemingly disconnected events, Townes lays the guilt of another failed love affair at the feet of a fickle woman:

> The drunken clown's still hangin' 'round
> But it's plain the laughter's all died down
> The tears you tried so hard to hide are flowin'
> And a blind man with his knife in hand
> Has convinced himself that he understands
> I wish him well Miss Carousel
> But I got to be a-goin'

Stylistically, the arrangement recalls the folk-rock of Simon and Garfunkel's *Bookends*. In the verses Townes gingerly strums his guitar accompanied by an electric bass, which also plays a wonderful introduction to the song. It all works just fine until the drums come stumbling in on the chorus with fills so awkwardly played they sound as if a pile of boxes fell over in the studio.

"Townes had a lot of girlfriends because he couldn't maintain a relationship," Kevin Eggers said, pointing to the lyric's inspiration. "All of his songs are very autobiographical. A lot of times he sang about himself in those love songs."

"It's a song about everyman's everywoman," Townes said of "(Quicksilver Daydreams of) Maria." "Caddo Parish Studdard III and I were spending a leisurely afternoon at the [now-defunct Austin club] 11th Door. Caddo invented a card game you play with beer coasters and I wrote this."

The archetypal female portrayed in Van Zandt's lyrics ranged from holy saints to deceitful whores with little or no room in between. Jim Pettigrew of *Country Style* magazine once observed that women in Townes's songs are "either the most incredibly lovely and untouchable or the most vile schemers and backstabbers. His losers [of both sexes] are so pathetic that they [could] bend the heartstrings of a stone figure."

"(Quicksilver Daydreams of) Maria" is a majestic waltz that reveals Van Zandt's ultimate vision of feminine perfection. It is as if Botticelli's

Venus emerged, not from a giant clamshell but as a brown-skinned beauty on a moonlit veranda in Mexico.

> A diamond fades quickly
> When matched to the face of Maria
> The harps they sound empty
> When she lifts her lips to the sky

Not merely sculptors and artists, but nature itself is awestruck by this woman's remarkable beauty:

> The sculptor stands stricken
> The artist he throws away his brushes
> When her image comes dancin'
> The sun she turns sullen with shame

> The birds they go silent
> The wind stops his sad mournful singing
> When the trees of the forest
> Start gently to whisperin' her name

In the last verse, Townes reveals himself as a hungry observer, "a lonely child" who "longingly looks for a place to belong." Like John Lennon who "stands with head in hand" in "You've Got to Hide Your Love Away," Van Zandt watches the scene from afar, brokenhearted.

"None but the Rain" depicts a heartbroken farewell in which Townes unflinchingly begs his departing lover to tell him gently who will be next in line. But unlike "Miss Carousel," there is no trace of jealousy and guilt in these verses. Van Zandt swears that once she has gone he will never devote himself to human love again: "None but the rain shall cling to my bosom," Townes sings as a pair of medieval recorders echo his strident vow. Only nature in its purest form can touch him from that day forth.

Townes Van Zandt includes four remakes from his disastrous first album: "For the Sake of the Song," "Waitin' 'round to Die," "(Quicksilver Day Dreams of) Maria," and "I'll Be Here in the Morning" (originally titled "I'll Be There in the Mornin'"). There is little doubt these versions, no matter how clunky and disjointed the drumming, were vast improvements over the originals. Meanwhile, Townes's career sputtered down the lost highway like an old Volkswagen Microbus with one cylinder out.

CHAPTER 9

NEW YORK TOWNES

She lives out on the D Train

But she's Texas as can be.

—TVZ, "Brand New Companion"

"It was a golden time. For about three years we lived a charmed life there," Kevin Eggers said, reminiscing about the old days at his brownstone at 54 Remsen Street in Brooklyn Heights. "When he wasn't somewhere on the road or in Texas, Townes would live at the house. Photographer Steve Salmierie lived in an apartment upstairs as well."

Although Salmierie would snap a number of album covers for Van Zandt, the portrait of Townes leaning in the doorway of New York's East Village that appears on the front of *Delta Momma Blues* was taken by Ken Beckles. With his hands in the pockets of his white chinos and a copy of Peter S. Beagle's classic fantasy novel *The Last Unicorn* poking out of the pocket of his suede jacket, Van Zandt glances at the camera with a win-some/lose-some grin. His head hangs down, while a young couple embraces in the corner.

On the flip side of the album Townes stands on a dock beside a mirror lake reflecting a grove of trees. Cigarette in one hand, bottle in the other, with wire-rimmed glasses and his hair a little longer, Townes resembles a hip English professor on a summer bender.

Released in 1971, *Delta Momma Blues* was recorded at Century Sound on Fifty-second Street in New York with Ron Frangipane producing. Frangipane, a pianist and string arranger who once studied under Igor Stravinsky, is best known for his work with John Lennon and Yoko Ono, the Rolling Stones, the Monkees, and Dusty Springfield.

"When Kevin chose an artist, and he chose artists who were not at all of the mainstream, he would really stand by that artist and push them, the producers, and the entire team to greatness," Ron explained. "Many record companies would go the commercial route with all the trappings and the bells and whistles, and they would force producers into copying anything that was on the radio at the time. That was not Kevin. He was trying to find the answer that would bring his artists a larger audience. That's different from being smitten with commercial success," Frangipane pointed out.

> Sometimes we producers get lost in the conundrum of looking to maintain an artist's vision. In trying to find something that could cross over into greater popularity, we might push them into domains that are inappropriate to their brilliance. In the seventies there was an explosion of commercialism. If it were today, I wouldn't have budged Townes one inch off the dime. I would have gone to Kevin today to convince him that what we needed was not to adjust the artist's work, but to develop a marketing strategy. You don't adjust their work. The minute you do, it's been infected. But in those days it simply was not under discussion. It was not a matter of marketing. It was about finding the magic moment that certain artists, no matter what you did, would never have. Kevin was always wondering what we were going to do to find the hit. But the hit, in Townes's case, would never be found in that fashion.

Looking back, one can understand how a producer in those days felt his only shot at topping the charts with a folksinger was to follow in the footsteps of Judy Collins's rhapsodic rendition of "Both Sides Now" (which the song's author, Joni Mitchell, apparently hated) or Dion's "Abraham, Martin, and John." Both tunes started out as gentle folk ballads but were pumped up with lavish arrangements in hopes of breaking through to the mainstream.

"If I saw anything I could have done to get at least one crossover hit with Townes, I would have done it," Ron admitted. "But I never read him that way. Townes was essentially an American storyteller, like a guy sitting on a porch, talking to you.

"Kevin had great taste and great commitment. There were a couple of blind spots, but they were not for lack of trying," Frangipane said in Eggers's defense. "Of the many producers I worked for, Kevin was one of the most sincere. And man, did he *love* Townes. He loved the daylights out of him. The road to hell is paved with good intentions, and maybe that's the light that Kevin should be seen in. I think there was a lack of understanding of the marketing aspect of the business [at Poppy].

"In every way, shape, and form Eggers embodied the impresario and entrepreneur," Frangipane continued. "But with all his love of music I think he felt frustrated and handcuffed by his own inability to create. If Kevin was a complicated person, Townes was even more so. He was very deceptive because he presented himself as a simple man but what was going on inside of that simple man was a festival of contradictions.

"Townes was not involved in the recording process in the traditional sense," Ron explained.

Whereas someone like Janis Ian would micromanage every eighth note, Townes was more like, sitting back in an old easy chair with holes in it, playing his guitar on the day before the session, saying, "Well, what are we gonna do?" He trusted that our reasoning was probably better than his, but he wanted to know where we were going. He was not just an "I'll show up, play it, and go home guy." There were times when I'd bring in sidemen that he wasn't quite comfortable with. I'd book a band and start the session with Townes, and then he'd come into the control booth very respectfully and say, "I'm not feelin' it that way." He was very much a solo performer. Sometimes playing with other musicians didn't allow him to stretch as much as he'd like. I would make charts of the song, but then he might not want to play four measures. He might feel the need to make it six. The players on the session were folk musicians as much as they were sidemen. The guys would take a break, go downstairs to the Carnegie Deli, and we'd cut Townes playing the song by himself. Then I'd take the lead sheets and adapt them. Sometimes the players could do it live. They could feel where he was breathing with the tempo.

Delta Momma Blues as an album didn't have any particular vision or flow to it. It was a mixed bag of whatever songs Van Zandt happened to have written at the time. There was little or no cohesiveness beyond that, other than perhaps being Townes's most rootsy recording. It was by no means his strongest batch of songs, yet the album contained some shiny nuggets that have held up quite well over the years. One reason is that Frangipane let the songs stand on their own without the kind of superfluous adornment that plagued Van Zandt's previous records.

Beginning with "F.F.V.," a remake of a traditional country song by the Carter Family, originally titled "Engine 143," Townes, accompanied by a slinky Dobro, earnestly delivers the fate of a young engineer named George Alley from Richmond, Virginia, who, according to Harry Smith's notes from the *Anthology of American Folk Music,* was killed in 1890 while driving the No. 4 train (known as the F.F.V.—which stood for Fast Flying Vestibule). Alley managed to survive for five hours before being "laid in a lonesome grave," as the lyrics recall. Although credited to the Carter Family, this grim ballad was supposedly written by a roundhouse worker in Hinton, West Virginia, just a few miles away from the site of the crash.

The front-porch pickin' session continued with the album's title song, which Townes claimed was inspired by a couple of soldiers he met while on leave in Oklahoma City. Van Zandt joined the pack of partying GIs, armed with a jug of Robitussin DM cough syrup that they nicknamed their "Delta Momma," and was soon extolling the pleasures of a cheap codeine-induced stupor.

Bob Myrick recalled the night in Boulder when Townes first introduced him and a couple of friends to those mean old Delta Momma blues: "The four of us walked over to a drugstore on the hill, and we each bought a bottle of Robitussin DM. Townes said, 'It's the best stuff. It's got dextromethorphan hydrobromide, but I just call it "Delta Momma," for short' (referring to the initials DM on the label). The lady behind the counter asked him if he wanted it in a sack. 'Nope,' Townes told her, 'I'll just drink it here.' And then he downed the whole bottle and set it back on the counter."

Myrick and his pals followed suit, gulping down the sweet, sticky concoction and setting their bottles back on the counter. Then together they all went swerving out of the store. "It was absolutely the worst high possible. It was just plain self-destructive," Bob groaned.

John Nova Lomax (the Houston-based journalist and son of John Lomax III) claimed he'd heard a story that Townes used to live above a pharmacy and was said to have "knocked a hole in the floor over the back room and used a fishing rod to angle for [bottles of] codeine." In an article Lomax wrote for the *Houston Press,* J. T. Van Zandt admitted that his dad was in the habit of knocking back about a quarter-pint bottle a day during the midseventies.

"If they weren't drinking it, they were looking for it," Lomax said, recalling his late mother, Bidy, a good friend of Townes's, driving from pharmacy to pharmacy in her VW van, searching for a druggist "with a corrupt, or generous, heart."

"As far back as Lightnin', everybody in Houston had a codeine song,"

Guy Clark told John Nova Lomax. "It's such a down drug, and Houston always seemed to have that down, kinda heroin vibe anyway. It was kind of pervading. Codeine kinda matches the weather down there."

Even stoned off his head on cough syrup Van Zandt managed to write "love songs that are so touching you know that love couldn't survive," journalist Jerry Leichtling said in the *Village Voice*. "Tower Song" was one of them. The tune, a monumental ode to sorrow, was written to Fran in a desperate attempt to save their crumbling relationship. Van Zandt addresses the failure of their marriage, full of regret, yet keeping his emotions somewhere tucked out of sight. You don't know whether to pity him or the woman he's singing to.

> So close and yet so far away
> And all the things I'd hoped to say
> Will have to go unsaid today
> Perhaps until tomorrow
>
> Your fears have built a wall between
> Our lives and all what lovin' means
> Will have to go unfelt it seems
> And that leaves only sorrow
>
> You built your tower strong and tall
> Can't you see it's got to fall some day

"We were living above Ma Carrick's when he wrote the 'Tower Song,'" Fran recalled. "He was doing some soul searching, trying to talk to me." In his notes to his songbook, *For the Sake of the Song,* Townes reminisced: "I thought when I wrote 'Tower Song' that I was writing it to someone else. Now I'm not so sure that I wasn't writing it to me."

Side two of the album opened with "Come Tomorrow," as good as a country ballad gets until a pair of happy-go-lucky recorders, like those adorning Paul McCartney's "Fool on the Hill," nearly nullifies the singer's emotions.

> Strange how many tortured mornings
> Fell upon us without warning
> Looking for a smile to beg or borrow
> But it's all over now, there's no returning

A thousand bridges sadly burning
Will light the way I'll have to walk alone
Come tomorrow

The album finally hits its stride with a pair of blues tunes. With "Brand New Companion," Townes proves that no matter how producers have tried to gussy up his songs with harpsichords and violins, that he *is* in fact the unwanted love child of Lightnin' Hopkins. With his Martin D-35 mixed right up front where you can't miss it, Townes bends and hammers the strings with raw emotion.

Having studied Lightnin' for years, Townes learned the effect of putting his finger "up around the 13th fret and bumming out just about everyone in the room." There is absolutely no trace of flash in his playing on "Brand New Companion." The notes just pour directly from his heart. The drums are in the pocket. A sizzling harmonica falls in behind him, tailgating his every phrase. Ultimately, the back-up band is just gravy, as this track is all about Townes, his words and guitar playing.

"Companion," with its sultry verses comparing his new girlfriend's sexy curves to those of his guitar, is followed by the funky, Bo Diddley–inspired groove "Where I Lead Me." Again, Van Zandt's guitar dictates the song's feel. On a good night Townes, by himself with a single guitar, could lay down the same deep, swampy feel that Creedence Clearwater Revival was famous for. Once again, everyone else on the track was, at best, just along for the ride. But within the jubilant boogie of "Where I Lead Me," Van Zandt paints a stark portrait of the ragged company he often kept. Whether he was shooting dice or junk, Townes doesn't say specifically, the only thing for certain is that the time has come to get movin'.

Ask the boys down in the gutter
Now they won't lie cause you don't matter
The street's just fine if you're good and blind
But it ain't where you belong
Roll down your sleeves, pick up your money
And carry yourself home

"For me, 'Rake' is unforgettable. It's like a tattoo," Ron Frangipane exclaimed.

I went in just with Townes and got the track. Then I had the chance to think about where I wanted to take it and wrote the arrangement. Townes allowed me a lot of latitude. I didn't think the song stood any chance of being a commercial crossover success, but I knew it would always live, which is far more important in the long run anyway.

At first we couldn't put our finger on it. We must have gone into fifteen to twenty hours of studio time to get it, which Kevin didn't like, as he wasn't too fond of going over budget. We just kept recording and recording. This went on for a couple of days. We'd both go home with a cassette and listen to it. Then Townes would call and say, "It's just not there yet." But when we finally nailed it, we knew it was the special moment on the album.

The first note from Van Zandt's guitar fans out like a drop of blood dispersing in water. Just as it's about to feed back, he falls into a slow minor-key waltz, and the dance of the vampires begins. The violins, which have betrayed him countless times in the past, are chilling, swelling into icy waves of sound. They suddenly recede, leaving Van Zandt and his guitar alone to tell the story, a tale dredged from so deep within his subconscious that Townes claimed not to understand its origin. Although the verses of "Rake" clearly portray the life of the "undead," Van Zandt claimed to be completely unaware of their meaning.

I used to wake and run with the moon
I lived like a rake and a young man
I covered my lovers with flowers and wounds
My laughter the devil would frighten

The sun she would come and beat me back down
But every cruel day had its nightfall
I'd welcome the stars with wine and guitars
Full of fire and forgetful

Van Zandt often claimed to be oblivious to the workings of his creative process. Years later, when Jeanene pointed out that the song depicted the life of a vampire, Townes, befuddled, replied: "Hmm... I guess I never thought of it that way."

In October 1971, Townes told WBAI DJ Ron Fass that he had written it in Wilmington, Delaware, after having just finished reading Nikos Kazantzakis's novel *Saint Francis.*

"Townes was in a fertile period at that time," Ron recalled. "He brought in 'Nothin' towards the end of the sessions. He called me about two or three in the morning and said, 'I want you to hear something,'" Frangipane recounted. "I didn't know if he had written it that day or if it just occurred to him to record the song. He had recently played it for Kevin and wanted to know what I thought. I said, 'We gotta do that tune.' Usually, the producer and the artist would make the choices about what songs to record. But when it came to Townes, Kevin had his hand on the repertoire. So we recorded it and then let Kevin hear it afterwards.

"One of the difficult things about working with Townes was his seemingly laid-back attitude. Beneath that easygoing demeanor you knew there was an incredible fire burning in his heart and belly. You couldn't miss it if you spent any real time with him," Frangipane said.

With "Nothin'" Townes leads the listener into a dark labyrinth of the human psyche, a place few songwriters dare visit. Van Zandt manages to simultaneously evoke the poverty and desolation of both the Mississippi Delta and the mountains of Appalachia by hammering a minor chord like a nail into your skull, on which he hangs a portrait of his haunted soul. The song has no chorus, just eight short verses that constitute a litany of dejection.

Once again a Kazantzakis novel inspired Townes to write a haunting ballad. He claimed the song came to him after immediately finishing *The Last Temptation of Christ,* while on tour in Oneonta, New York. Yet in many ways the lyrics seem to draw from the Buddhist concept of emptiness more than Christian philosophy.

In an act of renunciation the protagonist sheds his skin in hopes of finally freeing himself from his senses that, although bringing him pleasure, ultimately wind up deceiving him. In the third verse Townes sings:

> Almost burned out my eyes
> Threw my ears down to the floor
> I didn't see nothin'
> I didn't hear nothin'

In the seventh verse Townes invokes Jack Kerouac's compelling image, "the meat-wheel of conception" from "Mexico City Blues."

Being born is going blind
And bowing down a thousand times
To echoes strung
On pure temptation

Kerouac was referring to the bind of reincarnation, the endless cycle of birth, old age, sickness, and death that Buddhists claim to experience over and over again until nirvana is attained at last.

Ultimately, Van Zandt seeks refuge, as he did for many summers in the mountains of Colorado. In search of solitude, Townes turns his back on the chaos of the world and takes the path of the lone monk to a cave in the wilderness.

Sorrow and solitude
These are the precious things
And the only words
That are worth rememberin'

"The album seemed to take forever," Frangipane confessed. "We never cut more than one song in a day, which is very odd for this genre of music."

"I first met Townes in the Village. He had the look of a cowboy from the Texas range, which really went far. He was skinny, like the wind would blow him away," recalled singer-songwriter Paul Siebel (best known for his beautiful ballad "Louise," about a femme fatale of the Old West).

"Jerry Jeff Walker was on his way up to Hartford to play a gig at the University of Connecticut, and I joined him after a night of drinking. It was a summer Sunday around eight in the morning when we picked up Townes in Brooklyn. He was flyin' pretty high and insisted on driving on the way out of town," Paul recalled. "He ran three or four red lights, then crossed over the Manhattan Bridge and got on the FDR when he suddenly scraped the divider and bent the tire rim. He pulled off onto Houston Street and stopped on the corner of Lafayette to change the tire. I didn't think I'd see the end of the day, so I bailed out right there with my guitar and suitcase in hand. Jerry Jeff called me a coward," Siebel chuckled.

Over the years Van Zandt regularly returned to New York City to play venues like Tramps, the Speakeasy, the Lone Star, the Bottom Line, and Gerdes' Folk City (which have all since closed).

Folk City was a small pub on the corner of Sixth Avenue and Third Street in Greenwich Village. Known as "the house that Dylan built," the tiny dark room, covered in crimson wallpaper and ringed with head shots of famous folksingers, was a favorite haunt for local and touring musicians.

"At one of his gigs in the late seventies there was this weird carnival-like atmosphere in the place," Old Chief Rolling Papers recalled. "Townes was up on the stage, and the faces in the crowd began turning ugly and grotesque, like freaks in a Brueghel painting, or the type of people who go to the Indianapolis 500 and wait for a ten-car pileup. It seemed like, at any minute they were about to start placing bets on whether he was gonna make it through the set before he collapsed."

Butch Hancock neatly summed up the dynamic between Townes and his fans in a country waltz written in 2002 called "Toast of Townes (and Villages across the World)":

Some come to see if he lives
Some come to see if he dies
Some come to listen for truth
And some come to listen for lies

Some come to see if he stands
Some to see if he falls
Some come to stare at his face
And some come to stare at the wall

"After a show the fans used to flock around him, and Townes would entertain them. He'd be down on one knee orating, performing a monologue for them," the bluegrass bard Peter Rowan recollected. "When I saw him down on his knees I felt both embarrassed and in awe of him at the same time. It was unnerving. The fans were awestruck. You didn't know whether he was drunk or what to think. It was an old stage trick that Ramblin' Jack [Elliott] developed and Dylan copped—to look and act so twisted that you'd wonder if he was gonna lose it altogether and just fall off the stage. The promoters and the fans would feed into it. It was a drag, but there's nothing you can do about it."

"People romanticized Townes because he was a troubled soul. The audience loves that. They'll help pay and pave your way if that's the route you want to take," Bill Camplin imparted.

"Sometimes I'd see Townes, and I just couldn't watch him. I felt like a voyeur. It was too intense," Michael Timmins of the Cowboy Junkies admitted. "Some songs would be a complete shambles, and then he'd get totally focused and the whole room would become riveted to him. It would be so intense, and then suddenly the tension would break. He'd screw something up or go off on some tangent. But once in a while you'd get a show that would change your life."

Journalist Chris Dickinson recalled watching Van Zandt perform, "and something about it was God-awful lovely and freakishly honest, its aim so frightening and true, the effect was like catching a glimpse of a depth charge racing below the surface. Then all you could do was wait for the connection with the distant target of the heart. I once observed an entire club achieve a meltdown in his presence, people crying into their hands, a shared emotional participation I've never seen the likes of since."

And just as he did after cauterizing the crowd at Carnegie Hall, Townes would grin and then tell a little joke: "What's white and runs up your leg? Uncle Ben's Perverted Rice."

"My friends they all agree, there's no bigger fool than me," Townes sang years later in "Still Lookin' for You." Van Zandt never minded playing the fool. At times he seemed to relish it. Townes innately understood that healing the gaping wound of the world is the fool's true calling. He needed to clown around in order to balance out the overwhelming misery he clearly saw lying at the core of the human condition.

"Once Townes and Eric Andersen had a gig over at the old Lone Star on Thirteenth Street," Vin Scelsa recalled.

That night after the show everybody hung out at the Lone Star. A whole bunch of people was there, mostly old friends. I was sort of on the periphery and felt privileged to be there. Everybody, of course, was drinking. It was about 4:30 in the morning when Townes and I started playing liar's poker. Suddenly, he started staring at me. I hadn't seen him for four or five years, and I was beginning to feel a little uncomfortable, like I didn't quite know where he was goin' with it. I thought at any minute maybe he might bust a beer bottle and smash it into my face. There had been a brotherly love between us in the past, but now he was just acting weird. Finally, I said, "Hey, Townes, is there something wrong?"

And he squinted back at me. His face was all craggy, and he spoke real slow. "Vinny," he said, "how long have we known each other?"

"Well, Townes, it'll be going on twenty years soon," I told him.

Then his eyes became slits, and he said, "Vinny. . . how come you don't have any scars?"

"Shhhit, Townes!" I said. "I guess I must be livin' a good life."

Van Zandt squinted hard at his old friend for a minute, sizing him up with an inscrutable glare. "Yeah, I guess that's probably it," Townes reckoned. A moment later a big smile swept across his face, and Vin breathed a sigh of relief.

For a minute Scelsa felt like he'd somehow walked into the wrong bar in some old John Ford movie he'd never heard of called *Shootout at the Lone Star Cafe*.

"Some things you just can't make up. With Townes you never had to," Eric Andersen said, recalling a wild episode at the Gramercy Park Hotel after a Van Zandt gig at the Bottom Line in the early nineties. "We got a room and a bottle of wine or somethin', and Guy [Clark] started singin' these great songs I'd never heard before. Eventually, he got up and left when Townes looked at me and said, 'Y'know, man, you need a haircut.' I had this Swiss army knife with a pair of those little scissors on it. I was sitting on the bed in front of the mirror, and he just went at it and layered my hair. Townes gave me a hundred-fifty-dollar haircut. It took him a while, but once he started, I couldn't say no," Andersen laughed.

Andersen had first heard about Townes from Emmylou Harris when she stopped by his Spring Street loft in Soho in the midsixties. He would soon meet Van Zandt at a folk festival at Ohio State University in 1967. "He just knocked on my door," Eric recalled. "We had a physiognomy connection. We were both rail thin, like twin images of each other. He was southern, and I was a Yankee."

They spent the afternoon together, chain-smoking cigarettes, trading songs, and talking in the tiny dorm room the college provided for the performers. Suddenly, Townes pulled his hair back off his forehead and revealed a row of small red marks. "Shock treatments," he said, rolling his shiny black eyes. "He'd been in and out of the bin. So I liked him right away," Eric said with a big grin.

Just about anyone who picked up an acoustic guitar in the early days of the "Folk Boom" was compelled to learn Eric's songs "Close the Door Lightly" and "Thirsty Boots." The Colorado queen of blue-eyed soul, Judy Collins, would later make "Thirsty Boots," Andersen's wistful ode to the troubadour's life, famous on her *Fifth Album* in 1965.

"When you're writing, you have no idea who's listening or how you affect people's lives. Then they come up to you thirty years later," Andersen said. Not only was his "Violets of Dawn" said to have inspired Leonard Cohen, but Eric also discovered that Van Zandt and Guy Clark had been singing his songs for years before they met.

It was a gray April afternoon in Jersey City as he overlooked the Hudson River with the Empire State and Chrysler Buildings glowing in the distance. Eric, dressed in black, with a black fedora, talked on his cell phone while meandering around Fisk Park, followed by a gaggle of giggling children. A pack of neighborhood dudes shot hoops on the rain-black asphalt, while birds sang ethereal melodies as the sun began to set. As the first ice cream truck of spring arrived, Eric's posse suddenly fled. He'd been noticeably uncomfortable talking about Townes. Lighting a cigarette, he held it in his long, bony fingers, searching for the right words to come.

"Townes was a sad soul," Andersen sighed.

When you see and feel so much, it manifests in different ways. Some people get high. Some people are analytical. The world made him pretty sad. The sorrow of pain and separation was always on his mind, and those feelings are clearly portrayed in his work. It was also part of his humor. He'd threaten to slash his throat, and for a moment you might have to scratch your head and wonder. People just assumed that Townes was a depressed person because his songs were so sad. They used to say that Leonard Cohen was very down and funereal, but they are two of the funniest guys you could ever meet. We used to listen to Leonard to get cheered up. Of all the songwriters I think [Cohen] is the wittiest. But people always chose to see his downside.

Y'know how *Rolling Stone* rates new albums with stars? Well, if a song was really depressing, we would give it ten razor blades.

CHAPTER 10

HIGH, LOW, AND LOW AS LOW CAN BE

And if her shadow doesn't seem much company
Who said it would be?

—TVZ, "High, Low, and in Between"

While producing Van Zandt's fifth album at Larabee Studios in L.A., Kevin Eggers rented a three-bedroom apartment on the hip and happening Sunset Boulevard. "Guy and Susanna would come around, and we'd all hang out together. He was building guitars out in the valley [at the Dobro factory]. They were just married—a beautiful couple. Townes used to flirt with Susanna a lot, and it would really piss Guy off. My heart goes out to Guy, the way he used to fuck with him," Eggers said.

"It was wonderful to have someone like that in your life. He was my best friend for thirty-five years—at least *I* thought we were," Guy said, gazing up at Jim McGuire's black-and-white portrait of Townes hanging in his workshop.

Although Clark considered Townes his "best friend," there were plenty of times he wanted to kill him. Van Zandt, as Mickey White said, had a way of putting everyone he knew through "the paces," particularly his friends and family.

"And you always went for it. Goddamn you, motherfucker! I adore you, and you treat me like this?" Guy said scowling at Van Zandt's photograph.

Townes went out of his way to make people feel good—other guys who weren't as smart as he was and wanted somebody to just be nice to them.

Or he would fuck with people just to watch 'em squirm. It's not what I'd call a nice trait, but he did it. He fucked with everybody all the time. But he couldn't fuck with Susanna because she was as smart as he was, so most of the time he fucked with me. He and Susanna were much better friends than we were. They were like soul mates. They had a marvelous symbiotic relationship that worked best over the phone. They would talk every morning.

Susanna revealed the nature of her relationship with Townes in Nick Evans and Jeff Horne's biography of her husband titled *Song Builder:* "Every single morning at 8:30 for years Townes called me for our 'morning call.' Guy would usually bring me a cup of coffee, because he knew we'd be on the phone for at least an hour. He'd say, 'Hey, babe.' Townes was the only man I let me call babe."

Their discussions ranged from music to art and history and, of course, Texas. They ruminated at length over angels, demons, ghosts, birds, dogs, the Bible, Native American lore, and the *Andy Griffith Show.* Susanna was Van Zandt's confidante and sounding board. She knew Townes's private thoughts and was often the first to hear the details of his latest adventures or lyrics in their developmental stages. "He let me in his soul and I let him in mine," she confessed.

Although Susanna was his wife, Guy often felt like the odd man out whenever Townes was around. Clark frequently believed they were conspiring against him. One day he was driven so crazy by their routines that he slammed the bedroom door shut and nailed himself inside out of fury and frustration.

"Well, after some time I had to pee, and this old house we lived in had storm windows on it, you know, glass on the outside, and it was all painted shut," Guy said, describing the desperate scene. "I couldn't get the window open to pee out the window. So I decided I was going to swallow my pride, pull the nails; well, I had hammered these big ten-penny nails in the oak door and woodwork with a little bitty hammer, and it went in fine. But I couldn't pull it out of that oak with that little fuckin' hammer. And I was trapped. And it was just like, What have I done? And I don't remember how I got out, some combination of Townes pushin' and me pullin'."

In the December 1977 issue of *Omaha Rainbow,* Van Zandt recounted the tense atmosphere behind the drama: "I was livin with Guy and Susanna in East Nashville cutting the *Late, Great* and it was a little house, a real tense shotgun type house. It was real hot, we were real broke and we spent a lot of time sitting about the house."

"Well, Townes came down to be the best man at our wedding and he stayed for eight months. Townes had no money so in that little house the three of us stayed," Susanna recalled. Clark admitted she was "a little baffled at first" but soon adjusted to Van Zandt sleeping in her tiny art studio.

"It got so intense one day that Guy just nailed himself in his room to get away from everybody," Townes said. "He used big 16 inch nails and later had to climb out through the window because he couldn't get the door un-nailed. He'd used about five nails. Finally we had to break the door down."

In other versions of the story, Guy nailed himself inside the bathroom. Panic-stricken after smoking his last cigarette, he managed to somehow crawl out the window and run down to the store to buy more.

"Guy was a close friend to Townes back then. He loved him but was appalled by him at the same time," Fran said, attempting to explain the dynamics of their longtime friendship. "Guy was always protective of me whenever Townes was acting up," she added.

Although Townes regularly put his old friend through the wringer, it's clear, from an interview he did with *Omaha Rainbow,* that he had a genuine affection for the man: "Everybody in Nashville loves Guy Clark," Van Zandt said. "It's the way he is, he's so sincere 'n' all and so straight ahead."

In the fall of 1971 Mickey White broke up with his Austin girlfriend and moved down to Houston to begin a serious relationship with his guitar. "Townes had been out on the Bitter End coffeehouse circuit at the time and was playing at the Potpourri [the predecessor of Austin's Cactus Café] on a Tuesday night," he recalled.

I had a gig at the Old Quarter that Wednesday. Wrecks was playin' bass with Lightnin' at a gig at the Armadillo World Headquarters in Austin that Thursday, Friday, and Saturday. So I went to see Townes on the opening night. I'd seen him before at the Old Quarter and was impressed, so I went up and introduced myself. He told me, "Yeah, Wrecks is comin' up this week, and he's gonna bring my new Houston tomato with him." He was talkin' about Leslie Jo Richards. They had just met and struck up a relationship, and he had that little glimmer in his eye.

The next day I thumbed a ride back down to Houston and played my little gig at the Old Quarter and made my twenty bucks. Back then, that would get you a bus ticket back to Austin. But by this time Wrecks and I had become friends, so I got a ride up with him, Lightnin', his road manager, and Leslie. That was too much. I was an air force brat from Albuquerque and didn't even know who Lightnin' Hopkins was. Of course, once I heard him play, I knew *immediately* who he was.

We hung out at Townes's motel room during the day. I was really struck by his professionalism. He really knew his stuff both musically and lyrically. At the time Townes was really disciplined. You don't get that good unless you work at it, and Townes worked as hard as anybody. He cared about his music and wanted people to appreciate it.

Following the gig, Mickey caught a ride back to Houston with Van Zandt and company. Things were certainly looking up from his perspective: "Townes had this old green Ford Fairlane with a broken driver's-side window. Me, bein' the low man on the totem pole, I had to sit in the backseat behind him. It was November, and I was freezin' my butt off, thinkin' this is the *greatest fuckin' thing* that *ever* happened to me in my life. I have *arrived*. My application had been approved."

Earlier that summer, Smiley Harris, Darryl's little brother, was shot through the lung when a drug deal turned bad. Smiley had been recuperating at Darryl's apartment upstairs above Mickey's, while Leslie, a friend from Milby High School, nursed him back to health.

"I loved Smiley to death, but he could be a pretty crusty character," Mickey chuckled. "So to get away from him, Leslie would come down every morning, and we'd talk. We became pretty good friends."

Although Townes maintained a strict policy of "no slits on the road," Leslie Jo briefly joined him for one tour and traveled to L.A. while he recorded *High, Low, and in Between*.

One day Mickey found a letter from Leslie waiting for him.

Smiley handed it to me, and I read it. She talked about what was goin' on out there and Townes doin' the record, but she said she was goin' to be on her way back home soon. She didn't say anything about them breaking up, and I didn't get any impression that that was the case. She just said, "I'll be back in Houston soon. Looking forward to seein' you."

Then Smiley told me she was gone. He said she was hitchhiking, on her way back to Houston, when she was picked up and stabbed. She apparently made it to somebody's house and died. Townes didn't want to talk about it much, as their relationship had already ebbed and they were splittin' up. He never out and out said it, but she was leaving him.

The sudden shock of Leslie Jo's death devastated Townes. "It was a life-changing experience for him. I hadn't known him that long, but I'd known him long enough to see the effect it had on him," Mickey said, as he sipped his coffee at a Starbuck's on Sixth Street in Austin. Suddenly, Emmylou Harris's voice singing "Pancho and Lefty" came ringing through the speakers.

"Alright, there's a little 'Pancho,'" Mickey said with a big grin and picked up the story:

That fall me and Johnny Guess got a house that we called the Poodle Farm, 'cause it was next to a dog groomer around the corner from Anderson Fair [Houston's bastion of acoustic music in the Montrose district]. Townes had come back from the mountains. His hair was down to the middle of the back. It was the only time I ever heard him talk about Leslie. He described how he nearly fell apart at the seams and had gone to Aspen on one long bender. He was spiritually crushed by her death. I'd never seen him that way around any other woman as he was with Leslie. He never put her through the paces. He was in love with her—big time. When she died, somethin' about him changed. As far as his relationships with women went, it was never, *ever* the same again. She was his love, and it was a very difficult thing for him to go through.

Leslie Jo Richards would forever loom large in Van Zandt's memory. "In 'Greensboro Woman,' when he sang, 'For once there's someone waiting home for me,' he was talking about Leslie," White pointed out. "He also wrote 'Snow Don't Fall' for her."

The song's lyric is sparse, almost Zen-like, evoking the powerful cycles of nature as a metaphor for the sorrow and loneliness that Van Zandt experienced:

Snow don't fall on summer's time
Wind don't blow below the sea
My loves lies 'neath frozen skies
And waits in sweet repose for me

Her eyes did laugh, her lips did sing
Her legs did roll my soul to bring
Her hair did curl and her thoughts unfurled
Like birds upon the wings of spring

In the simple two-line chorus Townes acknowledged the powerful presence of his dead lover who, although gone, still remained close to him: "My love I need not see / To know she cast her glance at me."

The chorus of "Two Girls" also revealed Van Zandt's ongoing obsession with Leslie. Although the singer has moved on and is trying to make the best of it on the earth plane with a new girlfriend, she can only be, at best, a substitute for his dead lover. It seemed as if Townes was doomed to wander through life forever haunted by Leslie Jo's memory.

I've got two girls
One's in heaven, one's below
One I love with all my heart
And one I do not know

In "Two Girls" Van Zandt paints a surreal landscape peopled with a cast of oddball characters like Jolly Jane and her dozen husbands who come and go, caught in the oblique routines of their lives with no rhyme or reason.

Like the Band, Van Zandt felt a strong connection with a past that stood in stark contrast to the radical values of the late sixties. Townes was compelled to preserve what he could of what Greil Marcus coined "the old weird America" that he saw quickly disappearing around him. Townes was a man out of time, much like Dylan, who, at the height of the psychedelia, retreated to Woodstock's Catskill Mountains to raise his family and write a batch of bare-bones parables of biblical proportion that would become *John Wesley Harding*.

Van Zandt's world is a theater of the absurd where the clouds don't look like clouds and people listen with their mouths. The first verse begins with an odd, ominous description of the sky. But then things turn ugly fast. Either Townes is unduly paranoid, or it's time to get out of town before he finds himself lynched by a gang of his closest "friends."

The clouds didn't look like cotton
They didn't even look like clouds

I was underneath the weather
All my friends look like a crowd

The swimmin' hole was full of rum
I tried to find out why
All I know is this my friend
You got to swim before you fly

By the last couplet Townes is offering advice, suggesting we take trouble with a grain of salt (and perhaps a lime and a shot of tequila too) and remember to try to rise above our circumstances, no matter how strange they may appear.

In the second verse a pair of desperadoes on horseback arrives:

Two lonesome dudes on an ugly horse
Passed by not long ago
They asked me where the action was
I said that I did not know

As they disappeared into the brush
I heard the driver say
He's a little slow between the ears
He's always been that way

"He was alluding to these two guys looking to cop heroin," Mickey White explained. "The ugly *horse* was slang for smack. [It's about] two guys lookin' to score some dope at Johnny P's, where Townes was hangin' out. Johnny was a drug dealer from Pasadena, Texas, the industrial area outside of Houston. 'The air is greena in Pasadena,'" White said with a laugh. "It stinks there, and it's really depressing. Townes says, 'They asked me where the action was. I said I do not know.' When he sings, 'He's a little slow between the ears / He's always been that way,' he's just making a joke about himself."

The third verse portrays a grotesque woman whose hunger and sexual appetite rage on unabated, no matter how one man after the next tries his best to satisfy her. Although he might be "a little slow between the ears," the song's protagonist has enough sense to steer clear of her and not bother.

Jolly Jane just lays around
And listens with her mouth
She's had about a dozen husbands
But the last one just pulled out

Now who's gonna bring her dinner
Through the weary years ahead
All she'll get from me is sympathy
Got no time to see she's fed

By the song's fourth verse everything is completely askew. Nothing he grasps at makes sense any longer. Even nature, which Townes celebrated in Whitman-like epiphanies, can no longer be relied on or trusted. The opening lines of the song, "The clouds didn't look like cotton / They didn't even look like clouds," immediately tips the listener off that nothing is as it appears. Old definitions and clichés have no bearing on the dilemma he now faces. Like Dylan's "Ballad of a Thin Man," in which Bob sings, "Something is happening but you don't know what it is," Townes's salvation comes only in taking these bizarre scenes at face value.

It's cold down on the bayou
They say it's in your mind
But the moccasins are treading ice
And leaving strange designs

The Cajuns say the last time
This happened they weren't here
Beaumont's full of penguins
And I'm playin' it by ear

From the strange prophecy of the Cajuns we can ascertain that Armageddon is not far off. But as the one he loves is already dead, it doesn't matter much to him what happens next. Townes almost seems amused by the disintegration of the natural order happening all around him. There is clearly no escape from an absurd world that appears less and less familiar the farther he travels. For the time being he must remain "below," counting his blessings with a girl he does not know.

Not surprisingly, the tragedy of Leslie's death took on a life all its own, depending on whom you asked. "Leslie Jo Richards was the ideal girl to Townes," Kevin Eggers said. "He was head over heels for her. She was a free spirit, a beautiful hippie chick who was into free love. She used to walk around naked. If you asked her, she would have sex with you."

"Townes told me the story of Leslie Jo Richards many times," Jeanene sighed.

He was recording *High, Low, and in Between* with Kevin in L.A. when Leslie Jo, his girlfriend at the time, who was only about nineteen, went to get his pick bag. Townes had forgotten his picks that he used to carry around in one of those velvet Crown Royal bags. At that time everybody used to hitchhike. It wasn't any big deal. She said, "I'll go get it," and just left. Some guys picked her up and stabbed her a dozen times and threw her body in a ditch. She managed to live long enough to crawl up to a house and tell the woman inside that she was from Houston and she was with Townes Van Zandt and to call the studio. Townes was at the studio recording when he got a call from the police saying Leslie Jo was murdered and had died on the lady's porch. He really felt guilty about that. Townes was just a big pile of guilt.

"Leslie Jo's death didn't have *anything* to do with Townes," Kevin Eggers countered. "It was a typical random L.A. murder," he said. "We were in a recording session while she was out hitchhiking around somewhere. The police said she was found on the side of the road with fifteen stab wounds."

Like the stories of Leslie Jo's death, *High, Low, and in Between* teems with contrasts and contradictions. It is ultimately a difficult and unsatisfying album. The record plods along, hampered by hackneyed arrangements and production values. Kicking off the disc on the wrong foot is a white-bread gospel number called "Two Hands," a born-again clap-along with saccharine backup vocals praising "the glory of the Lord." Although Van Zandt's delivery seems sincere, the arrangement is enough to send you running, not down to the nearest river for a holy foot washing in Jesus' name but to the local liquor store for something cheap to quickly kill the pain.

If "Two Hands" isn't enough to scare you off, then "When He Offers His Hand" might do the trick. Once again Van Zandt's lyric is done in by an arrangement that sounds as if it would be right at home on a K-Mart Christmas compilation.

As the old saying goes, religion is the last refuge of a scoundrel. Perhaps Van Zandt, faced with the terrible ordeal of trying to kick his heroin habit and the recent murder of his girlfriend, had suddenly taken to writing gospel numbers in lieu of a little insurance.

"We're all Baptists," Fran explained.

We went to River Oaks Baptist Church on Sundays with his parents. Townes and I got married in the Baptist church. Townes's brother, Bill, is the deacon of the Second Baptist Church of Houston, and his sister Donna leads a Bible class in Boulder. They're teetotalers. They don't smoke or drink or anything. Both Townes's parents smoked and drank. Every night at five they would have two scotches with water, but no more than that. Then at dinner they'd have a little wine, and that was it. They always had a can of Lysol ready in case Dotsy's granny Aunt Jeanette, the matriarch of the family, happened to come by unannounced. They'd see her comin' up the sidewalk, and they'd spray the house to hide the smell of cigarettes.

Townes soon repudiates whatever comfort and joy he found trying to live the Christian life with "You Are Not Needed Now," in which he sings, "Heaven ain't bad but you don't get nothin' done." Over Don Randi's piano Townes gently croons "Lay down your head a while / You are not needed now," as a lullaby for the late Janis Joplin, whose tragic death he claimed inspired the song. Van Zandt adored Janis and used to joke that the statue of the Goddess of Liberty atop the capitol in Austin was actually fashioned after her.

The album is filled with moral dilemmas. Townes constantly wrestles with himself between living the righteous life versus stumbling along the primrose path. In "No Deal" he jokingly testifies:

Well, I come through this life a stumbler, friend
I expect to die that way
It could be twenty years from now
It could be most any day

But if there is no whiskey and women, Lord,
Behind them heavenly doors

I'm gonna take my chances down below,
And of that you can be sure

Townes then turns a cold shoulder to the advances of a "Greensboro Woman," warning her, "I do not feel like being comforted." The song is built on a familiar country-blues fingerpicking pattern similar to Mississippi John Hurt's "Creole Belle." Whereas Hurt's tune celebrates his "darlin' baby," Townes blows off a philandering "babe," explaining that "for once there's someone waitin'" for him back home.

With its theme of alienation and homesickness, "Greensboro Woman" brings to mind Paul Simon's "Homeward Bound," in which the weary singer yearns for his love who "lies waiting silently" for him. Except Townes, the loner, never had the faithful, curly-haired Garfunkel by his side to trace his every sentiment with honey-coated harmonies.

"Highway Kind" is a minor-key ballad that further explores the blue moods of the itinerant traveling troubadour. This pair of songs stands out as the album's finest moments not only because they were particularly well written but also because, for whatever reason, the producer finally got out of Van Zandt's way and let the songs simply speak for themselves.

"Townes wrote 'Highway Kind' in the fall of 1970 after he'd finished the Bitter End tour," Mickey recalled. "He always did his best writing on the road while he was alone. But he'd get lonely and want company, so he'd take Wrecks with him as his bass player. The Bitter End tour really helped get his name around the country. Kevin was trying to make Townes a star. They were 'Thinkin' big, makin' plans.' They always had a game plan, and at that point Townes really wanted to succeed. With *High, Low, and in Between* they were trying to put a folk-rock thing together. But it's a hard record to listen to," Mickey admitted.

"Townes could have been a star, but I think he chose not to play the game," Nina Leto surmised. "It was apparent that he was a smart cookie. He was so talented, so real, so charming and warm, with a great sense of humor. But he sure had a way of fucking up his life. He liked writing and performing, but I got the feeling he enjoyed the process more than putting it out there for the public."

"As far as being Kenny Rogers I can't see it. I keep my eyes closed when I sing and I'm just not a TV personality type. But I do okay in joints," Townes said in his own defense.

"The reason Townes was never a pop star was blindingly obvious,"

Paul K. said. "He couldn't be a big shot because it took so much dedication just to be Townes. The inner confidence and strength of purpose needed to put together a body of work like Townes's is beyond the abilities of most of us mortals. Van Zandt is a hero to me because he is no longer here, because his forthrightness hurts my shoulders, and because his lyrics make me cry," Kopasz said, claiming Townes wrote more "classic songs than Robert Johnson and Jerry Garcia put together."

Van Zandt's classic song, the tender "To Live's to Fly," first appeared on *High, Low, and in Between* in a less-intimate studio version than heard on *Live at the Old Quarter, Houston, Texas*. Townes claimed the tune came to him one early spring in Davidson, North Carolina: "It's impossible to have a favorite song," Van Zandt once said, "but if I were forced at knifepoint to choose one, it would be 'To Live's to Fly.'" The phrase would ultimately be etched in granite on his gravestone that stands in a small cemetery in Dido, Texas.

"To Live's to Fly," a simple three-chord tune of pure yearning, captures the transcendent imagery and lyricism found in William Blake's verse. Townes apparently shared a similar philosophy with Gustave Flaubert, who once wrote: "The principal thing in this world is to keep one's soul aloft." Guy Clark, who recorded the tune on a 1999 tribute album of Townes's songs titled *Poet,* believed the lyrics are "words to live by."

I won't say I love you babe
I won't say I need you babe
But I'm gonna get you babe
And I will not do you wrong

Living's mostly wasting time
And I waste my share of mine
But it never feels too good
So let's don't take too long

You're soft as glass
And I'm a gentle man
We got the sky to talk about
And the world to lie upon

Days up and down they come
Like rain on a conga drum

Forget most remember some
But don't turn none away

Everything is not enough
Nothing is too much to bear
Where you been is good and gone
All you keep's the getting there

To live's to fly low and high
So shake the dust off your wings
And the sleep out of your eyes

We all got holes to fill
And them holes are all that's real
Some fall on you like a storm
Sometimes you dig your own

But choice is yours to make
Time is yours to take
Some dive into the sea
Some toil upon the stone

Although spotted with great songs, *High, Low, and in Between* could hardly compare to the dark brilliance of 1969's *Our Mother the Mountain*. The album's uncredited cover photograph imparts an intense feeling of alienation. Van Zandt stands in an awkward-fitting, crumpled white shirt that oddly resembles a straitjacket, with his hands clasped behind his back, like a man in bondage. The studio lights behind him glow faintly, like dim lightbulbs or perhaps distant mushroom clouds. Townes's eyes are dark, shadowy, obscured by the soft focus of the photographer's lens. There stands a man in purgatory—someone who knows the deck is stacked against him and the water is wide and isn't sure if the fight for his soul is really worth the trouble.

With the recording sessions and Leslie Jo's tragic death behind him, Townes quietly slipped off once again to his beloved mountains of Colorado.

CHAPTER 11

NO ENVELOPE

If it all falls apart I'll just go back to playin' live
somewhere in Colorado probably.
   —TVZ

With the ongoing nightmare of the Vietnam War, the tragedy at the
Rolling Stones' free concert at Altamont Speedway, and the bizarre murder of Sharon Tate, the peace-and-love Woodstock generation was now
in full retreat, fleeing to pastoral settings in hopes of escaping the hard
(and increasingly weird) realities of the day. In the early seventies Colorado would become the mecca for bewildered hippies who wanted to
leave behind the conflict of the world and find a place to take their stand
and "take it easy," as Jackson Browne advised.

The majestic Rocky Mountains inspired dozens of singer-songwriters,
from Stephen Stills and Don Henley to John Denver, to grab their guitars and strum soft-rock country odes brimming with that "peaceful-easy
feeling." Gentle, reassuring lullabies as epitomized by Loggins and
Messina's "Danny's Song" soon replaced the nebulous, chaotic acid rock
roaring out of San Francisco. As the decade unfolded, even the Grateful
Dead toned down their wild feedback-laden jams to sing sweet three-
part harmonies on "Ripple" and "Sugar Magnolia" on their surprisingly
mellow *American Beauty*.

Although Townes had crossed paths with John Denver back in his
earlier days in Houston and both men shared an appreciation for the
same panoramic views and brisk mountain air, Van Zandt's songs were
the absolute antithesis of Denver's "Rocky Mountain High," a song that
sold more condominiums than an army of real estate brokers.

With nothing but an old guitar and the clothes on his back, Townes would ride his horse, Amigo, through the dazzling fields of wildflowers over Maroon Bells Pass from Aspen to Crested Butte and back. In this idyllic setting Van Zandt composed a batch of new tunes for what would become his sixth album, *The Late, Great Townes Van Zandt*. He'd originally heard about the little mining town of Crested Butte in Hoyt Axton's song "On the Natural."

Axton's influence on Van Zandt cannot be underestimated: "I learnt to finger pick from one of Hoyt Axton's records," Townes told *Omaha Rainbow*. "One of the first songs I learnt to finger pick was [the Reverend Gary Davis's] 'Cocaine Blues,' and I got the arrangement off his record. He's always been a favorite of mine. I played with him a couple of years ago. It really blew my mind when he recorded 'Pancho and Lefty.'"

The overwhelming beauty and natural charm of Crested Butte were awe-inspiring indeed. Whatever direction that Townes pointed his horse he found poetry, among fields of buckwheat and buttercups, thistle, columbine, and fireweed, down winding, sun-dappled trails and through cool, shady conifer-pine tunnels. The sky above him, the color of his old faded blue jeans, seemed to go on forever. But the weather was unusually rainy that summer and not the most ideal time for camping in the mountains, so Townes wound up spending most of his time in an old saloon called the Grubstake, where he played dice and blackjack with the locals.

"Everybody in Crested Butte was crazy, so he just fit right in," journalist Denis Hall remembered. "He'd come into the Grubstake and drink for hours and then sit down and start to play. It wasn't like a regular show. It was just part of the larger party. Sometimes he'd play half a song and then just slump over his guitar."

"It was a real robust scene—larger than life. Beyond the reach of anybody's rule," said longtime Snowmass resident "Bibs," who gained the nickname back in the seventies for her trademark overalls. "Everybody was so hammered all the time. And as drunk as everyone was gettin', who knew what we were eating in terms of drugs. There were plenty of psychedelics around. We'd snort cocaine and play pinball till four in the morning."

After a couple of rowdy nights of playing guitar and cards and shooting dice with the locals, Townes would light out for the mountains once more, disappearing into the wilderness for a couple days of precious solitude.

A photograph of Van Zandt at the time shows him healthy and smiling, riding his horse. Shirtless, basking in the summer sun, he looks

refreshed, as if the crisp, cool air had miraculously scoured years of cigarette smoke from the dank, gray caverns of his lungs.

"In some pictures he's just shining," Jeanene said proudly. "It was basically an either-or situation. The *either* was this adventurous frontiersman
guy that wanted to go canoeing and fishing; the *or* was a dilapidated,
junky alcoholic."

Out of cash and too stubborn to fold his hand, Crested Butte local Rick
Verplank literally lost the shirt off his back one night while gambling
with Townes and was surprised when Van Zandt expected payment on
the spot. Bare-chested and humiliated (it was his favorite cowboy shirt,
complete with pearl buttons), Verplank sauntered home.

"I went home half-naked," Rick said, chuckling at the memory. Yet in
the long run there was no love lost. To this day Verplank still admires the
way Townes could mesmerize a room when he picked up his guitar. "He
had an aura," Rick recalled. "He would just close his eyes and capture the
room whenever he played."

"Some people knew he was a musician, but he certainly wasn't be-
sieged by those who appreciated his celebrity," Bibs said. "He was definitely not *with* anybody. This girl I knew at the time brought him home.
He just tied his horse to the couch and stayed for three days. Townes
wasn't a cowboy. He was really a performance artist with a horse and
cowboy clothes," Bibs imparted.

He was a very dramatic person who put on some very bizarre shows.
He'd just start to rip his clothes up—which was no big deal really, except
that they were the only clothes he had. Then he'd have to put them back
on again. Nobody was offended. The cops didn't care. They were just
around to take people home who'd forgotten where they lived. People
were always pushing the envelope in Crested Butte, until of course they'd
find there *was* no envelope. The early seventies were some pretty lawless
days in Colorado. I'm sure Townes Van Zandt certainly wasn't the first
person to ride his horse into a bar in Crested Butte, but I can recall him
riding into the Grubstake one night and ordering his horse a beer, which
the bartender served up in a big bowl. There were lots of *real* animals—I
mean *nonhumans*—drinkin' at the bars in those days. Everyone appreciated Townes for his love of life and his sense of humor. He used to sing
with a local band called KY Jelly, which only gave a few performances.
They never had much of an audience, as nearly everyone in town was in
the band.

For such a small, out-of-the-way town, Crested Butte has had a long tradition and great love of music. While doing some research at the local library I discovered a small book called *The Mining Camps Speak* that contained this telling passage: "Music was so important. A forest fire swept towards the mining camp. There wasn't enough time to move the town's only piano so men quickly dug a hole and buried it, covered it with dirt, then found safety themselves. No buildings were left standing but they still had a piano."

Compared to Aspen, Crested Butte was truly squalid at the time. The main street wasn't even paved until 1975. After the mine closed down, Crested Butte fell on hard times. Other than mining, there were few jobs to be had. Most people considered Crested Butte the end of the road. It wasn't uncommon for a group of tourists to come to town, take a look around, and then quickly leave. It was, as Bibs said, "really just a bunch of hippies in a completely unsupervised place. But it really resonated with Townes."

Townes returned again to Crested Butte the following summer and took up residency at the Wooden Nickel, where he played a couple nights a week. Anyone wanting to jam with him was welcome to sit in. Some nights there'd be up to six or seven pickers joining in. Essentially, it was Townes's gig, but if anyone else had a song they wanted to do, Van Zandt was more than willing to share the little stage.

"Townes was always a joy to play with," David Amram explained. "He always had great musicians with him like Mickey White. Or sometimes he'd have people join him, members of his International Lifetime Sit-in Orchestra."

One member of Van Zandt's revolving-door band was guitarist Lee Ruth: "I was probably the best guitar player in Crested Butte at the time, so I could keep up with him no matter what he played," Ruth claimed.

He had a real driving rhythmic style with a flat pick and played the best version of "Mystery Train" this side of Junior Parker and Elvis.

Townes usually played bar gigs. But if somebody got busted and there was a benefit, he would be there on the back of a flatbed truck or playin' in the street. It didn't matter what shape he was in. Maybe four or five of us would be playing some street music, trying to get enough money for a watermelon, and Townes would come by and play with us, and we'd make that four or five dollars real fast. He was good at hustlin' folks with the tip basket. He used to do a number that was very funny that he never recorded called "Talking Crested Butte Blues" about a check that he bounced and wound up getting picked up and thrown in the Crested Butte jail.

> I was out in Crested Butte, Colorado
> Doin' a few things I hadn't oughta
> When up steps a man askin' "Are you cute
> 'Cause I'm the marshal of Crested Butte"

Most folks didn't pay him any mind. Townes played and sang in a real, unpretentious manner. Rock and roll clubs and bars were never the best place to see him. If you weren't paying attention you could easily miss what he had to offer. Townes knew where the music came from, not just historically but psychically. If he sang "Old Shep" it was *not* like he was doin' a cover. I think Townes really understood his position in the lineage of the music. He was the best songwriter east or west of Bob Dylan.

Ruth said, raising an eyebrow, "And between east and west, really how much space is there?"

CHAPTER 12

ONE SWAGGERIN' DUDE

I instinctively knew I had to watch myself so I didn't wind up
becoming Townes Jr.
—David Olney

"In the fall of '72 I got an insurance settlement check after this guy ran a
red light and broadsided me. So what did I do? I bought half an ounce of
heroin," Mickey White said, rolling his eyes.

Well, I got super-duper strung out on this good white Mexican dope, and
then it ran out. Townes came to town and showed up to support me at my
gig at the University of Houston. He took one look at me and said,
"Mickey, you're goin' down. You gotta get out of here." He told me about
the scene goin' on in Nashville, so I sold my car for a hundred and fifty
bucks and bought a plane ticket. I had my last little hit of dope and did it
up, nodded out on the plane, and got to Nashville and called Guy Clark.
He told me to call Rocky Hill who was stayin' over at Jack Clement's
house. I had enough money to get a cab over to Jack's place. Soon after, I
moved in with Richard Dobson and Skinny Dennis [Sanchez, the lanky
bassist immortalized by Guy Clark in "L.A. Freeway"] on Acklen Avenue, in Hillsboro Village. We'd sit around for hours at marathon picking
parties with Rodney, Townes, and Ricardo. We'd pick all day, and then
go to Bishop's Pub at night to play and pass the hat. Olney, Guy, and
Townes would play, whenever he was in town.

With so many great songwriters in his midst, White began to feel in-
timidated: "Between Richard and Townes, I felt like they were writin' all
my songs for me. I could play their songs and have my soul expressed in

them, so I began playing more lead guitar, and in a couple of months I got pretty good. Whenever there was a gap between verses, somebody would say, 'Take it, Mickey.'"

"Me, Richard Dobson, and Skinny Dennis were a bunch of bachelor songwriters livin' in this house with a juggler and a trapeze artist. It was a twenty-four-hour party," Rodney Crowell reminisced fondly.

People used to just blow through there all the time. We were all be sittin' on the porch drinkin' and smokin' dope, just waitin' for the sun to go down, when Johnny Rodriguez came by. He said he'd just cut this single called "Pass Me By (If You're Only Passin' Through)." We had this little old record player and went and pulled it out on the porch and played it. It was the first time he ever walked into a studio. He hung out with us all night, then left, and the next thing you know he was a big star.

I was twenty-one at the time and gainfully employed as a dishwasher. I'd go to work and wash dishes until about two o'clock in the morning. They'd bring in the bus trays, and I used to finish people's drinks. I'd go home sloshed and be right at the same level where everyone else was. They'd all be sittin' around, playin' songs, just chasin' the music. Skinny Dennis would be playin' upright.

Steve Earle and I got to Nashville around about the same time. I gravitated toward emulating Guy, while Steve gravitated toward Townes. I guess I emulated Guy Clark until I got somethin' of my own goin'.

Guy took Rodney to see Townes play live for the first time back in 1972: "He said, 'Listen and learn somethin', boy.' It truly changed the course of what I do," Rodney admitted. "Guy and Townes really changed me, as did Mickey Newbury. I had been a fan of Hank Williams, Bob Dylan, and the Beatles. But I think Townes was the first artist, with the exception of Dylan, that personified the poet-songwriter to me. We would all hang out together over at Bishop's Pub in Nashville. Townes was a mythic figure, a real troubadour. He'd come breezing through like he was Billy the Kid," Crowell recollected.

My first introduction to Townes was when he was withdrawing from heroin, so he was not really accessible. He was more like a rattlesnake in those days. I was always waiting for him to bite. I was a good seven or eight years younger than him. He was very smart and deeply committed to his art. Guy and I got to be really close friends, but it wasn't to be with

Townes. Actually, it was probably better that way—the genius poet that he was. Intimidation was good for his mythic image. If Townes didn't intimidate you, then you just weren't gettin' it. And *I got it*. He was right up there with Merle Haggard. He was just as vivid as Bob Dylan—just as mercurial and electric. To be around him made me aspire. I was inspired to aspire.

Whenever Townes showed up the whole scene would revolve around him. He had an unspoken magnetism. He would do things like grab my chick and take her off somewhere and bang her. I have no bitterness about that. I actually have a fondness for the poetry of the man. Whenever he walked into a room, the water in the toilet would start runnin' in a different direction. Like Miles Davis, Townes could be one intimidating motherfucker. I mean, look how smart and connected to his art he was. With that comes a swagger. The image of Townes from the early seventies that still sticks with me today is that of the swaggerin' dude. Townes was a freewheelin', ramblin', gamblin' troubadour, the wandering minstrel—the high-stakes dude. But when it came to gambling, I think it was more about the act than winning.

Most people's memory of Townes's gambling portray him as a hapless loser, but Chip Phillips recalled otherwise: "I'd seen him walk into the Gold Rush dead broke, borrow a dollar from somebody, play liar's poker, and walk out with close to two hundred dollars in his pocket," Chip said. "He used to gamble my wife, Bidy, for my cowboy hats while I was at work. I spent a lot of money on those hats, and I'd come home and Townes would be walkin' outta my house, wearin' my brand-new cowboy hat, sayin', 'Hey, man, ya like my hat?' I'd say, 'Yeah, I like it! I paid a lotta money for it.' 'Well, it's mine now. You talk to your wife about it. She gambled me for it.' He got three of my hats that way. It actually created a rift between me and Bidy."

"Bidy Lomax was a big, stout woman who loved to cook and party and always kept the house open for homeless artists and songwriters," Richard Dobson recalled. "She had been estranged from her husband John when Steve Earle called Chip in San Antonio and told him, 'I just met the girl of your dreams.'"

"As Bidy and Townes were best friends, it really helped sealed the deal," Phillips explained.

By the midseventies, Rodney Crowell headed west to L.A. to work with Emmylou Harris's band. It was Rodney who first turned Emmylou on to Townes's nostalgic outlaw opus "Pancho and Lefty" as well as the lovely, lilting "If I Needed You."

Seven years later, Crowell would cross paths with Townes and Guy again. "We were drinking, and Townes was so sweet and so gentle, telling those jokes. I don't think he felt any competition with me on a friendship level with Guy."

Singer-songwriter David Olney first met Van Zandt in January 1973, when he opened a show for him at a club in Athens, Georgia, called the Last Resort. Townes had just returned from a tour of Europe and was wearing a pair of white Beatle boots that David found "shocking." Overwhelmed by Van Zandt's fancy footwear, Olney found his performance even more amazing and was too inhibited to speak with him after the gig.

A year later Olney crossed paths with Townes again when he and Richard Dobson played a double bill in Houston. "He was just so crazy and had such presence. His magnetism was strong. I could easily have gotten caught up and become just another satellite around Townes. I thought, I can't *do* that, so I stayed back and didn't get to know him as well as I could've, I suppose," David explained.

"One afternoon Townes was completely wild. I remember him *eating* all the flowers in the flower bed. I thought there's no way I can keep up with that as far as innate craziness was concerned. So I steered clear of him a little bit," Olney confessed.

"I had written a few songs but hadn't really found my voice yet. That night Townes played, and he was stupendous, 'Pancho and Lefty' in particular." Eventually, Olney built up the courage to play Van Zandt his song "Illegal Cargo." Townes was so moved he wound up working the song into his set for a while. "I was very honored," David said.

Olney recalled a house party in Houston where Townes was gambling with Mickey and Wrecks when Cindy came strolling in: "She was unbelievably beautiful. I just saw a flash of red hair and then came to about ten minutes later. They quickly disappeared into a bedroom together, and I figured it's just another day at the office for that guy."

"Everybody used to worship Hank Williams and George Jones," Chip Phillips said.

It was just like Waylon Jennings sang, "Did ol' Hank really do it this way?" People felt if they were gonna be the "Real Deal," then they had to abuse themselves to keep up with those guys. Everybody used to go over to Bidy Lomax's house every night to hang out and get blasted. The guys were all tryin' to drink their wives under the table. Richard Dobson and his wife. Guy would try and drink Susanna under the table. My wife had an incredible constitution. And then along comes Cindy and Townes Van Zandt. But those women outdrank the men every time. And it wasn't like the men weren't tryin'.

With all the drinking and drugging going on, things were bound to get a little out of hand. Richard Dobson recalled Skinny Dennis as "a peaceable sort but prone to flip out on whiskey. One night walking through Hillsboro Village Dennis threw a brick through the window of the Pancake Pantry where the owner was hostile to people with long hair. We took off running, and Townes was amazed because Dennis, who had a bad heart, was already home when we got there."

"I had an old funky '52 panel truck with a single seat for the driver and a couple aluminum lawn chairs for passengers that weren't even bolted down. We were comin' home one night after we'd been out drinkin' at Guy and Susanna's house. It was me and Townes and Skinny Dennis," Rodney Crowell recollected.

Skinny Dennis was about six seven and weighed about one hundred and twenty pounds. He was insane. He and Townes were sitting in these lawn chairs, and they got into an argument. It was some kinda one-upmanship thing that was just crazy. I was drivin' drunk, just tryin' to get us home without windin' up in jail. I was outta my mind. We all lived in this hippie flophouse on Twenty-first Street. We were just comin' into town when Townes took this long-neck beer bottle and smashed it against the wall of the truck and jumped on Skinny Dennis, knockin' him out of the lawn chair onto the floor. I'm drivin' and kickin' 'em both, tryin' to get 'em to quit. Townes is on top of him with this busted beer bottle, sayin', "I'm gonna cut your skinny, motherfuckin' Mexican throat." Skinny Dennis is yellin', "I got a knife in my pocket, and I'll kill you!" I pulled over and flung the door open, and they just rolled out onto the sidewalk. They were still goin' at it. I couldn't figure out how to get 'em to stop. I reached in to stop Townes, and he just slapped me away. Skinny Dennis just wasn't that strong. Townes was holdin' the broken glass right up to his face, sayin', "I'm gonna cut your fuckin' jugular vein!" So Skinny Dennis yells, "Well, then, fuckin' cut!" And that's when Townes looks up at me real cool and calm and says, "I got him, didn't I?" He was just fuckin' with us. He was committed to the act right up till the last minute. Skinny Dennis thought it was for real, 'cause with Townes, you just didn't know. That was some electric shit.

Sanchez would soon die at age twenty-nine, not at the hands of a maniacal drunken prankster, but as the result of a combination of health problems. Well aware that he had heart disease, Dennis did nothing to help himself. Just two years younger than Townes, he appeared nearly ten years his senior. Standing at six foot seven and weighing between 125 and 140 pounds, he wasn't merely "skinny," as his nickname suggested; he was gaunt, born with Marfan syndrome, the same elongated bone condition that gave Abraham Lincoln his strange, emaciated appearance. Townes was quick to point out that the disease was "the *only* thing" the two men had in common. "He kept playing bass and drinking, [doing] a little cocaine every so often, weed and cigarettes," Van Zandt recalled in *Omaha Rainbow*. Although Sanchez had never ridden a horse before they met, Townes thought he looked completely natural in the saddle, "like he came right off the range for eighty years." Best known for his solid bass work, Sanchez, in Van Zandt's estimation, also "wrote about ten really good songs" and "a bunch of poetry as well."

"Skinny Dennis died with his boots on [Marfan syndrome sufferers have been known to literally drop dead] after playing a show in California with Rodney Crowell," Richard Dobson recalled (although others claim it was a gig at Sunset Beach with John Penn). "Townes and Susanna claimed his ghost haunted them." According to Ricardo, the recently disembodied towering Mexican bassist reached into his bag of typical spook tricks and made drinks disappear, moved chairs, and slammed a couple of doors.

"I lighted in Nashville for a good part of 1974," Jim Rooney recalled.

There was a beer bar called Bishop's Pub on West End Avenue where a bunch of singer-songwriters from Houston hung out—Guy and Susanna Clark, Rodney Crowell, Richard Dobson, and Townes. It was a pass-the-hat place. People were singing songs they had just written, but Townes was the one they were all looking to. He was a bit ahead of them.

Once in a while we'd go out to the country where Townes was living with Cindy. It was all very laid back. Joints were passed around, beer was drunk. Townes would be drinking something stronger. He would get into telling jokes and playing little games. People seemed to treat him as a source of some mysterious knowledge, with a bit of reverence, like Townes could do no wrong. I guess I'm not into idolizing people. I don't particularly like game playing. But I enjoyed his company, and he seemed to enjoy mine.

But games and drama were a regular component of Van Zandt's daily life, as David Olney recalled when he ran into Townes again at the Winnipeg Folk Festival in 1987: "He was skinny and ragged and somehow had managed to burn his hand badly. He told everybody that he had been bitten by a spider or stung by a bee. It was very swollen, much bigger than a bite. The water at the hotel where we stayed was unbelievably hot, and he'd scalded his hand."

"It was gory. When he got home Townes looked pale as a ghost and was shaking. He had fallen backwards into the bathtub and burned his hand and his ass. He'd lost the skin off his right hand and bun," Jeanene recalled.

"I ran into them at the airport after the festival. Guy was leading Townes around and asked me to look at his hand to see if I thought he should go to a doctor. When I looked at his hand, there was no skin on it. I said, "He's gotta go to a doctor NOW!" David exclaimed.

Olney flew ahead to Nashville and collected their suitcases while Guy took Townes to a doctor in Winnipeg, then got him on the plane back home to Nashville, where he finally checked into the Vanderbilt Hospital with third-degree burns.

"How much pain did he have to be in before he'd go to the hospital? He was gonna lose his hand. He was a guitar player, for God's sake! It would've turned to gangrene in a couple more days. But he was impervious," Jeanene sighed. "I called him 'Leather Man' 'cause his skin was tough as a leather hide."

CHAPTER 13

PANCHO, LEFTY, AND THE MAN WHO DIED TWICE

How thin you've grown.

Have you been suffering for your poetry again?

—Chinese poet Li Po to the poet Tu Fu

Many of Townes's darkest songs, fingerpicked ballads in minor keys like "Nothin'" and "Lungs," directly addressed the ravages of addiction. Although many thought Townes's excessive behavior was deliberate, Van Zandt believed he couldn't write with validity without firsthand experience. As an acolyte of Lightnin' Hopkins, Townes felt it was hypocritical to sing the blues if you hadn't lived them. Lightnin' didn't stop there, though. He believed if you're going to play the blues, you shouldn't even be able to stand up. And with fervent devotion Townes did everything within his power to prove his hero's theory valid. Indeed, Van Zandt was famous for taking anything he could get his hands on, from chugging vodka and codeine cough syrup to shooting heroin. In retrospect, it was a minor miracle that he managed to make it to fifty-two.

Jimmie Dale Gilmore felt that his friend's self-destructiveness was thoroughly self-indulgent and unnecessary: "Not only would he not take care of himself—he flat-out destroyed himself. I think he manifested it on purpose. Townes had acquired this idea that he was gonna be like Hank Williams, that he was gonna die and wouldn't be famous until after he was dead. But, y'know, in the long run he was right," Gilmore said, shaking his head.

"Not only was he a master of divinity, predicting his own death, but Townes lived to be fifty-two," Old Chief Rolling Papers pointed out. "That's a full deck."

Van Zandt and David Amram had performed together numerous times at the Kerrville Folk Festival over the years. One morning David was disturbed to find Townes drinking and confronted his friend about it. "Townes, I can't tell you what to do with your life," Amram said. "But your family loves you. Your friends love you, and a lot of people you don't even know love you. You've got to love yourself and stop all this mess so you'll be here for a while because we need you. We need your poetry and your music." Van Zandt glanced back at Amram with a pained but knowing expression. Destructive as it was, Townes had chosen his path long ago. Although he appreciated his friend's heartfelt advice, Townes was determined to carry on the only way he knew how, following Hank Williams's dust down the Lost Highway. "This is the way it's supposed to be for me," Van Zandt explained to his friend.

"Maybe he had to do it because he simply couldn't take the pain," Amram sighed. "But the amazing thing about Townes was that he was always uplifting to be with. He was always considerate of other people and made you feel good. Townes never wanted you to feel sorry for him, not for a second. This was just somethin' he had to deal with himself. On the other hand, he wrote some of the most beautiful and fantastic songs ever written."

"I wondered where his pain came from. I wondered why he did the things he did to himself," said Chris Eckman of the Seattle band the Walkabouts. "I wondered why he would thank audiences in Dutch, when he was playing in Germany. I wondered why he kept telling the same damn jokes. But with Townes you never wondered about his soul and his creative heart. In that department he was a giant."

According to Jason Wakefield, a former bartender at the Sand Mountain Café, the title of his sixth album, *The Late, Great Townes Van Zandt,* came about after Townes clinically died twice in one night in 1972, on the way to the hospital after a heroin overdose.

Fran recalls the traumatic event:

We were divorced in 1970, the year after J. T. was born, and had already started seeing other people. But we'd still see each other because Townes would come to visit the baby, and I still dreamed that we would get back together. He'd come over to see J. T. and would just assume that he'd have a place to stay and eat. J. T. loved Townes and was incredibly attached to him. He was more like an imaginary hero to him than a normal daddy.

Townes came back a week before I was supposed to get married, and I decided not to go through with it. I always had a sixth sense when he was in trouble. The hair would stand up on the back of my neck. He was comin' into town, and I asked him to be on time because J. T. was so excited to see him. I knew Townes was into somethin', and that's when he overdosed on heroin and was pronounced dead on arrival at Bentaub Hospital in Houston. I was pretty innocent at the time, and it was the first clue I had that he was into anything that heavy. I thought he was just drinkin' and smokin' some marijuana. Growin' up Southern Baptist, I never dreamed this stuff went on in the world.

All day long I kept callin' his mom's place. She was out of town at the time, and he was staying at her apartment in River Oaks. I called everybody I knew, sayin', "I know Townes is in trouble, but I don't know where he is." I'm not sure who found him. But whoever it was made an anonymous call. The ambulance arrived and raced him over to Bentaub. The family called saying that Townes was callin' for me and asked me to go to the hospital. I stayed up all night, talking to him, yelling at him, doing whatever I could to try and keep him awake. They had knocked his front teeth out in order to put the tubes down his throat. It was a terrible mess. But the amazing thing was he came back without any brain-cell loss. His constitution was so strong.

When word of Mrs. Van Zandt's wild child's OD spread through the apartment complex, everyone was horrified, and there was considerable pressure on Dotsy to move out, which only further compounded Townes's ongoing guilt over having failed to live up to his mother's expectations.

Fed up, Fran soon married again, in hopes of creating a normal environment for J. T. to grow up in. "It was the biggest mistake I ever made," she confessed. "I would've been a lot better off just taking care of J. T. and myself while being there when I could for Townes."

The photo on the back of the *Late, Great* record jacket reveals a bleary-eyed Van Zandt guffawing as he pops photographer Steve Salmierie the finger (another provocative moment courtesy of the folks at Poppy Records). It seems that Townes, having somehow survived dying (whether once or twice, as legend has it), was obnoxiously daring Death to a rematch.

Although understandably irked by the album's title, Van Zandt's mother, Dotsy, appreciated the genteel cover portrait of her son. But when she flipped the album over, she was appalled by the photo of some grinning lunatic making an obscene gesture and absolutely refused to accept that it was her boy.

"A lot of my friends saw it at the music store and tried to call my mother," Townes told *Omaha Rainbow*. "She didn't believe it was me on the back cover. When she and my aunt went to buy it in Houston, they had this argument with the hippie in the store. She said it wasn't Townes Van Zandt, he said it was, and she said, 'I should know, I'm his mother.'"

Salmierie's timeless cover shot portrays Van Zandt standing alone in Kevin Eggers's Brooklyn Heights townhouse, an alienated wallflower in a paisley shirt receding into the background, wedged between an oak table and a black marble fireplace. On the shelf sits a candelabrum along with various knickknacks. A portrait of an old Victorian woman (Kevin's ex-wife Ann Mittendorf's great-great-grandmother Emma von Keith) peers out from an ornate gilded frame. The fireplace is cold and empty. A vacuum seems to envelop the room. Townes's hands are folded gently over the headstock of his guitar. A thick, fuzzy black aura created by the photographer's flash shrouds his head and shoulders like a tainted halo. Van Zandt's hair is neatly combed. His dark eyes and lips are expressionless. There stands Tony Perkins as Ralph Waldo Emerson.

Milton Glaser designed the album cover to resemble an old-world funerary card, announcing Townes's premature demise in black Gothic letters across the top of the sleeve.

"It was a really half-assed and rather insulting idea if you ask me," painter and folksinger Eric von Schmidt said. "That was when Milton was designing his 'unknown' series, which included Chris Smithers without a face [for *I'm a Stranger Too*], me, looking like 'Mr. Anonymous,' holding an old army photo [for Eric's *2nd Row, 3rd Left* album], and *The Late, Great Townes Van Zandt*."

Kevin claimed to have conceived of the album's title as a comment on the nonexistence of Townes's career and hoped to draw attention to Van Zandt with a "Paul [McCartney] is dead" style hoax.

"The reason I named the album *The Late, Great* was because *nobody* was interested in Townes Van Zandt. Absolutely nobody," Eggers grumbled.

His fan base was zip, zero, nada. Townes had no commercial success. He was a blip on the radar screen. He worked very hard at being professional and had enormous exposure, but it was like we gave a party and nobody came.

I never made money on him. Nothing happened with "Pancho and Lefty" for almost ten years. Eventually, I sold Poppy to United Artists who instantly dropped Townes because he was only selling six thousand copies of a record, maximum. We got about thirty-five grand from UA, a lot of money in those days, which he quickly pissed away. We put him out on tour as the opening act for John Lee Hooker, but nothing came of it. I tried to get [Bob Dylan's manager] Albert Grossman to handle Townes, but he wasn't interested. Albert, who had the best taste of any manager in that era, didn't like his music. Neither did Peter, Paul, and Mary. We couldn't get them to cut any of his songs. He was just too far over their heads. It was like his work was in some kind of time warp.

"Jack Clement nearly had a fistfight with Charlie Pride trying to get him to record 'If I Needed You,' but he wouldn't do it," Eggers sighed.

Kevin Eggers often felt like he was leading a one-man parade when it came to championing Townes Van Zandt's career. Back in the fifties the Zen/Beat poet Gary Snyder claimed he used to hitchhike all the way from Oregon down to San Francisco just to find somebody that knew what was happening. Eggers and Van Zandt finally discovered that someone one night at New York's leftist listener-supported radio station, WBAI.

"There was this beautiful young girl singing 'Tecumseh Valley' who turned out to be Emmylou Harris," Kevin recalled. "She was the only one who got Townes's writing and was the first to record 'Pancho and Lefty.'"

"Emmylou sang 'Pancho and Lefty' on *Luxury Liner* because it was a great song. It was our honor and our duty to do it. It wasn't some kind of music-career-move bullshit," Rodney Crowell stated emphatically. Crowell, who was friends with Townes in Nashville before joining Harris's band in the 1970s, introduced her to Van Zandt's classic outlaw ballad.

First known for her lilting harmonies on Gram Parson's albums, Harris built a reputation as a fine singer-songwriter in her own right. Since her early days performing in Washington, D.C., folk clubs, she has continued to discover new, unknown singer-songwriters to cover and collaborate with. One night Jerry Jeff Walker caught her cooing his signature song "Mr. Bojingles" [*sic*] at the Old Cellar Door on open-mike night. Somehow Emmylou must've gotten ahold of a copy of Walker's tune before he cut it for Atco and gotten the old derelict's name wrong.

Released in 1973, *The Late, Great* was Townes's sixth and final studio album for the ailing Poppy Records. An underground classic of American roots and country music, the record mixed a pair of Townes's favorite cover songs, Hank Williams's "Honky Tonkin'" and "Fraulein," with a handful of Van Zandt's finest songs to date (including "Pancho and Lefty" and "If I Needed You," which appeared back to back on side two). The record opened with a curious ode to domestic bliss. "No Lonesome Tune" painted an idealized scene of family life that perhaps the perpetual rambler pined for in his heart of hearts.

"Jack produced the basic tracks to 'No Lonesome Tune' and 'Honky Tonkin'," Kevin Eggers pointed out. "I cut all the basic tracks to everything else and mixed it. The strings on the 'Silver Ships of Andilar' were arranged by Bergen White, one of the few black musicians in Nashville who happened to be the top string arranger in those days."

Closing out the album is a pair of songs about boats, as different as can be. Townes's bone-chilling "Silver Ships of Andilar," a seven-versed epic poem composed from the perspective of a dying man who slipped a message into a bottle in desperation, reflects Van Zandt's love of Samuel Taylor Coleridge's "Rime of the Ancient Mariner" as well as Lin Carter fantasies.

"It took thirty-six hours and an entire legal pad to get it on paper. I'd like to see Tiny Tim record it," Townes quipped. But perhaps the freaky, shrill-voiced ukulele strummer would have been better suited to cover the album's last number, "Heavenly Houseboat Blues." A lighthearted lullaby cowritten with Susanna Clark, with lyrics like "Welcome aboard you sweet, sweet pea," the song is more fitting to Tiny Tim's warbling than a grim ballad of death by drowning.

The album's masterpiece (and Van Zandt's signature song) is the ballad of a pair of hapless outlaws named "Pancho and Lefty." The tune is something of a sonic Rorschach test, drawing a different conclusion from everyone who hears it. Van Zandt never divulges whether Pancho and Lefty were friends or a pair of desperadoes thrown together in some ill-fated scheme on the desert plains of Mexico. Whatever the circumstances, betrayal lays at the heart of Van Zandt's tale. Some folks speculate that Lefty turned Pancho in for the money that paid for his passage to Ohio, where he lived out his final days in a cheap Cleveland hotel, after doing whatever it was that he had to do.

Jeanene's mother, Mary Locke Danforth, claimed that Townes once told her that Pancho was Jesus and Lefty represented Judas, and the mysterious "bread" that Lefty used to get to Ohio was a metaphor for the thirty pieces of silver that Judas was paid to betray Christ.

Mickey White recounted the first time he heard the song in the summer of '72:

Coming from New Mexico, I had a real affinity for the mountains and had gone up to visit my cousin who owned a hotel in Leadville, Colorado. By then Townes and I had become better friends and had connected musically, gettin' together to pick over at the Truxillo house [in Houston].

One morning I heard this pounding on my door while I was sleepin', and sure enough, there was Townes with a couple of friends. It was an honor that he even looked me up. I told him, "Hey, Townes, a friend of mine runs a little radio station up on the hill. What do you say we go over there and he'll put you on?" He said, "Yeah, sure."

Townes had a lot of energy and created a lot of excitement back in those days. Every time he came off the road all our friends would show up at the Old Quarter full of anticipation over what new tunes and stories he'd brought back with him. I said, "Well, Townes, what ya got, man?" And he slung his old guitar on and played me "Pancho and Lefty" and "If I Needed You" back to back while we were sittin' out in the parking lot, waiting to go into the radio station.

"I was at the session when they mixed 'Pancho and Lefty,'" Mickey recalled. "They were setting up the board, gettin' ready for the mix. Kevin had brought in a drummer and overdubbed a drum track. Townes was sittin' there at the board with Cowboy Jack. Kevin really wanted him to put drums on the track, but Townes said, 'No, we're not goin' with the drums.' Kevin told him, 'Well, I think you're passin' up a number-one hit.' He really believed that."

"Pancho and Lefty" stands beside "Ode to Billie Joe" as one of the great enigmas of the American songbook. No matter how one analyzes Bobby Gentry's moody, broody ballad, it's never clear exactly what was thrown off the Tallahatchie Bridge (although most people assume it was a baby). The only thing for certain is that the vague event makes the singer lose her appetite.

"Pancho and Lefty" always remained a mystery to Townes as well, who once confessed, "I still haven't figured it out. I remember thinking while writing 'Pancho and Lefty' that it was not about Pancho Villa," Townes said. "So many people feel that it is, however, that it might be. I've heard that a grad student at Harvard or Yale is doing his doctorate on the song, so the answer may be forthcoming," he joked.

Van Zandt claimed to have written "Pancho and Lefty" one night after he couldn't find a motel room in Dallas. In a bizarre twist of fate, both Billy Graham and the Guru Maharaji happened to converge on the city at the same time, along with thousands of their fervent flock. Having to seek shelter elsewhere, Van Zandt soon found himself holed up in a little seedy motel on the outskirts of town where he had nothing to do for three days but sit and talk with his buddy Daniel.

Townes relates one of the many "true" tales of how he came to write "Pancho and Lefty":

Billy Graham drew, like 500,000 young Christians from all over the world and the Guru had about 250,000 young gurus from all over the world. And I had, y'know, seven winos from downtown. Anyway, because of all these young Christians and young gurus, there were no hotel rooms for 50 miles from Dallas. So my friend Daniel and I finally found this place. It had no TV, no Coke machine, it had a swimming pool that had a big crack in it. There was nothing to do. Not a very fun place to be. So on the second day, I sat down in a chair and decided I'm not going to move from this chair until I write a song. I sat there for about three and a half hours and that's when 'Pancho and Lefty' kinda drifted through the window. And I wrote it down or else I'd still be sittin' there.

Here's the funny part of the story; Daniel wasn't even a hippy, he was a flower child, a whole different ball game. He had hair about down to his elbows and I didn't look too straight myself, I'm sure. The only ID Daniel had was an expired Georgia driver's license that had been expired, like 11 years. The only ID I had was a record album with my name and picture right there on it. So we're drivin' to the last night of the good ol' Dallas job in this old, broken down car and Daniel's swerving all over the highway. He didn't drink in the least or anything like that. He was just trying to miss all these young Christians and gurus hitchhiking into Dallas, hundreds of them. . . thousands, maybe thousands, on the side of the road. A big Dallas cop sees us swerving down the road in this broken down car, pulls us over and says "I better see some ID boys." I'm talkin', flat hat, mirror shades, the works. Daniel hands him his expired license. The cop's scowling at it when out of the blue, Daniel looks up at him and says, "Excuse me sir, but do you know Jesus?" The cop looks at him, hands him back his license and says, "You boys be careful." I figured that Billy Graham and the Guru Maharaji kinda co-wrote ["Pancho and Lefty"] but I never heard anything from them, so I guess it's okay.

Van Zandt, in his typical self-deprecating manner, believed that anybody could've written the song. "They just had to be sitting in the right chair," he professed.

"Townes's songs were more like paintings or moods," Jerry Jeff Walker surmised. "He said he wasn't really sure what 'Pancho and Lefty' was about. The first part sounds autobiographical. He could've been talkin' about himself in those lines. Then he spun it into two characters from there," Walker mused as he softly crooned the lyrics:

Living on the road my friend
Was gonna keep you free and clean
Now you wear your skin like iron
Your breath's as hard as kerosene

You weren't your mama's only boy
But her favorite one it seems
She began to cry when you said goodbye
And sank into your dreams

Steve Earle believed "Pancho and Lefty" defied every music-industry standard for success—that songs must be short, with a good beat, and not too literate or arty. "You won't find a song that's better written, that says more or impresses songwriters more," Earle emphasized.

"Even now when I'm driving to a gig and getting sleepy, I'll go over every word of 'Pancho and Lefty.' There are so many amazing things about that song. Every word really counts," David Olney marveled. "The first verse is delivered in the voice of the second person. From there it's all in the third person, which is really striking. You can imagine a Greek chorus singing it. And with each repeating of the chorus, a subtle change takes place. Townes connotes the passing of time when he sings 'a few gray federales say . . . '"

In his analysis David points out how Van Zandt suddenly broke character by employing modern slang when he sings the lines "Lefty split for Ohio" and "Where he got the bread to go" in a tale that obviously took place back in the Old West. "I think it makes it somehow more universal," Olney reckoned.

"You get the feeling from 'Pancho and Lefty' that someone close to you is telling you a very intense story. There's no words or music that can really convey that kind of intensity. It's beyond explanation. Whatever it was—Townes had it in spades," David exclaimed. "There are people who might've only had a five-minute conversation with Townes, but they'd walk away with this distinct feeling that they'd connected with him in some way. No matter how long you talked with him, he left you with the feeling it was really real somehow and worth remembering in some detail. That was the most unique thing about his personality. He gave so many people the feeling of having been close to him."

"Anytime anyone wanted to talk to him he'd stop and have as much of a conversation as they wanted to have," Darryl Harris said. "You couldn't walk five hundred feet through the Kerrville Folk Festival campgrounds with Townes. It would take you an hour and a half. He was incapable of telling someone, 'I'll catch you later.' He couldn't do it."

"The lyrics say that Lefty was an old poet and Pancho was the hero of the story he told. The song really shows the way that poets pass stories down from one generation to the next," Jeanene said.

Kevin Eggers complained that he's tired of all this "bar talk." (Townes wouldn't have been able to resist making some dumb pun in response to that statement.) Eggers believed it was time to clear the air of all the apocryphal stories that become more ridiculous with each telling and retelling over the years. Contradicting Van Zandt's story, Kevin claims "Pancho and Lefty" was written over a period of "many weeks" while Townes lived in Brooklyn Heights, and the song was actually a metaphor to describe their relationship. "Townes is in the song," Kevin pointed out, "but he is *not* Pancho."

Although "Pancho and Lefty" was one of the few Van Zandt songs to eventually generate any real revenue, it took several years before Townes would reap the reward of his labor. But the song paid off in a strange and unexpected way years before Townes received his first royalty check when he was driving from Houston to Austin and got pulled over for doing seventy-five through the little borough of Berkshire. Van Zandt wasn't sure what brand of illegal contraband he was carrying at the time. He just always considered himself "felonious while movin'." His driver's

Isaac Van Zandt (*top, left*);
Khleber Miller Van Zandt (*top, right*);
John Charles Townes II and his Great Danes (*below*)
(ESTATE OF DOROTHY TOWNES VAN ZANDT)

Mrs. Helen Markle Townes,
wife of John Charles Townes II
(ESTATE OF DOROTHY TOWNES VAN ZANDT)

Katie Belle Williams Van Zandt,
Katie Belle's namesake
(ESTATE OF DOROTHY TOWNES VAN ZANDT)

Townes's mother,
Dorothy Townes Van Zandt
(ESTATE OF DOROTHY TOWNES VAN ZANDT)

Townes with his father, "Van,"
going to the Shriner Circus, 1947 (*above*);
Townes with BB gun, age 3 (*right*)
(ESTATE OF DOROTHY TOWNES VAN ZANDT)

Townes, age 5, riding high in the saddle (ESTATE OF DOROTHY TOWNES VAN ZANDT)
Townes, second row, third from left, at Shattuck Academy Wrestling Team, 1962
(SHATTUCK ACADEMY YEAR BOOK)

Townes's graduation photo, 1962 (*left*)
(SHATTUCK ACADEMY YEAR BOOK)

Playing a sock hop (*below*)
(ESTATE OF DOROTHY TOWNES VAN ZANDT)

Fran and Townes's Wedding
The Petersons and the Van Zandts, August 24, 1965
(COURTESY OF FRAN LOHR)

Townes, Margaret Marable Lomax,
Antoinette Hopkins, Sam "Lightnin'" Hopkins
in Houston, Texas, 1969 (*above*)
(PHOTO BY JOHN LOMAX III)

The Young Poet. "He could be
so quiet and serene."
—Linda Lowe
(PROMO SHOT/TOMATO RECORDS)

Live at Carnegie Hall, November 26, 1969
(PROMO SHOT/TOMATO RECORDS)

Townes riding high
atop "Amigo,"
Aspen, Colorado, 1974
(PHOTO BY LAUREN CHANDLEE)

The Shack, Franklin,
Tennessee, 1974
(PHOTO BY WOOD NEWTON)

Townes and Uncle Seymour
Washington, Austin, 1975
(PROMO SHOT FROM
HEARTWORN HIGHWAYS,
CRIMSON PRODUCTIONS)

"This chicken only laid
double yolk eggs." —TVZ
(ROCKY MOUNTAIN NEWS,
JUNE 12, 1976)

Townes with axe
and Geraldine,
Franklin,
Tennessee, 1978
(PHOTO BY WILLIAM
J. DIBBLE)

"Hunting for a record deal." Franklin, circa mid-1970s
(PHOTO BY JOHN LOMAX III)

Blaze, Townes, and Wrecks, Austin, 1983 (*top*) (PHOTO BY JEANENE [JET] WHITT)

"Love—it's a bitch!" —TVZ. Townes and Jeanene
at Mickey and Pat's wedding (*above, left*);
Townes and Jeanene's wedding day, March 14, 1983 (*above, right*)
(PHOTOGRAPHER UNKNOWN, COURTESY OF JEANENE VAN ZANDT)

Townes in Willie Nelson and Merle Haggard's
video shoot of "Pancho & Lefty," summer 1983.
"I was the captain of the Federales. All I had to
do was look at people in contempt and disgust."
—TVZ
(PHOTO BY JEANENE VAN ZANDT)

Will's first birthday,
March 24, 1984.
Townes, Geraldine,
JT, Will, and Jeanene
(PHOTO BY CRAIG WINTERS)

Mickey White,
Harold Eggers,
Townes, and
Merrick, 1982
(PHOTOGRAPHER
UNKNOWN, COURTESY
OF THE ESTATE OF
TOWNES VAN ZANDT)

Harlan Howard,
Townes, and
Steve Earle
(PHOTO BY
BETH GWINN)

Townes, Susanna,
and Guy Clark at
record release party
for *At My Window,*
1987 (PHOTO BY
BETH GWINN)

Nanci Caroline Griffith
and Townes
(PHOTO BY JEANENE VAN ZANDT)

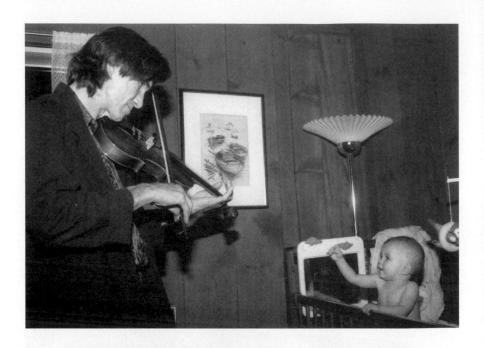

Katie Belle doesn't seem to mind Townes's fiddling, 1992 (*above*);
(PHOTO BY ALLEN MAYER)

TVZ and Jerry Jeff Walker (*below*)
(PHOTO BY JEANENE VAN ZANDT)

Family stack
(PHOTO BY ANTHONY LATHROP,
1994. COURTESY OF
JEANENE VAN ZANDT)

"Roll over Rimbaud and tell
Keith Richards the news!" 1994
(PHOTO BY ROY TEE)

Townes and Brownie McGhee,
Los Angeles, 1995
(PHOTO BY TOM ERIKSON)

Amsterdam, 1995
(PHOTO BY ROY TEE)

"Hell in a hand-basket," Los Angeles, 1995
(PHOTO BY TOM ERIKSON)

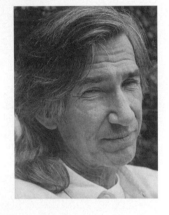

"You're talking to someone who just
came 20,000 miles, man." —TVZ
Steve Shelley, Townes, Cowboy Jack Clement
and Jeanene, 1996 (*below*)
(PHOTO BY WILLIAM J. DIBBLE)

license was surprisingly up-to-date, although it still showed an old address. But his inspection sticker had expired. Townes knew his bedrag-
gled appearance wasn't about to win any points with the authorities, and
in no time he found himself in the backseat of the police cruiser, in the
custody of a pair of mismatched highway patrolmen, straight out of that
old TV show *CHIPs*. The driver was a blue-eyed Aryan type with a
blond crew cut, while his partner was a bronze, dark-eyed Mexican.
They began grilling Townes with all sorts of questions, like what he did
for a living. "Well, I'm a traveling folksinger and songwriter," Townes
confessed. The pair of cops rolled their eyes and groaned, "Oh, great, another traveling folksinger-songwriter!"

With that Van Zandt wasted no time in playing his trump card. "Have
you ever heard that song 'Pancho and Lefty'?" he said. "Well, I wrote it."
The pair looked at him incredulously. "No, you didn't," they scoffed.
"Oh, sure I did," Townes answered earnestly. "I gave it to Willie," he said
and sang the opening line: "Livin' on the road my friend / Was gonna
keep you free and clean." The cops looked at each other and began to
grin. A moment later they huddled in the front seat for a quick confer-
ence. Meanwhile, Townes just sat there, "tryin' to be as nice as possible.
Not sayin' a word and tryin' not to even smell bad." Finally, the Aryan-
looking cop turned and said, "Well, Townes, we're gonna drop the
speeding ticket. Just remember when you get back to Austin to file for a
change of address on the driver's license. But we're gonna have to get you
for the inspection sticker, 'cause we already wrote it down. But that will
only be about five bucks."

"Well, thank you, officer," Townes replied appreciatively. Van Zandt
knew the code of the road, that once a cop lets you off, you don't say another word. Make no eye contact, just say thank you, and be on your
merry way as soon as possible. But curiosity got the best of him, and before he knew it Townes asked, "Hey, what prompted y'all to drop the
speeding ticket?" The cops explained that their police-radio code names
were Pancho and Lefty.

"Well, that sure is nice," Townes replied with a grin. "Thanks again,"
he said, as he got out of the car and started to walk off. But just as he
reached his car he couldn't help himself and spun around on his boot
heels and sauntered back to the car again to ask, "Uh, which one of y'all
is Pancho?" The Mexican pointed at the Aryan and said, "*He* is!"

David Amram recalled watching Townes sing "Pancho and Lefty" to
forty thousand people at the Farm Aid Benefit in 1993 at the Hoosier

Dome. The enormous crowd had Townes a bit nervous considering his usual turnout was somewhere between fifty to seventy-five people a set on a good night. (By the early nineties Townes's audience in Europe and Australia was routinely larger than it was in the States.) David bolstered his friend's confidence, reminding him, "Everybody loves your songs, Townes. Willie loves you, or he wouldn't have asked you to come. When the people in the audience realize that you wrote that song, they're just gonna flip out." Then he went out there just by himself and his guitar. There was a light breeze blowing in his hair, and he sang like an angel. It was one of the most beautiful things I've ever seen. A whole ballpark full of people quieted down and began to hum and sing along on the chorus together," Amram reminisced.

"Pancho and Lefty" eventually made its prime-time television debut in April 1993 when Willie and Bob Dylan sang the tune to millions of viewers for the Red-Headed Stranger's 60th Birthday Bash. Townes had just returned from another long road trip. Exhausted, he crawled into bed and was just drifting off when his son Will charged in the room hollering.

"Usually when I'm off the road, I go to sleep at like 9:00 or 9:30. I try to stay awake long enough for *F-Troop,* that's my favorite TV show," Townes told journalist Peter Blackstock in 1995. "I was kinda layin' there and goin' to sleep and my son Will comes screamin' around the corner, 'Dad! Get up! Get up! Dad! Get up!'"

Judging by the pandemonium, Townes figured the house was probably on fire. So he dragged himself out of bed and searched around for his boots, just in case he had "to kick something in." Stumbling into the living room behind Will, he found Dylan and Nelson, strummin' and singin' together on the TV set. There was Willie with a big black Stetson atop his head and his old beat-up nylon-string guitar. Beside him stood Dylan with his hurricane hair and eyes behind a pair of aviator shades. The crowd roared as Bob began to croak the second verse, "Pancho was a bandit boys," as if it was one of his own timeless songs.

"Well, it's about time, goddamn it!" Townes hooted. "I've sure done enough of his songs."

In yet another version of the story, Townes claimed the inspiration for "Pancho and Lefty" originally came from his old friend named Chito (a.k.a. Frank Greer), who not only attended the same school with him but wound up in the same mental institution in Galveston as well. "We were best friends, did everything together and his father owned a ranch in Mexico. Everyone called the old man 'Pancho,' so naturally his son was 'Panchito,' shortened to 'Chito.'"

"Once and for all let's set the record straight," Jeanene barked like a drill sergeant. "It's 'Pancho and Lefty,' not 'Poncho.' One is south-of-the-border for 'Frank.' The other is a goddamn raincoat."

CHAPTER 14

THE UNIVERSITY OF OLD QUARTER

**There are those of us who feel Townes is the leading poet
of these times.**
—Earl Willis

According to the album's producer and engineer, Earl Willis, the Old
Quarter was home to "stoned-out freaks and professional types, where
blue jeans and blue collars came together for the good music and cold
beer." Among the club's luminaries were Lightnin' Hopkins, Jerry Jeff
Walker, and Guy Clark, while lesser-known singers depended on the
mercy and generosity of the crowd who would pass the hat (actually an
old bedpan) around the 18 x 38–foot room.

In July 1973, despite stifling heat and humidity and a busted air condi-
tioner, Townes Van Zandt performed a string of five-night shows, to
nearly a hundred folks per set, packed shoulder to shoulder within the
club's bare brick walls. The room was so jammed that it was impossible
for a waitress to wend her way through the crowd to take drink orders.
People had to pass money hand over fist and wait, in hopes that a mug of
cold beer would eventually find its way back to them.

Recorded on a portable four track by Willis (whom John Lomax III
described as "an agreeable and rabid fan"), the tapes, seven twelve-inch
reels, lay dormant for four years until they were finally released on Kevin
Eggers's new label, Tomato Records.

Townes summed up the recording of his classic live album, the lull in his career, and his feeling about the future in a 1977 interview with *Omaha Rainbow:*

> Me and a guy named Earl Willis carried his Teac down there every night and did the whole deal ourselves. I kind of forgot all about them. Then Kevin Eggers took the tapes to a studio at Lima, Ohio, and came out with the record. It's okay. That's what went down and it's good to have. Getting that record out on Tomato meant to me that all the mire that the business end of my career got wedged into was finally evaporating. I was out of the chute on a brand new horse, right? With that album and the songs I'll be cutting on the next record, well, something's gotta give, and it ain't gonna be me.

Live at the Old Quarter, Houston, Texas (a.k.a. *The Green Album*) is considered by most of Van Zandt's fans to be the Rosetta stone of his recorded works. A lot would change since that hot summer when Townes held court at the OQ. Four years in the music business is longer than the life span of most bands. By October '77 *Rolling Stone* had boldly announced "Rock Is Sick and Living in London" and plastered two photos of a demonic Johnny Rotten across its cover. Overnight, the Sex Pistols would trash the mellow musings of Crosby, Stills, and Nash, while the crew of Jefferson Starship was instantly decapitated by Talking Heads' "Psycho Killer." Oddly enough, Townes felt an affinity with this new breed of misfits. With the arrival of punk Van Zandt began describing his music as "aggressive folk" and referred to himself as an "unrepentant punk folkie." An entire generation of singer-songwriters suddenly seemed hopelessly old hat. Although Townes's "Talking Fraternity Blues" and "Talking Thunderbird Blues" were two of his most entertaining songs, by the midseventies they were about as hip as Vaudeville. Bob Dylan hadn't touched a talking blues in years, and hard-core purveyors of the form like Arlo Guthrie and Ramblin' Jack Elliott were viewed by some as dinosaurs from a past era.

Antiquated or not, Steve Salmieri's cover photo of Townes was a different matter altogether. Only Iggy Pop and Jim Morrison (before he became bloated) played in that league. No other song-poet could flash that much flesh without looking pathetic (except, of course, for Joni Mitchell's delicious butt cheeks inside the gatefold to her *For the Roses*). There stands Townes bare-chested, as if to say, "Okay, folks, this is about as naked as I can get without gettin' arrested." Like the songs within, Van Zandt stands stripped of artifice except for his cowboy hat and a pair of John Lennon–like wire-rimmed glasses. He is wedged into a corner of an empty room, his head slightly tilted, gazing back at the camera. He appears unsatisfied, impatient, weary of obscurity. The window drenches him in light. For a junkie and a juicer he looks pretty damn fit. There stands the cow-punk poet as swaggering sex symbol. Leaning beside Townes is his doppelgänger, his menacing shadow self that was never very far away. His stooped profile against the gray bare wall resembles an ash smudge from Satan's stogie.

Yet Townes had misgivings about the album and its risqué cover from the start. Pittsburgh folksinger Frenchy Burrito remembered Van Zandt "fuming" over Eggers releasing the album without his permission. "He told me his mother would not appreciate him posing on a record cover without his shirt on," Burrito claimed.

"He cut the album after the fire in 1973," Mickey White recollected. "The fire was the event that marked the end of the Old Quarter's heyday to its decline. There was a semimusician who was a bit unstable that hung around and lived at the Old Quarter, helpin' out, sweepin' floors, and pullin' beer. I think Wrecks stole his girlfriend, and he started the fire in retribution."

"It was arson," Wrecks explained. "We let this guy stay there. He was a Jesus freak. Then we found out he was opening and selling beer after we closed. We kicked him out, and he came back and set the fire. Never did catch him. . . That was the end for me. My good friend Dale Soffar rebuilt the OQ and went on. I moved to Nashville, had a writer's contract, and thought I was going to be a star."

Although Townes was often criticized for his laconic delivery and droll sense of humor, Steve Morse of the *Boston Globe* hailed him as "a mesmerizing performer." When his magic was working right, Townes could hold an audience spellbound, breathlessly hanging on his every word. Drop the needle on an old copy of *Live at the Old Quarter* some time and listen, not to Townes but to his crowd. He made a pack of wild hell-raisers settle down and shut up. At the end of his first song, a gentle reading of "Pancho and Lefty," Van Zandt comments, sounding somewhat astonished, "I've never heard it so quiet in here."

"The Old Quarter was in an old two-story stone building on the corner of Congress and Austin in the backwaters of Houston," recalled Van Zandt's friend and sometime-manager John Lomax III.

It was *not* in a good neighborhood. Upstairs there was a pool table with a bunch of couches and some mattresses lying around where people would crash. You had to go out on the roof to smoke pot. The poor convicts would look out across at you from the city jail and wave. Needless to say, it was a bar where they didn't check IDs very often, so there were a lot of kids hanging out. But the cops never bothered them. There was a little itty-bitty stage with about ten or fifteen tables all around.

One of the highlights of my life was seeing the Allman Brothers Band play there sometime between '71 and '72. They had just ended a tour with Little Feat in Houston, and somehow the Allmans found out about the Old Quarter. After they got hooked up with their drugs and girls, they didn't have anything left to do but go home, so they decided to stay and play. They set up the whole band with the double drum sets, the organ, and two guitars, and Townes sat in with them singin' "Stormy Monday." They were all blues guys and knew another blues guy when they saw one.

"*The Old Quarter* is the most honest document of him. It's just Townes and his guitar. I was at the club when they recorded it," Lomax boasted. The grandson and nephew of folklorists John Avery and Alan Lomax, John III should know good music when he hears it. He believed Van Zandt was "one of America's greatest human resources," claiming Townes's lyrics "stick in your mind like burned beans to a Crock-Pot." Lomax was certain Townes was "destined for greatness" and would follow in the footsteps of legendary American troubadours like Jimmie Rodgers, Woody Guthrie, Hank Williams, and Bob Dylan.

Eventually, John took on the daunting and ultimately thankless task of becoming Van Zandt's manager in June 1976. It wasn't long before he realized the hard realities that Townes was up against. "I went out with him on a few tours, to get a feel for what it was like out there," Lomax chuckled. "I got him some shows in L.A., playing at the Troubadour, and was fishing hard to get him a record deal. This music lawyer, Brian Rowhan, told me he was making a package deal with Capitol for Paul Siebel and Townes. I said, 'Well, what does that have to do with my artist?' I was kind of new in the business at the time, and the next thing you know I got bounced.

"Part of Townes's charm is all the wild stories about him," Lomax continued. "Once he was at a bar but couldn't get a drink because it was too crowded. So he walked outside to a phone booth and called in a bomb threat to clear the place, then Townes came walking back in, sat down, and started drinking in the back while they emptied the bar out. The cops came running in and found him sitting there. 'There was a bomb threat—didn't you hear?' the cop yelled. 'No,' he told him, 'I guess I was in the bathroom, man.'

"Another time Townes actually crashed his car into the side of a bar, got out, and walked through the broken glass and into the bar and got himself a drink."

"I met Townes at Guy and Susanna's house in Houston," old friend Lysi Moore reminisced. "He came to town for a court date after smashing his car through a big plateglass window of a bar. I guess he got out of it because he didn't do any time. Back then drivin' drunk wasn't such a big deal," Moore said with a shrug. "Townes was twenty-five at the time, a nice, quiet guy. He was beautiful then. I remember him emptyin' out his pockets which were full of all these numbers that girls had given him."

Black Crowes' front man Chris Robinson was first catapulted into Townes's world when Mark Olsen of the Jayhawks gave him a copy of *Live at the Old Quarter.* "At the time I was goin' through a lot of heavy stuff, as most everybody does in their early twenties," Chris said. "That record really spoke to me. I listened to it constantly while on a tour of Europe. In rock and roll people tend to forget about the importance of songwriting. Townes has really inspired me to become a better songwriter. That motherfucker really had his antennas up. There's an intimacy with his songs, like he's standin' up there naked with just his guitar, doin' it like he used to say, 'for the sake of the song.' Townes really knew how to break it down to its most honest and human level.

"The sad songs are the most beautiful ones. In writing those songs, Van Zandt helped a lot of people deal with their problems and sorrow," Chris said earnestly. "They're just part of life, whether you choose to deal with it or not, and writing those kind of songs is a great way to deal with it.

"Like Thelonious Monk, Townes was a heavy guy with serious problems, but there was always plenty of humor in his music," Robinson pointed out. "On *The Old Quarter* he's tellin' those corny jokes, but that just makes it all the more real."

This Houston cop was workin' his beat
when he sees this guy cruisin' along in a convertible
with three penguins in the backseat.

He pulls the guy over and says,
"Hey man, you can't just cruise around with those penguins.
Not on my beat. You take those penguins to the zoo."
The guy says, "Yes sir," and off he goes.
The very next day the cop sees the same guy again
cruisin' down the road with the same penguins
except this time they're all wearing shades.
This really ticks the cop off.
So he pulls the guy over and says,
"I thought I told you to take those penguins to the zoo."
And the guy says, "Yes sir, I did,
and today we're going to the beach."
   —TVZ, "The Penguin Joke"

"Just listen to the *Old Quarter*. How many of his really great songs were on that album? Ninety percent of his really good songs were written before he drank heavily," Darryl Harris pointed out. "Although he certainly wrote some good songs while he was drinking, he also wrote some while he was drunk," Harris laughed.

"I never thought of Townes as a really depressing writer," David Olney said. "Rex's Blues" sounds like a person contemplating suicide, yet at the same time everything he says is uplifting. I play that song, but it never seems bleak to me. It's more like a lullaby."

Lyrically, "Rex's Blues" has a logic all its own. Townes's rambling stream-of-consciousness meditation springs from the cause and effect of something as mundane as having a nickel. He wrote the song for his pal Rex "Wrecks" Bell, who initially found its lyrics less than flattering. "I didn't like it for many years. But he really pegged me," Wrecks confessed. Bell considered Townes "one of the greatest writers that ever lived," claiming he "had more insight into life than anyone I ever knew."

Over a simple fingerpicked two-chord vamp, Van Zandt sums up the human condition with Zen-like scrutiny. Here, Townes's boiled down, finely crafted verse reveals his endless battle with depression and constant struggle to be free of the guilt that came from constantly hurting his family, wives, children, and lovers by remaining, at all costs, true to his own untamed nature.

The opening verse repeats again at the end as a bookend, leading us back to the conundrum we constantly face in life, riding the seesaw of joy and misery.

Ride the blue wind high and free
She'll lead you down through misery
Leave you low, come time to go
Alone and low as low can be

If I had a nickel I'd find a game
If I won a dollar I'd make it rain
If it rained an ocean I'd drink it dry
Lay me down dissatisfied

Legs to walk and thoughts to fly
Eyes to laugh and lips to cry
A restless tongue to classify
All born to grow and grown to die

So tell my baby I said so long
Tell my mother I did no wrong
Tell my brother to watch his own
Tell my friends to mourn me none

Chained upon the face of time
Feelin' full of foolish rhyme
There ain't no dark till something shines
I'm bound to leave this dark behind

"Townes could tell half-hour-long stories, but he was also a master of economy," David Amram pointed out. "His songwriting was concise, like great Japanese haiku writers or the way a sonnet writer says it all with just a few lines. In conversation he always had the ability to throw in the perfect one-liner at the right time and cool everyone out."

With *Live at the Old Quarter* came an avalanche of accolades in the press. The *Los Angeles Times* hailed Van Zandt as "a cross between Woody Guthrie and Leonard Cohen."

"Though this gifted songwriter has been a legend in and around the folk circuit of the Southwest for a decade, his albums have been harder to find than El Dorado," complained Sean Mitchell of the *Dallas Times Herald* in July 1977. The same day in the *Memphis Commercial Appeal,* Walter Dawson neatly summed up Van Zandt's predicament: "He came along too late for the sixties folk boom and too early for the progressive country movement." A local legend in Austin, Townes was voted third in a popularity poll, right behind Willie Nelson and Waylon Jennings.

With his new revamped label, Tomato, Kevin Eggers also reactivated the old Poppy catalog, rereleasing Townes's second, third, and fourth albums, while allowing his flawed first album to continue to wallow in obscurity a while longer.

For the time being, El Dorado seemed a little closer than Sean Mitchell thought.

CHAPTER 15

7 COME 11

One time I asked him, how long can it last? And he said,
"As long as you keep your 'mystical charm.'"
—Richard "Ricardo" Dobson

Townes was a passionate gambler who loved the electricity of chance and the thrill of taking risks. There are endless stories about him losing. Losing big, losing everything, walking out of a crap game with no hat, jacket, shirt, belt, or boots and not givin' a damn, for Van Zandt intuitively understood, as he sang in "For the Sake of the Song," that "to win is only to lose." Townes would bet on anything no matter how big or small, from pitching pennies to "raindrop races" (wagering on which raindrop would reach the bottom of the windshield first).

On tours of the East Coast, Van Zandt regularly played the (now-defunct) Bottom Line in New York City. After his set he'd walk into the office to settle up with Alan Pepper and inevitably try to coerce him into going double or nothing for his night's wages.

"He came upstairs one night and sat down and said, 'Alan, do you have a deck of cards? How 'bout we play double or nothin' for my guarantee?' I passed, but if my partner, Stanley, had been there, he would've played him," Pepper chuckled.

Steve Earle claimed that Townes was the worst gambler he'd ever seen. "The only person he could beat consistently was Guy Clark."

"The drunker you get the more bulletproof you think you are," Clark said with a shrug. "I figured I lost to him more than I beat him. Either way, it was just good fun."

"Oh, Townes was a *terrible* card player. You know that old line, 'If you get a three, Wrecks will get a two?' He had no patience to play cards.

Townes would literally gamble everything he owned on the roll of the dice or flip of a coin. He truly didn't care about money. He could always book another gig, and there'd be more money coming in," Wrecks explained. Bell would often approach club owners in secret to ask for the band's pay, hoping to get his hands on the dough before Van Zandt had the chance to squander it on whatever whim was sure to strike. "If they said, 'Townes has already been paid,' then I knew we were screwed," Wrecks laughed.

"Nobody knows where his generosity came from. I don't know if there's an answer to it. Townes was just one of those people who had an affinity for the downtrodden," Bell mused. "One night in Austin, he went out with all the money after the gig and took these two homeless guys out for a night on the town. The next morning I said, 'Hey, Townes, you got any money?' and he said, 'Aw, I spent it all last night.' He figured there would always be another gig."

If money meant nothing to him, material objects were worth even less. Every year for Christmas and his birthday Jeanene bought Townes a new handmade silk shirt. Whenever anyone appreciated something of his, no matter what the price or sentimental attachment, Townes felt obliged to give it away, freely, with no thought whatsoever of how someone else might feel. After his death Jeanene claimed Townes had only six shirts left hanging in his closet. "He'd just say, 'Here you go.' He was happy to trade one of those beautiful two hundred dollar silk shirts to some guy for his old greasy T-shirt with a hole in it. He'd just take it off at the bar and hand it to them. I have no idea where all those shirts went, but they're out there somewhere," Jeanene laughed.

For Townes, life was all about "the poetry and the pickin' down the line," as he sang in "Rex's Blues." "We don't care about material stuff," Townes told journalist Bill Flanagan in 1995. "We want to hear the guitar ring one note correctly and your voice ring the same note correctly with the proper meaning correctly for that instant . . . but if you hit that note, it goes around the world and maybe—this is not bragging but it's hopeful, kind of prayerful—maybe somehow connect up with a baby in England or Ireland or Ethiopia and somehow make a shade of a difference. Plus it keeps us off the streets."

An idealist of the nth degree, Van Zandt not only hoped to improve the sorry condition of the world with his songs but also attempted to create works that went beyond his own comprehension: "I'd like to write some songs that are so good nobody understands them, including me," he said.

"One time we were in a motel room at three in the mornin', and he was burnin' money—literally. It was ridiculous," Wrecks Bell said. "He finally said, 'Fuck it! Let's just go give this to the first person who is nice to us.' Next door was a café, and this lady served us coffee; she was real nice. He had several hundred dollars all wadded up in his pockets. He pulled it out and left this massive amount of money on the table. When we walked out the door we could hear her calling, 'Sir? Sir?' I'm sure to this day she is still tellin' the story about these two idiots."

"Oh, Townes *was* generous to a fault," drummer Leland Waddell said with a laugh. "One night in Nashville he won a blow job from a girl and then GAVE IT AWAY! She said, 'Are you serious?' He said, 'Hey, I won it. I can give it away.' Whether she went through with it or not, I can't say."

Townes's compulsive gambling was simply an excuse for what Bill Bentley deemed his "insane drama." Van Zandt, he reckoned, loved adventure for the sake of it and likened him to "the kind of guy who walks into a bar, finds the biggest guy, and punches him in the mouth so he'll get beat up."

In the early seventies Bill played drums in an Austin band called Lea Ann and the Bizarros. After their weekly Friday-night show the madness would continue until the wee hours of the morning at parties they called "twist-offs."

"One night everybody was over at Big Boy Medlin's on Pearl Street," Bill recalled. "We'd finished off several cases of beer, some joints, a little speed. About thirty or forty people were hangin out, chatterin', playin' records, going crazy, when around three or four in the morning Townes showed up. He had a girl with him. I can't remember her name. He immediately got into a dice game and lost whatever money he had. Then he said, 'Okay, I'm gonna put up the girl. *And he lost.* She had to leave for the night with the guy he lost her to. They're heading out the front door when Townes gave her this cute little wave and said, 'Don't stay out too late, honey.'"

By late 1974 Kevin Eggers and Cowboy Jack Clement had come to a final parting of the ways. Between Kevin's unpaid bills and some of Cowboy's more questionable production decisions (apparently the hatchet that chopped off the last verse of "Tecumseh Valley" was never buried deeply enough), there was still some bad blood behind them. And Van Zandt's dual Jekyll and Hyde personality could turn a shaky situation volatile in a heartbeat.

"Townes's personality ran the full gamut," Kevin Eggers explained.

"He could be the sweetest man one minute, soulful, bright, articulate, and then he could be a raving asshole, manipulative and mean-spirited, the next. I cut him off after he became a junkie. I would never put up with it."

"We were makin' an album at Jack's Tracks, the one that [Eggers] never paid me for," Clement recalled. "We'd been out drinkin', down off Broadway. I'd had a few cocktails and got mad at Townes 'cause he was bein' a horse's butt, a prima donna. At that point I was actually sidin' with Kevin. I just got pissed off and decided I'd beat him up," Jack laughed, recalling "the brawl of fame."

Kevin was incensed at Townes, who allegedly offered his song-publishing rights to the first person to score him some smack. This enraged Cowboy as well, who deemed Eggers questionable at best, but thought that Van Zandt ought to appreciate all they'd done for him over the years. A moment later Jack curbed his Cadillac, opened the driver's-side door, rolled up his sleeves, and pulled Townes out of the backseat.

"We started goin' at it. I had him around the neck and pinned him down on the ground when just then the cops came along and said, 'If ya don't quit, Y'ALL ARE GOIN' TO JAIL!' I was able to summon up my cool head and say, 'Look, officer, I'm in the music business, a writer-producer, and this guy's my artist. This is just a family squabble. Sorry, we'll be good. We shouldn't've done it and won't do it no more.' And they let us go. Just told us to go home. Ain't that the funniest thing? 'My producer took me out last night and beat me up.' Now that's a Music City story!"

Fed up with the pair of them, Cowboy Jack would no longer do business with Kevin again on anything but a cash basis and refused to hand over the tapes until he was paid in full for the sessions. Shortly thereafter, Poppy went bust. Eggers's "mystical charm" had come up snake eyes. Meanwhile, Van Zandt's master tapes mysteriously went missing. It was rumored that Clement recorded over the master tapes "out of sheer meanness."

Originally titled *7 Come 11, The Nashville Sessions,* as it was later called, Townes's seventh studio album, was not released until 1993. An acetate John Lomax III covets conveys a different album altogether. The original rough-board mixes reveal a stripped-down rhythm section providing solid support without the excessive overproduction that was added as an afterthought. There was also an earlier version of Townes's "If I Was Washington" (rerecorded in 1994 for *No Deeper Blue*), inexplicably left off the album.

The first glance at Milton Glaser's tormented portrait of Townes for the cover for *The Nashville Sessions* is nothing short of jarring, the visual equivalent of a Sylvia Plath poem. The intense red charcoal on a bright-yellow background screams with all the ferocity of Van Zandt in the depths of alcohol or heroin withdrawal or even Townes in the throes of electric-shock treatment.

"My intent was to capture Townes's intensity and convey emotion with just a piece of paper and charcoal, as directly as I could with a complete lack of artifice," Glaser explained.

Although Milton's illustration packs the punch of German expressionist George Grosz's grotesque art, one must question the handling of Townes's music and image in this manner and wonder if Eggers and company were not trying to intentionally hammer a stake, once and for all, through the anemic heart of Van Zandt's career.

If the objectionable production can somehow be overlooked, it's apparent that *The Nashville Sessions* was filled with great songs. But along with new gems like "The Spider Song" and "Buckskin Stallion Blues" were hackneyed versions of "White Freight Liner Blues" and "Loretta," which both appeared earlier, in more definitive versions, on *Live at the Old Quarter*. "Buckskin Stallion Blues" had been a staple of Townes's live set for the past few years and had become a vehicle for some of Mickey White's best lead work.

"In the late spring of '74 I had moved back down to Texas. By that time, lo and behold, I was a guitar player," Mickey chuckled. "Townes came by Darryl's house soon after and said, 'I'm playin' this gig tonight at the University of Houston. Do you wanna come along and play?' I said, 'Sure.' I already knew all of his songs anyway. So I became his guitar player. We *never* rehearsed. He'd just call a tune, and we'd do it. This was right at the end of his prime when he was still playin' really good."

Just before heading out to the Kerrville Folk Festival in May '74, Townes and Mickey flew back to Tennessee to complete work on the new album. "They left a track open for me on 'Buckskin Stallion,' and that was the first recording I did with Townes," White reminisced fondly.

I was there when the album was cut, and from my perspective, I think it was the one time they produced Townes without really losing him. There is some stunning harpsichord and guitar work on there. Garth Fundis [known lately for his work with Trisha Yearwood] engineered the session. The guy who really produced the album was Chuck Cochran, who also played piano and did all the arrangements and the "monastery"-type backup vocals on "The Spider Song." Guitarist Bobby Thompson played that great lick on "Two Girls," and Joe Allen played bass with Kenny Malone on drums.

(For whatever reason, credits were seldom listed on Van Zandt's Poppy and Tomato recordings.)

"Townes was *really* excited about that album. He was in on every note of it," White emphasized. But a minute later his enthusiasm suddenly waned as he rehashed the debacle over "White Freight Liner Blues."

"I remember disagreein' with the production on it. I know that Townes wanted me to play guitar on that song," Mickey grumbled, "but when I got there, it was already fully produced. There weren't any open tracks left for me to play on."

The song clearly begged for "a Telecaster and a Vibrolux turned up to ten," as John Hiatt sings in his roots rocker "Memphis in the Meantime." But, sadly, "White Freight Liner Blues" was dealt the same bad hand that drives Hiatt out of his mind and out of town, searching for something grittier than the tired old trappings of commercial country music.

Van Zandt's guitar on "White Freight Liner Blues" from *The Old Quarter* album evokes the funky, chugging rhythm of Elvis Presley's "Mystery Train." Yet the version that appeared on *The Nashville Sessions* resembled a square-dance number, complete with cheesy backup singers and a pack of fiddle, Dobro, and banjo pickers that sound like they have no clue what the lyric is about.

"White Freight Liner Blues," an obvious metaphor for the heroin barreling like a semi down the Interstate of Van Zandt's veins, addresses the dangers that he and his pals constantly faced for a brief moment of euphoria.

I'm goin' out on the highway
Listenin' to them big trucks whine
White freight liner
Won't you steal away my mind

It's bad news from Houston
Half my friends are dyin'
White freight liner
Won't you steal away my mind?

The song brought together two of Van Zandt's biggest inspirations—a driving rockabilly rhythm with a blues lyric reminiscent of "Trouble in Mind," a standard in Lightnin' Hopkins' set, in which the Houston blues man sang: "I'm gonna lay my head on some lonesome railroad line / And let the 2:19 pacify my worried mind."

Much like the perplexed man in Robbie Robertson's revamped version of Junior Parker and Sam Phillips's "Mystery Train," who runs down to the station in the middle of the night only to find a ghost train disappearing with his lover on board, something too has been stolen from Van Zandt—his "moment." As Townes sang in "For the Sake of the Song," "moments are rare." Somehow he understood that he would never capture this moment again and that if he grasped it, it would only "turn to butter" in his hands (as he sang in "Lungs").

Call it a case of coulda, woulda, shoulda, but "White Freight Liner Blues," as the Flatlanders, Mudhoney, Lyle Lovett, and dozens of others know (and often rely on to close a night of music on a high note), is a classic of American roots music that reaches back beyond Elvis and Hank Williams to Robert Johnson.

A simple twelve-bar rocker, the song is like a timeless snapshot from Robert Franks's photographic journal *The Americans*. "White Freight Liner Blues" contains the atmosphere of every greasy spoon and truck stop and the blare from every jukebox from every hole-in-the-wall joint from Barstow to Bangor. It's like looking out the window of a speeding car at a blurred, desolate landscape peopled by desperate loners, painted in muted hues by the "Van Gogh of lyrics." Like many others of Van Zandt's best songs, if handled properly, "White Freight Liner Blues" had the mojo that could've put him on the map from coast to coast. But once again, somebody dropped the baby. And like the ex-ballplayer and part-time grave digger Billy Phelan, played by Jack Nicholson in *Ironweed* (one of Van Zandt's favorite books and films that he claimed inspired his song "Marie"), Townes would never quite be the same again.

For whatever reasons, financial, personal, or artistic, Kevin Eggers claimed he didn't release *The Nashville Sessions* for twenty years because he had such "a bad feeling" about it. He was hardly alone.

CHAPTER 16

OF BIBLES, FIDDLES, AND MANGY MOOSE

If he hadn't been a songwriter he probably would've had a good life.
He could have been a brain surgeon.
—Bob Moore

"The record was in the can, and Townes was fully expecting it was gonna be released that fall. That was always the pattern," Mickey White explained.

He'd record in the spring or summer, then go to the mountains, and then tour behind the new album, in the fall. Meanwhile, Wrecks was tryin' to pull up [kick] off heroin and was playing bass with his brother at the Rocket Lounge out in Kemah, Texas. He'd gotten pretty good, having played with Lightnin'. Townes came back in September of '74, and we put a band together and had some promo pictures made. I called the Earl of Old Town in Chicago and the Rubaiyat in Dallas and put a little tour together. At that point we were making around five to seven hundred bucks for a four-night stint.

The week before we went on the road, we were sittin' around the Truxillo house when up comes Johnny Guess (a.k.a. Jimmy Joe Wanker) drivin' a brand-new motor home. This was during the Arab oil embargo, and the price of motor homes had plummeted, so Johnny picked this thing up really cheap. Townes immediately cornered Johnny and threatened him. "Look," he told him, "you're gonna take us on the road and be our road manager." Johnny's official job was to drive the motor home that

we called "the Blue Unit." He had a way of walking into a club and immediately pissing off every soundman.

So we took off on the road to Chicago, and I'm finally livin' the dream.
The tour was goin' pretty good for a while when along about Springfield
[Illinois], the first of the fights started up. The first one was between
Johnny Guess and Wrecks. Townes had to break it up. Then Townes and
Wrecks got into it after Wrecks threw one of his Bibles out the window.

Over the years Townes had become quite a connoisseur of the good
books that Gideon so generously left in every motel night-table drawer
from Maine to California. If the cover was odd or unusual in any way, or
a different color than the standard black, he'd immediately snap it up for
his collection. "That's what they're there for," Townes would point out.
"You're *supposed* to take them."

"He knew the Bible pretty well," Jeanene said. "Townes read all the
time, usually three books at once—anything from Larry McMurtry to
Louis L'Amour to Lin Carter, *Black Elk Speaks,* e.e. cummings, and Tennessee Williams. He preferred westerns, but if there wasn't anything else
around, he'd open up the Bible."

J. T. remembered his dad "lying in bed all day long and reading.
Though Townes wasn't very religious, I think he took his own ideas
from the Bible. He read it cover to cover a dozen times," he said.

At the end of Town Park Drive in Nashville (where Townes and
Jeanene moved in 1987) was a big field where the Southern Baptists held
their annual revival meetings. On the third anniversary of their return,
Townes walked in and announced to Jeanene, "It's time to load up them
Bibles, babe." They then emptied their basement of all the good books
Townes had collected over the years and stacked them in the back of the
Oldsmobile, drove over to the revival tent, and quickly dumped them on
a corner of the stage. Laughing like maniacs, they ran back to the car and
drove home as fast as they could.

Just before leaving on the "Blue Unit Tour," Townes met Cindy Morgan of Conroy, Texas, who was just sixteen at the time. "We're all sitting
around that morning at the Truxillo house when here comes this tall redhead," Mickey White recalled. "A few moments later Townes and this
pretty girl disappeared into the back, and we're all sittin' there just
shakin' our heads. He was one woman-gettin' son of a gun. Check out
the lyrics to 'Rake' when he sings: 'Whisperin' women how sweet did
they seem / Kneeling for me to command them.' It's really true, man,"

Mickey said with a grin. "Wrecks would say, 'If fifty women lined up for Townes, he was sure to get one of them.' And I was the one that would get skunked," White groaned. (Van Zandt often teased Mickey, calling him "Egg White, 'cause he'd only been laid once.)

Although Van Zandt's charisma attracted willing women by the score, Townes, when married, did his best to honor his vows no matter how desire wreaked havoc on his gentlemanly sense of decorum.

Chip Phillips recalled a wild scene in the early eighties:

All these women in the place were falling in love with Townes. They were melting into the wall, crying at the beauty of his poetry. There was a long line of women who, one by one, came up to him to express how much they loved his poetry while puttin' the moves on him. I guess they didn't realize that Jeanene, who was sitting beside him and pregnant with Will at the time, was his wife. And Townes, who was always the perfect southern gentleman, said, "I'm real flattered, but this is my wife, and she's pregnant, and her name's Jeanene." And then the next girl would come up and say, "You're so great. What are you doin' later?" And he'd say, "I'm real flattered, but this is my wife." It happened over and over and over again."

One night in Nashville the competition between the ladies reached a fever pitch. "There were girls literally fighting over Townes," Phillips chuckled. "David Olney and I had to pull him out to the car, 'cause these girls were fighting over him, goin' 'Hey, he's with me.' 'No, he's goin' home with me.' And Townes said, 'I'm not goin' home with *anybody!* Get me outta here!' They were literally pullin' at him. It was like a scene from *A Hard Day's Night,* and it was all because of the beauty of his poetry."

"Oh, women used to flock to him in droves," Jeanene said, rolling her eyes. "The first thing that had to go out the door when I met him was jealousy; otherwise, I never would have survived the relationship."

Chip's ex-wife Bidy was so obsessed with Townes that some considered her the original "Townes Van Zandt–gelist." "Bidy was in rehab, and they were trying to help her, but she kept goin' on and on to the shrink about Townes," Phillips recalled. "It was like 'Townes Van Zandt this and Townes Van Zandt that, and you just don't understand Townes Van Zandt! You've never met him. You've never seen him. So you don't know.' The shrink, frustrated with trying to get through to her, finally decided to go see Townes for herself. So they go to see Townes play a gig, and the shrink falls in love with him! . . . The next time Bidy's got a therapy session all the shrink wants to do is talk about Townes. Bidy's tryin' to talk to her, and she says, 'So, uh, tell me about this Townes Van Zandt guy . . .'"

"All the guys wanted to be like him, and all the girls wanted to be with him," Jeanene said.

"Yup," Chip agreed, "that's pretty much the way it was. It wasn't like he was tryin'. He'd just be playin', and suddenly some guy would be up in his face 'cause his girlfriend had fallen in love with his poetry and thought she was in love with the man behind it."

Townes told columnist and author Cynthia Heimel he first met Cindy Morgan in Houston, where he claimed that she picked him up. "One night, in the middle of a set, his guitar player leaned over and whispered, 'Cindy's only sixteen, y'know.' He recovered from the shock, married her anyway, even though he was thirty at the time," Heimel wrote.

Although Townes had already written "No Deal" a few years before meeting his teenage bride-to-be, Van Zandt described the sticky situation that both he and Jerry Lee Lewis found themselves in, either having to marry the girl or wind up doing time for messing around with jailbait.

When true love knocked upon my door
She'd just barely turned fifteen
And I was a little bit nervous
If you know just what I mean

But I've heard somewhere
That true love conquers all
And I figured that was that
Then I started having dreams 'bout
Being chased out of town
Wearing nothing but my cowboy hat

"By this time Townes had reached the end of his artistic and professional peak," Mickey White claimed.

Anyone that insanely creative can only keep writing that heavy for so long, and his alcoholism had physically started to catch up with him, and his career began to fizzle out. Everything seemed to get a lot harder for him. Townes tried to get tour support and advertising for the gigs. He clearly understood what promotion was about. He was loyal as the day is long and was still wonderin' when the new album was goin' to come out.

At first the gigs were good. We played the Earl of Old Town, Instant Karma, and Charlotte's Web in Rockford, Illinois. Then we came back down to Houston and played the Sweetheart of Texas and Castle Creek in Austin. Townes had brought a fiddle along with him on that tour. He wanted to learn how to play, but it became really frustrating for him. And, of course, we picked on him unmercifully. We used to call him "Papa John Screech."

Eventually his playing kind of turned into a Jack Benny routine. But the difference between Townes and Jack Benny was that Jack Benny could actually play the violin. He even stole Jack Benny's old line: "This is a Stradivarius. If it's not, I'm out fifty bucks."

Throughout his career Van Zandt experimented with a variety of instruments, from saxophone to trombone, banjo, and fiddle. Different tunings or tones often lead a songwriter to an unusual melody or a set of chord changes they might not have discovered on their primary instrument. Although Townes claimed the five-string banjo had inspired "Tecumseh Valley," he never played it much after writing the song.

"Oh, his fiddle playing was *bad,*" Jeanene groaned. "It was like creaking insanity. I used to revel in the demise of each fiddle. Somehow he managed to kill them all."

"Townes wound up smashing several fiddles in my sight. I guess it was his way of keeping the fiddle makers in business," Ruester Rowland quipped. "He really loved the sax, but he used to drive people nuts honkin' on it. There were times when he wanted to be Mick Jagger or Keith Richards, but thirty minutes later it would be Yusef Lateef. It was all part of his spontaneity," Rowland imparted. "He probably would have used a foghorn on a song if it seemed unreasonable enough."

"In Fort Worth there was this horrible hamburger joint called the Hop that we played for three nights," Mickey White recollected.

They didn't have a dressing room, so we parked the Blue Unit behind the club and hung out in there between sets. On the last night Townes got completely looped. He wanted to make a point and squander the gig 'cause he never wanted to go back there again. Nobody liked us. The manager hated us. The oil embargo was goin' on at the time, and there was a lot of anti-Arab sentiment around. So Townes took this checker-board tablecloth and wrapped it around his head [like a kaffiyeh] and pulled out the fiddle. If he took it seriously, his playing was passable at best. He could almost play "Dead Flowers."

One by one, we all left the stage with our instruments. That's when he decided to stand on his head and play "Farewell to Tarwathe" behind his back with this thing over his head. I'm sittin' there with my cousin who I haven't seen in years, trying to explain to him that Townes was in fact one of the greatest songwriters of the twentieth century. Meanwhile, the manager was in the back shakin' his head.

Well, Wrecks and Johnny Guess were out in the Blue Unit smoking a joint, and lo and behold, three cop cars converge on them all at the same time. They see a lid [an ounce of pot] sitting on the dashboard. So now they've got probable cause and start searchin' the motor home. Sure enough, they open up a little drawer, and there's a spoon with some cotton and a little rig sittin' in there. Double trouble! Johnny Guess, I love him to death, but he was the most obnoxious, tactless person I know. But for some reason he could talk to a cop like nobody I'd ever seen. He took the cops aside and said, "Look, I was in trouble with this stuff, but I pulled up, and these guys gave me a job as their road manager and saved my life. I'd be *dyin'* if it wasn't for these guys, man. I forgot it was in there. I swear. Whatever you can do for me on this, I'd really appreciate it fellas . . ." So they gave us thirty minutes to get out of town.

Meanwhile, Townes is still playin' the fiddle, and everybody has cleared out except me and my cousin. By now the manager is scowling. Johnny Guess and Wrecks come runnin' in the back door shoutin', "We got thirty minutes to get out of town or WE'RE ALL GOIN' TO JAIL!" They start packin' up as quick as they can. As I was the business manager for the band, I go over to the club owner and say, "Look, man, we need to get paid right away." I think he owed us a few hundred, but he saw how desperate we were and only offered me one.

So there we were, it was one in the morning, and we're being escorted to the city limits by a cop car and my cousin, to make sure we got to the edge of town. As soon as we reached the city limits the cop peeled off back to Fort Worth, my cousin peeled off toward Arlington, and we were on our way again.

As they say, you win some, you lose some, some get rained out, and some should never have been scheduled. *The Hop should never have been scheduled.*

By the winter of '74–'75, Townes had seriously begun to lose heart. There were no tours and no money for promotion coming from New York. And it was obvious the new album wasn't about to be released any-time soon.

"At that point we were just bookin' gigs to try and stay alive," Mickey admitted. "I got us a two-week gig at the Mangy Moose, a ski lodge in Jackson Hole, Wyoming, that I had played before with Mickey Clark. So I booked a winter tour around that gig, which included dates at the Ox-ford Hotel in Denver, the Grubstake in Crested Butte, and the Pioneer Inn in Nederland, Colorado."

As depressing as it was for Townes to get up on stage every night for two weeks at the Mangy Moose, he did his best to entertain the throng of vacationing families and ski bums who cared more for the party than the poetry. Frustrated by the scene, Townes was more than happy to trade sets with Mickey and Wrecks (who'd begun to develop a repertoire they soon performed as the Hemmer Ridge Mountain Boys [HRMB]). Richard Dobson, who would join the crew, also claimed to have gained some valuable stage experience at the time, filling in for Van Zandt.

"Me and Wrecks had begun to sing harmonies and play together, and Townes began handin' over more and more of the show to us," Mickey recalled. "We'd do stuff like 'What's Your Sign?' and 'Pig Latin.' We were the circus portion of the show. We'd argue about what song we were gonna do next and get into fake fights and do handsprings. Townes would get into it and do a pratfall on his back. One night I told Townes that after the tour we decided we were gonna focus on the Hemmer Ridge Mountain Boys, and he seemed pretty disappointed."

Eventually, the HRMB expanded their lineup to include second gui-tarist Andre Mathews and Mike Edwards on drums and became a viable band that could fill small venues. As Wrecks had previously played bass for Lightnin' Hopkins, the Boys began arranging gigs for him and pro-moted the shows. They would chauffeur Lightnin' to the gig and pay him, which in turn always ensured them of a solid turnout.

"Nobody endured like Townes, who was by turns droll, maudlin, lugubrious, gentle, caring, vicious," Richard Dobson wrote in his journal after flying up from Houston to join the tour, which he chronicled in his memoir *The Gulf Coast Boys*.

As every room at the Mangy Moose had been booked in advance and the management was not expecting Townes to arrive with such a large posse, Van Zandt and company were forced to hole up in the Blue Unit, huddled night after night around a butane heater with all the windows steamed over.

Dobson described the disheveled motor home on New Year's Day 1975 as "a shambles with coats, boots and sweaters piled everywhere. A stale effluvia of whiskey, cigarette butts, and flat cokes permeated the air."

Once again Townes had brought Cindy along with him on the tour. "All the guys resented that she'd come along, so Wrecks called up his girlfriend, Mary Dailey, who flew in and joined him, and Johnny Guess called his girl too. If I had had one I would've called her," Mickey chuckled. "Well, it was forty below outside with ten feet of snow, and everybody had cabin fever. It was a crummy gig, so we just sat around the motor home all day gettin' blitzed. What else was there to do?"

Even "the eternal brooding presence of the mountains," as Ricardo poetically described the ominous snow-laden Grand Tetons, had begun to wear on everyone's nerves. Finally, Townes let Cindy have it: "I'm gonna get another advance and fly your stupid ass home," he snarled at her. "It was Townes," Dobson pointed out, "who asked us to quit calling Cindy stupid. A Texas state–ranked champion in horse-jumping competition, Cindy wasn't exactly stupid. She only just turned seventeen and was running with a rough crowd. She liked to stay stoned and she talked only to Townes, ministering to him and hanging on with both arms around him, kind of like he was a horse," Ricardo wrote. "I always felt sorry for Townes's women with all they had to put up with."

On the morning of January 14 everyone piled into the motor home with Johnny Guess behind the wheel of the Blue Unit and headed off into a blizzard with a tape of Robert Johnson's *King of the Delta Blues Singers* playing repeatedly, an ominous soundtrack as they tooled along through the treacherous, winding roads of Wyoming.

"The weird got weirder that afternoon," Richard Dobson scribed in his journal, recalling the bizarre scene that took place after Mickey impaled Townes's stuffed dog, Spot, with a steak knife. "Townes became unglued, his face twisted in a mask of anguish," Dobson wrote. For whatever reason, Wrecks took full blame for Mickey's sick joke, while White sat silently watching the drama unfold.

"How could you kill Spot? You might as well put a knife in me," Van Zandt said, despondent, as tears welled up in his eyes.

Mickey White offers a somewhat different take on poor Spot's demise:

By the time we reached Crested Butte, things got completely ridiculous. He'd sit there holding Spot and give him little drinks of whiskey. We got so sick of hearin' about Spot. Townes was sittin' up in the front, in one of the captain chairs of the Blue Unit, when Wrecks impaled Spot with a steak knife and then came up behind him and dropped it over his shoulder. Townes looked at Spot and leapt out of his chair yelling, "Who did this?!" Wrecks screamed, "I did, motherfucker!" And they started goin' at it. Me and Johnny Guess had to break them up. Later on, Wrecks and Johnny Guess got into it. We were walking up to the motor home when Townes opened the door and Wrecks fell out, sayin', "Johnny Guess, he's threatenin' to kill me. He's got a knife!" He looks up and sees Johnny, who screams, "I still got it!" Townes reached up and caught his wrist with the knife in midstroke. Everything just stopped, and Johnny Guess dropped the knife.

With a week off before the gig at the Oxford Hotel the crazed crew of the Blue Unit cruised into Denver and crashed at some friends' house where they immediately blew all their money on heroin. "Excess for its own sake had achieved a momentum all its own," Ricardo observed.

"It was a two-night gig," Mickey recalled. "On the second night we got up to do 'Dead Flowers' with Townes on fiddle and Johnny Guess joinin' us on guitar. The gig hadn't been goin' that well. There were about fifteen people in the place. Suddenly, Townes stopped in the middle of the song, dropped the fiddle on the floor, and stomped it to splinters."

"One time in Madison, Wisconsin, he tipped a pizza delivery boy by givin' him his fiddle 'cause nobody could stand the way he played it," Ruester Rowland recalled.

"That was a weird sound, a man stomping on a violin—kind of like a delivery truck runnin' over a turtle. Townes picked up some pieces of the fiddle and tossed them out among the audience like party favors or Mardi Gras beads," Dobson recalled.

"He was *the world's worst fiddle player*," Wrecks declared. In Bell's version of the story, Van Zandt was scratching his way through Hank Williams's "You Win Again" when "all of a sudden he just stomped it into a hundred pieces. Every time he destroyed one I faced East and thanked someone. Once at Uncle Seymour's house this girl handed Townes a brand-new fiddle and without sayin' a word he walked over to the charcoals that were just getting ready for the goat that Townes bought for the picnic and laid it on them. It smoldered for a few seconds and then burst into flames. He liked to shock people, whether on or off stage."

"While the Mangy Moose was bad, the Grubstake was horrible, just ridiculous . . . ," Mickey White groaned.

Next we played the Pioneer Inn in Nederland, Colorado, where we stole the bartender and took her back to Texas with us. That spring Kevin was up and runnin' again, trying to get somethin' goin'. Kevin had taken up with Giorgio Gomelsky, who he hoped would help hustle up some money. [Gomelsky was the manager-producer of the Yardbirds who formed the short-lived Utopia Records with Eggers.] Kevin's expertise was in movin' money around, hustlin' it up, and coverin' it, and that's how he kept Poppy afloat, but it finally caught up with him. They were trying to bail out Poppy and rebuild it. Essentially, the idea was to create a new Liverpool and capitalize on the Texas songwriter scene with Don Sanders, Rocky Hill, and Townes. I'll never forget Giorgio, Kevin, and Townes sittin' in the back of the Blue Unit talkin' about their game plan. Townes was up for it—he wanted his album to get out. But whatever money they had went into Rocky Hill. They cast their lot with him. He finished his album, but it never came out. *The Nashville Sessions* never came out, and Don Sanders never even got recorded. The whole thing just fizzled out by spring of '75.

"Townes and Kevin were partners and friends. They had creative differences," White allowed. "But when Kevin couldn't follow through with his business commitments, Townes got his feelings hurt. He took it personally, but he never said a word about it to me. While driving from Texas to Vancouver, through all those long, lonely nights, across stretches of desert, he never bitched about Kevin once, not at all. Townes *never* felt that Kevin screwed him over. He thought he just didn't handle the business very well."

"It was mismanagement as well as bad choices on his part," Nina Leto concurred.

Kevin was always goin' in sixteen different directions at once—between jazz, blues, gospel, Phillip Glass, Jon Hassel, and John Cage. He was always frantically trying to get something to happen. There was so much anxiety. One day he came into the office with no shoes on his feet. He had left them in Long Island and spent the whole day walking around barefoot. People were always calling, wanting to get paid. But Kevin had a vision that was more powerful than such mundane matters. It became depressing to work [at Tomato] because it was always going down the tubes. Townes was taken in by Kevin who was so complimentary towards him and revered him. He thought that Townes was a legend, and he was. It's just that nobody else knew it at the time.

"Townes's business was goin' out the window. The gigs sucked. He started losing interest in bein' good, in bein' the great Townes Van Zandt, and he became careless," Mickey White said. "He was drivin' around the country with a band full of lunatics. His guitar player's gonna quit. The bass player stabbed his dog! He was just really, *really* disappointed. As far as women went—Townes would constantly test their loyalty and patience. He gave Cindy a lot of shit. She was young, vulnerable, and quite frankly didn't have the candlepower that Townes had, and he'd remind her constantly of that."

CHAPTER 17

BOONDOCK RHAPSODY

I think he had a real ambition to escape society. He would have loved to have lived unknown out on a ranch and had a happy family up in the mountains somewhere.
—JTVZ

I nearly became a hillbilly. I got out in the nick of time.
—TVZ

By the late sixties and early seventies it seemed like "moving to the country" was the all-purpose answer for a generation disgusted by urban decay, disillusioned with the corruption of Nixon, and freaked out by the horrors of the Vietnam War. The Foxfire book series and magazines like the *Whole Earth Catalog* and *Mother Earth News* extolled the virtues of the back-to-the-earth movement with "how to" articles on everything from canning fruit and vegetables to animal husbandry and building your own solar-powered geodesic dome. California blues rockers Canned Heat hit the Top Twenty with "Goin' Up the Country," encouraging everybody to quit "fussing and fighting" and permanently drop out of the rat race. Taj Mahal's funky "Think I'll Move Up to the Country and Paint My Mailbox Blue" longed for an ecological paradise "where there ain't no doggone smog around," while Joni Mitchell's utopian anthem "Woodstock" prescribed the best way to get your "soul free" was to simply "live out on the land."

Of course, those migrating to greener pastures soon discovered a whole new set of unexpected challenges awaiting them. Droves of middle-class refugees suddenly found themselves living rough, in the splendors of nature, with none of the conveniences of the modern suburbs they'd grown up with. The reality of running to the outhouse on a freezing-cold winter night was hardly as "poetic" as it first seemed. With no water heater, the simple pleasure of taking a bath became a chore of fetching and heating buckets of steaming-hot water. As the nearest Laundromat was miles away and having either a small generator or no power at all to run an electric washer and dryer, blue jeans and flannel shirts would hang for days on clotheslines until they finally dried, mildewed and stiff as cardboard. Yet all the hassles of country life would melt away with one whiff of the sweet perfume of a pine forest or the sight of the night sky spilling a million sparkling stars across your eyes.

Richard Dobson recalled driving David Olney twenty miles outside of Nashville, down a muddy road, to see Townes's thirty-dollar-a-month shack in Franklin, Tennessee: "It had two rooms—just bare walls and a tin roof. There was a kitchen in the back with a table and a sink with no running water—you had to draw it from the well. There was a porch in front with a swing, which was nice in the summer. Darryl Harris and I helped him dig the hole for the latrine, which was situated up on the side of a hill."

But on their way back to town, Olney, bewildered by the squalor in which he found the great singer-songwriter living, confided to Dobson that the farm looked like "something out of *Hee-Haw.*"

Van Zandt's attempt to live back in the woods with as little as possible was not merely a cop-out by someone who couldn't cope with the modern world. Townes had a strong connection to nature and the cowboy spirit. He loved to take off into the wilderness on his horse. With a jug of water and a couple slabs of jerky, he'd build a fire and make himself at home wherever he went.

"The promise of a song like 'Home on the Range' not only meant that you could feel at home not just anywhere in the entire state of Texas but that anywhere could be your home, not just physically but spiritually. You could live off the land, even if you had no house or address," David Amram explained. "The Kerrville Festival, where Townes played year after year, put a lot of people in touch with that spirit. Even though performers were provided with motel rooms, they often preferred to camp out in tents, or lie in the back of a truck or in the grass and sleep out under the open sky."

"It was natural for Townes to want to live out in the country," David continued.

In his heart, like with so many Texas songwriters, as well as many middle-class Texans who live in big cities, that went to big colleges and have all the trappings of modern life, there was still a strong connection to what folks on the eastern seaboard call "roughing it." For many Texans, "roughing it" means getting back to the nitty-gritty and living like a cowboy or pioneer or the immigrants who survived off the land. In Townes's case moving to the country wasn't a trendy or political thing at all. It was simply a way to get back in touch with nature and his own heritage and roots, which is a very Texas thing.

On his travels through Mexico in the 1950s, Jack Kerouac had witnessed the plight of present-day Indians living hand to mouth. He observed that although poor, they still possessed an indomitable spirit that stretched back to their Mayan ancestors. Jack referred to them as "the *fellaheen,*" an Arabic term for peasants that he picked up from Oswald Spengler's *Decline of the West*.

"The fellaheen did not worship poverty or glamorize suffering by any means, but rather understood that there's a beauty to it that you must rejoice in. I think that Townes managed to do that as well," David imparted.

Chip Phillips originally found the farm in Franklin, Tennessee. "This guy named Bobby Walker was livin' there and told me and my wife Bidy about it," Phillips recalled.

Townes didn't have much money at the time and had moved to Nashville with Cindy and begged me to let them have it. I turned it over to him so he wouldn't have to spend a lot of time hunting around looking for a place. It was a really big spread, on some eight hundred acres of undeveloped land. It was overgrown and run down and in need of a lot of work. Michael Ewah [described as either half-Japanese/half–Native American or Inuit] moved into the big farmhouse after Bobby moved out and was the "caretaker." But nobody was really takin' much care of it.

"It's real pretty, it's not like living in Nashville and it's only sixteen or seventeen miles away. It's real easy to go in everyday, but you're not in the smog, you're just not in the city," Van Zandt told *Omaha Rainbow*.

Although Townes's cabin had no plumbing or phone to begin with, it did come equipped with a wood-burning stove. Townes soon found the job of keeping warm absorbing an enormous amount of his time. "It was real cold last winter. The fuel is wood and for a month or two, eighty percent of my energy went into [chopping and hauling] wood. I had dreams about wood at night," Van Zandt joked.

In 1975 Steve Earle and Chip Phillips both worked for the Lamar Sign Company, giving them access to a surplus of billboard materials. As Townes's cabin was not insulated, the cold wind blew straight through its rickety walls. In lieu of traditional padding, Chip and Steve arrived one afternoon and pasted festive scenes of Christmas carolers to the kitchen walls, while in Townes's bedroom they plastered a giant glass of vodka above his bed.

Journalist Lola Scobey in her liner notes to *Flyin' Shoes* described Van Zandt's rustic palace as "truly beautiful. The kitchen table is a slab of wood gently swaying on chains hooked to the ceiling. One wall is papered with red foil Christmas wrap and one with a giant poster of earnest carolers fa-la-la-ing away."

"Beautiful" or not, the rural life gave Townes a feeling of being "more settled." He felt as though he could finally put some roots down and perhaps, at last, become successful in the music business. "Of course, if there wasn't any public I'd be all right," he told British journalist Edwyn Pouncey of *New Musical Express,* claiming he could always hunt his own food and subsist off deer and rabbit meat.

"I can hit a deer in the eyeball at a hundred yards," Townes boasted. "I can get the proper amount of money for the skin and I know exactly how to cut it. I'm a friend of the fleet deer and the silver raccoon. So, my family and friends are not going to starve and I don't care about no car. If I have to move back to the mountains tomorrow, no sweat, let's go."

Townes expounded on his philosophy on the sacredness of hunting to Bill Flanagan years later in *Musician Magazine:* "The Indians say every animal you ever shoot, if you don't use every bone, every feather, every marrow and every flesh, you have to carry it on your back to get into heaven."

But it was actually Townes's dog Geraldine who proved to be the best hunter in the family. At night she'd track down the neighborhood possums and leave her kill as an offering for Townes to find on the doorstep the following morning. He soon became quite skilled at skinning and selling their pelts for two bucks a piece. But if there were no raccoon or possum to be had, then a trip to Nashville's Parthenon was in order. On more than one occasion Townes was said to have been seen lurking about with designs on the ducks that flock around the pond at Music City's own replica of the gleaming-white marble temple dedicated to the virgin goddess Athena of ancient Greece.

Daily episodes of craziness and debauchery just came with the territory at the Franklin farm. Richard Dobson recalled the "semidangerous-when-drinking" Michael Ewah: "He was an outdoorsman and knew about raptor birds. They were all shooting guns and drinking whiskey, living a Daniel Boone kind of fantasy. Townes liked telling everyone that they were 'living off the land.' There were a couple of turtle ponds on the Franklin property," Dobson continued.

Townes told me that he and Michael Ewah had been shooting and eating the turtles: stewed, barbecued, and fricasseed. It was all a joke. Nobody was eating game when I was there, though I heard later that Michael killed a big deer. He would do just about anything Townes egged him on to do, like wrestling the refrigerator. Townes would shoot arrows off into the woods and tell Michael to go fetch them back, like a retriever. Ewah was just one example of the kind of people drawn to Townes or vice versa. He liked to have weird people around to provoke or provide some ready action. He saw them as a source of entertainment, to add to the climate of mayhem, a beggar's banquet about to spiral out of control. Townes liked that kind of scene, which usually revolved around some sort of gambling game. Gambling always bored me for some reason. But one time at the cabin he talked me into flipping coins with him, and I got on a streak and couldn't lose. I wound up winning his saddle. As I was flying back, I had to leave it behind at the cabin when I left. But Townes conveniently forgot it was mine and later told me the hillbillies stole it, along with his shotgun.

Although holed up in the boonies, there was never a dull moment around Van Zandt's "funny farm." Chip Phillips recalled a bizarre scene when he pulled up the driveway one day to the cabin in Franklin and found Townes standing on the porch wearing an aviator cap with a pair of goggles, holding a badminton racket. "What on earth are you doin'?" he asked his friend. "C'mon, you gotta see this," Townes replied. "Hold on, he'll be back in a minute." A moment later a gigantic shiny black beetle, about the size of a golf ball, came dive-bombing straight at Van Zandt's face. He drew the racket back, whacked the nasty insect, and sent him flying nearly thirty feet into the air. "Here, you gotta try this," Townes said, handing Phillips the goggles and racket. A moment later the beetle made a U-turn and was back with a vengeance, only to be sent hurtling into space once more by Phillip's mighty forehand. But beetle badminton and turtle stew were just the tip of the iceberg when compared to the murder of Moe the Rooster.

"Steve Earle and I were out at the house one time when Townes said, 'We gotta kill this rooster. It crows before the sun comes up every morning, and it keeps wakin' us up,'" Chip recalled. "We knew that Cindy loved her chickens and roosters, but Townes guaranteed us that he spoke to her about the matter, and she said it was okay. Besides, they didn't have any money to feed the cats, and they could use the rooster for cat food. Well, Townes wanted us to shoot the rooster, but we weren't gonna do it. And he couldn't do it because his arm was in a cast."

Van Zandt was in no shape to do the deed, as he had broken his right arm riding shotgun with Michael Ewah behind the wheel of his pickup truck. Returning from the liquor store, ripped out of their skulls, Michael suddenly blacked out as they pulled into the driveway of the Franklin farmhouse. Careening over Townes's homemade cattle guard, they crashed headfirst into a tree.

Richard Dobson showed up a couple days later to find Townes "doped up and in considerable pain. He couldn't play guitar and had to go out on the road soon," Dobson recalled.

"Steve finally flushed the rooster out while Townes leaned a shotgun over a fence and shot him," Chip continued with the sad saga of Moe the Rooster.

I was there, ready to administer the coup de grace if it didn't die quickly. So we plucked the rooster, boiled it, and fed it to the cats. They had a lot of kittens at the time. All the while Cindy was still sleeping. So Townes took the rooster's claw and went in their bedroom and said, "Hey, Cindy, Moe wants to say good-bye." Then he pulled on the tendon to make its claw wave at her. Of course, he hadn't made any arrangement with her. He'd lied to us all the time. There was a gun lyin' right beside the bed. When she saw what he'd done she grabbed it and took off after him. Boy, was she hot.

It wasn't long before Van Zandt's guilty conscience got the best of him. He tried to make it up to Cindy by giving her a horse. Nonetheless, Dobson remembers Cindy "always pouting or scowling at Townes." Soon enough, she would take revenge for Moe the Rooster's murder and a hundred other cruel pranks her husband had played on her over the years.

"Did you ever hear about the time that little redhead Cindy hand-cuffed Townes to the tree?" drummer Leland Waddell asked, with a king-sized twang—one part South Carolina, with a dash of Nashville and a whole lotta Texas.

Townes was livin' way out on a farm, right between two liquor stores. One was in Fairview, and the other was in Franklin. Every morning he'd get in his old pickup truck and drive sixteen, seventeen miles, one way to either one, it didn't matter. He'd buy half a pint and then drive back, six-teen, seventeen miles, sit on the porch, and drink that half-pint. When it got gone, he'd get back in his truck again. Instead of buyin' a half a gal-lon, he'd buy a half-pint at a time. That way he'd spend the whole day goin' back and forth. A bunch of us was out there partyin' when he de-cided he was gonna quit drinkin'. We told him, "Sure, Townes, whatever . . . We're goin' to town . . ." He told Cindy, "This is it. I'm really gonna quit now. Why don't you handcuff me to the tree just to make sure that I don't drink?" So she handcuffed him to the tree. [Jeanene Van Zandt claims that Cindy actually chained Townes to the tree, wrapping the chain around his ankle with a padlock.] And we all headed into town. I mean, who wants to be around Townes when he's sober?

We were at this place called the Gold Rush in West Nashville when Cindy comes walkin' in, just as happy as she can be. She was a drinker too. She could put 'em back. She got drunk and went home with one of her girlfriends while he was still handcuffed to the tree out there, all night. The next day we're toolin' around town and see Cindy in the truck here and there. She'd left him, a full twenty-eight hours before she came back—all that night and most of the next day Townes was out there handcuffed to a tree, goin' through the DTs. She had the keys, but she didn't even think about it. Cindy finally went home and let him loose. He jumped in that truck, man, and *hauled ass* to the liquor store, *squallin'* them tires. That was his last attempt at soberin' up for a while.

This was not the only time Van Zandt would have himself chained up like the Wolf Man on a full-moon night, hoping that locks and links of steel might help him beat the dreaded curse of alcoholism. Jeanene recalled when Townes demanded she chain him to their bed years later in 1993:

He said, "Babe, if I'm gonna get better, I'm gonna need to be tied up." Then he came back from the hardware store with a chain that was just long enough to reach from the bed to the toilet. I chained him to our waterbed, which was too heavy for him to pick up or drag or move. I wasn't too hot on the idea. I thought it was ridiculous. It might be bad for the kids to see him that way. After a couple days I decided to set him loose. "Well, I gave it a shot, babe," he said. Then he climbed into the truck and *hauled ass* down to the liquor store.

Although a lethal combination, guns and liquor were an integral part of Van Zandt's nouveau-pioneer lifestyle. "The first time I met Michael Ewah I had just come in from Texas," Dobson recalled. "I had a pint of whiskey with me and brought it out. We just barely had a sip when he grabbed the bottle and chugged the whole thing. I said something to him, and he started snorting and hyperventilating and charged off. I asked Townes, 'What the fuck kind of guy was that?' And he said, 'Michael's crazy. If he comes back with a gun, we're going to have to shoot him.' I said 'He's your friend—you shoot him.'"

"Almost everything about these guys is legend and its useless trying to get them to sort out the truth," Bill Flanagan wrote in an article about Townes and Steve Earle for *Musician Magazine* in which he related a hair-raising tale of gunplay that quickly became part of Van Zandt's legend:

Earle was over at Townes's house, shooting his mouth off and playing with Townes's guns. Townes, who speaks less often than a wooden Indian, got a little tired of the chatter and said, "See, Steve, you don't really understand guns. Let me explain." Townes picked up a pistol, put a bullet in the chamber, spun it around, put it to his head and pulled the trigger. Click. Earle jumped up yelling, "Townes! Cut it out!" Townes said, "See, you *still* don't understand guns." Put in a second bullet, spun the chamber, put it to his head and CLICK. "That's it," Earle said, "I'm not gonna sit here and watch you shoot yourself." And got on his motorcycle and split. Townes got his peace and quiet. If he'd killed himself? He'd have got some peace and quiet either way.

"My son had just been born and was crawlin' around on the bed," Chip Phillips recalled the story firsthand. "Steve was unhappy at the time. He was uptight, twirlin' a 357 Magnum in front of my baby. So I said, 'Oh, man, don't do that.' And he got all mad, sayin', 'I been around guns all my life.' He was upset with me, but I think he was really more angry with himself and realized he shouldn't have been doin' that. Then

I said somethin' to Townes about it. And that's why he did it," Phillips said. "Townes told him, 'You think guns are cool? I'll show you how cool they are, man.' Townes was Steve's hero, and he wanted to make sure he never did anything like that again, so he put some bullets in a gun and twirled the chamber."

"Townes was at his wits end. He couldn't get rid of Steve Earle. They were so ready for him to leave that he started to play Russian roulette," Richard Dobson's ex, Lysi Moore, said with a grin. "They called Steve Earle 'the Kid.' And the way they treated him was great impetus for him to become a great songwriter."

Although Dobson wasn't there, he concurs with Lysi that Townes told him he did it "to run off Steve Earle." Townes had told him, "Steve, a nonstop talker under any circumstance, was wired on speed and pestering him unmercifully. You might say he nearly pestered him to death." At the second click of the pistol, "Steve turned white as a ghost and fled."

"Steve likes the romance of danger but Steve doesn't actually want to die. He'd pull back. Townes might not care," Rodney Crowell later confided to Flanagan.

After Steve split, Townes was apparently so upset that he loaded up the pistol once more and blew his Epiphone to bits. He then offered the mangled guitar to Chip. When Phillips passed on it, he gave it to Michael Ewah. "Darn if Michael didn't patch the thing up," Phillips chuckled.

For years his father remained a mystery to J. T., who lived with his mother and a stepfather and didn't really get to know Townes until the fifth grade. "No one could have lived up to the ideal that J. T. had of Townes," Fran said. "He imagined him to be Elvis Presley or something. He kept his albums like a shrine on the dresser in his room. Townes wanted J. T. to come and stay with him and Cindy at the cabin in Franklin. He was just nine or ten, but I couldn't trust Townes at that time with all the drugs and alcohol. They were drugged out. It was just a horror. I had no idea they were in that condition, or I never would have let J. T. go," Lohr claimed.

"When I got off the plane, I had this picture in mind of a very young Townes who is clean-cut and athletic, and by this time when I saw him, he had long, greasy hair, gold teeth, and he was very skinny," J. T. recalled, flying to Nashville to finally meet his dad for the first time since he was a baby. "I knew it was him, and I was walking towards him off the plane and at the same time I was thinking, 'Oh, my God, what is this? What have I got myself into?" J. T. laughed. "It was quite scary. He was quite mad, you know?"

Townes not only got drunk but also did drugs in front of J. T., claiming he had nothing to hide from his son. In turn, John spent much of his time playing outside in the snow with Geraldine, waiting for Townes to pass out. Only then would he dare to venture back inside. "I felt safe as long as he was asleep," J. T. confessed. "I never tried hard drugs because I saw what they did to him. So in a way he led as an example of what not to do."

J. T. described Geraldine as "the smartest dog I have ever come across in my life. She really saved the trip for me. I was so nervous to be around my dad, but this dog had a natural affection for me, and I truly believe she understood the situation and was trying to ease my nervousness a bit."

What made Van Zandt constantly push himself to such extremes? Was it for the sake of song, or to add another wild story to his crazy ré-sumé of misadventures? Did Townes feel trapped by his legend, by people always expecting outrageous behavior from him if he were to always remain "the troubled genius" in their eyes?

"He knew he was creating a myth," Mickey White said. "I would always be amazed by all these incredible tales Townes told me. Then we'd go out on the road and run into some old friends who would bring up these stories without any prompting, and they were exactly the same word for word. My impression was he really didn't have to make that much up. It was so outlandish in the first place."

But what about such ridiculous and bizarre tales like how Townes supposedly killed a bear with his own hands? "That was a rumor that I started," Van Zandt confessed in *Omaha Rainbow*. "Someone called me one morning when I was staying in Colorado. My friend, Norman, woke me up and said there was a journalist on the phone. I'd just woken up and felt goofy, so I told him I was the local hero 'cause I'd killed a rabid bear. It was 100% bullshit."

Mad mammals aside, throughout his life Van Zandt found himself in plenty of tight spots, mostly due to his out-of-control drinking and gambling. But none of them, however (not even putting up and losing his girlfriend in an Austin crap game), compared to the absurdity of this episode: "Michael Ewah and Townes used to hang out by this tree together behind the house in Franklin. They called it their 'talking tree,'" Jeanene said. "One time they got to gambling, and Townes quickly ran out of money, so he wound up betting his gold tooth. Well, he lost the tooth too. Michael said, 'Man, I *can't* take your *tooth*.' But Townes insisted. He said he'd lost fair and square and demanded that Michael collect on the bet. So like some mad dentist, Ewah put a pair of pliers around Townes's gold tooth, but just as he was about to yank it out, he turned his head to look away at the last moment. The pliers must've slipped off, and somehow he pulled out the wrong one," Jeanene said with a laugh.

"Oh, stuff like that used to happen all the time," Chip groaned.

Townes had decided to pierce his ear, and Bidy wanted the honor of doing it. Well, he gambled her over it, and she won. They were in New York at the time, and he stopped outside of Bloomingdales. He said, "Hold on, I gotta run in here for just a second." He goes into the store, walks up to the jewelry counter, and asks the saleslady for their biggest butterfly brooch. She asked if he'd like to have it gift wrapped, and Townes said, "No, I think I'll just wear it out." Then he stuck it through his ear and goes walkin' out to the sidewalk where Bidy was waitin' for him. She sees this big thing hangin' off the side of his head and he's bleedin' all over the place. "Oh, Townes," she cried. *"I was supposed to do that."*

Yet amid all of his wild antics, Townes somehow managed to write a new batch of songs to add to the handful of unreleased gems from the lost *7 Come 11/Nashville Sessions*. In a newsletter, dated March 21, 1978, John Lomax III informed Van Zandt's die-hard fans that the basic tracks for fourteen songs had been cut and promised a new album would be in stores by May. With Chips Moman producing, *Flying Shoes* would be Van Zandt's first studio album in five long years.

Chips Moman's track record as a writer and producer remains impressive, to say the least. He effortlessly jumped genres from rock and roll to country and soul, and was behind one of Elvis Presley's greatest hit songs, 1969's "Suspicious Minds," as well as "Lukenbach, Texas" for Waylon Jennings and Aretha Franklin's "Do Right Woman." A prime architect of the legendary Stax soul sound, Chips produced records by Booker T and the MGs and Wilson Pickett, as well as Dusty Springfield's classic "Son of a Preacher Man." So both Kevin Eggers and John Lomax III had reason to pin a lot of hope on Moman's ability to work magic at the board on Townes's new album. At last it seemed that Van Zandt's songs might get the proper attention and handling they deserved.

For the *Flying Shoes* sessions Chips brought in a crew of top-shelf musicians that included guitarist Phillip Donnelly, an Irish import to

Nashville, known for his fine fret work with the Everly Brothers (and later Nanci Griffith and John Prine). Also on board were Randy and Gary Scruggs (Earl's boys) on guitar, mandolin, and harmonica along with Muscle Shoals stalwart Spooner Oldham on piano.

But as soon as they'd begun, a series of unexpected delays slowed the album's progress to a crawl. "Everything has gone smoothly as forty miles of speed bumps," Lomax quipped. Townes's strumming hand was still out of commission from the car wreck. Then Chips's wife delivered a baby (Casey Linc Moman on March 16, 1978, to whom the album was dedicated) halfway through the sessions. Meanwhile, Lomax joked, "the boys from the label have all gone bald."

Then there was Milton Glaser's original album cover for *Flying Shoes*. "It looked like a disco album," Nina Leto snickered. "The painting came to the office via messenger, and we all stood around expectedly to see it, and it was all these crazy-looking high heels and platform shoes. It was hysterical. It was a beautiful painting but not fitting for Townes at all," Nina laughed. "Kevin had told Milton that Townes had recorded a new album called *Flying Shoes* and just let him go with it."

In a noble attempt to further Townes's dismal career, Lomax pleaded with fan-club members to hound their local DJs who were content to pump out pureed pop like the Bee Gees, Billy Joel, and the Eagles. John goaded fans to pester local radio stations, suggesting they disguise their voices and request different albums.

"We need new recruits like a bird needs spring, like dry creeks need water, like vampires need fresh blood," Lomax wrote in desperation.

Start bugging sponsors of the station. Tell them you won't be using any of their products and they can go suck frogs until that station yields to overwhelming public demand and plays Townes Van Zandt. Tell them that you will buy six of everything if Townes gets on the air. Bombard your local record dealers; buy hundreds of records each time you go to a store. Wear Townes's name tattooed upon your forehead. Paste his picture on your back. Picket the stations. Write Jimmy Carter and in general make such a nuisance of yourself that a groundswell is created, thus alerting *Time* and *Newsweek* to the case.

Having gotten no response from the established news periodicals, John took out an ad in the then bible of counterculture, *Rolling Stone,* advertising the Townes Van Zandt Fan Club, to which he received nearly two hundred responses in one fell swoop. For just three bucks Lomax guaranteed members they would receive "all sorts of information on a regular basis." Membership fees cost five dollars for Canada, and ten bucks for "the rest of the universe."

Flyin' Shoes kicked off with "Dollar Bill Blues." Built on a lick reminiscent of an old Appalachian fiddle tune, the song contained one of Townes's most bloodcurdling lyrics of all time. It's dark, freaky stuff, like the kind of demented ditty William S. Burroughs might hum to himself while purposely stepping on every crack of a New York City sidewalk.

> Mother was a golden girl
> Slit her throat just to get her pearls
> Cast myself into a whirl
> Before a bunch of swine

The song makes a reference to Harlan County, Kentucky, the same destination the singer of another Appalachian classic, "Shady Grove," is returning to, looking for his true love. But Van Zandt's path is fraught with pitfalls and perils. With "a busted back and heavy load," Townes knows he "won't get there to save [his] soul." The verse ends with the traditional refrain of "early in the morning." But it is not the optimism of dawn that Townes infers here. The bright sun that he finds himself under casts a glaring, cruel light from which he must shield his hungover, bloodshot eyes.

Although Van Zandt found inspiration in and had a great love of traditional songs, he had little or no respect for the "more authentic than thou" stick-in-the-mud traditionalists in the crowd. He often introduced "Dollar Bill Blues" as "the only folk song I ever researched. I learned this from my grandmother," Van Zandt joked. "She told me she learned it from a friend of hers. I went and met her. She's about one hundred and five years old now. She learned it from her brother who's one hundred and ten. I went and met him in north Fort Worth and he learned it from me."

Simultaneously haunted and inspired by the Tennessee landscape, Townes wrote the album's title song while sitting by the Harpeth River where the Battle of Franklin took place. The Harpeth, a favorite canoeing spot for Townes, would also inspire one of his most astonishingly beautiful ballads, "The Catfish Song," which later appeared on *At My Window*.

Although many consider Van Zandt's time in Franklin a period of stagnation in which his alcoholism and drug use eclipsed his musical output, Ruester Rowland took an opposing view: "The time he spent living in the cabin, Townes produced his finest work," Rowland claimed.

Townes would walk out in the woods and soak up the atmosphere, and there were still earthworks out there from the Battle of Franklin. That's where he got the measure of inspiration to write "Flying Shoes." He imagined a miserable, wounded, sick soldier layin' there thinkin', "If I could only put on some flyin' shoes, I'd be out of this place." It's a wish song. But Townes had to have the experience to go out there and soak it up personally in order to imagine being that soldier. Townes first and foremost always considered himself a folksinger, and he understood the folk tradition. Most of his songs were drawn from personal experiences or from secondhand things. That's the reason he needed to live in a place like the farm, in order to write those kinds of songs.

"He did a lot of reading in that period about the . . . ," Ruester hesitated. "We call it the War between the States down here," he said firmly. "He'd soak it all up, and then things came out poetically."

Whether Townes was conscious of it or not, "Flying Shoes" seemed to have its roots in the nineteenth-century gospel tune "Golden Slippers." The song's author, James A. Bland (of Sprague's Georgia Minstrels, who also wrote "Carry Me Back to Old Virginny"), spells out that before entering heaven one must not only be pure of heart, but their "golden slippers must be neat and clean" and their age must be "sweet sixteen."

Whether a pure-of-heart teenage virgin ascending or a young rebel soldier dying on a blood-soaked battlefield, the ultimate destination of heaven is at hand, and the only sure way to glory, it seems, is to be carried on the swift wings of supernatural footwear.

From the opening notes of Spooner Oldham's piano to a trio of gentle, weaving guitars, this is truly one of the finest arrangements of Van Zandt's recorded career. "His melodies were surprisingly interesting and are sometimes overlooked," Robert Earl Keen pointed out. "The chord changes on 'Flying Shoes' always threw me a curve."

Although great songs are in abundance on this album, this time the blame for a lackluster recording cannot be placed on the producer. Townes's delivery is laconic at best. Throughout the album the playing and arrangements are solid, while Van Zandt himself appears to be lost in a fog of vodka.

Many of the album's tunes had been in Townes's repertoire for years before he cut them on *Flying Shoes*. Guy Clark recalled giving Van Zandt a taste of his own medicine one night when he performed "If I Had No Place to Fall" at show in Madison, Wisconsin: "Townes thought he could do pratfalls like Chevy Chase, but he was too drunk to catch himself. He hit the last chord of a song and fell over backwards, and crashed into a straight-back chair, while still holdin' his guitar. He started yellin', 'Is there a doctor in the house? Is there a doctor in the house?' This went on for nearly half an hour, and I gotta go on. I finally leaned over and said, 'Hey, Townes, you okay? 'Yeah, man, I'm alright.'" "Okay, then," Clark replied. "This is for you," Guy said and broke into a rendition of Van Zandt's "No Place to Fall." "I never liked that song anyway. It was the cheapest shot I ever heard," Guy said with a husky chuckle.

With a string of introspective ballads like "Pueblo Waltz," "Snake Song," and "When She Don't Need Me," the album begged for a rocker. That moment came courtesy of Bo Diddley's "Who Do You Love?" The rhythm section finally busts loose, as Bobby Emmons lays down a percolating organ groove and the guitars groan and snarl. Although people tend to peg him as a morose balladeer, Townes was never afraid to grab the bull by the horns and rock the joint.

Like the Grateful Dead's "Sugar Magnolia," who takes the wheel when Bob Weir's eyes see double, or the Band's Sweet Bessie in "Up on Cripple Creek," Van Zandt's "drunkard's dream" is personified by a vision of female perfection named "Loretta." While Sugar Magnolia's "got everything" Weir asks for and Levon Helm hoots the praises of his Bessie who boldly defends him and quickly mends him whenever he springs a leak, the perpetually "twenty-two" Loretta flits about, telling Townes lies he "likes to b'lieve." Compared to the funky rhythm that Van Zandt laid down on *Live at the Old Quarter,* this laid-back version of "Loretta" on *Flying Shoes* sounds pale, more like a lady grasping at her fading youth than a feisty barroom girl who's always has to be on top.

Although still nursing his broken wrist, Townes had little choice but to get back on the road before his career became no more than a memory. But first he needed to find a suitable guitarist who had just the right mix of folk picking and blues twang to cover for him.

"I knew I was gonna play with him before I met him," Ruester Rowland declared. "I was always searchin' for the best songwriter around who had the real stuff. That's one reason I worked with Guy Clark, who called me and asked if I'd consider goin' out to work with Townes. I said, 'Sure.' We had a meeting, and it happened."

John Lomax III would spirit Townes over to Ruester's house for their first meeting. As he walked in the door, Van Zandt spied an old Lightnin' Hopkins album sitting atop a stack of records piled on the living room floor. "You like Lightnin' Hopkins? Good deal," Townes exclaimed. That said, Ruester passed the audition without playing a note. Townes simply took it as a good omen when he saw Hopkins's gold tooth gleaming on the old album cover; besides, Rowland had already toured with and came highly recommended by his buddy Guy and already knew most of Townes's songs, having worn out copies of all of Van Zandt's records.

"It was me, Owen Cody on fiddle, and Jimmy Gray on bass. Townes had broken his arm, so he couldn't play. He would just hold the mike and sing. He was on pain pills, but still continued to drink," Rowland said, aggravated by the memory.

The trio began their tour on April 18 at the University of Iowa as the support act for their fellow Tomato Records label mate John Lee Hooker. It was the chance of a lifetime, not to be missed under any circumstances, although Townes's condition was clearly less than optimal.

Back in Houston, Van Zandt had learned the art of the boozy groove directly from Lightnin' Hopkins himself. Now, hanging with "the Hook," whose driving, hypnotic one-chord blues vamps were the personification of solid cool, Townes was hoping to pick up on a whole new brand of magic. Even if John Lee barely gave him the time of day, Townes still had plenty of mojo of his own—after all, he had Robert Johnson's guitar. Or so he claimed.

Van Zandt once owned a D-35 Martin that someone had customized with mother-of-pearl inlay at the twelfth fret with the initials R. J. Whenever anyone approached him after a show with questions about his songwriting or guitar playing, Townes would confide to them that his ax once belonged to the legendary Delta blues man who fell to his knees at a Mississippi crossroads one full-moon night and sold his soul to the devil.

Halfway through the "Broken Arm Tour," Townes called Cindy, asking her to come along. "They argued all the time, and then they'd kiss and make up," Ruester recalled. "We were all getting on each other's nerves, as you do when you're exhausted and drinkin' on the road. The tour was not conducive to getting any rest or practice in. Most of the time we had to cop it on the fly and improvise," Rowland explained.

"Ruester did a good job of copping Townes's licks that he played on the records," bassist Jimmy Gray recalled. "When I first started playin' with him, Townes was just singin'. Once I finally heard him play, I realized he was a good guitar player. I really think he was best when he was by himself, just him and the guitar. He didn't have to think about what he was gonna do. He just did it. When you got a band with you, you've all got to play together."

"You know that old line of his, 'You've gots to have your dynamics'? Well, Townes dreamed of having a band, but I don't think he really understood dynamics all that well," Rowland grumbled.

While Jimmy and Ruester laid down the rhythm and chords, Townes sat on a bar stool with his eyes shut tight, reciting his lyrics like poetic incantations, casting spells on crowds night after night, across the Midwest, to the East Coast and Canada.

"We were fortunate to have Harry Eggers as a road manager and a driver 'cause he didn't drink. I went a lotta miles layin' in the back of [Townes's truck] the Colonel on sleepin' bags, readin' books and drinkin' beer. It was a lotta fun," Gray recalled fondly.

Whereas Jimmy seemed happy to go along for the ride, Ruester was clearly not amused by Van Zandt's attitude and antics:

Townes didn't promote himself. He didn't even think about it. He didn't bother getting the box of records out of the trunk to sell them. He had no thought at all for the future. Whatever money he had, he'd blow. It all went in his arm or his stomach. He was always givin' money away. One time after a sound check at the Cellar Door in Washington, D.C., he was looking for a place to find a drink when a wino approached him on the sidewalk asking for money for something to eat. Townes knew better. He said, "What you need is something to drink." And took him in the liquor store and bought him a pint of vodka.

After the cast came off, Townes's chops eventually returned. Jimmy Gray stayed on, and soon after Cody returned to Houston and then mysteriously disappeared.

"He said he was headed for Hawaii, but no one ever heard from him again," Rowland claimed. "Cody's wife's brother wanted to kill him and broke his fiddle in hopes of forcing him to quit music and work a regular job as a chef."

"Last time I saw Cody he was in Houston. He either just got married or was just gettin' out of bein' married. I don't remember a hell of a lot," Gray confessed. "We ran so fast and so far."

CHAPTER 18

TRAILER PARK LOVE

Without his mental health problems and drinking
he would have been the perfect man, another Gregory Peck
but with Clark Gable ears.

—Jeanene Van Zandt

In the fall of 1980 Ron McCloud, "a would-be promoter," as Mickey
White described him, booked Townes for a six-week tour of Vermont.
"Around that time Reuster Rowland had enough of the music business
and went back to school, and the Hemmer Ridge Mountain Boys had
also run their course, so Townes asked me to play the gigs. The money
looked pretty good, and we had a place to stay, so I said, 'Sure, man.' Me
and Jimmy Gray drove the Colonel up to Vermont and met Townes to
play six weeks of gigs," White recalled.

It was September when they arrived. The leaves were still green, but as
fall started closing in they began to feel a distinct sense of foreboding. The
first gig had gone well. They split the bill with Billy Joe Shaver in the banquet hall of an old Vermont hotel, playing for about eighty people.

"Townes opened for us. It was a good combination," recalled Leland
Waddell, who played drums for Billy Joe on that tour.

We packed the place out, and the show was over by seven thirty, so we go
back to this old bed and breakfast where we're staying in this little post-
card-village town square. It had a small restaurant and bar. It was the
middle of winter; nobody was staying there. [One thing is clear, whether
it was fall or winter, it was a long time ago, and memories differ consider-
ably.] We were all sober, and the bar was closed. Everything was closed,
and it was cold. So they gave us the key to the bar, and we start shootin'

down the Jack Daniels. We go up to Billy Joe's room and start playin' poker and gettin' loud. The next thing you know we get to hollerin' and jumpin' on the furniture and actin' just as crazy as can be. We were drinkin' everything. Goin' from one bottle to the next. This guy comes up and says, "If you'll please be quiet and not disturb any of our guests, you can drink all you want. You'll have all the free liquor you want." We say, "Well, alright, we'll be quiet." So we get back to playin' cards, and I took all of Townes's money. I took all of Jimmy Gray's money too. So I took all Townes's money and his belt and his shoes, and he says, "One more hand." Once Townes gets into playin' poker, he *will not* let up. I say, "Okay, I'll play you for your shirt, man." The first hand, Wham! I had a full house. He didn't even have the chance to draw, and I had him whipped. He took that shirt off, and I took it. It was the only shirt he had. He's there with his pants and socks. No shoes, no belt, no money, and no shirt. The next mornin' we're rollin' out around nine in the mornin', and here he comes, stumblin' down the damn stairs with his socks on. No shirt and no coat in New England. We were headed back to Boston, and he didn't have fuckin' nothin. I wouldn't let his ass up, and he wouldn't dare ask for it.

"But I finally gave that skinny, shiverin' motherfucker his shirt back. That's the actual truth," Waddell said, howling with laughter.

For Townes's second show McCloud rented a large hall in New Hampshire, but nobody showed up due to a lack of promotion. McCloud still had to pay for the hall nonetheless. "But everything was cool," Mickey said. "We stayed in this old farmhouse, and Ron treated us like kings, keeping us in lobsters and whiskey. When the next gig came up, Ron walked in, shakin' his head. He said, 'Sorry, guys, they called to say the show is canceled.' Same with the next one. We started gettin' pretty nervous, but everything was still alright. We still had whiskey. The lobsters were gone after the first week, but we had chicken."

Luckily, Townes booked a gig in New York. So they jumped in the Colonel and headed down to play Gerdes' Folk City. Van Zandt was finally in his element at the little Greenwich Village club, home to Bob Dylan, Joan Baez, Phil Ochs, and Simon and Garfunkel. The crowd was there for one reason only: Townes Van Zandt had come to town, and they were primed for a night of pickin' and poetry.

"It was one of the high points of my career," Mickey reminisced. "Hittin' New York City with Townes Van Zandt to play a jammed-packed, prestigious room. Wrecks showed up unexpectedly, and there were people from Chicago and different parts of the country. Townes was brilliant that night. His playing was right on the money, and he was really funny. The crowd roared at his stuff. We got really energized by that show."

After a few days in New York the three road warriors triumphantly returned to Vermont. Luckily, the next gig came through, but soon the sight of Ron looming in their doorway meant only bad news. Before he could mutter, "Uh, hey, you guys, uh . . . ," they knew the rest. By now the chicken and whiskey were gone. Sardines and beer were the order of the day. The autumn wind had grown colder. The leaves had turned orange and scarlet and fell to the ground. By the first snowfall it was obvious the rest of the gigs would fall through as well. Each passing day grew gloomier until they bid Ron McCloud adieu and hightailed it south, nearly out of cash and with winter nipping at their heels.

Thankfully, Ron had booked Townes one last gig in Washington, D.C., at a little folk club called Childe Harold. Van Zandt and the boys sauntered in through the door when the bartender looked up, surprised to see them. "Hey, Townes," he called. "What are you doin' here?" Van Zandt replied hesitantly, "Uh, well, we've got a gig." "Uh, not here," the barkeep stammered. After a round of drinks on the house, the desperate trio piled back into the Colonel with just enough gas money among them to make it back to Nashville.

Townes's life was quickly coming unraveled. He was broke after a long, terribly mismanaged tour, and what was left of his marriage to Cindy was in the throes of disintegration. Van Zandt entertained the notion of trying to get back together with her for about a week but soon realized it was hopeless. Having dropped off Jimmy Gray in town, Townes and Mickey beat their retreat back to the Franklin farm, where things quickly went from bad to worse.

"We were wandering around the property threatening the chickens to lay eggs," Mickey said with a laugh.

Townes had a club and was about to whack a bunny when tears suddenly started streaming from his eyes. Right about then, we heard a chicken squawk, so we split the egg with a can of beans that we had. The woodpile was gettin' low, and winter was closin' in fast. We didn't have *any* money, no gigs, no nothin', and we were stuck out there without any gas in the truck.

One Sunday morning a couple hillbillies stopped by, and Townes arm-wrestled one of them for their whiskey. So we had enough whiskey to get by. Luckily, the electricity and phone was still on. We were gettin' really depressed with nothing to do and nowhere to go. What actually saved us was *The Godfather* saga, which we watched on TV for four consecutive nights.

The hapless pair were down to one log with no ax to split it. Just as they were contemplating busting up the furniture for fuel, the phone rang. It was John Cheatem on the horn from Austin. He had just started a new place called You Scream, Ice Cream and wanted Townes to come back and play the grand opening.

"He was gonna fly Townes down, and then he'd come back to pick me up later. I grabbed the phone out of his hand and said, 'Cheatem, you son of a bitch. You called me and hooked me up with this damn tour in the first place, and if you don't get me on a plane back to Austin I swear I'm gonna wring your fuckin' neck the next time I see you,'" Mickey laughed. "So Cheatem coughed up two tickets, and Lomax had to drive out to give us a couple dollars so we could buy enough gas to drive the truck over and leave it at his house."

Some might say it was fate or perhaps it was just the percentage of available consenting adults in a small Texas town, but when John Cheatem went to pick up Townes and Mickey at the airport that day he happened to meet a girl named Gradi Sterling. Gradi was waiting to pick up her friend, who was on the same flight as Townes, sitting beside him. In the meantime Gradi's friend and Townes had hit it off and decided to get together after landing in Austin. Meanwhile, Gradi and John had paired up.

The next morning Townes awoke in the woman's bed to find a couple of kids running around the house. "Uh . . . where's your husband?" Van Zandt asked hesitantly. "On a gun run down to Mexico," she replied. That was all Townes needed to hear. He pulled on his boots, grabbed his hat, and was gone a minute later.

It was November 1979, when Van Zandt and White returned again to Austin to discover a little folk-music revival in full swing. Between Spellman's, the Alamo, the Other Side, the Outhouse, and John Cheatem's new joint, there was actually a possibility of making a living, or something pretty darn close to it.

"It was great," White enthused. "You could pass the hat at Spellman's, make a hundred bucks, and get free food. We came back, and Townes was a star. Blaze [Foley] had moved up from Houston. Jimmie Dale Gilmore and Butch [Hancock] were around as well. Lucinda [Williams] was playing and gettin' a lot of attention, as well as my soon-to-be wife Pat Mears."

Having survived exile in Vermont and near starvation in Tennessee, things were actually beginning to look up for Townes and Mickey. "At least we were eatin'," White laughed. "Then somebody in the family gave Townes a white Ford sedan, which we drove back to Tennessee to retrieve the Colonel. So we caravanned back to Austin, talkin' back and forth over the CBs the whole way."

In the meantime, Mickey had perfected his pool game to where he could actually hustle a couple bucks. He was just about to sink the eight ball for a dollar when he heard the news that John Lennon had been murdered outside his home in New York City. "I went ahead, made my shot, and made my crummy dollar," White confessed.

Shocked and bewildered, Mickey headed over to a South Congress club where a throng of pickers and singers gathered to pay homage to the bespectacled ambassador of peace and love. "I just played my way through the night," Mickey sighed. "Townes wasn't a huge Lennon fan, but he knew I was. I think he was more worried about how his friends were handling it."

The following night Townes Van Zandt would meet Jeanene Munsell.

"I wasn't quite sure what it was, but somehow I saw somethin' there. Townes was *totally* different from anyone she'd dated before," Gradi Sterling said. Gradi, who had rescued Jeanene from her former old man at gunpoint just a few months earlier, kept telling her friend about a guitar-playing pal of Cheatem's who she thought was "just perfect" for her. "Jeanene said, 'He's a FOLK MUSICIAN? Are you CRAZY?' "I said, 'Look, girl, I'm tellin' you.' Jeanene is *very much* a character, a real spitfire," Sterling said. "She is who she is, and she changes for no one. She's also a helluva good storyteller. I think that's where they really connected. They were always trying to outdo one another with stories."

On December 9, 1980, there was a candlelight vigil for Lennon at Austin's Zilker Park. Along with three hundred stunned and grieving Beatles fans, Gradi and Jeanene stood holding hands in the cool December night air, singing "Let It Be" (even though it's a Paul McCartney song). Straight across from Jeanene stood her ex-boyfriend with his new girlfriend sporting a fur coat. Fuming, she turned to Sterling and said, "Where the hell is that guitar player you been tellin' me about?"

"Nanci Griffith happened to be playing at You Scream, Ice Cream that night, so we went down there, and before you knew it Townes asked Jeanene if she liked to gamble, and they started playin' a couple hands of kissy-face poker," Gradi recalled.

The way Jeanene recalls the scene, Townes was surrounded by a handful of pretty girls when she came sashaying through the door. Ever the gentleman (with an eternal roving eye), Townes stood up, tipped his hat, and said, "Pardon me, ladies," and sauntered over to Ms. Munsell's table. Van Zandt's pickup lines, like his jokes, were awful but always managed to work. Townes pulled out a chair, threw his long leg over it, and plopped down. "Hey, darlin'," he said with a big grin, looking her up and down. "Do you gamble?"

"I took one look at him and said, 'I must,'" Jeanene laughed.

"Well, I got three cards here. Whoever gets the queen of hearts has to kiss the other one," Townes said, explaining the rules of his obvious ploy.

"We played cards for about half an hour and then went out for a night of clubbing. He was a wee bit gamey and in need of a bath," Jeanene said.

In a dark corner of Austin's famous Continental Club, Munsell suddenly recalled where she'd seen her future husband before. At the time she'd been into bands like Journey as well as new wave and punk rock. "I wasn't too up on folk music," Jeanene admitted. "I thought it was something you had to wear a costume for." It was then she remembered where she'd first seen this lanky, charming stranger. He was that folksinger she heckled to "get the hell off the stage" seven years earlier at the Armadillo World Headquarters so that bluesman Taj Mahal could get his mojo workin'.

Jeanene claimed her first date with Townes was so strange that she "went home and took some acid just to feel normal again." "Although we slept together I absolutely refused to have sex with him until he had a bath," she said, recalling that long week and a day she dubbed the "Eight-Day War."

Townes could be pretty stubborn at times. As many have testified, he never had a manager for very long as he was simply unmanageable. And nobody was going to tell him when he had to take a bath.

"On the morning of our second day together, Townes looked over at me in bed and asked, 'Do you remember what you said last night? You suddenly sprung up out of a sound sleep and popped your eyes open and said, 'Would you like some cold dog soup, sir?' Then you laughed hysterically, fell back on the pillow, your eyes slammed shut, and you fell back asleep,'" Jeanene recalled. "Then he asked me 'Do you know what cold dog soup is? That's what they used to call water back in Civil War times.' I immediately knew at that moment that we'd been together in another lifetime, during the Civil War, and that he was my lieutenant and I was the water boy."

"From then on it seemed like they were always together," Sterling said. "He'd been on some kind of a binge at the time. Townes, like most everybody else in town, was on the sauce a little too much. I didn't know him like I *got* to know him. I didn't realize he had so many problems, or I might not have steered her in that direction. They came over to my house, and Townes hadn't had a bath in I don't know how long. So there was nothin' goin' on with them until he got in the tub. The boy *needed* a bath," Gradi laughed. "Finally, Jeanene got him in the damn bathtub, and he got cleaned up, and they had some whoopee. But I still don't appreciate her not cleanin' up the tub afterwards."

At the time Munsell had been the foreman of a landscaping crew and had her own groovy little bachelorette pad. She would soon inherit the jukebox from Cheatem's failed beer and ice cream parlor, and Townes and Geraldine could be heard howling along to Warren Zevon's "Werewolves of London" every morning while Jeanene cooked up a batch of steak and eggs. In short order Townes became "a full-time deal," Jeanene said.

I was just trying to keep him alive, fed, and out of jail. Townes did weird stuff when he was drunk. He had to be watched. You didn't know when he was just suddenly going to go off the deep end and start pounding on things in public places. All the cops in town knew him by first name. They'd wait outside the door while I'd try to get him in the truck and take him home. They'd say, "Do ya think we're gonna need the cuffs tonight, Townes?" Sometimes he'd tell them, "Yeah." And sometimes he'd go, "Naw, I think I'll be alright." Then we'd kiss goodnight in front of the police, and I'd get in the truck and go home, and one of his buddies would go pick him up the next morning.

At the time he was actually still married to Cindy. *I did not know* he was married when God handed him to me. I do *not* date married men. That's a big taboo. He was married but hadn't been with his wife for over a year and just never bothered to divorce her. One day out of the blue Townes told me, "Well, you know, babe, I'm married, and one of these days I gotta roll." So one morning, after several months of his flip-flopping, I said, "Well, looks like today's the day!" and threw all of his shit out in a big grease spot on the driveway. I said, "Darlin', the door is open, but I am not going to put up with this shit anymore. The time has come when you gotta make up your mind. If you want to be with me, then be with me. If you want to go home and be with your wife, then go home and be with her. I think now is just as good a time as any for you to pack up your shit and get your ass back to Tennessee and see your wife. He said, "Well, I think you're right." He had left her at that little shack with Geraldine. So he went back to Tennessee and called me up and said, "I don't think this is gonna work out. Will you marry me?"

"I didn't want to jump right in and get legally married, but it was like we were already married anyway—so I figured what the fuck, we didn't have nothin' to lose," Jeanene said with a laugh.

Brash at times, stubborn, and highly opinionated, Ms. Munsell was not an immediate hit with Townes's friends: "I thought she had her nails in his back," Houston folksinger Linda Lowe confessed.

"At first I was lookin' at Jeanene like *who is she?*" Lysi Moore said, lighting a cigarette. "But over time Jeanene has won my respect, and now we're close friends. I'd go to jail for her, and I might have to punch somebody out in the process."

Townes soon returned from Tennessee with Geraldine and some of his things. "The first time he left town and left Geraldine with me, I went outside the next morning and found a dead possum on the doorstep. I called Townes, and he was delighted. He said, 'Oh, good, that means she likes you,'" Jeanene laughed.

They soon moved out of town to a trailer park beside Lake Austin. "We found these two trailer houses that had been stuck together in the shape of a T which I took as a sign," Jeanene said.

So we ended up moving in there. One of my high school girlfriends moved in and took one of the rooms, so we had a roommate for a little while. That was a wild scene. We had a pet tarantula named Furry Lewis [in honor of the great bluesman] that escaped. One night we rescued a hooker, but she started doing the whole neighborhood, so we had to take her back to her pimp. I thought I was saving this girl, and she just looked at it as a business opportunity. But Townes was very compassionate.

Our kitty cats had ripped up all the screens in the house, and the flies were terrible. Townes and I would lay in our bed together with one of those Daisy BB guns and shoot at the flies that were all over the wall. The flies just liked this one wall. I don't know why. Maybe there was a dead woman behind there. Both of us were deadeye shots. The whole wall had all these little ping marks with blood splatters around 'em. That's what we used to do for fun.

We'd been together for about a year and a half when he happened to mention that he had a son. Townes was always very hush hush about everything, and I was never one to quiz people. I said, *"Excuse me? You have a son?"* Then he told me all about his marriage to Fran and J. T. So I immediately called up Fran and said, "Hi, I'm Townes's wife." He was calling me his wife. I was using his name, but he was still legally married to Cindy. He never bothered to get divorced. It was just too much to deal with. I told her I just found out about J. T. and didn't think it was right that they never saw each other. J. T. was twelve at the time, living in Houston. So he came to visit for the summer and lived with us in the trailer house while we shot flies off the wall. When he showed up he was the spittin' image of his daddy. It was scary.

J. T. visited every summer after that until he was fifteen, when he came to live with us. When he turned sixteen, he said he didn't feel like gettin' up to catch the school bus anymore. So Townes went into his room and told him, "Hey, sport, you're sixteen years old now—if you want to go to school, then go to school. If you don't—it's not my problem." Then he went back to bed. After that J. T. went to school every day and ended up going to college.

When it came to talking about his past Townes preferred to let most things go unsaid. Not only was Jeanene in the dark about his son and two past wives, she barely had a clue what Townes did for a living. "I was pissed off 'cause he said he was 'goin' on the road,' and I didn't know what it meant," she confessed.

That was the first time I'd heard that line, "no slits on the road," which kind of angered me. He and Mickey were gettin' ready to take off when he opened the door, leaned in, and said, "Hey, babe, here's one of my records," and whirled a copy of *Our Mother the Mountain* across the room at me. I said, *"You got records?"* That was the first I'd heard of it. He was in the driveway, loadin' up the car, when I put the record on and started to freak. I just started bawlin'. By the end of the first song I was a puddle of tears. I was so clueless. I didn't even know what he did. I knew he played guitar, but I had no idea he wrote *those* kind of songs. By then he was pullin' out of the driveway, and it was all I could talk about until he got back.

Although Townes epitomized the devil-may-care rambler, headed down the freeway of life, living for the moment, his guilt over his drunken fiascoes, sloppy good-byes, and other unresolved issues of his past had a way of catching up with him in the middle of the night. With the success of Emmylou Harris and Don Williams's rendition of "If I Needed You" topping the charts, Townes felt it was time to settle some old scores.

It was two in the morning when Fran received a surprise phone call from Townes. "Ronny and I had just gotten back from our honeymoon. It was our first night back after a Caribbean cruise," Lohr recalled.

Ronny answered the phone and said, "It's for you." It was Townes. He was just exuberant. He said, "Babe, our song is at the top of the charts. I can buy your dad the Cadillac. We can get back together. J. T. can have a big house." He just went on and on about all the things that were gonna be different. And he was straight. Maybe he'd had one drink. Then he said, "By the way, is that a nice man who answered the phone?" It was a heartbreaking moment to hear him so excited and so straight. It was like hearing him ten years back. I was so happy to hear that things were going well. I've told many people, including my husband, that I never quit loving Townes. It was never a doubt about how much I loved him, it was just how do you *live with him?*

CHAPTER 19

THE PHANTOM HARPSICHORDIST AND A BOY NAMED TACO

Being a folk singer is 10% playing and 90% drivin'.
—TVZ

"Although Townes had this policy of 'no slits on the road,' he finally gave in and asked me to go along on a tour of Canada and California. He said, 'Uh, babe, we're going on the road, and I want you to come with us' . . . Mickey was bringing Pat along, so I guess he figured he had to ask me," Jeanene recalled.

At age twenty-six, Jeanene had never been out of Texas except for an occasional Mexican shopping spree. Now she was getting a firsthand look at her troubadour's life, for better or worse. Night after night she watched as the audience sat riveted to Townes's every utterance. She knew that if he had any clue that she was pregnant he would have sent her home in a heartbeat. Jeanene managed to hide her morning sickness for the entire leg of the Canadian tour, but by the time they reached California the charade would soon be over.

"We were going down this mountain road through the Redwood Forest, and they were blithering drunk, driving the truck," Jeanene recalled, puffing on a Black and Mild cigar. "I'm in the back, and speakers are flying all around. I'm banging on the window screaming, 'Slow down, goddamn it! I don't want to die!' They're dodging redwood trees, going down this mountain, and I've got morning sickness, tryin' to get them to pull over so I can puke. It was one of the most grueling experiences I'd ever been through."

In San Francisco Townes opened for his old friend Mickey Newbury at the Great American Music Hall. Each night of the tour Jeanene religiously popped a cassette into the soundboard to record the show. Heading out of town after the gig that night, they listened back to the tape as they tooled along in the Colonel. Suddenly, they heard something that sounded like somebody playing a harpsichord along with Townes. Inexplicable as it was, it was there for all to hear—clear as a bell, bigger than Dallas. Van Zandt sang and played guitar while Mickey White picked lead, and someone or some *thing* plunked away on a harpsichord. Jeanene began to freak out. "Oh, my God, who *is* that?" she cried. "It couldn't have been anybody in the audience." "Oh, that's just a ghost," Townes said flippantly. With that the hair on Jeanene's arms stood up, and she began to cry.

It wasn't bad enough that Townes was persistently plagued by harpsichords foisted upon him by his producers on his first couple albums; he was now dogged by the frilly baroque keyboard on the astral plane as well.

But with each listening of the tape the harpsichord began to grow fainter. They decided to put the tape away for safekeeping before the phantom harpsichordist finally disappeared for good. "It's around here, somewhere," Jeanene assured me. "I promise I'll dig it up for you sometime soon." (But she never did.)

With its red-velvet wallpaper and decaying Victorian vibe, one doesn't need to possess a fantastic imagination to believe that the Great American Music Hall might host spirits, musical or otherwise. Granted, something strange may have occurred that night, but the very next evening after the show the phantom harpsichordist appeared on the tape once again. And the following night as well.

"Holy shit, Townes! That ghost or whatever it is is following us," Jeanene said in a panic. Townes, ancient soul mariner that he was, innately understood that one must be gentle when dealing with spooks. They're in the business of haunting and respect no artificial limits. So he began to address the spirit directly, speaking to it softly.

"Hey there . . . Are you still with us?" he asked the source of the sonic apparition as his onyx-black eyes scanned the motel walls. The next afternoon, on their way to the next gig, Townes confidently announced that the phantom harpsichordist was gone. "He just got off at the last stop," Townes said, trying to assure everyone that everything was "normal."

Many of his friends claim that Townes was a lightning rod for disembodied spirits and that he openly acknowledged diabolical demons or the occasional angel perched on the edge of his bed.

"Townes suffered delusions and lived constantly with ghosts, spirits and hallucinations," Richard Dobson wrote in his memoir. "Being around him was frequently an exhausting ordeal. It was like when you hear the neighborhood dogs start howling in pain from an ambulance siren—only with Townes those sirens never stopped wailing and his pain never ceased. It was the pain of his existence, no less and he dealt with it the best he could."

"I didn't take a lot of things he said in the latter part of his life real seriously," J. T. confessed at his father's funeral, recalling a grueling tour to Alaska he did with Townes and Harold in 1994.

But he always spoke of a white angel who would spread her wings around him, and he knew he'd be alright on the road in Europe or here in the states. That was his savior. Otherwise, he saw goblins or whatever else his mind at that point brought to his vision. And I'd say, "Yeah, yeah, Townes, whatever gets you through the night." Following a show in Juneau, Alaska, a shaman Eskimo priestess was escorted to him, and they spoke on a level that I can't comprehend and not many of us can. She told him that he didn't fall off of his stool and was able to play that night because a white angel was supporting him. And I thought he truly does have the strongest and most spiritual connection to this world and all that is real.

Meanwhile, back in 1982, Townes and company arrived in El Paso for the last gig of the tour. The next morning the weary travelers decided to go to Mexico for the day and do some discount shopping. Before leaving, Jeanene sneaked off to the drugstore to pick up a pregnancy test. She was hardly surprised when it came up positive. So she marched back to the motel to make the big announcement. Townes was gonna be a father again.

"Oh, hey, babe, that's just great," Townes said, throwing his lanky arms around her. Leaving the Colonel on the U.S. side, they grabbed a cab across the border, with Townes carelessly carrying all the tour money in a big wad of cash, bulging out of his breast pocket. They were having a great time. He drank tequila. She shopped for switchblades. As they entered the main marketplace, Jeanene looked through the souvenirs when suddenly she heard a commotion behind her. She turned around to see what the ruckus was. A crowd of children had surrounded Townes while he towered above them, pulling money out of his pocket, saying, "Here, take this home to your mama. Take this home to your pop." Money was falling out all over the place in little wadded-up bills. Tens, twenties, fifties. The kids began to lunge and grab for the cash. Suddenly, the kids got bigger and bigger until Townes found himself getting crushed by a crowd of hungry, angry Mexicans who were not about to wait any longer for the tall, skinny gringo to slowly dole out the cash. They were on the verge of tearing him apart when Jeanene ran over to the cabstand and grabbed the biggest driver she could find. "Go . . . Go get him! Now! *Andelle!*" she screamed, pointing at her husband. The cabby ran over and grabbed Townes, picked him up, and threw him over his shoulder and plowed his way through the mob. Townes was still peeling off bills, tossing money away as he was being carried off while Jeanene shouted, "Hurry up! Hurry! Put him in the car!" The cabby tossed Townes into the backseat. With his feet dangling out, she reached over, pulled him in, and then pulled the door shut, while the crowd chased the car down the street, yelling, with their hands out.

"I had just gone through a month and a half of hell with him," Jeanene sighed. "I'm pregnant and he'd given away all the money at the end of the tour. *Just gave it all away.* I cried and cried for hours wondering what I'd gotten into. It was my first tour with Townes, and I was stunned. We had a kid on the way, and I thought, Now how the hell is this going to work?

At the border I stashed my switchblades in the cab, and we walked through customs. The customs agent asked Townes, who was dressed in a poncho and turquoise sombrero, if he had anything to declare. He tossed the poncho around his neck and announced, "I'm drunk, I'm broke, and my wife is pregnant," Jeanene said, howling with laughter. "I sat in silence all the way back to El Paso. But that was just a typical day for Townes Van Zandt."

"Jeanene was goin' nuts—wonderin' how they were gonna pay the rent when they got home," Mickey White recalled.

Once he saw her freakin' out, the price immediately went up. Now he's gonna put her through the paces. That's the way Townes was. He did it

just to get to her. If he detected a weakness, if you freaked out over his behavior, then he would gladly accommodate it.

That night we had another gig, which gave us just enough money to
get back home. The bigger issue was if we could sober up in time to play a
show at this folk society. It was at a church, in a stucco Spanish chapel,
and we played really well.

After many a gig Townes was known to head straight to the poorest
section of town and give his money away to the first homeless soul he
could find. Like Jerry Jeff Walker's "Mr. Bojangles," Van Zandt eulo-
gized his pal Mr. Sinbad, in his song "The Blue Ridge Mountains."

Sinbad, as Wrecks Bell recalled, was "an elevator operator who hung
around the Old Quarter. He was an upper-class wino with only one lung,
but he loved to smoke pot." He had been picked up and thrown in the
drunk tank, where he died from alcohol withdrawal. Since then Townes
was on a mission to make sure that winos everywhere got their bottle to
keep them from suffering from the DTs.

One night after a gig in Houston, they cruised along in Dotsy's old
Oldsmobile with Jeanene at the wheel and Townes riding shotgun, di-
recting her through the deserted city streets. It was nearly three in the
morning, and Townes was searching for some poor soul to give his
money to. Suddenly, he spied a homeless man slowly pushing a grocery
cart along. "Follow that guy!" Townes cried. "Hey, buddy. . . Hey,
buddy!" he yelled, hanging halfway out the window. The frightened
bum began to run away. Jeanene followed, driving alongside him for half
a block, but the old man refused to stop. To their amazement he actually
started to pick up speed. Townes jumped out of the car and chased the
poor fellow down the street, shouting, "Hey, buddy!" The guy was about
to have a heart attack. He pushed his cart over the curb. Rags and bottles
went flying everywhere. Townes finally caught up to him and shoved a
wad of bills into his hand. Then like some kind of wobbly Robin Hood,
he climbed back in the Oldsmobile, and they roared off into the night.

"Dotsy loved Townes's father, Van," Jeanene said. "In twenty-five
years after he died she never took off her wedding ring. She would always say she was waiting for the day when they would be reunited in
heaven. Townes admired that. He could appreciate a great love story. Before Will was born Townes went down to the hospital to see his mother
where she was dyin' of lung cancer. She pulled the ring off her withered

finger and handed it to him and said, 'Go home and marry that girl. Don't let her get away.' He came back, woke me up, and we decided to do the legal thing."

The day after Townes and Jeanene were married (March 14, 1983) Van Zandt appeared as a guest on Bobby Bare's TV show. Before going on the air Jeanene pleaded with him: "Whatever you do, don't say we just got married and we're havin' a baby in the same sentence. Either say my wife, Jeanene, and I are gonna have a baby any day now, or say we just got married."

TVZ—"I'm s'posed to mention that my wife, Jeanene, and I are havin' a baby any minute."

Bobby Bare—"Oh, that's right."

TVZ—"And there's a law in Texas that once you get divorced you can't get remarried for thirty days. And it was gettin' close. We got married a couple days ago." (Audience laughs.) "It was gettin' close, and I decided, well, we can always go up to Oklahoma. I phoned my mom and said, 'Look, Mom, with this thirty-day law we might have to rush up, we might have to go to Oklahoma and get married. She said, 'Now, don't you do that, Townes. You don't want that baby born in Oklahoma.'" (Audience roars.)

Apparently Townes took the responsibility of parenthood a bit more seriously than he had the first time around. As he told one interviewer, "I'm a father and that's a goal in itself."

Will was born on March 24, 1983. The day after Jeanene brought the baby home from the hospital Townes wrote a good-time country-blues romp called "Ain't Leaving Your Love."

"He had written all these beautiful love songs, and I used to ask him, 'When do I get one?' The following morning he woke her up with a surprise. "Babe, wake up," Townes said. "I finally wrote that love song you wanted." Jeanene propped up her pillow, anxiously awaiting a stirring ballad, as Townes started to warble:

Mr. Gator is sliding down the bayou
Mr. Buzzard, he's flying through the air
Mr. Turtle'll be hittin' the highway
But I ain't goin' nowhere

"That's my *love* song?" she asked incredulously.

"Yeah. I haven't found the melody for it yet, but I think it's great," Townes replied.

"Oh, okay," Jeanene sighed. "If you like it then I guess I do too."

Following Will's birth came a long stretch of silence when Van Zandt walked away from recording altogether. After the debacle of *7 Come 11* and the highly anticipated *Flying Shoes* just barely getting off the ground, Townes turned his back on a process he felt little love for. Besides, the steady stream of songs that once spontaneously gushed from his brain had now slowed to a mere trickle.

Long before "Pancho and Lefty" hit the charts they'd decided to name the baby Will for Townes's grandfather William Lipscomb Van Zandt. Will's middle name is Vincent. As a two year old Will would brusquely inform everyone that his full name was "Will Van Zandt Gogh" and would become aggravated at anyone who failed to call him such. Whether named in honor of Townes's pal songwriter Vince Bell or the delusional Dutch painter Vincent Van Gogh is not certain, although Townes was obsessed with Van Gogh. Perhaps the kinship was inspired by the overwhelming rejection they mutually endured (although Townes was infinitely more popular during his lifetime) or the turbulent madness and alienation they suffered. Vincent's blazing canvases and the deep emotions his swirling brushstrokes evoke mesmerized Townes. Painting was the channel for Van Gogh to express his emotions, as songs were for Van Zandt.

The powerful mood of Townes's songs often rivaled their content. This is not to infer that his lyrics were murky or unclear unless he was purposely being cryptic. Van Zandt's poetry was as well defined as the bold brushstrokes of the nineteenth-century master. Both men grappled with the notion of suicide throughout their lives. No longer able to endure his existence, Van Gogh snuffed himself out at age thirty-seven, while Townes took the more socially acceptable path by methodically poisoning himself with alcohol.

"'Pancho and Lefty' was number one the day that Will was born," Jeanene said proudly. "We used to joke that the next time he had a hit song we'd have another baby. Nine years later the Cowboy Junkies did 'To Live's to Fly,' and we had Katie Belle.

The undisputed poet of the family, Townes, named both babies. When Jeanene became pregnant again, she had an overwhelming craving for

Taco Bell every day. Townes said that if it was a girl he would christen her Katie Belle after his paternal grandmother. But if it was a boy, his name would be Taco Bell. "We hoped it was a girl or we were going to have a boy named Taco," Jeanene laughed.

CHAPTER 20

THROUGH A SHOT GLASS DARKLY

Townes showed his innermost pain under the spotlight. He'd start crying in the middle of a show. I mean, nobody does that.

—Joe Ely

The late seventies and early eighties were a rough time for performing singer-songwriters. As punk exploded across the United States, acoustic music suddenly seemed like an artifact of the past. The raw energy of Patti Smith, Television, and the New York Dolls had practically obliterated what was left of the old New York folk scene. There were very few left from the old days: Dylan would soon begin his endless tour, slugging it out in the stadiums. Joni Mitchell had turned to jazz, and Leonard Cohen traded in his gut-string guitar for a Casio keyboard and an air-tight Euro-trash beat. Meanwhile, Eric Andersen and Townes were somewhere on the road in Texas and New Mexico. Tom Paxton performed rarely. Phil Ochs and Peter LaFarge had both committed suicide. Buffy Sainte-Marie moved to Hawaii. Patrick Sky retired. The two Tims, Hardin and Buckley, had both overdosed, and Fred Neil had disappeared and was living off royalty checks from *Midnight Cowboy* while allegedly combing the beaches of the Florida Keys.

"It was very weird because we didn't play pop music. We weren't the Eagles or Jackson Browne, yet there were plenty of people that still wanted to hear us," Eric Andersen explained. "Recording was uneven. Back then I spent a lot of time between labels . . . Johnnie Walker Red and Johnnie Walker Black!" Eric said with a grin.

We weren't getting any radio play at the time. We grabbed whatever gigs we could. This was before the next wave came along. Suzanne Vega and Shawn Colvin were still opening acts at Folk City. These days, acoustic music is a cottage industry. It's all over college radio, but it was never that way when I started back in the Village. In the seventies FM radio rock DJs like Alison Steele on WNEW played *Blue River* [Andersen's finest album]. Townes's writing was always too sophisticated for the country scene, so he didn't get much airplay. It certainly wasn't acceptable in Nashville. He had to carve his own niche.

In November 1981, Linda Lowe tried her best to help further Van Zandt's career by booking him a small tour of Arkansas, bringing him to Fayetteville, Eureka Springs, and Little Rock. A singer-songwriter with a lilting voice, Lowe opened the shows each night.

I wanted to bring my Texas songwriter friends to my home and start a concert series with shows by Townes and Nanci Griffith. I was trying to get everyone out of the clubs. I got some investors together to do the concert and talked to the people at the Fine Arts Concert Hall at Little Rock University. It was mostly used for classical concerts. They never gave it to a folk singer before. I talked them into giving me the hall with the sound system. At five dollars a ticket we sold out the show. The local press got behind it, and Dorothy Palmer [sister of journalist Robert Palmer] wrote an article for the *Arkansas Gazette*.

The first gigs went off without a hitch. Everything was fine until the afternoon of the Little Rock concert. "At that time Mickey was straight. The problem was they were never straight together," Linda said, rolling her eyes.

They were sober and made it on time to the gig. But then the security guard met them at the door with a bottle, which they drank together in a matter of twenty minutes, while I was up on stage opening up for him. Then I introduced him. There was a spotlight on the stage, but he didn't come out. After about three songs Townes started speaking Egyptian. Being from Texas, he started bad-mouthing the University of Arkansas football team. Mickey, who was sober, quit right there on stage. Then Townes fired him and spilled the rest of the whiskey all over a five thou-sand–dollar rug that was on the stage floor. Of course, all the people got up and left and demanded their money back. My brother was the only one left.

As the producer, I took the blame. Townes stayed at my place that night after the show. He was so drunk he pissed on our dishes. I think he thought he was in the bathroom and the sink was the toilet.

Linda didn't sleep a wink all night. The next morning she sat outside her house on the curb when Townes sauntered up and sat down beside her.

He said, "How bad was it?" I told him I was probably gonna have to leave town. He apologized and said, "You don't have to pay me." I got on the phone and called Guy, but he wouldn't talk to me. He probably thought I was just another of Townes's little idiots. But I managed to talk to Susanna and told her, "You gotta get Harry [Eggers] or somebody to road manage them if they're going to make it to New York and play the rest of his gigs because this is *not* gonna work." So she got Harry to come and pick them up and take it from there. But what happened that night was really my fault.

"Townes had a reputation for blowin' gigs, and he would—here and there. . . But the real reason he blew Linda Lowe's show in Arkansas was because it was a self-fulfilling prophesy," Mickey White explained.

Linda was so worried that he was gonna blow the gig that Townes simply obliged her. He would never blow road gigs, even after the alcohol began to affect his ability to play. If Townes was gonna blow a gig, he'd usually do it at home. He did it just to keep things *interesting*. I've seen him drunk as a skunk and perform beautifully. I've also seen him sober as a judge and get up on stage and totally blow it. For Townes, blowin' a gig was just part of the act. He was no fool. He knew he couldn't go someplace like Folk City or the Great American Music Hall and choke. They'd never hire him again. But he'd go to the Cactus Café, blow the gig, and still get rehired. If he blew a gig there he'd could always come back again and play a great show.

Townes could be kind of mean to people, especially those people he was close to. He was really smart and intuitive. He understood personality quirks and knew just what to say to cut someone to the bone. He tested your loyalty and put you through the paces. If you held up, then you'd be his runnin' buddy. But if he tried it with me, I'd leave. He knew better than to get into it with me in the car. We'd get into philosophical arguments, but generally he wouldn't pull that kind of shit while we were traveling because it was a professional situation. Besides, Townes depended on my ability to recall exactly which exit or U-turn or location in seventy selected cities across the United States that we could find a liquor store in the shortest amount of time.

"If there wasn't a circus going on he'd get bored in a hurry. Then we'd *really* be in trouble," Jeanene chuckled. "He loved to get people so agitated that their eyes would start buggin' out of their heads. He had an amazing ability to create chaos and laugh about it. He'd come into the bedroom and say, 'Watch this, babe—I'm gonna have 'em all crazy out there.' And the next thing you knew, people would be screamin' and jumpin' up and down. Then he'd come back in the room laughin' like an impish kid. Actually I had three kids," Jeanene said, rolling her eyes. "One of them was six foot two. The worst thing he ever could have done was bore me, and I can happily report that for fifteen years I was *never* bored. But there were times that I wanted to kill him."

"By 1983 I was in pretty sorry shape from all the drinkin' and druggin'," White confessed.

Townes finally got fed up and fired me. We were "divorced" for nearly a year. In the meantime, I'd been soberin' up, and he admitted that he missed my guitar playin'. There was a real tension between us in our playing. Steve Gillette once described us as watching a trapeze act. Just at the very moment we were about to lose it, we'd always catch it again. Townes couldn't get a record deal at that point. So he said, "Fuck it, let's put a band together, play a bunch of gigs, and record an album on a four-track recorder at home."

Townes's new posse of musical misfits was perhaps the closest he'd ever come to finding a Crazy Horse (Neil Young's quintessential backup band) of his own. The band featured the Waddell brothers—Leland on drums and David on bass—along with Mickey on lead guitar and the token Yankee of the group, Boston transplant Donny Silverman, on saxophone and flute. Although they gigged frequently around Texas, Townes found taking a band with him full-time on the road was a logistical nightmare.

"Unfortunately the rehearsals just turned into big drunken orgies with everybody arguing all the time. We'd just get drunk and wind up screaming at one another," White admitted. "If we'd been sober, we woulda been a great band. Leland was a really tasteful drummer."

Although their ragged and inspired music is long gone, their legendary hell-raising adventures live on. Leland Waddell recalled a wild ride to an ill-fated show in Lubbock in Dotsy's Oldsmobile:

It was an outdoor concert at a ball field, an all-day-long deal. It was an early mornin' ride, just me, Donny, Mickey, and Townes. Everything was fine. We were sittin' back, cruisin', not drinkin' a whole lot. We got about fifty, sixty miles outside of Lubbock when we stopped off the highway for drinks, and just as we were pullin' back on the on-ramp to the expressway, the car started slippin' and the transmission went out. I said, "If we're lucky there'll still be some clutch left in reverse." I put the car in reverse, and it backed up real good. So I backed it real slow down the side of the Interstate, till I could get it off at the next ramp. Well, I whooped that baby around and tooled along backwards, slow to begin with, then I got the feel for the car and cocked my mirror and said, "This ain't too bad." We were rollin' along with the trucks brushin' by us . . . Vhooom! We got up to the first exit. Hell, everything was fine, and we were makin' time. Had plenty of gas. I said, "Townes, we only got forty more miles." He said, "No way, man, pull off!" I said, "I'm getting the hang of this. Let's go down one more. I'm lookin' at the mirror, and the reflectors on the Interstate are shootin' by—boom, boom, boom. I mean, we were cruisin' good, runnin' up around thirty, thirty-five. We stayed on the side the whole time. I figured we'd catch a nail in the tire for sure. People lookin' at us, just freakin' out. Steerin' backwards is a whole lot different than steerin' forward.

We're bookin' along, backin' up, and the next thing I know I'm passin' an old pickup truck. This old farmer's eyes were buggin' out! I figured, okay, maybe we'll get off at the next ramp. We get there, and I say, "Townes, we ain't but thirty miles away." He says, "Goddamn!"

None of us was drunk. We didn't have any drugs. We'd get some when we got there. I said, "Look, if we get pulled over, I'll just explain to 'em that we're tryin' to get the car to the next exit." So zoom, we pass the next ramp. Townes says, "You gotta stop." I say, "No, let's go. Let's chase it!"

I got it hummin' in reverse, dust flyin' out from the front of the car. It was cool. Silverman was behind me. Mickey was behind Townes, who's ridin' shotgun. I was gettin' tired, so we roll backwards off the ramp and into a 7/11. I jumped out, go in and grab a cup of coffee, got back in the car, and backed it down the next ramp and onto the expressway. I said, "Damn man, it's twenty miles to Lubbock! We got a chance at it." So we were startin' to get outside of Lubbock. I backed that son of a bitch up into a motel so we could get a room and call the promoter to come get us. We come sailin' right in there backwards into the parkin' lot, and this guy was there, hoein' his flowers. Turns out he's a cop. He says, "Where'd you come from?" I tell him, "Austin." He asks me, "How far have you been backin' that car?" And I said, "About forty miles." He said, *"And the police didn't stop you?"* I told him, "We didn't *see* one." He thought that was a kick, man. The cop said, "I tell you what, I'll take you into Lubbock." Mickey and Donny had both been lookin' outta the back of the car for the last hour and a half. When they got out of the car, they both had a crink in their necks. Mickey couldn't straighten his head this way, and Donny couldn't straighten his head that way. Anyway when we finally showed up there wasn't a goddamn soul at the concert. It was a bust. Townes says, "Aw, that's alright. Don't worry about it . . ." They gave us a couple hundred dollars, and we stayed at a motel.

"When we got to the speedway there was nobody there," Mickey White recalled.

It was freezin' cold, and there were a dozen bikers standin' around a fire they'd started inside a big barrel. Indian Gary, who'd booked the gig, started apologizing to Townes. We'd spent all our money getting there and were expecting to get paid so we'd have enough to get back. It looked like another situation where we'd have to call and get some money wired to us. We were supposed to make six hundred bucks, but we told him we'd let him off the hook if they gave us the money for a couple motel rooms, some food, and enough whiskey for the night. Indian Gary was goin', "Oh, God, thank you, thank you." From there, the gig turned into a two-day drunk. We just wound up tearing up the motel rooms and yellin' at each other. Leland, being the car man, went out and bought this three hundred dollar Chevy and rented a tow bar from U-Haul and hooked up the Oldsmobile and drove it home.

"The next mornin' we had no transportation," Leland said, picking up the story again.

The car was sittin' at this motel five miles out of town. Townes said, "My mother gave me that car. I can't leave it!" Townes always liked to say he was broke and livin' on the edge, but there was always some money stuffed away somewhere. So we bought this old car for three hundred dollars and a clamp-on bumper for another seventy-five, went back to the motel, and hooked up his car with a tow bar. We put that baby in neutral and pulled out. We're rollin' now, on our way back. Everything's cool. We spent the night, got drunk, had a great time, and it looks like we're gonna make it back to Austin. The next thing you know Mickey says, "Somethin's wrong!" The left front tire on the Olds had blown out a long way back, and the rim was ground down, nearly completely off. As far as you could see, for twenty miles, we had ripped up the highway, gougin' rocks out of the asphalt. We pull off to the side of the road, and I say, "Mickey, here's some money, get your ass into town, and get us a tire and a wheel." We were all drunk by then, and we had drugs on us, which we got in Lubbock. The first time Mickey stuck out his thumb this old guy picked him up. Just as he pulls out of sight, here comes this burly-assed country county cop. What's left of that tire is just hangin' off the rim, smokin'. He said, "I been followin' you for twenty miles by that scratch in that highway. I'm gonna charge you for every inch of it. What are you gonna do?" We were dirty and had been up for days. I told him I got a guy on his way to town to get a tire and a wheel. He said, "Get in the car." We head into town, and there's Mickey at the first service station, rollin' the tire, about to thumb a ride back. He saw I was tellin' him the truth, so we stop and pick Mickey up with the tire, brought us back to the car, and said, "You've got fifteen minutes to get out of my county. If I catch you in my county when I roll back by here, ALL OF YOU ARE GOIN' TO JAIL!"

We got that tire on there and drove, but halfway to Austin we got into a fight. Mickey was just yak, yak, yakkin', "Goddamn it, this thing has been a bust from the beginning." Finally I said, "Mickey, you gotta shut up, man!" My fingers was getting tight 'round that steerin' wheel. We were all on edge. None of us could stand to go to jail. Mickey keeps goin' on, "Goddamn you, Townes! This happens every time." Finally I said, "Mickey, if you say one more word I'll knock your head off your shoulders! So shut up!" He said, "What the fuck are *you* gonna do?" I slammed on the brakes, got out of the car, and said (calmly), "Come on . . ." He got out, knowin' he was about to get his ass whipped. I said, "Right over here in the bushes, motherfucker!" He's just a little old thing, so I said, "Alright now, young man, cool out or I *am* gonna kick your ass!" He said, "Okay . . . Okay . . . I'll be quiet . . ." So we drove back to Townes's house, and he gave the Oldsmobile to Blaze Foley. He had a little money and got the transmission fixed but then just left it out at some girl's house when the battery died, and it wouldn't start.

"The band had no real name to speak of, though club owners called us all sorts of things," Donny Silverman quipped. The group's short, bumpy ride lasted less than a year. Townes's group played their last gig as a band at Poor David's in Dallas. "The place was packed, and nothin' was goin' right," Leland recalled.

The sound wasn't right. The guitars wouldn't stay in tune. It was a terrible set. I said, "Townes, let's take a break and get ourselves together." We go over to the bar, and I start shootin' vodka down as fast as he could fill 'em. Townes starts playin' an acoustic set with Mickey while my brother's chasin' some skirt. I get *totally* drunk and said, "Fuck it, I'm never playin' drums again!" My bar tab came to about seventy dollars, so I traded my drums to the bartender for my tab and left without tellin' anybody. I got in my pickup truck so fuckin' drunk I could barely walk. Somehow I drove eighty miles, got twenty miles outside of Waco, pulled over to the side of the road, and fell asleep. About an hour later, I hear somebody beatin' on the window. It was Townes and all of 'em in his truck. He had bought my drums back from the bartender! Paid for 'em and loaded 'em up into the truck and woke me up on the side of the road ten miles outside of Waco. My brother drove me the rest of the way home. Nobody ever said a word.

"That was just another gig with Townes," Wadell said, shaking his head.

Although a couple of board tapes still exist, Townes would never record with the Waddell brothers. As it became obvious that he couldn't cart the whole gang around with him on the road, Van Zandt started gigging as a trio with Mickey and Donny.

"We just couldn't pull it off with the whole band, but we could always pile two guitars, a sax, and a flute in one car and go," Mickey explained. "Little Harold booked us at Twelfth and Porter on April 17th, 1985, and set it up to record the show. He advertised it quite well, as Townes's big return to Nashville. Everybody showed up that night—Guy and Susanna, Rodney [Crowell] and Rosanne [Cash], and Neil Young were all there. But the album" [culled from the evening's performance, titled *Live and Obscure*] "was not mixed properly," Mickey groused. "I didn't like the way it was recorded and tried to talk Townes out of releasing it."

Cowboy Jack Clement was also in the house that night and was taken by the trio's chamber–folk ensemble sound. Clement suggested they come down to his studio to cut some tracks. "The sax was kind of strange, but it had its place," Cowboy Jack surmised.

"For a little while Townes tried to be a saxophone player," Mickey explained. "He never played it on stage. He really liked the low honk of the tenor. That's why he included Donny as part of the sound."

The sax in Van Zandt's hands would meet a similar fate as the fiddle. Aggravated by his own caterwauling, Townes eventually hung the horn from a tree branch and blew it to smithereens with a shotgun.

If his earlier work showed an effortless knack for meticulous rhyme schemes and stunning imagery, then Townes's long-awaited 1987 release, *At My Window,* revealed a mature simplicity that could only have come with experience and age. Like Dylan before him, who was accused of "going soft" during his much maligned late-sixties and early-seventies *Nashville Skyline/New Morning* phase, Townes too would settle down by the mid-eighties to raise a family.

For the first time in his life Van Zandt seemed almost content, or about as content as Townes Van Zandt could ever be. The domestic bliss he once sang of in "No Lonesome Tune" had almost become a reality.

"Townes wrote beautiful songs about family and love, but he never lived those things out; he was off in a corner creating them while his family was wishing that they had a father or a husband," J. T. said, offering some perspective on his father's devotion to his art. "He sacrificed his personal life to describe to the rest of us what true beauty and love is. He didn't experience it, so he became the poet off in the corner beating his brains out [in order to express] what the essence of human emotion is. You can choose that, or you can be a simple man who follows his heart and behaves honestly and treats his family well."

"Really, I'm just a folksinger who's made a lot of friends, and I can write good songs," Van Zandt told journalist Holly Gleason. "I have good business deals and bad business deals, good motel rooms and bad motel rooms. I've finally found a good wife, good children, and a good guitar."

"It was the first time in his life that Townes felt stable," Jeanene imparted. "He never dreamed he could have a family. Townes was always a big gigger. We basically lived on gig money. He'd been out there for twenty years straight."

As Townes's popularity and workload steadily increased, his busy tour schedule was just one more thing Jeanene would learn to adapt to: "He'd be home for a month to a month and a half, and then he'd hit the road for another month to a month and a half. Sometimes he'd be gone for two to two and a half months at a time. But that was all I could handle," she confessed.

From Jeanene's description of him, Townes at times resembled a revenant from an Ann Rice novel:

> He was an energy sucker. It might sound bizarre, but it's true. He really *physically* sucked your energy to keep going. It was like, "I don't have time to chew, babe. You eat the food, and I'll just suck your energy." Sometimes before he would go on stage, he'd plop me in the corner, and I could feel him sucking my energy. Before he'd leave to go on the road he would just suck all my energy. I would be at the point of collapse. Then he'd go, and I'd take to my bed for two or three days. I wouldn't answer the phone. I would just go to bed. When he came home it was just the opposite. I'd be so excited and energized. Even if I was thoroughly pissed off at him when he left, it didn't matter. I'd be yanking my garter belts on underneath my jeans, runnin' down to the airport to pick him up. It kept the relationship really fresh and alive. It was really perfect for me in a lot of ways. When I was worn out he'd go away, long enough until I'd want him to come back again.

"I hadn't toured with him much after the first time," Jeanene continued. "If he was touring around Texas I would go along. Then, after Will was born, he let the band go and decided to take "the slit" on the road. We went full-time, just me, him, and the baby those first five years.

"All of a sudden he started getting these royalty checks in the mail. At first I didn't know where they were coming from," Jeanene exclaimed. "After Townes got some money from Emmylou Harris singing 'If I Needed You,' he bought a little sailboat he named *The Vincent,* after Van Gogh, of course."

As a boy, Van Zandt's parents owned a beach house in Galveston Bay where he went sailing with his dad. Townes loved boats and throughout his career wrote a number of odes to heavenly houseboats, golden galleons, and silver ships.

Whenever a decent sum of money from publishing royalties came in he would run right out and buy another boat. Jeanene and Townes spent most of their time on Lake Travis living on *The Vincent* (an eighteen-foot sailboat that slept two to three people in the hull). After Jeanene cracked up singer-songwriter Blaze Foley's avocado-green Ford Escort, she appointed Townes's buddy the official "caretaker" of the Van Zandt household while they lived out on the lake. Foley was homeless without a car to sleep in.

"We spent a lot of time on the lake fishing. We'd be the only boat out there in February. It was the best time of my life, and I think it was of Townes's too," Jeanene reminisced fondly.

More boats soon followed. With the first checks from Willie and Merle's recording of "Pancho and Lefty," Townes purchased a twenty-two-foot Windstar that slept four. He christened it *The Dorothy,* in honor of his mother. In turn, Jeanene named her little paddle boat that she used to get to shore, *The Toto Too.*

The following year Van Zandt bought *The Lightnin'* (a thirty-two-foot houseboat that slept five), which eventually wound up in a watery grave under the command (or lack there of) of those wild Waddell brothers.

"During the school year Townes toured with Harold, but over the summer, we'd travel as a family," Jeanene recollected.

He'd try to book gigs around sites that we wanted to see. One of my favorite times was when we spent two weeks in Yellowstone Park camping in our Swinger conversion van. One of the worst was when Townes jumped out of the van somewhere in East St. Louis and disappeared into a bar, taking every penny with him. I couldn't find him, and it was a very dangerous neighborhood, so Will and I spent the night in the police station parking lot. They were very kind except for one high-ranking cop who wanted to throw me in jail for vagrancy and put Will in state custody. The other cops talked him out of it and instead brought us hamburgers and magazines. The next morning I washed Will in a bucket in front of the police station with a hose. Then the police took us in a squad car from bar to bar looking for Townes until we found him. When I had told them how much money he had on him and of his habit of giving it away and putting it in wads that fell out of his pocket every time he pulled some out, they were convinced that we'd find him dead in an alleyway.

We finally found him in a bar connected to a brothel where he'd spent the night. He was already having his early-morning refreshment when the police called the bar asking about him. The bartender said, "Mr. Van Zandt, the police are on the phone looking for you." Townes, of course, thought we were in the parking lot sleeping in the van and was reluctant to answer, but he did. They told him, "Mr. Van Zandt, don't move, we've got your family here, and we're coming to get you!" They were pretty angry and brought him out in handcuffs and said they were going to charge him.

"Thank goodness he charmed the pants off them and soon had them standing in line with copies of *For the Sake of the Song* songbooks to get his autograph. After everybody was all buddy-buddy we headed out for Nashville and stopped in Oakley, Kansas, to see Prairie Dog Town. I still have the souvenir magnet of two prairie dogs screwing on the fridge," Jeanene laughed.

The cover snapshot of *At My Window* portrays Townes in the kitchen again . . . Cowboy Jack's to be specific. This is not the primly painted, antique dollhouse he inhabits on his self-titled 1970 release, where he sits, eyes closed, dejected, unable to face the world. Here "the lost high roller" leans casually against the sink, his black eyes gleaming, peering gently through Jim McGuire's lens. Gone is the fork-bending glare of yesteryear. Townes's eyes are soft, friendly, resigned. His gold-coin belt buckle and cowboy shirt, embroidered with a winning poker hand, let you know that although he's now a family man, he's still up for a friendly wager. Warm and cozy as the scene is, there is something obviously askew. McGuire's image, a squiggly, manipulated Polaroid snapshot, conveys a jittery sensation, much like what the human nervous system experiences with an oncoming rush of a mescaline trip.

Although *At My Window* is Townes's best studio outing and certainly his finest album that was not part of his Poppy/Tomato heyday, it was not exactly the fresh batch of songs his fans had hoped for. Interspersed throughout the album is the fourth remake of "For the Sake of the Song." Although the arrangement is understated and tasteful, it lacks the sense of urgency the lyric conveys. There are also a handful of songs from the lost *Nashville Sessions,* including "Buckskin Stallion Blues."

"I worked out 'Gone, Gone Blues' with him," Mickey recalled. "And we'd been doing that double-guitar arrangement of 'Buckskin Stallion Blues' since back in the seventies." Townes's standard intro to the song sounded like a line stolen from Henny Youngman: "'Buckskin Stallion' is half about a woman and half about a horse. I still miss the horse."

"Townes really wanted to get those songs out from the unreleased *Nashville Sessions,*" Mickey explained. "It was Jack's idea to recut 'For the Sake of the Song.' He wanted to take some of Townes's earlier repertoire he'd cut before and do it with a live feel. The album sounds a bit tentative in spots 'cause we didn't use headphones and missed some of the nuances goin' on. And by the time we did *At My Window,* Townes's skills were not consistent," White confided. "After he broke his arm a couple of times [Van Zandt had broken his wrist a second time after falling off a horse], he didn't fingerpick as well as he used to. And he started getting a little lazy as a singer. As his voice matured, it got deeper and more reso-nant, but he tended to not sing with as much energy and lung power as he used to and started shaving off his notes and phrases more and more."

"I think the best album of Townes's that I was involved in was *At My Window,*" Cowboy Jack said. "We cut the basic tracks, and when some-body would come by I'd have 'em overdub and sprinkle some stuff on it here and there and then set it aside. Nine months or a year later we ze-roed in on it and finished it up."

Some of Nashville's finest pickers weighed in on the sessions, includ-ing Mark O'Connor, whose mandolin danced lightly around Townes's lyrics on the majestic "Snowin' on Raton," while Willie Nelson's har-monica man, Mickey Raphael, blew high and lonesome, and Roy Huskey Jr. gently bumped the songs along with his solid upright-bass playing.

"Truth be known it was a really Jim Rooney record," Mickey White claimed. "Jack was out of the state, down in Florida. He came in once to remind us that it only takes three minutes to cut a hit record and then disappeared."

Wherever he was, Clement had clearly taken more of a hands-off ap-proach to Townes's music this time around. Jeanene recalled hanging out with Cowboy up in his office, "smoking a fatty," while the sessions took place without him: "Jack had it all wired up where he could just flip a switch and listen in on the proceedings whenever he felt like it," she re-called. "He listened to 'em for a minute or two, flipped the switch off, and said, 'Sounds like they got it under control,' and then went about his business."

"Over the years I would run into Townes occasionally," Jim Rooney recollected. "He was traveling a lot, playing. If he played in town I would always go. There was a humor and sadness in his singing that moved me. Townes had made the traditions of the ballads and the blues his own. By the mideighties Jack Clement had persuaded me to learn how to run the board, so I became his recording engineer," Rooney explained. Most important, Cowboy Jack gave Jim free reign of his studio, the Cowboy Arms Hotel and Recording Spa, to produce some of his own projects. "It was a great gift, and I did albums with Richard Dobson, Nanci Griffith, Dave Mallett, Jerry Jeff Walker, and others."

One day Rooney noticed Van Zandt's name on the blackboard that listed upcoming projects for Jack's studio.

> I knew that Townes and Jack had been spending some time together, and it looked like they were going to do some recording. I went into Jack's office and asked who was going to engineer it. He said, "Why don't you?" So I did. It was all very simple. Townes brought in Mickey White and Donny Silverman on sax and flute. Jack added pianist Charles Cochran, the wonderful bass player Roy Huskey Jr., and the equally wonderful drummer Kenny Malone. So we got started. Jack was the producer, but he was downstairs in his office, "listening through the walls," which meant I started making a few decisions on my own. After a couple of days I went to see Cowboy and said it seemed to me that we might be actually producing this record together. He agreed, and on we went.

"Townes was in a good place," Jim reckoned. "I think he felt he was in good hands with Cowboy and me. He was with people who loved him and would do him no harm. He didn't have to play games with us. The musicians responded to his songs and his singing. It was all seamless. To make it sound as good as we could, I brought in Rich Adler, a real engineer, to mix the album. Together with the earlier albums that Townes did with Cowboy, I think *At My Window* turned out to be one of his best. It shows why all those other writers looked up to him."

Rooney has always approached recording as an organic, natural process, capturing what the artist does without changing it or getting in their way. The album's sparse production was the antithesis of the approach that Poppy had taken with Townes's music. Finally, Van Zandt's poetry took a front seat and was able to shine through unfettered. Many of Townes's songs celebrated his hard-living ways. His weathered voice, full of resignation and melancholy, was now that of a grateful survivor. Although it seemed he'd found a bit of stability and contentedness, old themes of alienation could be found bubbling just below the surface.

Townes sang in "Buckskin Stallion Blues," "If love can be and still be lonely / Where does that leave me and you?"

"Nobody writes songs about love affairs gone wrong with as much tenderness and insight," wrote Robert Palmer in the *New York Times*. With "a strong, weathered voice, the texture of a lived-in leather jacket," Van Zandt delivers his verses brimming with "prickly uncomfortable truths and unsentimental reflection. There's a catch in it on certain words," Palmer pointed out, "an almost yodel that's country music's equivalent of the bluesy quaver black singers call soul."

Nowhere does Van Zandt's soul pour out so freely on the album as on the last number, "The Catfish Song."

> Down at the bottom of that dirty old river
> Down where the reeds and the catfish play
> There lies a dream as soft as the water
> There lies a bluebird that's flown away

Over a simple piano accompaniment Van Zandt recites the lyric as if delivering a timeless hymn. Here the bluebird, the old clichéd symbol of happiness and brighter tomorrows, lies lifeless at the bottom of cold, dark water. Townes, ever aware of the brevity and preciousness of life, addresses the universal power in hopes that he, as well as this fragile creature that has fallen from the heights of the sky only to plummet into the abyss, will be judged kindly when his time inevitably comes. The mood, like that of many of Van Zandt's songs, can be seen as morose or foreboding, but within this existential prayer lays a greater understanding of the breadth of our emotions and the cycles of life, aging, and death:

> All you young ladies who dream of tomorrow
> While you're a listenin' these words will I say
> Cling to today with its joy and its sorrow
> You'll need all your memories when youth melts away

Van Zandt's voice, tough and enduring as the bark of an old oak tree, belies a genuine tenderness with the power to make time stand still just long enough for us to recognize our true selves.

"Some songs you write, and other songs you *gotta* write. You've seen it, so you gotta report it like a journalist," John Prine explained. "Townes, Bob Dylan, and Leonard Cohen absolutely *had* to write. They had no choice in it. They had to get it out of 'em. I always think I'm writing songs. I never sat in front of a typewriter and said, 'This is poetry!' You're always shootin' for the top, for the best image you can get. You're tryin' to get this sore out of you, y'know? Townes walked around with that weight on him. It was apparent. He wrote songs that were sent from heaven . . . and hell," Prine chuckled. "He was always curious enough to peek behind the curtain. And he paid a heavy price for it too."

"The songs come up through him from a deep source," Jim Rooney agreed. "He sings them to us in a voice as burnished and dark as the whiskey he loved. His was an old soul telling and retelling old stories that show us how to pass through this life and go on to the next."

Although Townes appreciated his pals' kind words, he became irate when he discovered Steve Earle's quote on a sticker on the cover of *At My Window*. He felt it was preposterous that Sugar Hill should rely on an endorsement from "the Kid" to promote his music. He grabbed the phone, punched the record company's number, and demanded they "get that stupid sticker off the album!"

No matter what sort of hassles and fiascoes Townes put him through, agent Keith Case maintained it was always worth the grief representing him. "It was a real labor of love," Keith confessed. "But Townes was just a trip. It was a delight to work with such a genius. He was one of a kind, and you don't often get an opportunity to be associated with anybody like that," Case said. "When I took him on, I was aware of the difficulties up front. His reputation definitely preceded him. I saw the signs when he first got to Nashville. He could hardly stay sober long enough to make the record. And that pattern continued on through the rest of his life."

In 1987 Jeanene headed to Nashville in search of a suitable home for Townes, Will, and herself:

I thought I'd never find it. I called back home to tell Will I was staying a few more days 'cause I hadn't had any luck. Little Will, who was only three at the time, said, "Oh, that's okay, Mom. Just find the yellow house, and that will be our home." I'd nearly called it a day, but there was one more house on the list to check out. Townes had to be close to the airport, and this one was. As I pulled into the driveway on Town Park Drive, I'll be damned if it wasn't yellow, just like Willie Boy said. I was a little concerned about the liquor store being right at the end of the block but decided it was probably a good thing, as there would be less of a distance for him to drive and less of a chance of Townes getting into trouble.

Not only was the house conveniently located near the airport and liquor store, but the mental hospital was just around the corner as well. Just as they were hauling their first load of junk to the new house, Townes spied the state mental hospital, where he had done an earlier stint, and suddenly began to panic. Jeanene had no clue when she rented the house that it had a similar view from the bathroom window of the orange and white water tower that Townes once had from his hospital room.

CHAPTER 21

A FAR CRY
FROM DRUNK

The water is gonna run out in about 1988,

if the terrorists don't get the atomic bomb first.

They're gonna stop making whiskey in 1979 + 1/2

Not only are we gonna die

but we're gonna be stoned sober when we do it.

—TVZ

Some of Townes's friends believed it was the birth of his daughter, Katie Belle, while others thought the forty-five days he did in the detox program in Huntsville, Alabama, was what did the trick, or maybe it was the combination of the two. But whatever inspired him, in 1989 Townes entered the longest period of sobriety he'd known since before his college days in Boulder. Within those couple years of clarity Townes recorded the basic tracks for two (posthumously released) albums and played some of the most inspired live shows of his career.

Bob Moore, an old drinking buddy of his, would also hop on the wagon to join Van Zandt for a tour of New England and New York State. Moore was amazed by Townes's renewed focus, energy, and mental clarity: "A lot of stuff was goin' through his head at the time. He was working on a couple new songs like 'The Hole,' but I never saw him write anything down."

Linda Lowe thought the arrival of Katie Belle gave Townes the impetus to start playing good shows again. "After she was born he was so happy. He was in love with that child," she claimed.

"I toured with Townes and Guy for a year to a year and a half [between 1990 and 1991] when Townes didn't drink . . . maybe he'd drink a little beer. We'd go out for two weeks at a time, so I got to see a lot of great shows," Robert Earl Keen recollected.

"In October 1989 I got a call from Jeanene saying that Townes was fixin' to go to New Zealand," Mickey White recalled. "He'd sobered up and thought it would be a good idea if I went with him to play the tour. So I flew up to Nashville, and we flew to New Zealand together and played a ten-day tour. We did two gigs in Aukland, a radio show, one in Wellington, and a college town. It was great. He didn't drink the whole time."

Before heading Down Under, Townes signed a new contract with Kevin Eggers to record an ambitious sixty-song, three-CD box-set overview of his career.

"From '90 to '92 he was clean," Eggers recalled. "There was a time when he was in his heroin period when it all fell apart, and I couldn't continue with him. But this was a spiritual reunion. There was a lot of love between us. There was a lot of joy. Townes came to play on these sessions. His voice was at its peak. Harold told me he didn't even look for a drink the whole time he recorded these tracks."

Over an eight-month period in 1990 Van Zandt would recut the best of his repertoire in a series of duets at the Fire Station in San Marcos and Willie Nelson's studio in Pedernales with a veritable King Arthur's court of Lone Star nobility. Joining Townes was Willie Nelson, Freddy Fender, Emmylou Harris, Doug Sahm, Augie Meyers, James McMurtry, Jerry Jeff Walker, and a vocal group called the Chromatics.

Engineer Eric Paul took on the enormous task of mixing hundreds of hours of songs that were in various states of completion. While in the thick of this daunting project he became friends with Jeanene Van Zandt, a precarious position to be in, as Kevin and Jeanene have been at each other's throats since day one, continually fighting and threatening each other with lawsuits over the rights to Townes's legacy.

"I did my best!" Eric said, rolling his eyes. "I was an engineer, so it was my job to do whatever the producer wanted." Paul was in a tight spot between Kevin and Jeanene, who vehemently hated the production on the album, particularly the backup singing by the Chromatics, which she felt was not merely superfluous but "cheesy."

"I know for a fact that Townes was very proud of the sixty-song project," Eric claimed. "I was in the studio working with Townes and Kevin on that record while Townes listened to the chick singers, and quite frankly he didn't think there was anything wrong with it. Townes *liked* the Chromatics."

"Townes was a big Elvis fan," Kevin explained. "He *loved* the Jordanaires." Hence, the controversial addition of the Chromatics (whom Jeanene dubbed "the Johnson Wax Singers") can be heard adding their vocal "shine" to "Two Girls."

"While working on the sixty-song project Townes did a benefit one night where he heard the Chromatics and asked them if they wanted to stop by the studio to sing on a few songs," Jeanene recalled. "They came in and sang on six or seven songs, and it was cool. They added the dynamics that Townes liked. After Townes finished recording he left the studio with copies of the rough mixes of the whole project. He was so proud of it. He played those tapes for everyone who came to the house. I knew those recordings by heart.

Then in 1997, three months after Townes died, Kevin came to Nashville hustlin' to finish the project. Pedernales had been holding the tapes for nonpayment of studio bills, but Kevin had a new backer who bailed him out. Kevin wanted me to bring Townes's master from *No Deeper Blue* for the song "Marie." At the time Townes had refused to record it for him, as he hadn't recorded it himself yet. Kevin had Willie sing the whole song, and he wanted to add Townes's vocal. I agreed to bring it down to see if maybe we could work something out. That's when I met Eric Paul. I was amazed at his skill. He separated out Townes's vocal and laid Townes's part in seamlessly for a new "duet" with Willie Nelson. Kevin said we'd talk about "the deal" later. As I stood there with him in the studio listening to the tapes I couldn't believe my ears! Eggers had taken those singers back into the studio and added them on to thirty songs. My heart just broke. So much for "the dynamics." Of course, I got the usual deal from Kevin for using "Marie," which amounted to "Screw You."

When asked about the project in an interview in August 1995, Townes told journalist Tim Perlich:

I figure the label is waiting for me to die before releasing it. You might laugh but I believe it's true. I made sure everyone who played on the sessions including myself got paid. So it's up to the people at Tomato/Rhino to make the next move. If they really are waiting till I'm dead, they're making a big mistake. If I was a business person, I'd much rather deal with me than my wife Jeanene. Over the years she's learned a whole lot about how the record business works. Jeanene's very sharp and doesn't take any crap from anybody. Believe me, I know.

Eggers's desire to shoot the works and carve Van Zandt's oeuvre in granite once and for all was in part driven by the slew of low-budget, off-the-board recordings of live shows produced by his brother, Harold, that have flooded the market.

"We already have classic folk versions of all these songs. We wanted to have a new conversation with the material," Eggers explained. "He'd made all these bad live albums. It was a form of reverse snobbism. If it wasn't coming out of a toilet, it's not *authentic,*" Kevin groused. (However, Eggers himself would be guilty of watering down Townes's legacy with the lackluster *Acoustic Blue,* released on Tomato in the fall of 2003.)

For all of his supposed lack of business acumen, even Van Zandt had trouble with the logic behind the big production: "If I have trouble selling records for $7.99, what makes them think I'm gonna all of a sudden sell them for thirty bucks?" he asked a reporter from *Goldmine.* Ironically, the proposed three-CD box set, complete with lyric book and biography, tentatively titled *Newology,* would feature no new material.

Eventually, the project came to a grinding halt due to a lack of available funds. A number of unsubstantiated stories claim that Eggers left town, stiffing the studio with a rubber check. In return, they wouldn't let him have the tapes unless they were paid in full.

"I don't want to get in the middle of it," Eric Paul replied diplomatically when asked about the problems plaguing Kevin's extravagant plans.

In 2001, the newly revitalized Tomato Records released a dozen tracks from the sessions as a single disc titled *Texas Rain.* The album's stand-out cut came from Freddy Fender, Augie Meyers, Doug Sahm, and Rubin Ramos and the Texas Revolution joining forces and heading south of the border on "Pancho and Lefty." With the addition of accordion, bajo sexto, and a bit of mournful mariachi brass, they breathed some much-needed new life into Townes's oft-recorded outlaw ballad.

Of the three posthumous projects of Townes's he was involved with, Paul thought his production work on *A Far Cry from Dead* created the definitive-sounding record of Van Zandt's career. The album was constructed after Townes's death from three cassette work tapes he'd made during a streak of sobriety in the early nineties.

"Jeanene came up with these tapes of twenty-four or twenty-five songs, which I meticulously cleaned with pro tools, taking out whatever hiss, pops, and snaps until I had a clean lead vocal and guitar," Eric explained. Paul then called a group of his favorite pickers and singers to build the tracks.

"I made it sound as if he was in the middle of this wonderful jam session, but he was never there!" Paul explained. Eric considers the album "a miracle." Perhaps . . . At the very least there was some hoodoo involved.

Paul recalls an unexpected "visit" from Townes while in the thick of it:

When we were making *A Far Cry from Dead* it was a very spiritual experience. There were lots of candles burning and mood. Jeanene had brought Townes's ashes into the studio. This was the craziest thing. I have never seen anything like this. One morning there were three of us in the room—myself, an assistant engineer, and Steve Henning, who owned the studio. It was the only time I've ever seen levitation. There was a candle on top of the speaker. There was nobody near the console. Suddenly, the speaker jumped up and flew across the control room and smashed. The candle went to the back wall and broke. I'm tellin' you, this *really* happened. I was wondering if I was doing the right thing or not. Townes might've been trying to knock me out. I don't know. We stopped for a few moments and then just kept going. Townes was definitely hanging out during that record, and somehow he physically did that. I think he was having a blast and dug it. That was some weird stuff.

Jeanene remembered "Townes's visit" a bit differently: "I was in the break room getting a drink when I heard this commotion. The speaker sitting on the console started to levitate. The candle sitting on top of the speaker suddenly did three flips in the air and landed on the floor, under Eric's chair, still burning. I told him, 'It was just Townes tryin' to start a fire under your ass.'"

The first pressing of thirty thousand copies of the album immediately sold out. But a month after it was released, the Austin division of Arista Records bit the dust. While missing in action, *A Far Cry from Dead* was nominated for a Grammy Award in the Contemporary Folk category, while *Poet,* a tribute album to Townes that Paul also worked on (featuring Guy Clark, Emmylou Harris, Willie Nelson, Nanci Griffith, Steve

Earle, and John Prine), was nominated for two Grammies as well. Both lost to Bob Dylan.

"After working on the Eggers sessions I finally got the chance to make him sound the way I heard him," Paul explained. "But there was a lot of controversy over *A Far Cry*. While many people loved it, the press and record people, the Townes 'purists' felt I overproduced it."

Although the album featured the usual mix of folk, blues, and country, it was the first Van Zandt record that actually rocked. The guitars on "Sanitarium Blues" soar and scorch with the kind of intensity heard on old Velvet Underground records.

"Unfortunately, the records of Townes's that I produced were all after his death, which is a shame as I would've liked to have had the pleasure of having Townes approve my work," Eric said wistfully.

CHAPTER 22

SMACKED OUT
IN THE SADDLE

I'm the mold that grunge grew from.

—TVZ

As a songwriter, troubadour, and hard-living legend, Townes somehow managed to survive long enough to become an inspiration to a new generation of young rockers, including Mudhoney, the Black Crowes, Tindersticks, the Walkabouts, and the Cowboy Junkies.

In 1990 the Cowboy Junkies' Margo and Michael Timmins invited Townes along as their opening act on an extensive two-month tour of North America beginning in June. Traveling with the band on the tour bus, the Junkies would get to know their hero pretty well.

"We initially asked Townes to join us because of his writing," Michael Timmins explained. "We'd been touched by his music long before we ever met him. He was a huge inspiration to us as a songwriter. As a person he was a real complex guy who carried a lot of demons around with him. At the same time he was a really, really gentle soul, a gentle character on many levels, and that's what allowed us to live with him for those few months being in a very confined space, on a bus with people he didn't know that well. It was a terrific experience.

"Townes was addicted to lots of things and gambling was one of them," Michael said with a laugh.

He taught us how to throw dice and play craps, which was fun! He just loved it but didn't know when to stop. He couldn't control it, and that was a problem. Townes didn't give a darn about money one way or the other. It was the thrill of gambling. We'd be sitting around, waiting, and he'd pull a quarter out of his pocket and flip it. "Okay, let's go," he says, "Ten bucks! Call it—heads or tails." One time we took a twenty-four-hour trip with him from Boulder to Houston. The whole trip was taken up with us gambling and the flux and flow of the money going around the table while throwing dice. He told us he used to make that trip all the time between Texas and Colorado. He loved the Colorado hills.

Had Townes, the Texas troubadour–smack addict been the original inspiration for the band's name?

"The funny thing about our name was it was chosen arbitrarily and with not a lot of thought or concept behind it," Michael claimed. "In the end it really made sense considering the kind of music that we create. Or maybe it was just a subconscious thing.

"Townes felt he was a channel. He didn't pretend to understand where the music came from, he just bore the burden and we're all the better for it," Timmins continued. "Sometimes at night after shows he would entertain us. We could join in if we wanted to, but Townes was tough to back up."

Like his hero Lightnin' Hopkins, Van Zandt performed best solo, unadorned. He had his own sense of timing and pushed and pulled the rhythm however he felt it, allowing his voice and guitar to become one.

"Townes with a single guitar on a real good night could stop folks cold," Ruester Rowland declared. "Some songs were absolutely best when he played them alone."

Wrecks Bell, like most of Townes's friends and fans, loved his music straight up and raw: "I loved when it was Mickey White on acoustic and me on bass, but I also think when he went out with just Mickey it was really probably better. But I loved playing with Townes. He didn't really need a bass player. He just liked me or felt sorry for me. He was at his finest alone, back when his guitar picking was just about perfect. Man, I watched him silence many an audience until he hit his last note."

"He was a very unique spirit," Michael Timmins imparted.

I talked with Jimmie Dale Gilmore about him, and we both agreed the only reason Townes stayed alive as long as he did was that he had more songs to write. That was the only thing that kept him on this earth. He had this spirit that really shouldn't have been here. He was much too sensitive for this world. The power kept him grounded here so these songs could be channeled through him and given to us. When those songs were done, it was time for him to go. There's so much poetry in his lyrics, yet at the same time they're really down-home. He's got a beautiful use of words, and at the same time he really cuts to the bone. That's what I've always loved about Townes's work.

In return for the Cowboy Junkies covering his heartbreakingly beautiful anthem "To Live's to Fly" and "Lungs," Townes penned "Cowboy Junkies Lament" for his pals while on the road during that two-month period.

"It's the only song I've ever wrote on purpose for somebody to play," Townes told Irish journalist Patrick Brennan. "I've written songs about people but I don't think I've ever written any for somebody else specifically to play. I wrote it to their rhythm. Bomb-be-bomb-be-bomp! And I would ask Michael, 'What do you think about this line? Is this too corny?' [And he said,] 'No, that's great.' It was real fine."

"He wrote quite a lot of the songs from *No Deeper Blue* during that time," Timmins recollected. "It was a real active songwriting period for him. It seemed like Townes was always getting on the bus in the morning with a new song. As we went along on the tour he told us he was writing a song for us, but he wouldn't reveal any of it until it was finished. By the end of the tour it wasn't finished, so he sent us a tape a couple months later. We sat down and listened to it and tried to decipher it. Finally I called Townes and said, 'Man, you gotta give us a clue here,'" Michael chuckled. "He said, 'Well, the first verse is about you. The second verse is about Margo. And the third verse is about Pete,' and he left it at that. We listened to it again, and it eventually fell into place and made sense. That was the biggest honor that's ever been bestowed upon us, havin' Townes Van Zandt write a song for us. It's pretty spectacular. In response to that we wrote a song for him called "Townes' Blues," which appeared on *Black-Eyed Man*.

"He truly *was* the black-eyed man," Jeanene said. "When we were out sailin,' with the sun light shinin' on them, you could actually see the color of his eyes. They were real dark brown, but when he was inside, they were black as night."

CHAPTER 23

ULTRAMARINE

I have a lot of heavy-duty songs. I've always thought if you took enough of them or any particular one seriously enough, you'd be in trouble.
   —TVZ

By April 1993, Jeanene handed Townes a final ultimatum: "If you're gonna drink—you can't live here!" she hollered. In return (or retribution), Townes rented an apartment at the Third Coast Hotel (a.k.a. the Rock 'n' Roll Hotel), Nashville's haven for raving alcoholics and notorious hell-benders.

"It doesn't take a rocket scientist to figure out what happened next," Paul K. said. "Living there, Townes only drank more. When he'd go on the road he was drinkin' too. But when he was at the house he'd have to be on his best behavior, which meant he was rather lifeless."

Jeanene hoped that by some small miracle Townes might rent a nice apartment with a swimming pool where he could bring the kids. "But instead he went and moved into the raunchiest motherfucking hell-hole he could find, in hopes that I'd say, 'Oh, Townes, you *can't* live there,' and take him back home again—which is of course just what I did—eventually."

As a compromise they bought a small cabin from Guy and Susanna Clark in Mount Juliet (as seen in the parting shot of *Heartworn Highways* where everyone is sitting around the dining room table drunkenly warbling "Silent Night"). Like his old tree fort back in Clarksville, Townes once more had a place where he could party 24/7 with his drinkin' buddies and not have to worry about the wife and kids. He christened his new home "Bayou Self."

Jeanene claimed their "no-strings relationship" continued to grow stronger until Townes's death. Every couple of days he'd show up at the Ponderosa, or she'd stop by every so often "to scare off the freaks and to make sure he had something to eat."

By spring 1994 Townes and Jeanene were legally divorced, although they maintained a common-law marriage in order to keep the family together. "We took everything out of his name and put it in mine just in case he hit a kid with his pickup truck while driving drunk. That way we would still have a home and his song publishing wouldn't be up for grabs. They could sue Townes Van Zandt as an individual, but they couldn't touch me and the kids. In twenty-twenty hindsight I probably should've stayed married to him. After he died I got a lot of grief from everybody over the nature of our relationship," Jeanene confessed.

Their relationship was complex to say the least, and outsiders didn't always know what to make of their passionate dynamic. A few days before Christmas 1995, Townes took a three hundred dollar cab ride to Dickson, Tennessee, to buy Jeanene a diamond ring. When he pulled it from his pocket he told her: "I'm not givin' you this as a Christmas present. I want you to *have* it because I love you. You are my wife no matter what."

"From that day on, whenever he called from the road he'd ask, 'Are you still wearin' my ring?'" Jeanene said. "I'm *still* wearin' it!"

"My wife and I don't live together. We live not far from one another. I see her and I see the kids almost every day. But as far as being a family man and coming home from work, we decided that because of my lifestyle and [for] tax reasons and insurance reasons and credit reasons, for her to build credit, we had a very loving divorce and we still love one another," Townes explained.

"Our lives didn't really change much," Jeanene said.

Townes gave me the power of attorney so I could continue conducting business for him, and the kids were used to him comin' and goin' all their lives. After a tour he'd come straight to the Ponderosa or call me from Bayou Self sayin', "Hey, babe, I made it back safe and sound," and we'd make plans to get together over the next day or two. He tried to honor our agreement, not to drink around the kids, the best he could. He'd leave the bottle out in the truck and go out for maintenance sips. I figured out all sorts of tricks to play on him. I'd sneak out there and shove it over, up against the door on its side, so when he went to get it, it would fall out on the driveway and break. But soon the bottle started makin' its way closer to the house. First he hid it the garage, then behind a sofa cushion.

"Then one day I was preheating the oven and a giant blue fireball blasted the oven door wide open," Jeanene said, shaking her head. "I said, 'Goddamn it, Townes!' The heat had melted the cap off the bottle and it was hell gettin' that fire out."

"I've given up my family, my liver and everything else. When you're traveling 40,000 miles, sleeping three hours a night in a little rat hole, having sound checks, then gigs and then parties afterward, you're not the ideal married man," Van Zandt confessed with typical self-deprecating humor.

"They got divorced, but I don't think they meant it in the traditional sense," Darryl Harris said. "I think he transferred his assets to Jeanene to keep his family from losin' everything. He could've killed somebody when he was drunk, or he could've died after a lingering million dollar illness. In his later years I think he developed more of a sense of responsibility. He hadn't been so straight up with Fran and J. T."

"Townes worked his butt off to keep Jeanene and the kids livin' in a nice house. He'd signed the songs over to her and the kids. It wasn't anything she had to litigate over. It was somethin' that he just did," Chip Phillips explained. "He wanted to be a good provider for his family."

Try as he might to steer a steady course, Townes was well aware of the toll that his inner demons, depression, and alcohol had already taken. In turn he often worried about his son Will's future: "That kid," Townes once said, pointing at Will, who was four years old at the time, "will probably never live to see twenty-one."

It's been a pretty wild ride so far, but somehow Townes's youngest boy has managed to make it to twenty-two, even after a hip replacement after getting run over by a truck at age seventeen.

Will sat on the front porch of the Ponderosa in a rocking chair on a warm afternoon in April 2005, sipping a beer, feeling good, considering he was about to turn himself in the following Monday to do a forty-five-day stint in the big house for DUI while already on probation.

"When I'm in the shit hole and things can't get any worse, I listen to my dad's most sad, horribly depressing songs, 'Nothin',' 'Marie,' 'Waitin' 'round to Die,' and it usually gets me feelin' a little better," he said. "Anybody with half a brain can realize that Townes ain't bullshittin'. All my friends are fans and listen to his music, even when I'm not around. I can't handle most music these days," he groaned. "I'd rather listen to Lightnin' Hopkins, John Lee Hooker, or Sonny Terry and Brownie McGee."

Will is a first-rate graffiti artist. While driving into Nashville he pointed out his latest work, done the night before on the wall of an abandoned garage off Route 24.

"Tonight I'm goin' back and chainsawin' those goddamn trees so you can see it better from the highway," he said with a fiendish grin.

One night while crashing at the Third Coast Hotel, Townes had a lucid dream instructing him to fly to Ireland and record his next album with Phillip Donnelly.

"When I woke up it was real vivid in my mind still," Van Zandt later recalled.

> So I went through to the other room where the phone and the light was. I had my hand on the desk and my finger on the light bulb, trying to get the light to work. I was still asleep and had no clothes on. I picked up my hand and there's Phillip Donnelly's phone number, who I hadn't called for two years. Phillip played on *Flyin' Shoes* and an album that was never released. He's such a [fine] player but in the meantime he'd turned into a producer also. It's three thirty in the morning and I have this dream telling me this is what I'm supposed to do.

It was nine-thirty when Donnelly answered the phone. After heartfelt greetings, Van Zandt told him of his plan to record his next record in Ireland. "I want you to produce it. You pick the players. What do you think about that?" "Splendid! Lovely!" Phillip replied exuberantly. Townes explained that he would still need some time to write another half-dozen songs and get the money together.

One morning Jeanene awoke to find Townes's writing pad lying on the coffee table. As he was fast asleep, she felt safe taking a peek at the lines he'd scribbled down the night before. As she read the tragically beautiful words to what later became "A Song For," she began to cry.

Hearing her sob, Townes wandered out of the bedroom to find out what the matter was. "Townes," she said, "this new song is so beautiful. It's bound to be my favorite." Van Zandt shrugged, wiping the sleep from his eyes. "Song my ass . . . That's a suicide note," he said.

Ribbons of love
Please keep me true sane
Until I reach home on the morrow
Never, never to wander again
I'm weak and I'm weary of sorrow

London to Dublin
Australia to Perth
I gazed at your sky
I tasted your earth
Sung out my heart
For what it was worth
Never again shall I ramble

There's nowhere left
In this world where to go
My arms, my legs they're a-tremblin'
Thoughts both clouded and blue as the sky
Not even worth the rememberin'

Adding the final verses, the unused death letter was transformed into an emotionally pulverizing song:

Now as I stumble and reel to my bed
All that I've done
All that I've said
Means nothing to me
I'd soon as be dead
All of this world be forgotten

No words of comfort
No words of advice
Nothin' to offer a stranger
Gone the love, gone the spite
It just doesn't matter no longer

My sky's getting far
The ground's getting close
My self goin' crazy

The way that it does
I'll lie on my pillow
And sleep if I must
Too late to wish I'd been stronger

"That's a real strange song, 'cause I don't really feel that way," Townes later explained. "I might have felt that way in the middle of the night when I woke up and wrote it down, but I don't feel that way."

That May, Townes and Harold Eggers flew to the Emerald Isle where Phillip Donnelly met them at the airport and spirited them off to Limerick, where they holed up at Hanratty's Hotel. The sessions for the album took place at Xeric Studio where journalist Aidan Corr of the *Limerick Leader* found "the atmosphere totally in contrast to the outdoor sunshine."

Grim as the environment may have been, for Townes, "the whole ten days were a real treat. It was just me and Harold and the boys." The band, composed of "all good, top of the line players," as Van Zandt described them, cut two songs each day. "This is the first one I've done that I've laid back and said, 'You guys play and I'll sing.' And they were such good players that it was a real joy, there were no nuances lost.'

Some might argue with Van Zandt, who often underestimated his own musical contribution to his albums. Townes's guitar playing, particularly on his earlier records when his picking was pristine, would always dictate the feel of the song. On *No Deeper Blue,* that feel is sadly nowhere to be found (except on the final cut, "Gone Too Long").

The album's blues numbers ("Goin' Down to Memphis" in particular) ultimately suffer from the absence of his guitar playing, sounding a bit generic, while some of the ballads ("Hey Willy Boy") beg for his instrumental presence as well. Yet there are some wonderful touches that never would've happened if Townes hadn't hopped a plane to Ireland. Percy Robinson's haunting steel guitar on the opening track, "A Song For," sticks to your mind like cobwebs. The intricate accordion and fiddle fills on "Niles River Blues" recall the Band working out on a catchy Cajun waltz. Declan Masterson's uilleann pipes weave and wheeze through Townes's most surreal narrative since he crashed his silver ship against the rocks of Andilar.

"Billy, Boney and Ma" is a hilarious, rambling tale of a kid who takes up a life of crime after "seein' socket to eye" with a skeleton he happened to meet while poking around in a graveyard. A little old lady with bad eyesight figures into the picture, cooking up something "hot and greasy" for Boney, in hopes of putting some meat on his sorry frame.

Van Zandt felt that *No Deeper Blue* was "a beautiful album. When you listen to it, put on some earphones, it'll drive you straight into the ground!"

"I was honored to be asked by his producer at the time, my old friend Phillip Donnelly, to play on the album that he made in Ireland," Donovan Leitch fondly recalled. "The tunes he recorded are quite astonishingly unique, and I played my harmonica with a will that day in Limerick, knowing I was with a master of our craft."

"That was the first time I ever got to meet Donovan," Townes enthused about the Hurdy Gurdy Man's guest appearance on his album. "He's a really good guy and a very fine harmonica player."

Donovan, the avatar of Flower Power, whose funky acid anthem "Sunshine Superman" and ultragroovy "Mellow Yellow" defined sixties hip, was quite taken with Van Zandt as well: "Townes is a classic of the genre. He is sadly missed now," Leitch lamented. "I recall a song to his darling little girl ["Katie Belle Blue"]. Sad she won't grow to know him when she's a woman. *No Deeper Blue* indeed!"

Townes's tender waltz to his "beautiful daughter," "Katie Belle Blue," is sure to put a lump in your throat. The song contains the album's misleadingly dark title within its opening verse:

> There is no deeper blue
> In the ocean that lies
> As deep as the blue
> Of your laughing eyes
> No sweeter sound
> Than your gentle sigh
> No heart was ever so pure

Once the basic tracks were cut, Phillip got down to the chore of mixing, while Harold and Townes hit the bumpy, winding roads for a twenty-day tour of Ireland and then hopped over to England before returning once more to Nashville.

"Townes was in Dublin when he heard a song playing in the background that he suddenly realized was something that he'd written, a punk version of "Kathleen" by a band called the Tindersticks. It was in heavy rotation on the BBC, and he didn't know anybody had cut it," Chip

Phillips said. "He had just hired an agent to track his royalties. I went over to his house, and he had gotten a platinum record for 'Pancho,' and I congratulated him for it. He said, 'Ya wanna help me burn it?' He was mad 'cause it was a huge record and he hadn't gotten any royalties off it."

Looking back at the recording of *No Deeper Blue,* Van Zandt later told the *New York Times:* "From the time I had that dream until somebody handed me the finished cassette was about a year. I can't believe I pulled that together."

In 1994 Sugar Hill Records also released *Roadsongs,* an album comprising Van Zandt's favorite tunes by everyone from the Rolling Stones, Bob Dylan, and Joe Ely to a superb version of Bruce Springsteen's "Racing in the Street." The set was rounded out with some old Lightnin' Hopkins numbers, "The Wabash Cannonball," another version of "Fraulein," and Clarence Ashley's "The Coo Coo Bird."

"He did my favorite versions of a lot of old songs that weren't his," Butch Hancock enthused. "His voice was incredible. It had that plaintive feel. I love it more than Hank Williams'."

But of the pair it was *No Deeper Blue,* Townes's first collection of new tunes since 1987, that packed the wallop. "You can't listen to it without throwing up blood," Townes quipped.

"He called it his 'dance album,'" Jeanene said jokingly. "Dance of death was more like it."

Among the standouts on *No Deeper Blue* was "The Hole," which Townes jokingly subtitled "Green Eyed Lady of the Lowlands." The song, another of Van Zandt's eerie, twisted tales, rivals the best of the Brothers Grimm; a minor-key odyssey in which Townes stumbles through the dark forest of his psyche where he meets a lonely hag who works some nasty magic on him, stopping short of turning him into a toad.

Van Zandt's "Marie," said to be originally inspired by Meryl Streep's character in the movie *Ironweed,* is a harrowing ballad of a homeless couple facing unfathomable hardship. The minor-key ballad manages to pack the punch of William Kennedy's novel in under three and a half minutes. The song's protagonist sleeps at the mission and spends hours waiting in line for unemployment checks. Soon after meeting Marie they "do a little settlin' down" beneath a bridge for the summer until she becomes pregnant. Things quickly go from bad to worse until she dies with their unborn son "safe inside" her. From there, the singer catches the Chesapeake freight heading south, where he believes fate will soon reunite him once more with Marie. Even by Van Zandt's standard, the song was a milestone—unquestionably "a ten razor blader," as Eric Andersen would say.

"He did 'Marie' live for years before he recorded it," Michael Timmins recalled. "But it was such a disappointment the way the producer handled it. The song really got lost in that production. They should have just let the man tell his story. But I just don't think Townes cared that much," Timmins reckoned. "His thing was songwriting; by the time he recorded a song, his attitude was well, whatever . . . "

Townes wrote "Marie" in Santa Monica, where he and Guy Clark were booked to play McCabes' Guitar Shop. Arriving a day early, they holed up at a cheap hotel across the street from the tiny club. The next morning they met for breakfast and then returned to their respective rooms to hang out, write, and watch TV. That afternoon around five o'-clock Townes knocked on Clark's door and sauntered in with his guitar.

"He sat down and played this song," Guy recalled. "I said, 'Wow, man, that's beautiful.' And I'll be a son of a bitch if he didn't walk out on stage that night at nine o'clock and play it! Townes said, 'Man, I don't know where that came from. It just came out!' That was a one-day song! It was breathtaking. He wasn't showin' off. He was the Real Deal . . . But I don't like the way it was recorded," Guy grumbled.

In response to a near decade of silence, Van Zandt told the press, "I'm not going to try to churn out new albums. I'm in competition with Mozart, Beethoven, Lightnin' Hopkins, the Rolling Stones, and the Lord. I can't just make up some silly song and put it out there."

"It's amazing what he produced in his lifetime," Michael Timmins said. "Even at the end."

CHAPTER 24

LAST CALL, Y'ALL

Everyone keeps buying me drinks.
I think they're trying to kill me.
   —TVZ

Like his hero Hank Williams, he was running himself into a wall.
   —Harold Eggers

"Townes, like Kerouac before him, was brought up in a time when being able to hold your liquor was considered a virtue. It was a sign, not just in Texas, but all over, of being 'a real man.' The outstanding feature of Townes's life was not that he drank too much but of the beautiful work he left us," David Amram pointed out. "We unfortunately live in a society that glorifies the barfly rather than the work of the habitué that the bar created."

"I had a hard time with his alcoholism. I just couldn't embrace it," Rodney Crowell confessed. "One of the last times I saw Townes was about six months before he died. He was drunk, and it was just too sad."

"He dried out so many times; he just ran out of insurance after a while," Keith Case said. "The last couple of detoxes were so tough they almost killed him. They put him into an ICU. It was that intense."

Encouraged by his friend Ricky Skaggs, Peter Rowan (author of an ode to the notorious dope-running outlaw named "Panama Red") moved to Nashville to record *The Walls of Time* with Jim Rooney in 1982. Although they occasionally ran into each other around town, it wasn't until a tour of England with Guy and John Stewart in the early nineties that Peter really got to know Van Zandt.

"I tried hard to get on Townes's wavelength, but I'm a real failure when it comes to alcoholism," Peter laughed. "Townes never acted drunk. He just kept a steady buzz goin'. Townes was like a junky, in the way he measured out his alcohol. He had it down to a science. He'd carry around little bottles of vodka and soda with him all the time. First he'd drink half of the bottle and then top it off with soda water and sip on it throughout the day. Every time I'd see him he'd say, 'Listen to this!' and then he'd recite some rhyme that was just brilliant. You had to dig 'em, whether they became songs or not."

"Townes was an anomaly, like a western [Charles] Bukowski," Chip Phillips said. "When the inspiration was flowing, lyrics would just roll off the tip of his tongue. Once I was over at his house on Town Park Drive when he told me, 'Man, I can write a song about anything. If you don't believe me just pick up the newspaper.' So I did. And we played pin the tail on the donkey with the newspaper. I closed my eyes and pointed to a story, and he read it and wrote a song about it. Most of it was decent, as good as anything you'd hear."

"In 1994 Townes became deathly ill with the flu and was hospitalized for over a month. He called me to say he was coughin' up blood," Jeanene sighed.

I told him to get his ass to the hospital. He walked into Vanderbilt, and some doctor immediately declared he had TB and threw him into isolation. Then the DTs kicked in. I said, "He's gonna die if he doesn't get a drink!" Seven days later he was lying there, tied to the bed, having terrible hallucinations and convulsions. He kept screamin' that Katie Belle was flyin' around the room and was gonna fly out the window just like Loop did. But she wasn't even there. They finally put him in a drug-induced coma in intensive care and put a breathing tube down his throat, which really screwed up his voice. You can hear the difference in his singing on *No Deeper Blue*.

It turned out he had inhalation pneumonia from the construction they'd been doin' at the Rock 'n' Roll Hotel. They were refurbishing the restaurant in the front of the building, and he was breathing in tons of dust and dried-up rat shit. They'd told Townes and the other tenants they could stay, and there was nothing to worry about.

In the meantime Jeanene canceled his lease, threatened to sue the hotel, and brought Townes home, temporarily. As a solution they bought the Clarks' lake house. Townes then flew to Ireland to cut his new dream album while Jeanene moved in furniture, set up the kitchen, and made the place nice and comfortable for her ex-husband's return.

While being treated for pneumonia, Van Zandt's doctors determined that his deteriorating health had little chance of improving unless he was willing to submit to a thorough detoxification program. The last time Townes had detoxified was nearly two years earlier when he'd spent a month and a half in Huntsville, Alabama.

"When he went into convulsions, you couldn't go near him. He needed to be tied down as he could fly out of bed and hit his head. It's *not* a pretty picture," Jeanene said. "There was plenty of puking and shitting. And then there were the hallucinations."

In one of Townes's more vivid and bizarre visions he claimed to have seen an Indian princess sitting in the branches of a tree while her husband sat below, cross-legged on the ground. Their son was playing nearby when an airplane flew overhead. The boy pointed up at the plane and asked, "Mama, what's that?" "That's just some humans that think that they can fly," she answered. Then the little boy pointed at Townes sitting beside his father and asked, "Who's that, Mama?" "That's just some poor soul waiting around to die," she replied.

Without a slow, steady intake of alcohol Townes would eventually go into convulsions. Harold Eggers learned how to pace him and keep him together enough to play a show. But as Townes grew increasingly frail over the years, drying out had become less of an option.

Eric Andersen believed his friend's battle with addiction was intrinsic to his persona: "If you take a look at most creative people, whether they're writers, painters or musicians, from Proust to Baudelaire, to Rimbaud to Hemingway or Fitzgerald, any incandescent talent or anybody who really feels deeply or sees far, within three feet of them you'll find a bottle or a vial. Just take a look at Charlie Parker, John Coltrane, or Mozart," Andersen insisted. "None of these people could take life straight. They *all* did drugs just to attain equilibrium, just to feel normal. In Townes's case, it was about maintenance. He wasn't getting high. He didn't enjoy it."

CHAPTER 25

THE GLORIOUS TRAIN WRECK (INCLUDING THE BLAZE FOLEY DETOUR)

Mr. Clean I ain't! But instead of raising hell, I'm more interested in reaching people in the audience.

—TVZ

"Townes and I were just good friends. We never thought what we were doin' was *legendary*. We were just lookin' for the next bottle of whiskey or the next piece of ass we could find," Wrecks Bell laughed. "He had everything that anyone wants in life. Fame . . . money . . . Townes *had* success."

Bell sat talking in the back room of the new Old Quarter in Galveston, which doubles as his office and performer's dressing room. A big Texas flag hangs on one wall. Various performers' set lists are stapled to another. There's a couple of neon beer signs, a poster from a Richard Dobson gig, and above his desk his prized poster from the night Bell played bass with Lightnin' Hopkins at Carnegie Hall on a bill called "Boogie 'n' Blues" with John Lee Hooker, Clifton Chenier, and David "Honeyboy" Edwards on April 10, 1979.

"I introduced Townes to Lightnin' at the old Old Quarter," Bell said proudly.

I don't know how influenced he was by his playin' really . . . Townes already had his own style when he was so young. He was a great performer too . . . Could take an audience and just shut 'em up. They wouldn't say a word. I can't say where his inspiration came from. He was very intelligent and very well read. He could sit in a hotel room in the middle of nowhere and write a song because he had that gift. He was always prolific, wrote on airplanes, buses, trains . . . on the college circuit from North Carolina up the East Coast to New York City. He wrote 'To Live's to Fly' on that tour. Y'know that verse "The bottom's low and the treble's clear"? He was talking about a college gig we played in Kimborough, North Carolina, at an all-guy's school. They shipped in the girls from a nearby all-girl college, and Townes ran off with some girl that night. She was supposed to go back to her college but wound up staying with us. Townes kicked me out of the room. Then he got busted and wound up gettin' in all kinds of trouble. These days, of course, it would be nothing.

In the original version to the song Townes immortalized his friend, singing:

Get up Rex my friend,
It's time to go again
Think of all the poetry
And the pickin' down the line

"That song has one of my favorite lines he ever wrote," Bell said and began to sing in a warm, friendly voice: "Everything is not enough / And nothing is too much to bear."

"Boy that pretty much sums it up. Maybe I'm biased, but he was the greatest writer that ever lived. I think Townes is in an echelon by himself."

THE BLAZE FOLEY DETOUR

Every year on the anniversary of his death, Wrecks continues to hold the Annual Townes Van Zandt Wake, an open mike where anyone can get up and perform a song or two by the legendary Texas troubadour. Over the past ten years the club has turned into something of a shrine to his old friend. The wall behind the stage, covered with old photographs and gig posters, is dedicated to Van Zandt's memory. Perhaps the most fantastic artifact of all is Blaze Foley's duct-taped wallet, which Wrecks found a few days after Blaze's funeral, shoved down into the recesses of his couch, upon which Foley had been crashing during his last couple nights on earth.

"Blaze stayed at my house and slept on my couch, and I listened to his songs but I just didn't get it," Guy Clark said, shakin' his head. "He was one of those guys who was drunker than Townes and didn't know why. Blaze wanted to be as crazy as Townes, but he wasn't as smart so it never worked. I think Townes tried to make him feel better about himself. That's only my opinion. Maybe I didn't get it because I was tired of Blaze sleepin' on my couch, I don't know . . . Maybe Blaze was one of the few guys I ever met who was more fucked up than me," Guy laughed.

"Blaze just came with the territory. He played Uncle Fester to Townes's Gomez," Jeanene groaned.

"Ah, Blaze Foley, the duct-tape man," old friend Marvin Williams sighed.

Blaze was an adventurous lad who never took very good care of himself. He was a sweet man with a slightly rough exterior. A real piece of work. Wonderfully talented and so nice, he'd do just about anything for anybody . . . Give you his last dollar. He'd give you anything he had. He didn't care about anything remotely material. He once gave me his most prized possession—his Swiss Army knife. It was about the only thing he owned. All he cared about was his music and his friends.

I remember early one morning Bill Bentley and I were sitting in the Split Shift in New Orleans' French Quarter, a place filled with ladies of questionable virtue and sailors passed out on the bar. It was about four o'-clock in the morning when Blaze walked in. This was before he called himself Blaze and was known then as "Deputy Dawg." He just got off a plane from Chicago and was carrying a suitcase. Having just taken an il-legal substance, he was tripping when two of the four people sitting at the bar shouted, "Hey, Deputy Dawg! What's goin' on?" With that he turned, grabbed his suitcase and fedora hat, and broke for the door.

One time we were sittin' up at the bar at the Hole in the Wall on Twenty-sixth and Guadalupe, and I was buyin' the drinks when the Shiner truck pulled right up on the sidewalk. Several cases of Shiner soon mysteriously found their way into Blaze's station wagon, which we then took over to the Continental Club on Congress and traded for an afternoon of rounds of whiskey. Then Blaze drove us somewhere out to the country, pulled up this dirt road to a shack, went in and brought back a handful of brightly colored capsules and tablets, none which were identifiable. He asked if I'd like to try one. I don't remember how, but I managed to get back to town before things got completely out of hand.

Townes first met Michael David Fuller of Austin, Texas, at the Bitter End, on Bleecker Street in Greenwich Village. Foley had a room at the Gramercy Park Hotel, paid for, courtesy of an "interested" record company. Sharing many of the same passions (songwriting, art, liquor, and drugs), the two hell-raisers had become fast friends.

There are nearly as many bizarre stories about Blaze that surrounded his friend, champion, and inspiration, Townes Van Zandt. And most of them are just as surreal, hysterical, and ultimately heartbreaking.

After his death, Foley's pal Jubal Clark and some friends plotted to steal his body from the funeral home and duct tape him to the door of a tiny club called the Austin Outhouse, where a cast of local luminaries was holding a benefit to raise the cash needed for his burial.

Blaze had a lifelong fetish for duct tape. He loved its color and texture but most of all its remarkable versatility. Foley used it for everything. He wrapped his old dilapidated boots up with the stuff, mended frayed lapels of sports jacket, and even fashioned some pretty spiffy hatbands too.

Even after Willie Nelson and Merle Haggard recorded Foley's "If I Could Only Fly," he continued to sleep on friends' couches, under porches, and inside trash bins, preferring BFI (Browning-Ferris Industries) Dumpsters in particular.

An old poster for one of Blaze's gigs still hangs on the wall of Will Van Zandt's bedroom. In the box under the words "Blaze Foley Appearing At," somebody scrawled the words, "Your house when you least expect it!"

"He was my best friend since I can remember," Will said. "He was like a big teddy bear, always bringin' me toys and trinkets. His death didn't really affect me at first. I was only five or six at the time. Then one day I found some pictures and realized what happened to him and how he went out, and it just tore me up."

In 1987 the Van Zandts loaded up the truck and moved to Nashville "to get Townes away from the constant entourage of misfits and hangers-on," Jeanene explained. There were just too many "old friends" sleeping on their couch or buying Townes another round every time he went to town. Van Zandt needed to clear the zone, but unfortunately Music City was hardly the ideal environment for Townes to get healthy and turn his life around.

On February 1, 1989, Blaze was killed after an argument with Carey January who testified that he shot Foley because he "feared for his life." Both men accused each other of taking advantage of Carey's father, Concho, an ailing alcoholic who lived off Social Security and veterans' benefits. Carey claimed he was hired by a state agency as his father's caregiver and worried that Blaze was trying to take his job. He claimed Foley repeatedly kicked him out of the house and once whacked him across the back with an ax handle.

January testified that on the day before the shooting, Blaze and his father were drinking heavily and Foley began to harass him again. The following morning, after Blaze chased him with a broom, Carey grabbed a loaded .22 from the hall closet and (claiming he first fired a warning shot through the floor) killed him. January feared Blaze was going take the rifle away from him. But investigators found no evidence of a struggle or bullet holes in the floor.

"He was coming at me," January told the court, with "fire in his eyes."

Singer-songwriter Pat Mears claimed that Blaze had the ability to "look right through you. If you weren't an honest person, you couldn't handle his eyes." Perhaps Foley's Old Testament glare triggered something in Carey he couldn't control.

January's father, Concho, told the jurors that he didn't understand why his son had shot Blaze. He claimed Foley was sitting beside his bed in a chair, showing him his drawings, when Carey burst in the room and blasted him in the chest. In his original testimony Carey, hoping to save himself, told the police that Blaze had stolen the old man's government checks and beaten his father.

In the end Carey January was acquitted, claiming he acted in self-defense. The cops wrote off the murder as an "unfortunate homicide." "Blaze would have laughed at that, then gotten mad as hell," said Casey Monahan of the *Austin Chronicle*. "To someone like Blaze, there was no such beast as a fortunate homicide."

Foley, a big old bear of a man, stood six foot two and weighed nearly three hundred pounds. Some described him as "a walking contradiction" given to fits of sudden rage while under the influence. Yet Marvin Williams described him as "a gentle, gentle man. It was a big blow when he was shot. He was so interesting to talk to. I'd be happy to just sit there and buy him beer all day, which happened on more than one occasion. He never had any money, but he had stories. He probably gave it away to people who had less than he did. Everything sprung out of his love for music . . . and duct tape, the two ruling passions of his life."

It was Townes who first turned Larry Monroe of KUT 90.5 onto Blaze. Larry was one of the few DJs who dared to play Foley's music on the radio—not just in Austin, but *anywhere*. In Monroe's *Austin Weekly* eulogy for Blaze he recalled the night Foley helped Townes, fresh out of detox and struggling through a set at emmajoe's. When Van Zandt faltered over the lyrics to "If I Needed You," Blaze came to his rescue. Standing beside him, he began singing a gentle harmony that helped Townes to regain his focus. "Townes grew stronger from that point, and it almost seemed that a direct energy transfer from Blaze had occurred," Monroe recalled. From that point on Larry considered Foley more than just another lost soul and eventually gained a genuine appreciation for his idiosyncratic songs. He was not alone. Willie Nelson, Merle Haggard, Lyle Lovett, and most recently John Prine have all recorded Blaze's tunes.

Townes would later write "Blaze's Blues," which chronicled the misadventures of a pair of ramblers as they bounced from gig to gig and town to town. Van Zandt recorded the tribute to his friend on *No Deeper Blue,* but it was really Phillip Donnelly's sizzling slide guitar that made the tune memorable.

Blaze "certainly looked up to Townes," Lucinda Williams told Lee Nichols of the *Austin Chronicle*. "I think Townes was his hero. Unfortunately, I think he romanticized that whole self-destructive, outlaw lifestyle."

Lucinda Williams, whose heartbreaking portrait of Blaze in "Drunken Angel," which appeared on her 1999 roots-rock masterpiece, *Car Wheels on a Gravel Road,* considered him both "a genius and a beautiful loser."

Foley was indeed both. And he had the reputation to match it. The following year after being permanently banned from the Kerrville Folk Festival, Blaze managed to get through the gate dressed as a woman in a flowery skirt, in a blonde wig with bright-red lipstick (with his full beard and mustache). Once Kerrville's director, Rod Kennedy, got wind of Foley's crazy charade, Blaze was promptly hunted down and dragged out. Blaze was shunned from nearly every bar in Austin as well, except the Austin Outhouse, which was the only joint in town that dared book him and allowed him to sleep under their pool table.

"Even the police didn't take him seriously," guitarist, songwriter, and producer Gurf Morlix told Monahan, recounting the night they saw a fire on their way back from a gig. "Blaze got on a pay phone and reported it to the police, and they asked him who he was and when he said, 'Blaze Foley,' they hung up."

Bumpin' into Blaze always had a way of rearranging whatever plans you had in mind. Butch Hancock recalled unexpectedly taking the Blaze Foley detour:

> One night at this little ol' club called the Beach, just north of the campus in Austin, the gig was all over and we'd been hangin' around when we wandered out into the parking lot. I had this old clunker Volkswagen when Blaze came up and said to me, "Hey, uh, wait a minute! Hold on there! You're gonna take me around the block on your Volkswagen." I said, "Okay, hop in." He said, "No. I'm gettin' on top!" Then he crawled up on this funny rack I used to carry 'round my PA with and started hollerin' directions at me. I figured, oh, hell, the sooner I got around the block, the sooner he'd get off the car. We went zoomin' around, then he crawled down off there and said, "Hey, that was fun!" I was like, "Yeah, yeah, that was great Blaze . . . Well, I'll see ya . . ." Then he said, "No, wait, you get up there, and I'll drive *you* around!" I said, "No, man . . . No way! And sure enough, there I was, ridin' around on top of my Volkswagen with Blaze Foley at the wheel.

On June 26, 1986, Larry Monroe got a phone call informing him that Bob Dylan was in Austin, shopping at Electric Ladyland. He grabbed his daughter Sara, hopped in the car, and zipped over to find Bob trying on a variety of masks and jackets. Monroe hung around wondering how to break the ice until Sara dragged him away, wanting to show her dad something interesting she'd found. A moment later Dylan made his escape. Suddenly, Blaze Foley appeared and approached Larry, offering to introduce him to the legend, who was standing outside talking with Townes and his ragged company, which included the concert promoter Indian Gary and a friend named Pussycat.

"They had all been on a binge, and none was seeing too straight," Monroe later described the "summit meeting." In the meantime, Blaze hit everyone up for a couple of spare bucks to buy a Ronald Reagan mask, which he then used as a cassette case.

"Ah . . . the late Blaze Foley. He was late all his life!" Darryl Harris quipped. "I was a eulogizer at Blaze's funeral." With just a couple words Harris summed his friend up in a nutshell: "I don't think there's a person here who hasn't been embarrassed by his honesty," he told the crowd.

Musician and producer Gurf Morlix remembered Foley's funeral as "a chaotic clusterfuck." Blaze was laid to rest on the coldest day in the history of Texas. The ground was so frozen it took a backhoe to bury him. Of course, there wasn't enough money to pay for a police escort, and nearly everyone got lost on the way to the graveyard. "About two-thirds of the people heading for the cemetery never found it," Gurf said. "It was perfect." Those who managed to arrive received a piece of duct tape that they either wore as an armband or used to seal Blaze's coffin.

"We were a funny bunch of guys, at least the ones of us who are still alive," Darryl chuckled. "Blaze was so into duct tape everybody wanted to mummify him with it! If it weren't for Townes, they probably would've gone ahead and done it. You know it's pretty scary when Townes Van Zandt is the voice of reason."

Soon after Foley's funeral, Townes began circulating a story about how Blaze had hocked his guitar just days before his death, and in the midst of all the shock and grief nobody grabbed the ticket out of the pocket of his suit jacket, which he wore when he was laid to rest. Van Zandt then enlisted the help of the Waddell brothers, drove over to the cemetery, and hired a guy with a backhoe to exhume Blaze's grave so they could get his guitar back from the pawn shop.

Even by the pale light of a moonless winter night no one needed to question if they'd dug up the right casket or not. Across the top of the late singer-songwriter's coffin somebody had taped the initials BFI in big silver letters, which of course, as he once said of the Dumpsters of Austin, stood for "Blaze Foley Inside."

We now return to Wrecks Bell, tending bar on a slow winter's night at the Old Quarter in Galveston: "Townes played here on Saturday, October 5th, 1996, for the grand opening of the new Old Quarter and then went up to Austin, played the Cactus Café, did Larry Monroe's radio show, and that was pretty much it."

Although Bell clearly missed his old running buddies (he'd printed a T-shirt with Jet Whitt's old photo of Blaze, Townes, and himself to commemorate the Eighth Annual TVZ Wake), he seemed to have come to a point of resolve about their passing. In fact, he was quite surprised to still be here himself. And in the spirit of the notorious hell-raiser, singer-songwriter Warren Zevon, who recently passed on, he's determined to "enjoy every sandwich."

After the wake, lost in the Galveston fog, I drove in circles, searching for Highway 35, to get back to Houston. Turning a corner, I suddenly found myself face-to-face with the looming wrought-iron gates of the University of Texas Medical Branch Hospital where Townes had once been treated for a nervous breakdown. Just then the Surfaris' "Wipeout" came blaring through the dashboard speakers. The reverb-drenched guitars twanged as the drums frantically pounded out the perfect movie soundtrack to Townes Van Zandt's life.

"No matter what shape Townes was in, he had the songs, and that's what people came to hear," Griff Luneberg said. Van Zandt's last Austin shows took place at Luneberg's Cactus Café on October 11 and 12, 1996. Griff remembers them as "pure magic," with the audience hanging on every word and sending back a huge outpouring of appreciation after every song. "They even laughed at his jokes, which are the same jokes he'd been telling for twenty years," Griff recalled.

Diagonally across the street from Austin's famous dive, the Hole in the Wall, on the University of Texas campus is the Cactus Café that Griff Luneberg has managed for the past twenty-three years. It's a beautiful old bar built in 1933, complete with stained-glass windows and a ceiling with molding strips depicting holy relics of the Old West, kind of like a tiny Texas version of the Sistine Chapel. There's a pistol in a holster with a belt full of bullets, a hat and pair of gloves with a lasso around it, a powder horn and canteen, and a longhorn skull and a pair of boots with a rattlesnake wrapped around them. "There's a lot of history here," Luneberg said, proud but weary.

Griff first got to know Townes back in the midseventies when he bought Emmylou Harris's *Luxury Liner* album and immediately fell under the spell of "Pancho and Lefty." It wasn't long before he caught Townes live at Liberty Hall in Houston, accompanied by the Hemmer Ridge Mountain Boys. A few years later, in the early eighties, he chanced to see him again at the Hole in the Wall: "I went in to get a beer, and he was playing but I didn't recognize him at first. I thought this guy sure writes some really great songs, but he doesn't sing very well. There were only a handful of people in there."

In 1982 Griff went to a "gettin' out of jail party" for Austin singer-songwriter Calvin Russell at the Soap Creek Saloon and found Van Zandt playing a couple songs but mostly shooting pool. Luneberg remembers:

I'd been booking the Cactus for a year or two but hadn't had any major talent there yet—Nanci Griffith and Lyle Lovett, before his first album came out. I was real nervous, just a kid, about twenty-three. But I went over and talked to him. I said, "Hey, Mr. Van Zandt . . . uh, my name is Griff, and I run this little songwriter club called Cactus Café, and we'd sure love to have you play." Townes was real genuine. There was no pretension there whatsoever. He immediately said, "Really? Well, that sounds like a wonderful idea. Here's my number; give me a call." Then he said, "Good lucks to ya." He always said "good lucks" in the plural, not the singular. I called him two days later, and we booked a gig a month later for two hundred bucks.

Griff recalled that for his first gig at the Cactus, Townes was "real together. He didn't blow that show, though he blew a lot of 'em. But having Townes Van Zandt on our stage was real special, and I thought we had arrived. Back then," Lunberg confessed, "I was kind of a romantic. We went out drinkin' afterwards. We were with my girlfriend, Mary, and I said, 'Townes, isn't she the prettiest girl you've ever seen?' He said, 'Well . . . the second prettiest—*my wife's* the prettiest.' I had bought into the myth and tried to keep up with him and wound up on all fours," Griff said with a laugh.

There's plenty of stories about acolytes hoping to prove themselves to Townes by trying to match his voracious appetite for drink, drugs, and lunacy. New York singer-songwriter Richard Julian recounted his own folly:

Once he took me fishing, out on Percy Priest Lake [in Nashville] on his boat with Jeanene, Will, and Buddy Mondlock. I was twenty-one at the time and determined to become this hard-boozing musician. I brought along a bottle of Jack Daniels, but Townes wasn't drinkin' hard stuff at the time, only beer—which he hated. Over the course of the afternoon I drank the entire fifth by myself. Then it started to rain like crazy, and we had to go down into the cabin. Townes was up on the deck and found the empty bottle. I was lyin' down with my feet up, feelin' ill, when I heard Townes ask everybody if they'd drank any of it. Then he came over, grabbed me by the collar, and dragged me up onto the deck of the boat in the middle of a rainstorm to get some water on my face. He called me "an idiot" and said, "Man, you could fuckin' *die* from this."

"The next day I remember thinkin' to myself, I had the most famous alcoholic in the world drag me around his boat, lecturin' me. That really got me to clean my shit up after that," Richard said with a laugh.

"If it hadn't been for Townes, I never would've got sober," Bob Moore explained. When Bob went in for treatment, Townes regularly stopped in to check on his friend.

"He'd gone to Europe, and I started drinking again," Moore confessed. "When he got back he was surprised that I was drinking again. He knew very well what the consequences would be. Townes was like a medicine man—like a shaman to his tribe. He said to me, 'You can do what you want. Go ahead and get a beer. But if nothing else you'll have cleaner heartaches.'"

"I never gave up on him, and he never gave up on us," Griff Luneberg said.

He could've played bigger places, but he knew we would book him through thick and thin. When he lived in Austin he'd play here once a month. In the nineties, after he moved to Nashville, he'd come back and play two nights at the club. Invariably, he'd blow the first night. But there were always nuggets of beauty no matter what was goin' on. Then he'd feel guilty and stay straight for the second night. People in the know would always come for the Saturday show because they knew Friday night would usually be a train wreck, but a glorious train wreck nonetheless.

His turnout was consistently good. In the last few years we'd have to do two nights to get all the people in. Most other people who've blown shows here don't come back. People aren't gonna waste their money. They'd lose their crowd, but Townes's only got bigger. There were some amazing shows, and you'd hope to get one of those. And if you didn't, there'd always be something magic about the dark shows, where if you could just grab one nugget, it would make it all worthwhile. Sometimes, with Townes, it was like you pay your money, and you take your chances.

Journalist Chris Dickinson recalled going to see Townes perform one night, describing the amazing sort of rebound he'd make just as you were about to grab your hat, pay your tab, and slide out the door: "The first set cleared out most of the place long before it collapsed to its conclusion. His public disintegration was like watching an aggressive virus devouring its host from the inside out. I figured he would not return for a second set. He came back like some focused Lazarus, limbs jerking back into motion, from his descent into the tomb . . . sucked down into the bottomless blur-hole of his life . . . the hair of every dog that ever bit him."

"Between 1983 until when he died in 1997, Townes must have played here somewhere between eighty and a hundred times. In nearly fifteen years he only missed one show!" Griff recalled. "No matter what kind of shape Townes was in, he always walked through that door except once in 1984."

He played here several times before and never did a sound check, so I wasn't worried. Townes would usually show up around eight o'clock and go to the bar next door and have a few drinks before he'd walk through my door. So I figured he was over there. The doors were openin', and I'm lookin' around for him. Usually, he'd be shootin' the breeze with people out on the patio. I started lookin' around the building for him. No Townes. It's nine o'clock. No Townes. We put the opening act on. No Townes. Nine thirty rolls around. Intermission. I'm startin' to get a bad feeling. Mickey White was here. He said he talked with him just the day before, and the gig was on. We held out as long as we could. It's ten o'-clock. No Townes. I knew he wasn't gonna show up. So Mickey played a set. We didn't tell anybody that Townes wasn't here. They'd all paid their seven bucks. Lyle Lovett walked in, this was before he was "Lyle Lovett." He'd played here frequently and came to see the show. I pulled him aside and said, "Lyle, man, Townes isn't here. Could you go on and do a few tunes?" So he borrowed Mickey's guitar and played "Flyin' Shoes." It's 10:45, nearly eleven, and there's no Townes. So I got on stage and made the announcement. Then we played *Live at the Old Quarter,* and the funny thing was *nobody* left! I said, "You can get your refunds at the door." And hardly *anybody* asked for their money back! It was amazing!

"About a week later I got ahold of Townes and said, 'What happened to you, man? Where were ya?' He said he was stranded on the houseboat with a broken arm. I didn't believe him at the time, but apparently it was the truth. If he had a commitment, he'd always make the gig no matter what shape he was in. That's the kind of guy Townes was. I think there were a few times when he shouldn't've showed up," Griff said with a chuckle.

We eventually learned how to handle Townes's drinkin.' The bartenders would just ignore his requests. We knew who the enablers and the hangers-on were, who didn't have his best interests at heart. We knew when they were trying to get drinks for him. He was in the throes of alcoholism towards the end of his life, and he'd have to have a shot of vodka to play or else he'd go into DTs. So we'd give him a "Townes" shot, which was one-third vodka and two-thirds water. I think he knew it all along, but he respected us for it. Most clubs would just give him whatever he asked for.

Townes always took time for his fans. He'd ask people how school was goin' and knew all the bartenders by name. He always made people feel special. He was a magnet and he just invited people into his spirit. You could be a pauper or a king, and he'd treat you the same way. I'd only seen him be mean a couple times.

"I'll always love Harold Eggers for the way he treated Townes," Griff continued. "He has my undying respect. Harold was there with him through thick and thin. He took care of Townes. He babysat him, put up with him, and loved him. He went all over the world with Townes. My feeling is whatever live albums that he releases is all right with me.

"For a couple months in 1995 Jeanene and Harold got into it over the records he put out. I think he got fired 'cause he wanted a couple more dollars. He deserved three times as much to road manage Townes."

"Harold was a dear and sweet friend," Jeanene said. "We used to joke about him being Townes's road manager and me being his business manager, as Townes was impossible to manage. What it really meant was that somehow we managed to get things done. Harold has been through it all. He kept all the 'good folks' away from Townes, trying to become his buddy with drink and drugs. He's had Uzis held on him at airports. He got Townes in the truck and to the next gig when he'd rather start a crap game in an alley of the most dangerous part of Anytown, USA. Got him to the hospital . . .

"It wasn't over money or all those live records he's been releasing. Harold had said something to Susie Nelson (Willie's daughter) about Townes, and it got back to him," Jeanene said, attempting to set the record straight. "Townes was angry, called Harold, and fired him. We spoke about it, and Harold was remorseful."

"So Townes showed up at a gig with no Harold," Griff added.

He's with this cowboy who drove him up from Houston who has no clue how to handle him. From the moment he walked in I knew the show was gonna be a disaster. Townes was blitzed, and I'm freakin' out because this was a two-nighter, and it wasn't startin' off too well. I got on the phone and said, 'Harold, where the fuck are you?" He says, "I got fired, man." I said, "WHAT?" I always relied on Harold 'cause I knew I couldn't do it alone. Me and Harold knew how to keep Townes straight and make a successful gig—between the bartender ignoring him and putting ice cubes in his vodka. For years there was always Harold giving a report about how much Townes had drank before the gig. I said, "Man, you *got* to get your ass down here!" He came down to the gig, and that's when they made up. The gig was a complete disaster. Harold sat in the back. I went up to him and said, "Man, he can't go on the road without you." So at the end of the gig he went over and talked to Townes, and they patched things up again and Harold was back on the road with him.

Those two nights in October 1996 turned out to be the final shows Van Zandt would perform in the United States. Griff continued,

Townes was in bad shape. He was *not* healthy, just skin and bones. I knew in my heart that that was the last time I'd see him. The first night was kind of fucked up but still good somehow. The second night was really, *really* good. But I could just tell he was slippin' away. I knew he was gettin' close to the end of his road. He was sittin' at my desk in the back room, havin' delusions, seein' parrots . . . "evil fuckin' parrots." I loved him but couldn't do anything for him. I didn't know how to get him out of it, but Susan, our bartender, knew exactly what to do. She very calmly said, "Townes, those are *nice* parrots. They're really *good* parrots." And somehow he came down out of the delirium and stopped hallucinating.

After the show, they all went over to see Larry Monroe at his Saturday overnight program on KUT. "I was watchin' my friend die . . . ," Griff groaned.

He had a quart of cheap vodka that he'd brought along in the car. We asked him if he wanted Stoli or Smirnoff, but Townes always liked the cheap stuff. While he was playing one of Townes's records I said to Larry, "Go on and ask him the *real* question, Larry." He said, "Nah, I can't do that." I said, *"Ask him the fuckin' real question, man!"* And Larry said, "No." So I got on the mike and said, "Townes, it's been great havin' you at the Cactus again for the last two nights, blah, blah, blah ... Tell me, why are you waitin' 'round to die?" I had to do it. I did it because I wanted to save my friend's life. He said, "Life is too painful. There's animals and birds and pain ..." It was real surreal, poetic and nonsensical.

Perhaps if Townes was in better shape at the time he may have articulated a similar sentiment he shared with Irish journalist Patrick Brennan back in February 1995: "I have a feeling though that I've had a very blessed life. I've had so many good friends and loved ones. A job that I like to do and I feel is useful in this world. You can't do much better than that. I couldn't care less about money or having things. I don't need all that much. I'm just lucky to be here. Man I'm just trying to stay alive. I'm not trying to live up to nothing. I'm just trying to live."

"It was three or four in the morning, and we went over to my house and listened to the *Freewheelin' Bob Dylan,*" Griff recalled.

This was the first time he'd come over to my house in all these years, and I knew this would be the last time I ever saw him, and I just wanted to fuckin' save him somehow. I started talkin' to him, but he said, "Shut up! I haven't heard this record in forever." He wouldn't let me talk. He listened to the whole record, and then I gave him my favorite shirt that I was too fat to wear. But he didn't appreciate it. The sun was comin' up, and I walked him out to the truck, and I said, "Y'know, Townes, you're a mean fuckin' drunk!"

"And those were my last words I ever said to him," Luneberg said, weary, regretful, and a little drunk.

We both just sat in the empty barroom in silence for a while. "Lemme get ya another beer," Griff said and got up and wandered over to the icebox. We had another drink. For Townes, of course, and for Griff, to take the sting out of memory and as a medicine to bolster himself to continue the task of rehashing his friend's demise. And for me, to take the edge off the double-bladed sword of Townes's tragic-comic life that seesawed continually from one extreme to the other. I was exhausted from howling with laughter one moment to drowning in an undertow of sorrow the next. For every outrageous, hilarious adventure, there was always a tale of devastating tragedy equal to it.

Suddenly, something Kevin Eggers said in an interview a few years ago came back to haunt me: "He worked at being a tragedy. That was his full-time occupation. There were a lot of funny stories, but they often grew out of his own desperation. You wind up laughing out of both sides of your mouth."

CHAPTER 26

BAYOU SELF

The end is coming soon, it's plain
A warm bed just ain't worth the pain
And I will go and you will remain
With the bitterness we've tasted
   —TVZ, "Tower Song"

"For Townes, I think the playing and singin' was the most fun he found in being alive. But there's that waiting-around time that you've got to fill with other things. It was hard for him to break the cycles of addiction," Jerry Jeff said knowingly. "When he got into a town, all the old people he used to run with would show up again. If he had time on his hands, the next thing you know he'd fall in with them and was doin' all the same things over and over again. There were periods where he'd try and straighten out. When I cleaned up I'd have all my phone calls sent to another room first," Walker said with a chuckle.

Somebody would screen 'em and then send 'em over to me. The old friends knew what hotels you liked to stay in, and the next thing you know, they're in the lobby bar, lookin' you up. You need to have some kind of alternative. That's why everybody started to play golf while they're on the road. It gets you out in the sunshine and grass for a few hours. If you just go to the hotel and check in, you're bound to wander down to the bar to see what's goin' on; then you're back at it again. There's always camaraderie at the bar or a party at someone's house. You stay with people to save expenses, but then you're livin' their lifestyle. They invite some friends over, and the next thing you know—they're breakin' it all out.

"We didn't get to see each other a whole lot after the early days in Houston," Jerry Jeff confessed. "Either you're out on the road touring or home spending time with your family. He was livin' in Nashville while I'm in Austin. When I cleaned up my world, I eliminated a lot of temptations. If I went to see Townes, I knew what was goin' on, and I didn't wanna be drinkin' and hangin out."

"In the early nineties he didn't drink. He had a year or so of sobriety. That's when I have these nice memories that are not particularly exciting. I remember him throwing a football with his kid. Little by little he got back into drinking, which became a downhill slide," David Olney recollected. "A year before he died I saw Townes and he was in *horrible* shape."

David heard Townes was leaving for a tour of Europe, and judging by the shape he was in the last time he saw Van Zandt, he figured he'd never make it. Concerned for his friend's welfare, Olney drove down to the airport to see him off. He knew Van Zandt loved boats and was fond of the epic poem "The Rime of the Ancient Mariner." A couple verses of his songs clearly bore traces of its inspiration. Feeling awkward, searching for something to say to a friend he might never see again, Olney began to recite the Coleridge classic to him. A moment later Townes's eyes began welling up with tears. David put his friend and inspiration on the plane and bid him farewell, expecting to never see him again.

"A week later I was over in Europe and I kept hearing all these terrible stories about his concerts," Olney recalled. "Everyone said they were *awful,* that he was incoherent and drunk and falling off his stool. When I got back to the States I called him up. I said, 'Hey, Townes, how you doin'?' He said, 'Good.' 'How'd the tour go?' 'Oh, it was great,' he told me. I must've heard twenty stories about Townes bein' at death's door, yet to him the gigs were great."

A month earlier, in November 1996, Townes joined Joe Ely on stage for half a dozen songs in a little town just north of Milan, Italy. "I got Townes up for the last song, which we played together," Ely recollected.

There was a full house, about a thousand people in this big room. I told everybody, "Thanks y'all! Goodnight," and waved and started walkin' off stage with Townes. Halfway off the stage Townes planted both his feet and grabbed me and dragged me back on. Of course, the crowd went crazy. I didn't know what else we were gonna do. Townes started playin' a song, and fortunately I knew it. They clapped and I said, "All right!

Thanks y'all!" and started walkin' off again when Townes stopped me and pulled me back again. Then he started playin' some songs I never heard before. He was so drunk he couldn't play the guitar, so he handed it to me, and I was playin' these songs that I've heard but didn't know the chords. He started singin' and said, "This is in C." I'm thinkin', "What the fuck! I don't know this song!" As it worked out, it didn't matter 'cause Townes was four sheets to the wind, and all these Italians were lovin' the whole thing. It was somethin' they'd never seen before. It was a complete jam session. We ended up playin' song after song. It was really fun. That's just the way he was. You never knew what he was gonna pull on ya.

While in the midst of a divorce, Chip Phillips began spending more time in Mount Juliet with Townes.

He told me to quit my job and come live out at the lake with him. I said, "I can't quit my job." But I did appreciate the offer. It was a real tranquil place, and me and the kids loved Townes. So I took him up on that and went out there almost every day after work. Me and the kids would get in the car and go hang out with him and shoot BB guns and fish and whatnot.

It was Christmastime, and me and my kids went to Texas for a vacation. I called Townes as soon as I got back. We were best friends at the time, and I wanted to know how he was doin. Townes told me he had fallen in a bathtub in Europe and didn't realize it at the time, but he cracked his hip and never had it taken care of. He was also badly burned, scalded by the water. He told me he'd recently fallen out of bed and re-aggravated his hip. He couldn't stand up and was scootin' around on his butt for days and couldn't prepare any food for himself. He said luckily his dog Feather had enough food and was willin' to share it with him. Townes wasn't afraid of eatin' dog food. He said he used to eat it with the Indians on Skid Row in Crested Butte in order to save enough money to buy alcohol.

It was Christmas, and he was supposed to go out to Smyrna to see Jeanene and the kids. He called her and said he couldn't get up in his truck and asked her to come out and give him a ride. She told him, "Townes, you're welcome to come out and have Christmas with me and the kids, but I'm really busy right now and I got all this stuff to prepare, so you're gonna have to get out here on your own." That ticked him off. He was too proud to say, "No, baby, I really can't." He'd been down on his butt for days when his neighbor Jim found him. He was goin' to check his mail and saw Townes's truck and realized he was s'posed to be in Smyrna. He got him back in bed. I asked him if he needed me to come out there. He told me, "No, Harold is on the way, and we're goin' to Memphis to do this album." I said, "Man, you need to go to the doctor." He said, "If I don't do this album now I might never get a chance to do it."

The irony of the situation is astounding. Townes was signed to indie rockers Sonic Youth's label, Ecstatic Peace. A subsidiary of Geffen Records, Ecstatic Peace was the first major label to offer Townes a record contract. The sessions, produced by the Sonics' drummer, Steve Shelley, at Easley Studios in Memphis, would ultimately yield just a handful of unfinished tracks. (Unfortunately, Shelley declined to be interviewed, as on all accounts, the sessions were an unmitigated disaster.)

Shelley had no clue how far Townes's health had deteriorated until he arrived at the studio. He planned to pair Van Zandt with the Memphis-based band Two Dollar Guitar. According to Harold Eggers, Townes had been very flattered that "these younger cats wanted to play with him."

Van Zandt arrived in a wheelchair. Work soon began on the album but he was in constant agony. Certain this would be his last record, Van Zandt (or "Leather Man" as Jeanene had started calling him) pushed on, determined to finish it, no matter what shape he was in.

Listening to the board mixes of the sessions was a dreadful experience. Van Zandt wrestles through "Old Satan," a blues number in E. His guitar playing is loose and sloppy. His voice, weary. He stumbles over the words. Townes sounds as if he, at last, had become the bluesman he set out to be all those years ago. It's chilling to hear Van Zandt mumble the foreboding lyrics:

I used to get lonesome
Can't remember why
I used to love
Now I don't even try
I come from the country
Ain't goin' back no more
Guess its Ole Satan knockin'
On my door

Townes then attempted a take of "Harm's Swift Way," a fingerpicked Appalachian-style minor ballad. Shelley, Two Dollar Guitar, and "H," as Townes called Harold, do their best to keep the session rolling. They alternately suggest that he "take a break" or compliment him on "finding his groove," for making it through a song.

In turn, Townes complains, "After a while it hurts so bad I can't concentrate. Really, H, I can barely sit up. I'm tired and in pain. Ain't no doubt about that! I'm not tryin' to be a fussbudget, but, man I think I should go to sleep!"

Eventually, Van Zandt laid his guitar down with the intent of improvising a blues. The band, a group of young alternative country rockers, attempt to follow him, much like the bewildered white boys who once tried to figure out which way Lightnin' Hopkins was headed. After a couple takes it sounds as if the song is taking shape. But it never gets there, as Townes needs a drink—badly. "No more of those stupid little cups," he snarls at H, who tries to maintain him and keep him functional. "I'll pour a gallon down ya!" Eggers replies, fed up. They sound like an old married couple going through the same routine for the umpteenth time. "This is ridiculous!" Van Zandt sneers. "This life is ridiculous!" Harold snaps back, "So just take a drink will ya?"

"We'd talk on the phone every day, but he didn't want me to see him," Bob Moore said. "He told me he didn't know how or when it happened, but he felt like he'd been stampeded by a herd of buffalo. He was in so much pain."

"Townes was telling everyone he'd pulled a muscle after a bad dream caused him to violently thrash around in bed. It was the most ridiculous story I'd ever heard in my life," Jeanene exclaimed.

"He predicted his own death years before to the point where it became crying wolf," J. T. confessed. "He would say: 'T, I don't have much longer, you know that.' I heard it so many times, basically since *The Late, Great Townes Van Zandt* came out in the seventies. So I had come to accept it long before it happened."

But this was not just another wolf cry for attention. It wasn't long before Harold called Jeanene back at the Ponderosa to tell her the sessions were canceled and that Townes finally agreed to go to the hospital once they got back to Nashville. Fearing the worst, Van Zandt convinced Eggers to take him to a neighborhood health clinic instead.

The phone rang again. It was Harold calling with more bad news. After inspecting the huge mystery bruise, the doctor at the clinic warned

Townes he could have a blood clot that could kill him instantly. "Meet us at the lake house," Harold told Jeanene. "He won't let me take him to the hospital. He said he'd only go with you."

On the way to Summit Hospital in Nashville, Townes began talking as if he was on his deathbed. "You love me, don't you, babe?" he prodded Jeanene. "Of course I do," she replied. "You know I've loved four maybe five women in my life, but none as much or for as long as I've loved you," he told her. "And I always will, and that's forever . . . "

Townes's guilt, this time, was over an affair he'd had with a German lawyer named Claudia during his last European tour. "He still loved Jeanene," Chip Phillips maintained. "But they were separated at the time, and I guess there was still some fire in the furnace."

In the meantime, Jeanene met a millionaire, and their flirtation only added more friction to her ever more complex relationship with Townes.

A minute after arriving at the hospital, the emergency room instantly transformed into their stage, as Jeanene and Townes began to fight before the small crowd. "Send the bill to him! I don't want it," Jeanene growled at the nurse signing him in. Filling out the forms, Townes wondered aloud, "Hey, babe, are you my wife or my ex-wife? I'll just put "friend." She's my *best* friend!" Townes told their captive audience. "And you're mine too!" Jeanene snapped back sarcastically.

Although Jeanene was shocked, the doctor was hardly surprised to discover Townes had broken his hip. At this point the huge bruise had become as big and purple as an eggplant. Townes's eight-day-long crazy charade was finally over.

"He had been goin' around in a wheelchair like that for eight days," Jeanene said, rolling her eyes. "It was another Eight-Day War. It took me eight days to get him to take a bath just so we could have sex. Then it took another eight days to get him to go to a hospital after he broke his fuckin' hip!"

Van Zandt had plenty of reasons to dread the hospital. He knew if the surgery didn't kill him, quitting drinking again surely would. But he finally acquiesced after Jeanene put it to him bluntly: "Townes," she said, "do you want to be able to walk out on stage, or do you want to have to be wheeled out from now on? It's already been eight days, and you are obviously not getting any better."

"The surgeon, Dr. McHugh, understood the situation and agreed to get Townes back home and to his bottle as soon as possible. I promised him I would not keep him there, as it could be very dangerous. Before he went in Townes made me swear to God I would not let them try to detoxify him because the last time he nearly died. Dr. McHugh said, 'Okay, let's just get him stable, and we'll send him home ASAP.'" The doctor then advised her go home and get some sleep. It was midnight, New Year's Eve 1997.

"This is it. This is it, babe," Townes repeated over and over again as she said good-bye. Unbeknownst to her, Townes had already given the doctor orders not to resuscitate him under any condition.

Around two in the morning Dr. McHugh called Jeanene to say that Townes's surgery had gone well, and he was stable, and she could retrieve him early the next morning. But the following day the doctor on the morning shift refused to prescribe any painkillers if Townes was going to go home and drink.

"The man just had a pin put in his hip and needs pain medicine," Jeanene pleaded. "I'll be there to monitor his drinking," she promised. But the doctor was obviously not impressed with her custodial skills.

Townes was in serious shape. He'd already begun to shake and vomit. Jeanene pleaded with the nurse to sedate him before he had a heart attack. "It turned out her father was also in the hospital with a broken hip," Jeanene recalled. "He was an alcoholic too. So she knew exactly what to do." The nurse immediately gave Townes a sedative, which knocked him out. "Everything would have been fine if I could have just brought a bottle into the hospital, but of course, they wouldn't let me," Jeanene groaned.

Everyone expected Townes to go home and drink himself to death, and perhaps he would've, but he sure as hell wasn't going to die in a hospital, not if Jeanene had anything to do with it. "Give me the goddamn papers. I'm taking him out of here!" she snapped at the nurse at the front desk.

At approximately five o'clock on New Year's Day, Wednesday, January 1, 1997, Townes signed out from the hospital, as the autopsy report later revealed, "against medical advice."

"We couldn't even dress him because we couldn't get his clothes on. I had a jug waiting underneath the car seat, which went against everything in my power that I did to keep him away from the bottle until the end. He was just a mess. He was shaking so bad he couldn't get the lid off. I opened it for him and practically shoved it down his throat before he went into violent convulsions. By the time I got him back to Bayou Self he was lucid and wasn't shaking as bad."

Back at the cabin Jim Calvin lifted Townes out of the car, put him into a wheelchair, and wheeled him into the house. He kept an eye on Townes and the kids while Jeanene and Jim's wife, Roy Ann, went to fetch some Tylenol and a couple of bags of groceries. Jeanene called the nurse at the hospital and begged her again, to no avail, to call in a prescription to the local pharmacy. Upon her return Townes mumbled something about having taken a couple of Ibuprofen that had been in the nightstand drawer. "And you'd better give me three of those Tylenol, babe. I'm really hurtin'," he added.

Sometime around ten o'clock, Jeanene went into the kitchen to make Townes some supper—a plate of roast beef with some sliced cheese and apples and a cluster of grapes. "I said, 'Try and eat something.' He told me, 'Thanks, babe.' Those were the last words he said to me."

As Jeanene left the bedroom, Will stuck his head in the door to check on his dad. "You need anything, Dad?" Will asked. Townes assured his son he was all right. "He said, 'I'm fine. I got everything I need,'" Will recalled. "As I started walkin' off, he called me back and told me, 'Will, I just want you to know I love you.'"

Those were the last words Jeanene heard him speak. Will went to the bathroom a moment later while Jeanene called Susanna Clark to give her the full report. "He's back home and doin' fine. But goddamn it, Susanna, one of these days I'm going to cut these apron strings for good," she said with a sigh. A moment later Will rushed into the kitchen, yelling, "Mom, you'd better come look at Dad! He looks dead!"

Jeanene claimed from the moment she entered the bedroom she knew he was gone: "His spirit was simply not in the room. I still had the phone in my hand. I screamed, 'Oh, God, Susanna, Townes is dead, I gotta go!'"

Jeanene frantically punched 911 as Katie Belle stood silently beside her father, watching cartoons. She was just one month shy from turning five. "Hurry! Please hurry! I think he's dead!" Jeanene cried. Throwing the phone down, she began administering CPR to Townes's lifeless body. Pulling the sheet off him to pump his chest she discovered Townes with one hand over his heart and the other tightly grasping his flask. "Goddamn it, Townes!" she cried. Being the typical alcoholic's wife, she yanked the flask from his hand and promptly hid the evidence beneath the bed.

For the next twenty minutes it took the ambulance to arrive, Jeanene continued to give Townes CPR, even though she knew he was gone. All the while she swore she heard his spirit talking to her, saying, 'Oh, babe, just stop doing that now! That's just silly.'

"It was like I had one foot in reality and one foot in the spirit world," Jeanene said. "One moment I was on the ceiling looking down at myself and the kids having a telepathic conversation with Townes, telling him, 'I have to do this! It's what's expected of me!' The next moment I was slammed back down to the human world, screaming Townes's name between breaths."

Finally, a volunteer fireman showed up and pushed her aside to administer CPR. "He was trying to resuscitate Townes by rolling his fist up into a tube and breathing into him but he wasn't getting any air!" Jeanene recalled. "I pushed him aside and said, 'You do the compressions—I'll breathe for him!'"

The paramedics finally showed up, too late. They loaded Townes's lifeless body into the ambulance at the top of the driveway and continued to work on him, but finally left silently, with the siren off. "He was already dead and gone into another realm," Jeanene sighed.

After the ambulance left I called Guy and Susanna back. They said they'd meet me at the hospital. I was too shaken to drive so I called Jim and asked him to drive me while Roy Ann stayed with Will and Katie Belle. When I arrived at Summit Hospital and saw the way everybody was looking at me, I knew it could only mean bad news. Jim and I were ushered into a private waiting room and shortly a doctor came in and said, "I'm sorry, but Mr. Van Zandt didn't make it." Even though I already knew Townes was gone, hearing it come out of a stranger's mouth made it a very earthly reality. I just lost it. Jim put his arms around me, and I just wailed and buried my face in his big belly. He sat me down in a chair, and I burned through a box of Kleenex. Then I asked to see Townes.

Jeanene entered the curtained room and stood beside him. Townes was covered with a sheet up to his neck, which she immediately pulled away. It was hard to see him like that, with that big blue tube shoved down his throat, still protruding from his mouth. She picked up his lifeless hand and held it in hers. "I always loved his hands. They made me feel safe," Jeanene said. "But they didn't even look like Townes's hands. They looked so meek. Townes's hands were so powerful in life, powerful, strong, and magical. But all that was gone."

She tried to joke with him. But this time Townes didn't joke back. "I said, 'Okay, Townes, you've really gone and done it this time. What am I supposed to do now?' I was in there for about fifteen minutes, but it felt like a lifetime."

When I came back Guy and Susanna had arrived, and she asked if I thought she should go in and see Townes. I told her that he still had tubes in him from when they tried to resuscitate him. I said, "If you want to remember him like he was, I wouldn't recommend it." She decided against it.

Then we all drove back to Bayou Self, and Roy Ann met us at the door. I asked her, "How are the kids? Do they know?" She said, "No, I don't think so." Then she told me, "After you left Katie told me, 'Daddy had a fight with his heart.'" I went in and took Will and Katie by the hands and took them into Townes's bedroom. We sat down, and I put my arms around them and said, "Will, Katie, your father loves you more than anything or anybody on earth and he always will . . . but he won't be coming home this time." Katie asked, "My daddy died?" "Yes, baby, he did," I told her. "I'm so sorry. Will, I'm so sorry." We just huddled together crying for a long time. Then Will got angry and got up and kicked a hole in the closet door and ran off into the woods, while Katie clung to me for dear life. I tried to find J. T. I called every number I had but couldn't find him. I didn't want him to hear it on the news.

It was about five in the morning on January 2 when J. T. heard that Townes was gone. He was on his way out of Austin headed for Corpus Christi on a fly-fishing trip. Driving through a thick fog on I-35, he began surfing the dial looking around for something to keep him awake. Suddenly, he caught the tail end of a Townes song, immediately followed by a second one. J. T. claimed he was in "disbelief" but then realized, as it was a Tuesday, perhaps by some miracle the DJ had chosen Townes for a "Twofer Tuesday" block.

"Then the guy came on and said, 'That was a song by the late great Townes Van Zandt.'" At that point John "completely lost [his] mind." Enraged from hearing about his father's death over the radio, he began pounding on the dashboard and tried "to pull the fucking steering wheel off."

"I was a wreck and then I turned back to my girlfriend's house. I still hadn't cried. I hit the back door, and she came to the door and said, 'What are you doing here?' Then, when she saw my face, she just figured it out. There was something written on my face. I crawled into bed and wept for the entire day, and then in the night I pulled myself together and said, 'I'd better get a suit,' and went to Nashville to join the rest of my family."

Stoic, in his new suit, J. T. managed to create a moment of levity at the funeral: "I misunderstood the guy on the radio a little bit, and I heard he had jumped from a train. I immediately suspected Harold," he quipped.

Jeanene recounted making the dreaded phone call to Donna Spence, Townes's sister in Colorado: "She, of course, was heartbroken, but there were practical matters to attend to." It soon became apparent that Townes needed to have two funerals: one for the public in Nashville and one in Texas for family and friends who couldn't get there.

She asked me if I would handle the funeral plans for Nashville, and we discussed a plot for Townes in Dido. She said she would call the rest of the family and not to worry about the cost, that she would cover everything. God bless Donna. She was always there for Townes after his mom died and things got tight.

Then after I called Harold, Katie and I went and lay down on Townes's bed and cried ourselves to sleep. I remember as I was finally drifting off the phone ringing constantly. I could hear Guy or Susanna in the next room saying over and over again, "Yes, it's true. No, she can't come to the phone."

Townes's autopsy revealed the pills in the night table drawer he'd swallowed had actually been antihistamines and not ibuprofen, as he had thought. The combination of the powerful antihistamine and Tylenol PM (which also contains antihistamine) along with the stress of surgery and his body craving alcohol had most likely caused his heart to fibrillate.

"Everybody naturally assumed it was a blood clot because he died the day after having surgery. But Townes had heart disease. He was on anti-coagulants and had a massive heart attack. They called me up to say they wanted to do an autopsy. I said, 'Great! I'd like to know what killed him.' They probably thought *I* killed him!" Jeanene said with a laugh.

In the end no autopsy was necessary. Anybody who knew Townes knew what killed him—just being Townes Van Zandt was enough to kill anybody.

During the last twenty years of his life Van Zandt repeatedly said, "I'm never going to make it past fifty-two. I'm going to go just like my dad." He also predicted he would achieve fame only after death. Oddly enough, Townes died on New Year's Day, the same day as his hero, Hank Williams, forty-four years earlier.

"Both men live in their music, as if singing and writing and being human were the same thing and as natural as breathing," wrote Robert Palmer, who would also die later that same year. Palmer recognized Van Zandt's songs, like those of Hank Williams, as "the direct, untrammeled expression of a man's soul." In the long run, their voracious appetites for alcohol and drugs did them both in.

Ironically, Townes, the quintessential rambler who lived most of his life on the road, carrying a guitar and suitcase, died at home in his own bed.

CHAPTER 27

MOURN ME NONE

It's a thin line between mournful and whiny.

—TVZ

"Townes died on New Year's Day 1997, and I already had two dates for him booked on the calendar," Griff Luneberg said. "So we decided to turn those two dates into a celebration. Everybody played . . . Jimmie Dale . . . [along with Joe Ely, Kimmie Rhodes, and a handful of others]. We did two nights of Townes's songs and put roses on all the seats and gave away posters.

"It broke my heart, man . . . Broke everybody's heart," Griff sighed.

It seemed like there was a void in the singer-songwriter community after that for ages. The King was *gone*. I wanted to quit this place after he died. As far as I was concerned it was over. There was no reason to do what I do because I put so much heart into it, and it felt like the soul was gone. Townes always made you feel that it was about *you*. And I wanted to fuckin' die, man!

I went to his funeral in Nashville, and there was this horrific thunderstorm while I was on the plane. It was the day before the funeral. Mickey White and some other Austin people were there too. I got loaded, and I really didn't care if that plane crashed or not. I was devastated. I didn't want to do it anymore. I was just goin' through the motions. It was just so important to me. But at the same time I was really pissed off at him. I knew he was dyin'. I said, "Townes you have so much to share with the world. You have so much to give. Why are you waitin' 'round to die?" And do you know what he said? "I just can't do it anymore." He really *wanted* to die.

"Townes was a really complicated guy," Richard Julian reckoned. "He pissed off a lot of people, but at the same time he also inspired a lot of people. Once he died, it suddenly became this beautiful picture, and you could see him from top to bottom—how he lived his life and the songs he wrote and everything he left behind."

"I had expected a call about Townes for a few years," Jerry Jeff Walker said. "When I finally got it, it was still very sad when it came."

Townes's first funeral took place at Belmont Church on the afternoon of January 5, 1997. Songs and eulogies were read by Steve Earle, who acted as emcee, Rodney Crowell, and Guy Clark, who quipped that he'd "booked this gig thirty-seven years ago."

"That phone call telling us Townes had died was a phone call all of us who knew him had been expecting for twenty years, though the circumstances were very unexpected," Nanci Griffith said. "But we were happy that he was at home, with his family."

"This I can tell you for a fact: Townes Van Zandt was no different when he was nineteen years old as he was the day he died, as far as his singing and performance went," Mickey Newbury told me. "He was always Townes. A lot of people are not what they were thirty-five years ago. I can think of a bundle of superstars that if you knew 'em when I met 'em, you wouldn't recognize them today. But Townes was exactly the same person, except he was just a more worn-out version of it."

The last time Vin Scelsa saw Townes, he played at a singer-songwriter series that Scelsa hosted in the early nineties called "In Their Own Words" at the Bottom Line. The show was based on Nashville's Bluebird Café's weekly showcase where four or five performers would gather to swap songs and stories.

After the show everybody hung around until it was finally time to pack it in. Vin offered to drive Townes back to his hotel but wound up getting lost in the tangled maze of highway that surrounds Newark Airport.

We just kept goin' around and around in circles, and Townes started getting nervous. He said, "Vinny, are you sure you know where you're goin'? Do you want me to drive? You're from New Jersey, aren't ya?"

We finally found the place, pulled up to the Holiday Inn, and got out of the car. We hugged, and I got back in the car and watched him walk into the hotel, carryin' his guitar case. He was wearin' a suede jacket and cowboy hat. I remembered vividly thinking, "There goes a fuckin' legend." Part of me wanted to run into the lobby of that hotel at three in the morning and yell "DO YOU KNOW WHO THE FUCK IS STAYING HERE? TOWNES VAN ZANDT!" And that was the last time I saw him. He looked just the same as the first time I met him, only slightly more bent. That moment is permanently etched in my heart and memory.

"It's as if one day a cloud just appears in front of you," Vin continued. "And the curtain parts, and out steps Miles Davis, fully formed. Or out steps Billie Holiday or Hank Williams. And Townes, except for Leonard Cohen and maybe Jimmie Dale Gilmore, is the only person I've ever met who stepped out of that cloud. It's like, where the fuck did he come from? A cloud picked him up from somewhere, some other time realm, and plopped him down in ours. And we were lucky to have him."

"Townes was like some weird cosmic unit for humanity," Jeanene said. "We don't know why he was here, other than to write songs. But goddamn, he was vital to our existence. *We* weren't vital to his existence at all! Not me, not Guy Clark, nobody! I tried to feed him and carry on the next generation for him, but I was not *vital* to Townes Van Zandt. I was just a fringe element, but still part of God's plan."

"It was very painful to be around Townes towards the end," David Olney confessed. "I didn't want to sit around and watch somebody that I cared for dying right in front of me. It made me angry. It's taken me a long time to get over it 'cause I miss him. I just hope his legend doesn't obscure how good those songs were."

Shortly after Townes's death Jeanene was presented with a phone bill for twelve hundred dollars. It turned out that he'd called nearly every one he knew, in the United States and Europe, during the week before he died—from old runnin' buddies to favorite high school teachers.

In the last phone conversation she had with Townes, Linda Lowe recalled him talking about his friends and family and meeting his maker.

I asked him how he was doing, and he said, "Sometimes I get so sad I can't breathe. I'm worth so much more dead." He also brought up the time he blew the concert in Arkansas, and I said he needed to let go of that. Townes remembered everything he did and spent years of his life trying to pay people back for all the things he'd done when he was drunk. I told him that my "Writers in the Round" concert series would never have grown into what it's become without him. He told me on his last tour of Europe he'd fallen off a stool, and it scared him because he was completely sober when it happened, but his legs were so weak from the extent of the damage that alcohol had done to his body. His legs just gave out on him and weren't steady enough to hold him.

"His voice was soft and clear. I don't know if he was reading something or rambling," Linda said, regarding the fragments of a poem that she wrote down as Townes spoke (they were in fact the lyrics to Van Zandt's unreleased song "Harm's Swift Way").

There is a home out of harm's swift way
I set myself to find
I swore to my love I would
Bring her there
Then left my love behind

It was January 2, 1997, in Norway when the phone rang at seven in the morning. The sudden, incessant ringing didn't merely aggravate Eric Andersen, it gave him chills. He knew at that hour it could only be bad news. Who the hell would call him so early in the morning? Andersen fumbled for the receiver only to find it was "the call from hell," informing him that Townes was dead.

"It was a terrible, terrible way to start the New Year," Eric confessed, taking a long drag on a cigarette. "Townes often joked about death. It was always on his mind and in his conversation," Andersen said, recalling the sight of Van Zandt and Robert Palmer standing outside of Tramps in New York, hugging, stoned, and dripping with sentiment. "Palmer had this fifty-pound satchel full of writing and records that he always carried around with him. They said good-bye to each other in tears. It turned out it was the last time they ever saw each other."

Soon after Van Zandt's death Eric discovered a batch of old tapes of live shows from the Bottom Line and the Lone Star, along with a work tape of four songs he coauthored with Townes in 1986. The tapes had gone missing for nearly twelve years. Andersen, it seemed, had completely forgotten about the tunes.

"It was all very painless," Andersen said, recalling their collaboration. "Townes lay on the couch while I ran the tape recorder and played guitar. We went back and forth on the lyrics a few times. It was just whoever came up with something good. [Robert] Palmer was around too. He came over with his clarinet."

Their song "Night Train" was originally inspired by an empty bottle and a single shoe they discovered in a doorway while wandering the streets of Denver together. A fifth of Black Bush Irish whiskey provided the inspiration for a New Orleans–style funeral march of the same name. After killing the bottle they immediately wrote the song at the bar.

"As far as I knew Townes had never really written with anybody before. Or it had always been piecemeal, a little something here and there. Townes was a very, very close friend of mine, and he's sorely missed," Eric said, lighting another cigarette. "He would come out to my house with just a suitcase, two pairs of underpants, a clean shirt that Jeanene had ironed, an extra pair of blue jeans, a bottle of vodka, a trench coat, his guitar, and his glasses.

"Before he died I saw him in Oslo, and he told me he intended to record 'The Meadow Lark' and 'The Blue March,'" Andersen recalled. "He'd been playin' the song as a three-chord blues while on tour in Germany. 'The Meadow Lark' meant a lot to him because he'd spent part of his youth in Montana. When you're driving you can hear them singing as they fly over the road. I spent some time with the tape, rounding out the music a bit, but I didn't alter any of the lyrics. They're all intact," Eric said, referring to his recording of the four songs they'd cowritten on his 2000 release, *You Can't Relive the Past.*

In his last years Townes had grown terribly frail. Standing over six-two, his weight dropped down to barely 130 pounds. Journalist Ed Ward recalled watching his hands tremble as he "pulled a small bottle of vodka from his pocket and surreptitiously refilled the shot-glass."

"Each time you saw him it was clear that he was one step closer to dyin'," Linda Lowe said. "Every time I saw him for the last five years I figured it would be the last time, and I'd start to cry."

"The last time I saw him at McCabes' he was pretty shaky," Bill Bentley recalled. "He was dissipated. You could feel the life force draining out of him. But he never lost the ability to move you with his music, even though he was barely holdin' on."

"After Townes died I ran into Guy. We were both shit-faced," David Olney recalled. "I said I been playing these tributes, and people keep telling me how I was influenced by him. Even though he was dead, he could still swallow you up. Guy looked at me like, 'You don't know the half of it.' I can't imagine what it was like for him."

But true to Townes's character, in the midst of overwhelming sorrow came a moment of levity and magic: "After the funeral we went home and everybody was sittin', crowded around the couch, watchin' the tape from the funeral," Will Van Zandt recalled. "Townes's old roulette wheel was sittin' over there at the bottom of the stairs when all of a sudden I heard it take off, spinnin'. Everybody heard it. It was still spinnin' when J. T. got up and walked over to see what was goin' on. That's when the ball landed on double zero—which means the house wins."

Even before Townes's ashes had the chance to "ride the blue wind high and free," a steady slew of venomous accusations and barbed insults began to fly, fast and furious, among friends and family: "Kevin Eggers actually had the gall to go to the funeral and get up and speak," John Lomax III sneered. "Then he went over to Guy's house afterward. I was amazed that somebody didn't go up and hit him in the head with a whiskey bottle."

"I never figured Kevin out," Fran Lohr said. "I still don't know to this day if he was a friend or a shyster. Was he a supporter or a thief? I don't know."

"We were very close, like spiritual brothers," Eggers countered. "He was the best man at my wedding. Townes and I had a great collaboration and friendship."

"They say I'm a villain, yeah. But you know what? I'm the only one who bellied up to the bar. Fuckin' made the records, supported him for many years, was his friend. He died a friend of mine. He apologized to me for what he did to me. People like to get their names in print and shoot their mouths off, and I can't stop 'em," Kevin told the *Houston Press.*

"You know what the bug up Jeanene's ass is?" Kevin groused. "She thinks she's Townes Van Zandt in a dress. She wants to be Townes Van Zandt. She hated the guy's guts when he died, and she basically wants to be him now."

"Jeanene is *not* Townes's widow. She's his ex-wife," Guy Clark pointed out. "They were divorced for a year and a half before he died, and she's still playing the grieving widow while assuming all the legal rights that go with it, which she does not really have. I was the executor of the will. It was one last joke from Townes. Besides, he's dead, goddamn it!" Guy grumbled.

"Townes named me executrix to his will," Jeanene countered. "I was told by the lawyers that I couldn't do the job because I was his ex-wife. Guy was named next if I was unable to handle it. Once I faxed Guy the list of chores involved, he quickly bowed out and reassigned me to the task. It took six years to finally close his estate. There is still unfinished business left to take care of," Jeanene said, referring to her ongoing battle with the Eggers brothers.

In the midst of all the blame and resentment, the tax man soon appeared, looking for his piece of the action. "Not long after Townes died the IRS showed up wanting $25,000. I fought 'em. I don't put up with shit from anybody," Jeanene growled. "I went through six agents. They were hoping to catch him without receipts. They didn't know they were going to encounter *the rabid Jeanene!* They weren't going to allow any of his traveling deductions. I said, 'If he didn't travel there, he didn't show up and get paid. How the hell do you think he got to the gig? Transcendental meditation?'"

When asked his criteria for choosing Van Zandt for his "Favorite Dead Americans" list, Kinky Friedman, the wild and wooly Texas Jewboy (who joined the 2006 gubernatorial race for the Lone Star State—and lost), replied, "Townes was a very special guy who not only wrote some really brilliant songs—magical songs—but interwove his life and his art so completely that you couldn't tell one from the other. I see him very much like Hank Williams. In fact, he died on the same day Hank Williams died. And his weight was precisely the weight of Jesus Christ at his death—about 107 pounds. So he was very Christ-like and very Hank-like."

"The similarity is made a lot, but in my own mind I think that the Hank Williams and Townes Van Zandt correlation is that Townes lived long enough to dictate what Hank felt like in the last days," J. T. reckoned. "He warned that his end was coming—thirty years before his death, he said that it could be thirty years from now, but he basically warned you all the time that he was skating on that edge."

POSTSCRIPT

THE ROAD TO DIDO

To Live's to Fly

—inscribed in granite on Townes's tombstone

At age sixteen, Khleber Van Zandt made the long journey from Marshall, Texas, to Franklin, Tennessee, to attend college. Upon his arrival, his grandparents presented him with a mare named Dido, "on the condition that I gentle [saddle train] her," Khleber later wrote in his memoir, *Force without Fanfare*.

After graduating school a year later, Van Zandt planned to return home to Texas, but a terrible epidemic of yellow fever and cholera was sweeping the land. The water was low, and the river boats sat, tied up in their docks. No one dared board them for fear of contracting a deadly disease while in such close quarters. Instead, Khleber, along with a couple friends, made the long trek home, riding over a thousand miles on the back of his gallant mare, Dido, for whom the small community of Tarrent County, Texas, was soon named. Four years later Van Zandt sold his prized horse for one hundred dollars to help raise the money needed to build a church.

"It's really complicated to find Townes's gravestone," Darryl Harris said, sitting beside a Christmas tree glittering with antique ornaments. "Dido is not actually a city, and it's not a town. It's a retirement-home district. You *can* get there, but if you stop at convenience stores or roadside restaurants and ask 'Where's Dido?' They'll say, 'Hell, I don't know about *no Dido*.' It's unbelievable. You see lots with mobile homes in total collapse that have gone unattended for so long they've become compost. It's so weird. There are a few other Van Zandt family gravestones up there. His grandparents had donated the land for the cemetery. But I think Jeanene only put a few of his ashes up there," Darryl said. "She divided 'em up and then dropped the rest over Fort Worth by helicopter."

Jeanene had divided Townes's ashes into three parts. One-third were split between her and the kids and kept in urns, to always keep Townes near. One-third she took to Dido to scatter at the old family plot where Townes's paternal grandparents, William Lipscomb and Katie Belle Williams Van Zandt, were buried, and the last third would be scattered in various places that Townes loved.

"I never got in that helicopter," Jeanene confessed. "I was drivin' around, lookin' for the place, when I heard Stevie Ray Vaughn on the radio and took it as an omen from Townes. Even if I didn't feel much like livin' at the time, I still have a couple of kids to raise."

It was bitterly cold when Jeanene went to Dido to plant some of Townes's ashes at his headstone. The next day, there was a terrible ice storm, and all the planes were grounded at the Dallas–Fort Worth airport.

The kids and I had to wait out the storm at the Worthington Hotel while the rest of the relatives went home. We were standing together at a plate-glass window looking out at the stillness of Fort Worth under a blanket of solid ice. I told the kids that the hotel was probably standing on their Great-great-uncle Khleber's farm. As I looked out at the sky, high above the city, there was a lone mourning dove struggling against the freezing wind. He was the only thing moving as far as the eye could see. We watched him through our tears as he fought his way across the horizon until he disappeared. We knew who it was . . .

The next morning the city had thawed, and we got ready to leave. I felt bad about not goin' through with the helicopter idea. On our way to the airport I was thinkin' about how Townes never liked to fly very much, but he sure loved the highway. So we opened the sun roof of the limo and released him right there. I guess it just felt right. Townes blowin' down the highway again . . .

BIBLIOGRAPHY

BOOKS

Alden, Grant, and Peter Blackstock. *No Depression: An Introduction to Alternative Country Music*. Nashville: Dowling Press, 1998. "Mickey Newbury," by Kurt Wolff, 22–30. "Guy Clark," by Bill Friskics-Warren, 31–36. "Steve Earle," by Peter Blackstock, 37–43.

Cox, John Harrington. *Folk Songs of the South*. Cambridge: Harvard University Press, 1925.

Davis, John T. *Austin City Limits: 25 Years of American Music*. New York: Billboard Books, 2000.

Dawidoff, Nicholas. *In the Country of Country: A Journey to the Roots of American Music*. New York: Vintage Books, 1998.

Dickerson, James L. *Goin' Back to Memphis*. New York: Cooper Square Press, 2000.

Dobson, Richard. *The Gulf Coast Boys*. Bryan, Tex.: Greater Texas Publishing, 1998.

Evans, Nick, and Jeff Horne. *Song Builder: The Life and Music of Guy Clark*. Kent, England: Amber Waves, 1998.

Griffith, Nanci, and Joe Jackson. *Nanci Griffith's Other Voices: A Personal History of Folk Music*. New York: Three Rivers Press, 1998.

Guralnick, Peter. *Lost Highway*. New York: Perennial Library, Harper and Row, 1989.

Hinton, Brian. *Country Roads: How Country Came to Nashville*. London: Sanctuary Publishing, 2000.

Hudson, Kathleen. *Telling Stories, Writing Songs: An Album of Texas Songwriters*. Austin: University of Texas Press, 2001.

Jenkins, Margaret Elizabeth Hall. *A History of Van Zandt County*. Austin: Pemberton Press, 1976.

Reder, Alan, and John Baxter. *Listen to This*. New York: Hyperion, 1999.

Santelli, Robert. *The Big Book of Blues*. New York: Penguin Books, 1993.

Sanders, Leonard. *How Fort Worth Became the Texasmost City*. Fort Worth: University of Fort Worth Press, 1973.

Scaduto, Anthony. *Dylan*. New York: Signet Books, 1973.

St. John, Lauren. *Hardcore Troubadour: The Life & Near Death of Steve Earle*. London and New York: 4th Estate Publishers, 2003.

Unterberger, Richie. *Eight Miles High: Folk-Rock's Flight from Haight-Ashbury to Woodstock*. San Francisco: Backbeat Books, 2003.

_____. *Unknown Legends of Rock & Roll*. San Francisco: Backbeat Books, 1998.

Van Zandt, General K. M. *Force without Fanfare: The Autobiography of General K. M. Van Zandt*. Edited and with an introduction by Sandra L. Myres. Fort Worth: Texas Christian University Press, 1968.

Van Zandt, Jeanene. *Townes Van Zandt: The Last Songs*. A small press, limited edition of seventy-five copies of TVZ's last songs and lyric fragments, 1997.

Van Zandt, Townes. *For the Sake of the Song: A Limited Edition Book of TVZ's Chords and Lyrics*. Houston: Wings Press, 1977.

NEWSPAPERS AND MAGAZINES

Alarik, Scott. "Townes Van Zandt: At My Window." *Boston Globe,* date unknown.

Blackstock, Peter. "Townes Van Zandt Interview." *Rocket,* September 27–October 11, 1995.

Brennan, Patrick. "Townes Talk." Publication unknown, February 8, 1995.

Corr, Aidan. "Nashville Comes to Limerick." *Limerick Leader* (Ireland), date unknown.

"Country Singer-Songwriter Townes Van Zandt Dies at 52." *Washington Post,* date unknown.

D. H. "Townes without Pity." *Melody Maker* (U.K.), October 10, 1987.

Davis, John T. "Tejano Pop Stars Gather Here for Townes Van Zandt Project." *Austin Light,* October 25–31, 1989.

Dawson, Walter. Title unknown. *Memphis Commercial Appeal,* July 17, 1977.

Delgado, Berta. "Austinite Acquitted in Musician's Death: Shooting of Blaze Foley Called Self-defense." *Austin American Statesman,* September 29, 1989.

_____. "Self-defense Claimed in Singer's Death." *Austin American Statesman,* September 28, 1989.

Dickinson, Chris. "Townes Van Zandt: In Memory." Publication and date unknown.

Drew, Joan. Title unknown. *Country Style,* November 1976.

Flannagan, Bill. "Ragged Company: Steve Earle and Townes Van Zandt." *Musician,* August 1995.

Flippo, Chet. "Songwriter's Songwriter Townes Van Zandt Dies." *Billboard,* January 18, 1977.

"From Townes Van Zandt." *New York Times,* November 24, 1994.

Gleason, Holly. "Great Music Comes from Hard Livin'." *Tower Pulse,* August 1987.

Goldsmith, Thomas. "There's Not Much Van Zandt Hasn't Tried." *Nashville Tennessean,* April 20, 1987.

Gray, Michael. "An Appreciation of Townes Van Zandt." *Nashville Banner,* January 3, 1997.

Greenfield, Robert. "Townes Van Zandt: Space Cowboy." Publication and date unknown.

Hall, Michael. "The Great Late Townes Van Zandt." *Texas Monthly,* March 1998.

Hanks, Matt. "A Gentleman and a Shaman." *No Depression,* January–February 1999.

Hedgepath, William. "Townes Van Zandt: Messages from the Outside." *Hittin' the Note* (Atlanta), May 1977.

Heimel, Cynthia. "Townes Van Zandt: Melancholy Cowboy." *Soho Weekly News,* May 25, 1978.

Henderson, Joe. "Townes Van Zandt: The Legend Came to Visit." *Cashbox 50,* June 13, 1987.

Hill, Jack W. "Bluesman on Guard against His Demons." *Democrat* (city unknown), 1990.

Jarvey, Paul. "New Album Is Dream Come True." *Westboro (Mass.) Telegram and Gazette,* March 2, 1995.

K., Paul. "High, Low, and in Between." *New Times* (Los Angeles), January 16–22, 1997.

Kelso, John. "Sticking with Blaze Foley." *Austin American Statesman,* February 9, 1989.

Langer, Andy. "Townes without Pity." *Austin Chronicle,* June 14, 2002.

Leichtling, Jerry. "Townes Van Zandt: Out of the Shadows." *Village Voice,* October 3, 1977.

Leigh, Spencer. "Livin' on the Road, My Friend." *Country Music People* 22, no. 3 (March 1991).

Lomax, John, III. Title unknown. *Hank Magazine,* October 1976.

Lomax, John Nova. "Codeine Country: Houston Was the City of Syrup Long before DJ Screw Came on the Scene." *Houston Press,* May 5, 2005.

———. "Out of Townes: Wrecks Bell Finally Steps into the Spotlight." *Houston Press,* October 19, 2000.

"Luxury Liner: Emmylou Harris." *Playboy* 24, no. 5 (May 1977).

Mitchell, Sean. Title unknown. *Dallas Times-Herald,* July 17, 1977.

Monahan, Casey. "Blaze of Glory: Friends, Musicians Remember Singer-Songwriter Foley as 'Honest' but Troubled Man." Publication unknown, February 11, 1989.

Nichols, Lee. "The Dean of Texas Songwriters." *Austin Chronicle,* date unknown.

———. "The Legend of Blaze Foley: A Walking Contradiction." *Austin Chronicle,* December 24, 1999.

O'Brien, Peter. "Townes Van Zandt: Become Involved with a Legend." *Omaha Rainbow,* no. 36 (Spring 1985).

————. "Townes Van Zandt: The Legend Returns." *Omaha Rainbow,* no. 15 (1977). The article is composed of a series of interviews by Richard Wootton on Saturday, August 20, 1977, and Scott Giles on Monday, August 8, 1977. Additional material taken from articles by Bob Claypool of the *Houston Post,* published June 1, 1977, and Joel McNally of the *Milwaukee Journal,* published Sunday May 1, 1977.

Palmer, Dorothy. "Recluse Ready to Share His Music with Arkansans." *Arkansas Gazette,* November 11, 1981.

Palmer, Robert. "A Hard Road, Seldom Taken." *New York Times,* June 7, 1987.

Pareles, Jon. "Sung Tales about Just Plain Folks." *New York Times,* November 11, 1990.

Perlich, Tim. "Provocative Blues Poet Shakes the Death Rattle." *Now,* August 10–16, 1995.

Pettigrew, Jim. "The Growing Townes Van Zandt Cult." *Country Style,* no. 25 (November 1977).

Picking Up the Tempo. Issue no. 15, date unknown, midseventies.

Pop Top: The Record Buyers Guide. Vol. 2, no. 12, date unknown.

Pouncey, Edwyn. "Rocky Mountain High." *New Musical Express,* November 7, 1987.

Puckett, Jeffrey Lee. "The Shadowy Poetry of Townes Van Zandt." *Scene,* June 10, 1995.

Ruhlmann, William. "Townes Van Zandt: Legendary and Obscure." *Goldmine,* October 5, 1990.

Sanders, Don. "Talkin' with Townes." *Houston Press,* June 21, 1990.

Stern, Edward. "Townes Van Zandt: A Local Legend." *Crested Butte News,* date unknown.

Trost, Isaiah. "Townes Van Zandt: Sad but True." *Country Guitar* 2, no. 5 (December 1994).

Tyer, Brad. "End of the Road." Publication unknown, January 13, 1997.

"Van Zandt: Taking Inspiration Wherever He Finds It." *Anchorage Daily News,* March 27, 1995.

Wolff, Kurt. "Darkness on the Edge of Townes." *Huh Magazine,* February 1995.

Ziemer, Joe. "TCB." *Goldmine,* March 14, 2000.

Zollo, Paul. "Townes Van Zandt: For the Sake of the Song." *Song Talk* 2, no. 15 (Spring 1991).

LINER NOTES, NEWSLETTERS, WEB SITES, E-MAILS, AND LETTERS

Amanda. An e-mail account of a Barnes and Noble Web chat with Kinky Friedman, September 11, 2000.

www.austin360.com

Burrito, Frenchy. "The Mosquito Diaries Entry #1: My Adventures with Townes Van Zandt." Web site posting, May 2003.

Hamilton, Josh. An e-mail account of Steve Earle at Old Town of Folk Music, June 5, 2000.

Mosser, Jonnell. *Around Townes*. Liner notes by Jonell Mosser. Winter Harvest Records, 1995.

Lomax, John, III. "Eighter from Decatur." *Townes Van Zandt Fan Club Newsletter,* between 1976 and 1977.

_____. "Pless Crippings." *Townes Van Zandt Fan Club Newsletter,* between 1975 and 1977.

Scobey, Lola. *Flyin' Shoes*. Liner notes. Tomato Records, 1978.

Smith, Harry. *The Anthology of American Folk Music*. Liner notes. Folkways Records, 1952.

www.trad.music.com. J. T. Van Zandt interview.

FILMS, VIDEOS, DVDS, CDS, AND RECORDINGS

Brown, Margaret. *Be Here to Love Me*. Rake Films, 2005.

"Butch Hancock's Dream." From *TVZ Tribute Show*, McCabes' in Santa Monica, Calif., February 1997 (from the private collection of Jeanene Van Zandt)

CMT/Opryland Studios. *The Bobby Bare Show,* March 28, 1983.

Holland Television. *All along the Watchtower*. Broadcast April 19, 1992.

Szalapski, James. *Heartworn Highways, 1981*.

Van Zandt, Townes. *Last Rights*. Produced by Nick "Chinga" Chavin. Gregor Records, 1997.

TVZ Records. *Townes Live in Amsterdam, 1991*.

Although I have tried to be as thorough as possible with this bibliography, there are instances in which source information was photocopied (sometimes multiple times), and some of the print was either lost or unreadable. My sincere apologies to anyone who has been overlooked or gone uncredited.

TVZ SELECTED DISCOGRAPHY

This discography of Townes's music is hardly complete, but the albums are listed in sequence based on when they were recorded rather than their release date, which reflects a truer time line of Van Zandt's output as a songwriter and what his live sets were like. There have been a plethora of live albums released over the years with multiple versions of the same songs, so I have chosen to include just a few of them— hence the title, "TVZ Selected Discography."

IN THE BEGINNING

Released 2000, Compadre Records,
52402-1

1. Black Widow Blues
2. Maryetta's Song
3. Hunger Child Blues
4. Gypsy Friday
5. Waitin' for the Day
6. Black Jack Mama
7. When Your Dream Lover Dies
8. Colorado Bound
9. Big Country Blues
10. Black Crow Blues

TVZ—vocals, guitar
With uncredited studio musicians
  (although Charlie McCoy was said to
  have played on some tracks)
Produced by Jack Clement
Recorded 1967

FOR THE SAKE OF THE SONG

Released 1968, Poppy Records,
PYS-40,001

1. For the Sake of the Song
2. Tecumseh Valley
3. Many a Fine Lady
4. Quicksilver Daydreams of Maria
5. Waitin' 'round to Die
6. I'll Be There in the Morning
7. Sad Cinderella
8. The Velvet Voices
9. Talkin' Karate Blues
10. All Your Young Servants
11. Sixteen Summers, Fifteen Falls

TVZ—vocals, guitar
With uncredited studio musicians
Produced by Jack Clement and Jim
  Malloy
Recorded at Bradley's Barn, Nashville

OUR MOTHER THE MOUNTAIN

Released 1969, Poppy Records,
PYS-40,004

1. Be Here to Love Me
2. Kathleen
3. She Came and She Touched Me
4. Like a Summer Thursday
5. Our Mother the Mountain
6. Second Lovers Song
7. St. John the Gambler
8. Tecumseh Valley
9. Snake Mountain Blues
10. My Proud Mountains
11. Why She's Acting This Way

TVZ—vocals, guitar
With: Ben Bennay—harmonica; James
*   Burton—Dobro, guitar; John*
*   Clauder—drums; Jack Clement—*
*   guitar; David Cohen—guitar; Mike*
*   Deasy—guitar; Chuck Domanico—*
*   bass; Donald Frost—drums; Jules*
*   Jacob—flute; Charlie McCoy—bass,*
*   guitar, harmonica, organ, recorder;*
*   Harvey Newmark—bass; Don*
*   Randi—keyboards; and Lyle Ritz—*
*   bass*
String arrangements by Bergen White
Produced by Jack Clement, Jim Malloy,
*   and Kevin Eggers*
Recorded in Los Angeles and Nashville

A GENTLE EVENING AT CARNEGIE HALL

Released 2002, Dualtone Records

1. Talking KKK Blues
2. Rake
3. Like a Summer's Thursday
4. Second Lover's Song
5. She Came and She Touched Me
6. Lungs

7. Tecumseh Valley
8. A Joke
9. Talking Thunderbird Wine Blues
10. The Ballad of Ira Hayes *(Peter LaFarge)*

TVZ—vocals, guitar
Recorded live at the Poppy Records
*   Showcase, Carnegie Hall, November*
*   26, 1969*

TOWNES VAN ZANDT

Released 1970, Poppy Records,
PYS-40,007

1. For the Sake of the Song
2. Columbine
3. Waitin' 'round to Die
4. Don't Take It Too Bad
5. Colorado Girl
6. Lungs
7. I'll Be Here in the Morning
8. Fare Thee Well, Miss Carousel
9. (Quicksilver Daydreams of) Maria
10. None but the Rain

TVZ—vocals, guitar
With uncredited studio musicians
Produced by Kevin Eggers and Jim
*   Malloy*
Recorded at Bradley's Barn, Nashville

DELTA MOMMA BLUES

Released 1971, Poppy Records,
PYS-40,012

1. FFV *(Trad. arranged by TVZ)*
2. Delta Momma Blues *(TVZ, Caddo Parish Studdard III, Richard Moore)*
3. Only Him or Me
4. Turnstyled, Junkpiled
5. Tower Song
6. Come Tomorrow

7. Brand New Companion
8. Where I Lead Me
9. Rake
10. Nothin'

TVZ—vocals, guitar
With uncredited studio musicians
String arrangements by Ronald
  Frangipane
Produced by Ronald Frangipane
Recorded at Century Sound Studios,
  New York

HIGH, LOW, AND IN BETWEEN

Released 1972, Poppy Records, PYS-5700

1. Two Hands
2. You Are Not Needed Now
3. Greensboro Woman
4. Highway Kind
5. Standin'
6. No Deal
7. To Live Is to Fly
8. When He Offers His Hand
9. Mr. Mudd and Mr. Gold
10. Blue Ridge Mountains
11. High, Low, and in Between

TVZ—vocals, guitar
With: Larry Carlton—guitar; David
  Cohen—guitar; Harvey Newmark—
  bass; Donnie Owens—guitar; Don
  Randi—piano, organ, finger cymbals;
  John Sumner—drums; Ann
  Whitsett—hand claps
Produced by Kevin Eggers
Recorded at Larabee Studios, Los Angeles

THE LATE, GREAT TOWNES VAN ZANDT

Released 1973, Poppy Records, LA004-F

1. No Lonesome Tune

2. Sad Cinderella
3. German Mustard *(TVZ and Rocky Hill)*
4. Don't Let the Sunshine Fool Ya' *(Guy Clark)*
5. Honky Tonkin' *(Hank Williams)*
6. Snow Don't Fall
7. Fraulein *(Lawton Williams)*
8. Pancho and Lefty
9. If I Needed You
10. Silver Ships of Andilar
11. Heavenly Houseboat Blues *(TVZ and Susanna Clark)*

TVZ—vocals, guitar
With uncredited studio musicians
Arranged by Chuck Cochran
String arrangements by Bergen White
Produced by Jack Clement and Kevin
  Eggers
Recorded at Jack Clement's Studios,
  Nashville

LIVE AT THE OLD QUARTER, HOUSTON, TEXAS

Released 1977, Tomato Records,
TOM-2-7001
Announcement by Dale Soffar

1. Pancho and Lefty
2. Mr. Mudd and Mr. Gold
3. Don't You Take It Too Bad
4. Two Girls
5. Fraternity Blues
6. If I Needed You
7. Brand New Companion
8. White Freight Liner Blues
9. To Live Is to Fly
10. She Came and She Touched Me
11. Talking Thunderbird Blues
12. Rex's Blues
13. Nine Pound Hammer *(Merle Travis)*
14. For the Sake of the Song

15. Chauffeur's Blues (*Lightnin'
    Hopkins*)
16. No Place to Fall
17. Loretta
18. Kathleen
19. Why She's Acting This Way
20. Cocaine Blues (*Trad.*)
21. Who Do You Love? (*Elias
    McDaniel, a.k.a. Bo Diddley*)
22. Tower Song
23. Waitin' 'round to Die
24. Tecumseh Valley
25. Lungs
26. Only Him or Me

TVZ—vocals, guitar
Produced by Earl Willis
Recorded live, July 1973

THE NASHVILLE SESSIONS

*Released 1993, Tomato/Rhino Records,
R2-71542*

1. At My Window
2. Rex's Blues
3. No Place to Fall
4. Buckskin Stallion Blues
5. White Freight Liner Blues
6. The Snake Song
7. Loretta
8. Two Girls
9. The Spider Song
10. When She Don't Need Me
11. Pueblo Waltz
12. Upon My Soul
13. If I Was Washington (*unreleased*)

TVZ—vocals, guitar
*With: Chuck Cochran—piano, vocals;
   Bobby Thompson—guitar;
Mickey White—guitar; Joe Allen—bass;
   Kenny Malone—drums
Arranged by Chuck Cochran
Produced by Kevin Eggers*

*Recorded at Jack Clement's Studios,
   Nashville, 1973*

FLYIN' SHOES

*Released 1978, Tomato Records, TOM-
7017*

1. Loretta
2. No Place to Fall
3. Flyin' Shoes
4. Who Do You Love? (*Bo Diddley*)
5. When She Don't Need Me
6. Dollar Bill Blues
7. Rex's Blues
8. Pueblo Waltz
9. Brother Flower

TVZ—vocals and guitar
*With: Eddy Anderson—percussion,
   drums; Billy Burnette—vocals;
   Tommy Cogbill—bass; Jimmy Day—
   steel guitar; Phillip Donnelly—guitar,
   vocals; Bobby Emmons—keyboards;
   Billy Earl McClelland—guitar,
   vocals; Chips Moman—guitar, vocals;
   Spooner Oldham—piano; Gary
   Scruggs—harmonica; Randy
   Scruggs—guitar, mandolin; Toni
   Wine—vocals
Produced by Chips Moman*

ROADSONGS

*Released 1994, Sugar Hill Records,
SHCD-1047*

1. The Ballad of Ira Hayes (*Peter
   LaFarge*)
2. Dead Flowers (*Mick Jagger and
   Keith Richards*)
3. Automobile Blues (*Lightnin'
   Hopkins*)
4. Coo Coo (*Clarence "Tom" Ashley*)

5. Fraulein *(Lawton Williams)*
6. Hello Central *(Lightnin' Hopkins)*
7. Indian Cowboy *(Joe Ely)*
8. Racing in the Street *(Bruce Springsteen)*
9. My Starter Won't Start *(Lightnin' Hopkins)*
10. Texas River Song *(Trad.)*
11. Wabash Cannonball *(A. P. Carter)*
12. Short-Haired Woman Blues *(Lightnin' Hopkins)*
13. Man Gave Names to All the Animals *(Bob Dylan)*
14. Little Willie the Gambler *(Bob Dylan)*
15. Cocaine Blues *(Trad.)*

TVZ—vocals, guitar
With: Owen Cody—violin; Jimmie Gray—bass; Danny "Ruester" Rowland—guitar; Mickey White—guitar
Produced by TVZ
Executive producer: Harold Eggers
Recorded "in joints all over America" between the midseventies through the early eighties.

LIVE AND OBSCURE

Released 1987, Heartland Records, HLD-004
Released 1989, Sugar Hill Records, SHCD-1026

1. Dollar Bill Blues
2. Many a Fine Lady
2. Nothin'
3. Pueblo Waltz
4. Talking Thunderbird Blues
5. Rex's Blues
6. White Freight Liner Blues
7. Loretta
8. Snake Mountain Blues

9. Waitin' 'round to Die
10. Tecumseh Valley
11. Pancho and Lefty
12. You Are Not Needed Now

TVZ—vocals, guitar
With: Donny Silverman—flute, saxophone; Mickey White—guitar
Produced by Stephen Mendell and TVZ
Recorded live, April 19, 1985, at 12th & Porter Playroom, Nashville

AT MY WINDOW

Released 1987, Sugar Hill Records, SHCD-1020

1. Snowin' on Raton
2. Blue Wind Blew
3. At My Window
4. For the Sake of the Song
5. Ain't Leavin' Your Love
6. Buckskin Stallion Blues
7. Little Sundance #2
8. Still Lookin' for You
9. Gone, Gone Blues *(Townes Van Zandt and Mickey White)*
10. The Catfish Song

TVZ—vocals, guitar
With: Jack Clement—guitar, Dobro; Charles Cochran—keyboards; Mark Howard—guitar, steel guitar; Roy Huskey Jr.—bass; Kenny Malone—drums, percussion; Joey Miskulin—accordion; Mark O'Connor—mandolin, fiddle; Mickey Raphael—harmonica; Jim Rooney—guitar; Donny Silverman—flute, saxophone; Mickey White—guitar, slide guitar
Produced by Jack Clement and Jim Rooney
Recorded at Jack Clement's Cowboy Arms Hotel and Recording Spa, Nashville

NO DEEPER BLUE

Released 1994, Sugar Hill Records,
SHCD-1046

1. A Song For
2. Blazes Blue
3. The Hole
4. Marie
5. Goin' Down to Memphis
6. Hey Willy Boy
7. Niles River Blues
8. Billy, Boney and Ma
9. Katie Belle Blue
10. If I Was Washington
11. Lover's Lullaby
12. Cowboy Junkies Lament
13. BW Railroad Blues
14. Gone Too Long

TVZ—vocals, guitar (on "Gone Too
Long")
With: Fran Breen—drums; Robbie
Brennan—drums; Sven Buick—bass;
Pete Cumins—guitar; Phillip
Donnelly—guitar, percussion;
Donovan—harmonica; Adrian
Foley—tuba; Brendan Hayes—piano,
organ; harmonium, baby chimes; Paul
Kelly—fiddle; Declan Masterson—
whistle, uileann pipes; Brian
Meehan—clarinet, tenor sax, tin
whistle; Martin O'Connor—accordion;
Brendan Regan—bazouki, mandolin;
Percy Robinson—steel guitar
Produced by Phillip Donnelly
Executive producer: Jeanene Van Zandt
Recorded at Xeric Studios, Limerick,
Ireland

THE HIGHWAY KIND

Released 1997, Sugar Hill Records,
SHCD 1056

1. Still Lookin' for You
2. Dublin Blues *(Guy Clark)*
3. Lost Highway *(Leon Payne)*
4. A Song For
5. The Hole
6. Highway Kind
7. (I Heard That) Lonesome Whistle
   (Hank Williams and Jimmie Davis)
8. No Deal
9. Blaze's Blues
10. Darcy Farrow *(Steve Gillette and*
    Thomas E. Campbell)
11. My Proud Mountains
12. Wreck on the Highway *(Dorsey*
    Dixon)
13. Rake
14. The Ballad of Ira Hayes *(Peter*
    LaFarge)

TVZ—vocals, guitar
With: Roy Ann Calvin—guitar; Jim
Calvin—guitar, mandolin, fiddle; Rise
Payne—fiddle, vocals; Kelly Joe
Phelps—guitar on "Ira Hayes"
All tracks recorded while touring
throughout the United States and
Europe, except "Dublin Blues,"
"Lonesome Whistle," and "Wreck on
the Highway."
Produced by TVZ
Executive producer: Harold Eggers
Recorded by Michael Catalano

A FAR CRY FROM DEAD

Released 1999, Arista Records,
0782218888-2

1. Dollar Bill Blues
2. To Live's to Fly
3. Rex's Blues
4. Sanitarium Blues
5. Ain't Leavin' Your Love
6. Greensboro Woman

7. Snake Mountain Blues
8. Pancho and Lefty
9. For the Sake of the Song
10. Waitin' 'round to Die
11. Many a Fine Lady
12. Tower Song
13. Squash

TVZ — vocals, guitar
With: Richard Bennett — guitars; Jim
Calvin — banjo; Russ Hicks — steel
guitar; Larry Knechtel — keyboards;
Craig Krampf — drums, cymbals,
tambourine; Kenny Malone — drums,
congas, percussion; Susie Monick —
squeeze box; Charlie McCoy —
harmonica, vibes; Michael Spriggs —
guitar, Dobro, tipple; Bob Wray —
bass; and the Squash Singers
Produced by Eric Paul
Executive producer: Jeanene Van Zandt
TVZ's original vocals and guitar tracks
were recorded between 1989 and 1996
at Texhoma Music Group Studio and
Jack Clement's Cowboy Arms Hotel
and Recording Spa, Nashville.
All other tracks recorded in 1998 at
Imagine Studios, Nashville.

TEXAS RAIN: THE TEXAS HILL COUNTRY RECORDINGS

Released 2001, Tomato Records

1. If I Needed You (with Emmylou Harris)
2. Pancho and Lefty (with Freddy Fender, Rubin Ramos and the Texas Revolution, Doug Sahm, and Augie Meyers)
3. Waitin' 'round to Die (with Calvin Russell)
4. Blue Wind Blew (with Jerry Jeff Walker)
5. Kathleen (with the Chromatics)
6. No Lonesome Tune (with Willie Nelson)
7. Brother Flower (with Kimmie Rhodes)
8. Two Girls (with Doug Sahm)
9. Marie (with Willie Nelson)
10. (Quicksilver Daydreams of) Maria (with Freddy Fender, Rubin Ramos and the Texas Revolution, Doug Sahm, and Augie Meyers)
11. Snowin' on Raton (with James McMurtry)
12. At My Window (with Kathy Mattea)

With: Riley Osborne — keyboards; John
Inmon — guitar; Ernie Duwa —
drums; Wilbur "Junkman" — drums;
James Fenner — percussion; Augie
Meyer — accordion; Doug Sahm —
guitar; the Texas Revolution — horns;
Irving Charles — bass; Gene Elder —
fiddle; the Chromatics — vocals;
Rubin Ramos — vocals
String arrangements by Wardell
Quezergue
Produced by Kevin Eggers
Recorded at the Fire Station, San Marcos,
Texas, and Pedernales Studios,
Pedernales, Texas

ACKNOWLEDGMENTS

Thanks to everybody who took the time to share their memories, insight, and dreams about Townes for this book. They include:

Eric "Roscoe" Ambel, David Amram, Eric Andersen, Rex "Wrecks" Bell, Bibs, Bill Bentley, Brooks (bartender at the Hole in the Wall, Austin), Frenchy Burrito, Bill Camplin, Keith Case, Guy Clark, Cowboy Jack Clement, Rodney Crowell, Mary Locke Danforth, Richard "Ricardo" Dobson, George Dolis, Steve Earle, Kevin Eggers, Ramblin' Jack Elliott, Joe Ely, Alejandro Escovedo, Ron Frangipane, Marshall "Marsh" Froker, Jimmie Dale Gilmore, Jimmy Gingles, Robbie Gjersoe, Milton Glaser, Keith Glass, Jimmy Gray, Seymour Gunther, Denis Hall, Butch Hancock, Darryl Harris, Charlie Hunter, Nora Jones, Richard Julian, Paul K. (Kopasz), Robert Earl Keen, Victor Krummenacher, Donovan Leitch, Nina Leto, Fran Lohr, John Lomax III, Linda Lowe, Griff Luneberg, Jim Malloy, Joel McNally, Alyse Moore, Bob Moore, Bob "Mav" Myrick, Mickey Newbury, Old Chief Rolling Papers, David Olney, Eric Paul, Alan Pepper, Chip Phillips, John Prine, Dan Rather, Jerry Rau, Chris Robinson, Gradi Sterling Rocamora, Jim Rooney, Peter Rowan, Danny "Ruester" Rowland, Lee Ruth, Don Sanders, Vin Scelsa, Blaine Schultz, Jonathan Segel, Luke Sharpe, Richard Shindell, Paul Siebel, John Sieger, Donny Silverman, Stanley Smith, Donna Spence, Peter Stampfel, James Szalapski, Richard Thompson, Michael Timmins, Jeanene Van Zandt, John (J. T.) Van Zandt, Will Van Zandt, Rick Verplank, Eric von Schmidt, David Waddell, Leland Waddell, Jason Wakefield, Jerry Jeff Walker, Ingrid Weigand, Mickey White, and Marvin Williams.

Special thanks to: Marilyn Cvitanic, Sonnie Kruth, Steve Kruth, and Jeanene Van Zandt. To my agent, John Michel, and to Ben Schafer at Da Capo Press and Christine Marra at Marrathon Production Services. And to Anya Gallas, Rob Dunning, Bruce Eckel, May Cobb, Chuck Scherrer, Nancy Fly, Linda Lowe, and Munch, for their cuisine, couches, cars, and phones. And to Louie "Cannonball" Dupree for his hard-nosed dedication, ruthless humor, and bullet-proof faith. And a couple hoots and hollers out to: Patrick J. B. Flynn, Kevin Calabro, Peter Basta Brightbill, and Mercer Street Books. And to all the journalists whose work I quoted from. And anyone else I snagged some illumination from and tossed it into the mix. Thanks! And "Good lucks to ya!"

RIP Sonnie Kruth, Old Chief Rolling Papers, Jim Szalapski, Dale Soffar, Roxy Gordon, Jim Calvin, and LeAnne Romano Bell.

> **"Remember. Time flies like an arrow . . .**
> **Fruit flies like a banana."**
>
> **—TVZ**

INDEX